FIFTY YEARS OF
COLLECTIBLE GLASS

1920-1970

EASY IDENTIFICATION AND PRICE GUIDE

VOLUME I:
TABLEWARE, KITCHENWARE, BARWARE AND WATER SETS

BY TOM AND NEILA BREDEHOFT

A Division of Landmark Specialty Publications
Dubuque, Iowa

ISBN: 0-930625-79-X
Library of Congress Catalog Card Number: 97-74599

Editor: Kyle Husfloen
Editorial Assistants: Ruth Willis, Pat B. Scott
Designer: Virginia Hill
Production Assistants: Lynn Bradshaw, Aaron Wilbers,
  Barb Brown, Carla M. Heathcote-Goldhammer
Cover Design: Jaro Sebek

Front Cover: top left to right: Tea Room vase; Iris Golden
Iridescent pitcher. Bottom left to right: Patrician plate, sugar
& cream; Fry covered casserole.

Back Cover: A grouping of blue Mayfair pieces.

Please Note: Though listings have been double-checked and every effort has
been made to insure accuracy, neither the editors nor the publisher can assume
responsibility for any losses that might be incurred as a result of consulting this
guide, or of errors, typographical or otherwise.

Printed in the United States of America

To order additional copies of this
book or a catalog please contact:

Antique Trader Books
P.O. Box 1050
Dubuque, Iowa 52004
1-800-334-7165

 **Antique Trader Books**
A Division of Landmark Specialty Publications

CONTENTS

FOREWORD

We are often asked about glassware, and the two most common questions are: What is it? and What is it worth? This book is our attempt to answer both of these questions in a different way. Identifying glass if you have no idea of its name or the name of the company who made it is very difficult—the only way is to look page by page in many books. This book makes it easy to find a pattern name by actually looking at the piece of glass and then turning to the proper category, i. e., circles, flowers, swirls and many other pattern motifs. We are listing patterns with most of the pieces known in each along with prices to be used as a guideline. In order to present as many patterns as possible, we have limited the number of illustrations. We believe that all patterns can be identified from the photographs, catalog pictures and drawings shown.

We hope this presentation of patterns by motif is helpful for both the advanced collector and especially for the beginner who is unfamiliar with pattern names. We made the book easy to use, and we hope that all of you will find it so.

Happy Glass Collecting!
Neila and Tom Bredehoft

SPECIAL THANKS

Most books are not the creation of one or two individuals but draw on the collective information and specialized knowledge of many people. Many friends, both collectors and dealers, have graciously helped us with information and suggestions for this book. Several have chosen to remain anonymous, and we are as indebted to them as well as to the following:

Susan and Lee Allen
French Batten
Susie and John Determan
Joan and Odie Finchum
George Fogg
Neda and Harry Freed
Mart Groesser
Dianne Hermes
Kyle Husfloen
Leora and Jim Leasure
Milbra Long
Frank Maloney
Jo and Bob Sanford
Emily Seate
Annie Shatrau
Dean Six
Green River Depression Glass Club, Kent, WA
Weston Area Glass History and Study Group, Weston, WV

DEDICATION

Early in the 1960s, two ladies began to publicize and research what now is called Depression Glass. The credit for raising all collectors' awareness of this type of glass began with these dedicated ladies who, each in her own way, provided invaluable information to collectors.

We wish to acknowledge and dedicate this book to Hazel Marie Weatherman. Mrs. Weatherman became the foremost researcher of Depression Glass and unequaled in the accuracy and depth of her research. With her early books on the subject, she was the most influential person to bring Depression Glass to its present height of popularity.

The second person we wish to recognize in the dedication is Nora Koch, former editor of *The Daze*, known for years as *The Depression Glass Daze*. Nora published a monthly newspaper devoted to Depression Glass, creating a forum for researchers, buyers, sellers and those who needed to have answers to their questions. Her legacy continues to this day.

INTRODUCTION

Glass made during the 50 years from 1920 to 1970 represents the most collectible glass in America today. More people collect American glassware from this era than from any other. During these years companies made what is now called Depression Glass and Elegant Glass. Spurring interest in glass of this period are several national clubs devoted to the entire period such as the National Depression Glass Association, or to the products of specific companies such as Fostoria, Cambridge, Heisey, Imperial and others. While these organizations have done an excellent job "spreading the word" about collectible twentieth century glass, the glass itself is its own best ambassador.

What attracts people to this particular glass even if they know nothing about it? In a word—COLOR! In the early 1920s color began to be used in glassware after a period of ten or more years when crystal glass reigned in popularity. At first color was mostly enamels in both vivid and pastel colors applied to crystal glass. These designs were mainly florals with some geometrics fitting in nicely with the Art Deco period. The first mentions we have found of true colored glass of this period were of sets of salad plates to be used as colorful accents to china tableware.

In the mid 1920s glass companies in the United States began to make entire tableware sets in color—green, pink, amber and yellow predominating. Within a period of several years the Elegant companies added stronger and more exotic colors to the spectrum. Cobalt blue, black, red, amethyst, orange and wonderful orchid hues were developed to tempt the housewife. Colored stemware was added in a multitude of designs. Lemonade and water sets in many styles were also made in profusion.

The 1920s and 1930s also saw color used in kitchens. Housewives eagerly bought colored measuring cups, reamers, mixing bowls, canister sets and even rolling pins to brighten their kitchens. After all, at that time much of a housewife's time was spent in the kitchen—preparing food, preserving food, washing dishes—with none of the labor-saving devices to which we have become so accustomed. No wonder color appealed to her to brighten her workplace. These colors attract homemakers today and kitchenware is one of the fastest growing of the glass collectible fields.

The repeal of Prohibition in 1933 made liquor again legal, and the glass companies saw a ready market for various barware and companion items. Mostly this was a variety of stems and tumblers, the shapes and sizes of which were designated for serving specific drinks. But pieces such as cocktail shakers, decanters, ice buckets and bowls and many other accessory pieces for the home bar were also added. Naturally, color again played an important part in the success of these pieces.

The Second World War and its material requirements put a stop to much colored glass production. Color did not disappear entirely, but crystal again regained its popularity. However, in kitchenware this was not true, although the colored pieces began to be replaced by milk glass with fired enamel decorations.

Eventually in the 1950s enamel decorations in color were the most popular in barware, kitchenware and beverage sets. Some glassware companies continued to make tableware in color—Anchor Hocking continued its Jade-ite and Hazel-Atlas developed new colors of amethyst and aquamarine blue.

By the 1960s many glass companies were out of business, many others barely managed to remain viable. Elegant glass companies such as Heisey, Cambridge, Duncan & Miller had all vanished. Tiffin was in the process of going through the hands of several owners, eventually succumbing in 1980. Imperial and Fenton were still in business but struggling to find new markets.

Fenton and Indiana Glass are still in business today. Interestingly, Indiana still has a large business in *its own* old patterns and patterns first made by Heisey, Imperial and Fostoria. Fenton is now making primarily giftware and decorative glass, especially hand-decorated pieces. While glassware for table use is still available in stores today—both in discount stores and higher class department stores, increasingly the glass available is made in foreign countries. For the most part, manufacture of tableware in America has ceased to exist.

WHAT IS DEPRESSION GLASS?

The term, Depression Glass, describes glass made primarily during the late 1920s and 1930s. For the most part it is machine-made glass and does not have hand finishing. It is usually pressed in a mold. It was cheaply made and may have flaws such as sharp or prominent mold lines, extra bits of glass on edges and other imperfections typical of a quickly and cheaply made product with little quality control. Often quantity, not quality, was the goal of factories that made Depression Glass. This has not dampened the enthusiasm of collectors for this colorful glass.

Many Depression Glass patterns were made by a process known as mold-etching. The design was etched into the mold resulting in a busy, decorated surface resembling true etched glass which has elaborate designs etched by acid into the glass after it is in its final form. However, because the design was in the mold, the lengthy, expensive process of etching the glass with acid was eliminated. Mold-etching still produced the light, airy designs found on etched glass but utilized a much cheaper technique.

Many factories produced Depression Glass tableware almost as a side line—their main product line being such items as fruit and jelly jars, simple and sturdy restaurant and bar tumblers, pitchers and other items. Many made soda fountain items—sundae and soda glasses, straw jars, crushed fruit jars, syrup dispensers and other more mundane, day-to-day items of glass used in both businesses and homes.

Depression Glass originally was often given away as premiums at movie theaters or in soap or cereal boxes. As a general rule, smaller pieces were given away so many basic luncheon sets are fairly common. Consequently, in most patterns, larger pieces and serving pieces such as pitchers, vegetable bowls, and dinner plates are more difficult to find.

Some companies that produced machine-made Depression Glass include Hocking Glass Co., Hazel-Atlas Glass Co., D. C. Jenkins Glass Co., McKee Glass Co., Lancaster Glass Co., Federal Glass Co., and Indiana Glass Co.

WHAT IS ELEGANT GLASS?

Elegant Glass is a term which has come into general use to describe the better, hand-made glass manufactured by companies during the 1920s through the 1960s. Hand-made glass is not completely handmade; molds were used to give form to the glass items. In contrast with machine-made glass which was almost always in a complete, finished form when it left the mold, hand-made glass often had extra finishing manipulations done by glassworkers after the piece had been pressed and taken out of the mold. Extra forming was often done to rims by flaring, cupping or crimping. Sometimes feet and handles were hand applied, often in a contrasting color from the body of the article. Pieces were usually fire polished—a technique in which the piece was reheated in the glory hole (a small furnace) to soften the outer surface and smooth the rough edges left by the mold. After all these operations, many pieces were given a ground and polished base rim resulting in a flat, smooth surface on which the piece rested. Look for these special extra finishing features when trying to decide whether your pattern is Depression or Elegant.

Glassware produced by Elegant companies was sold by better quality gift shops, department stores and jewelry stores who carried a sideline of china and glass ware. Elegant Glass tended to be sold for several years from matching stock. Depending on the popularity of the pattern, pieces were added to or dropped from these patterns as sales indicated. Because of this, many of the Elegant Glass patterns are much more extensive than the true Depression Glass patterns. Many of the most popular were available in over 100 pieces. Some long-lived patterns such as Fostoria's American, Duncan & Miller's Early American Sandwich and Canterbury, and Imperial's Cape Cod and Candlewick grew to immense proportions because of their lasting popularity. Pieces in these patterns were continually being added and dropped from the line, resulting in extremely rare pieces today.

Some companies that made Elegant Glass include: Fostoria Glass Co., A. H. Heisey Glass Co., Duncan & Miller Glass Co., Imperial Glass Co., New Martinsville Glass Co., Paden City Glass Co., Cambridge Glass Co., Dunbar Glass Co., and Louie Glass/West Virginia Glass Specialty Co.

TERMINOLOGY

Many specialized terms are used by collectors of glass and by the companies that made glass. The following are terms which might be confusing to beginning collectors. In our lists we have used the original company terminology for the names of pieces. This preserves the original company names which is important historically. Collectors need to be aware that the same piece made by two different companies may have different names. To further confuse the issue, the same company sometimes used different names through the years for what we today would think are the same pieces. As you study the patterns, you will see that each company had its favorite nomenclature for pieces.

Bar Glass or Whiskey—A small tumbler used for serving liquor. A shot glass.

Cocktail—A footed glass with small capacity (usually about 3 oz.) for serving cocktails. The bowl is usually shallower and more broad than a wine glass.

Comport or Compote—A bowl, usually footed, for serving fruits. The foot may be either tall or short depending on the item.

Cover—A lid.

Flip Vase—A vase with tapered sides, looking much like a large tumbler.

Goblet—A footed glass for serving water. Now these are often used for serving wine. Goblets usually hold about 8 or 9 ounces.

Iced Tea—When made these were for serving iced tea, lemonade and other drinks. Now they are often used for serving water. Iced teas can be flat or footed and usually have capacities in excess of 9 ounces.

Jelly—Usually a small bowl with one handle. Sometimes called an olive. Another variety is a small comport which is often called a footed jelly.

Jug—A pitcher. A variety of pitcher or jug is a tankard, which has tall, straight sides.

Molasses or Molasses Can—A container, usually with a metal top, for serving syrups or molasses. Now usually called a syrup.

Muffin Tray—A plate, sometimes handled, with opposite edges turned up.

Oil—What is now usually called a cruet, used for vinegar or oil for salad.

Olive—Usually a small bowl with one handle. Sometimes called a jelly.

Parfait—A tall, slender footed glass used for desserts.

Pokal—A term used mainly by Imperial Glass for large covered urns or candy jars.

Reamer—A citrus juicer with a cone shape for squeezing out juice and a shallow bowl shape to catch the juice and seeds.

Rolled Edge or Turned Edge—A way of hand finishing the edge of a plate or bowl. In this case the edge is slightly turned up or turned down on the rim.

Salver—There are 2 styles of salvers listed in this book. One is a flat plate, often with handles for serving cake. The other, also for serving cake, is either on a tall stem or on a short pedestal.

Sandwich Plate or Tray—A plate with either a center handle for serving or with 2 handles. Fostoria called its center handled sandwich plates luncheon trays.

Sherbet—Different companies made different styles of sherbets. Some are flat bottomed while others are stemmed. In most cases, the bowls of all hold about 5 or 6 ounces and are broad and shallow. Duncan & Miller usually used the term, sundae, for what others called sherbets.

Soda—A drinking vessel, very similar to a tumbler, but usually taller and more slender.

Spider—A term used by Imperial Glass for iron-skillet-shaped pieces, especially in their Cape Cod line. Spider is an old fashioned term for a skillet or frying pan.

Tumbler—A drinking vessel, usually for water and often having no foot, but sometimes also listed as footed. In the case of footed tumblers, the foot is usually directly below the bowl with no stem between the two.

Ware—The term used by glass companies to describe the glass they produced. All glass is ware, and ware is divided into patterns or line numbers or names.

COLORS

Colors are most important to glass made during this period. When we have known the name used by the company originally we have tried to use this in listings. Often these are self-explanatory such as emerald (a shade of green), rose (pink) and others. Some others are not so obvious such as sahara (yellow) and zircon (turquoise).

Duncan & Miller made three opalescent colors; Jasmine Yellow, Shell Pink, and Cape Cod Blue. Imperial Glass Corp. called their opalescent colors Sea Foam Harding Blue, Sea Foam Moss Green and Sea Foam Burnt Almond.

In the case of Milk Glass, most companies used either the term Opal or Milk Glass. Hocking called their product, Vitrock and Hazel-Atlas called theirs Platonite. Black glass was usually called Black or Ebony. The color now called Vaseline was called Canary by most manufacturers.

The following table lists company names for colors.

COMPANY	PINK	GREEN	YELLOW
Bartlett-Collins	Nu-Rose	Nu-Green	
Cambridge	LaRosa	Emerald, Pistachio	Gold Krystol
Dunbar	Pink, Rose Pink	Green, Bermuda Green	
Duncan & Miller	Rose	Biscayne Green, Chartreuse, Avocado, Green	
Federal	Rose Glow		
Fenton	Velva Rose, Pink	Green, Jade *	Topaz
Fostoria	Rose	Green, Empire Green	Gold Tint, Topaz
Hazel-Atlas	Pink, Sunset Pink	Green, Killarney Green	
Heisey	Flamingo	Moongleam	Sahara
Hocking (Anchor Hocking)	Cerise, Rose, Flamingo	Green, Forest Green Jade-ite *	
Imperial	Rose Marie, Rose	Green, Imperial Green Steigel Green	Golden Ophir
Indiana	Pink	Green	
Jeannette	Pink, Wild Rose Shell Pink *	Green, Jadite * Jeannette Green	
Jenkins		Green	
Louie	Pink	Green	
Macbeth-Evans	Pink	Emerald	
McKee	Rose Pink	Green, Grass Green Skokie Green * Jade Green *	Topaz, Seville Yellow *
New Martinsville	Rose, Peach Melba	Green, Emerald Jade *, Stiegel Green Evergreen	
Paden City	Pink, Cheri-glo	Green, Forest Green	Golden Glow
U. S. Glass	Pink	Green, Light Green	Mandarin Yellow
Westmoreland	Rose, Roselin	Green	

* denotes opaque colors

AMBER	BLUE	RED	AMETHYST
Madiera	Royal Blue	Carmen Burgundy	Heatherbloom
Amber	Blue Sapphire Blue	Ruby	
Golden Glow	Madonna Blue		
Amber	Royal Blue, Celeste Blue Victoria Blue, Aquamarine Mermaid Blue	Ruby	Wisteria
Amber	Blue, Regal Blue, Azure	Ruby	Orchid, Burgundy Wisteria
Topaz	Blue, Ritz Blue		Moroccan Amethyst Burgundy
Amber	Stiegel Blue		Alexandrite, Hawthorne
Topaz	Blue	Royal Ruby	
Amber, Topaz	Blue, Ritz Blue	Ruby	
Amber			
Amber, Topaz	Delfite*, Ultra-Marine		
Amber			
Topaz			
Topaz			
Amber	Blue, Sky Blue Chalaine Blue * Poudre Blue *	Ruby	Amethyst, Orchid
Amber	Blue, Alice Blue Ritz Blue	Ruby	Wine, Amethyst
Amber	Blue, Royal Blue Ceylon Blue, Cobalt Blue	Ruby	Mulberry
Amber	Blue, Royal Blue Light Blue	Red	Amethyst
Amber	Blue		

* denotes opaque colors

FOCUS & CONTENT

FOCUS

This book focuses on the patterns made in tableware by American companies from the 1920s through the 1970s. In order to present an overview of patterns of this era, guidelines were established for including patterns in this book. There are dozens of patterns not included due to lack of space. For this book we have defined tableware patterns as those patterns comprised of a dinner or luncheon service. In other words, the pattern must have a plate and either a cup and saucer, a tumbler or goblet to complete the setting. Some patterns have little more than this basic setting, but many have extensive lists of pieces, sometimes hundreds.

For added interest we have also included brief chapters on collectible kitchen glass and barware and beverage sets. Both of these areas are immense and would require a book or several books to cover them thoroughly, but we have chosen representative examples of types of glass which collectors will encounter when looking for glass in these categories. This book will give an overview and a guide for similar pieces not actually listed or illustrated.

CONTENT

The patterns in the book are arranged in visual categories to speed identification. That is, when examining a piece of glass, first determine the most predominant feature in the design—a circle, a flower, a square. To use the book effectively, use this predominant feature to then refer to the chapter of the book representing this feature. Some patterns could easily be put into two or three categories, so it might be necessary to look in more than one chapter before finding your pattern.

Chapters are arranged in alphabetical order, and patterns in each chapter are also arranged in alphabetical order by pattern name. We have used the original name, if known, as we feel that it is historically important to retain these names. If original names are not known, we have used names which are familiar to today's collectors. If more than one company used the same name for patterns (and they often did), it is necessary to refer to a pattern by both the name and the company which made it in order to identify it properly. For instance, Radiance by New Martinsville or Radiance by Duncan & Miller.

We have given a beginning date for each pattern although sometimes this date is not certain and can only be estimated. We also provide the name of the company making the pattern and the colors in which we know the pattern was made. If we have pertinent information about the pattern, including reproductions, we have given this information in a small paragraph. Following this is a list of pieces made and the values of the pieces in various colors. If not all pieces of a pattern were made in all colors, a percentage value is assigned to a color. If possible, we have used the original company terminology for the names of pieces listed.

In order to present as many patterns as possible, we have limited the amount of information presented. For detailed information about patterns we suggest you consult other books, especially those devoted to specific companies such as Cambridge, Duncan & Miller, Fostoria, etc. There are also books on only one pattern, such as Cambridge's Caprice, Imperial's Cape Cod and Candlewick. Our book is meant to provide basic information only; and other books, including catalog reprints, may give you much more detail.

You may be surprised to find that some "patterns" listed in other books are not listed in this one. For the most part, we have included only true patterns in this book—those of a specific design or line number of the company, not a grouping of pieces of one color such as Royal Ruby, Jade-ite or Moroccan Amethyst. These combine many line numbers under one umbrella heading.

The kitchen and barware sections are less comprehensive than the pattern category, and are presented to introduce you to the great possibilities of collecting glass in these categories. Again, many books are available with specific information, such as books on Fire-King and Pyrex, books entirely about stemware (some of only one company) and other specific subjects. If these categories become your main collecting interest, we again urge you to consult these other sources for detailed information.

Chapter 1
ANIMALS

GEORGIAN

Date: 1931 to 1935

Manufacturer: Federal Glass Co., Columbus, OH

Colors: Green, Crystal

Georgian is the original name. Sometimes called Love Birds because birds appear in the design on most pieces. Baskets also are part of the design. Only the basket motif appears on the tumbler and ice tea. Sugar lids are difficult to find. Crystal pieces are valued about 50% of Green. Prices given are for items in Green.

Georgian Covered Butter, Sugar, 4½" Berry Bowl

Bowl, Berry, 4½" *(Illus.)*. $10.00
Bowl, Cereal, 5½" 30.00
Bowl, 6½" 75.00
Bowl, Large Berry, 7½" 80.00
Bowl, Oval Vegetable, 9" 85.00
Butter & Cover *(Illus.)*. 90.00
Cream, Footed, 3" 15.00
Cream, Footed, 4" 18.00
Cup & Saucer 14.00
Hot Plate, 5" 62.00
Iced Tea, 12 oz. 165.00
Plate, 6" 5.00
Plate, 8" 9.00
Plate, 9" 24.00
Plate, 9" (center design & edge design) 38.00
Platter, Handled 11½" 78.00
Sherbet 12.00
Sugar, Footed, 3" *(Illus.)*. 15.00
Sugar, Footed, 4" 18.00
Sugar Lid, Small. 42.00
Sugar Lid, Large. 140.00
Tumbler, 9 oz. 75.00

SYLVAN

Sylvan Butter Dish & Cover

Date: 1931 to 1932

Manufacturer: Federal Glass Co., Columbus, OH

Colors: Green, Amber. Limited items in Crystal and Blue.

Sylvan is the original name, although many people still call this pattern Parrot. It is difficult to find today as it was made for only about one year before the molds were reworked into the Madrid pattern. Sugar lids are quite scarce.

	Amber	Green
Bowl, Berry, 5"	$22.00	$35.00
Bowl, Soup, 7"	40.00	55.00
Bowl, Large Berry, 8"	90.00	80.00
Bowl, Oval Vegetable, 10"	85.00	75.00
Butter & Cover *(Illus.)*	1,100.00+	425.00+
Cream, Footed	38.00	48.00
Cup & Saucer	65.00	70.00
Hot Plate, 5" (2 styles)	800.00+	
Iced Tea, 12 oz.	160.00	190.00
Pitcher, 80 oz.		2,500.00+
Plate, 6"	28.00	38.00
Plate, 7"		56.00
Plate, 9"	38.00	54.00
Plate, Square, 10"	55.00	65.00
Plate, Grill, Round, 10½"	55.00	
Plate, Grill, Square, 10½"	34.00	
Platter, 11¼"	75.00	65.00
Salt & Pepper, pr.		350.00+
Sherbet, Cone Shape	20.00	28.00
Sherbet		320.00+
Sugar	32.00	38.00
Sugar Lid	400.00	150.00
Tumbler, Footed, (pressed), Cone 10 oz.	165.00	
Tumbler, (blown) 10 oz.	145.00	170.00

Chapter 2
CIRCLES & RINGS

BUBBLE

Date: 1934 to 1965

Manufacturer: Anchor Hocking Glass Co., Lancaster, OH

Colors: Crystal, Light Blue. Limited Production in Pink and Light Green. Forest Green, Royal Ruby. Rarely found in Milk White and Amber.

The original colors were Crystal and Light Blue. Forest Green and Royal Ruby were made much later. Amber and Milk glass are found only in a few pieces, not the entire pattern.

Bubble Dinner Plate, Cup & Saucer

	Crystal	Blue	Ruby	Green
Bowl, 4"..................	$5.00	$22.00	$	$8.00
Bowl, 4½".................	4.00	12.00	10.00	7.00
Bowl, 5¼".................	5.00	16.00		12.00
Bowl, 7¾".................	6.00	20.00		35.00
Bowl, 8¼".................	6.00	24.00	24.00	18.00
Bowl with Rim, 9"...........		350.00+		
Candlesticks, pr............	24.00			35.00
Cream....................	6.00	32.00		15.00
Cup & Saucer *(Illus.)*.......	6.00	7.50	12.00	14.00
Iced Tea, 12 oz.............	10.00		16.00	
Iced Tea, 16 oz.............	12.00		22.00	
Juice, 6 oz.................	5.00		12.00	
Lamp (various types).........	40.00			
Pitcher, Ice Lip, 64 oz........	87.00		60.00	
Plate, 6¾".................	2.00	4.00		6.00
Plate, 9¼" *(Illus.)*.........	5.00	9.00	20.00	20.00
Plate, Grill, 9¼"............		25.00		
Platter, 12"...............	9.00	20.00		
Sugar....................	4.00	28.00		15.00
Tidbit, 2 Tier..............			40.00	
Tumbler, 9 oz..............	8.00		15.00	

CIRCLE

Circle Pitcher

Date: 1929

Manufacturer: Hocking Glass Co., Lancaster, OH

Colors: Pink, Green

Both colors are valued approximately the same.

Bowl, 4½"	$12.00
Bowl, Deep, 4¼"	20.00
Bowl, Flared, 5½"	12.00
Bowl, 8½"	18.00
Cream	10.00
Cup & Saucer	7.00
Decanter, Handled	45.00
Goblet, 8 oz.	20.00
Juice, 4 oz.	10.00
Pitcher, 60 oz. or 80 oz. *(Illus.)*	40.00
Plate, 6"	2.50
Plate, 8¼"	6.50
Plate, 9¼"	14.00
Sherbet, 2 sizes	6.50
Sugar	10.00
Tumbler, 8 oz.	14.00
Wine, 4¼"	20.00

IPSWICH, NO. 1405

Ipswich 11" Floral Bowl

Date: 1931 to 1946. Crystal only from 1951 to 1953

Manufacturer: A. H. Heisey & Co., Newark, OH

Colors: Crystal, Sahara, Flamingo, Moongleam. Limited production in Stiegel Blue (Cobalt)

Reproductions: Imperial Glass Corp. made candy jars and a bowl with a crimped edge (not originally made by Heisey) in several colors. These are found with and without the Diamond H.

Ipswich was inspired by early Sandwich Glass (Comet) but produced by Heisey in contemporary shapes. First advertisements called it Early American Scroll, but the name was changed almost immediately to Ipswich. All items are not available in all colors, Sahara being the most common color found. Most pieces are marked with the Diamond H. Goblets in Alexandrite are $750.00+. In Stiegel Blue, (Cobalt), the floral bowl is worth $350.00, the cocktail shaker $1,000.00, the complete centerpiece with vase and prisms, a pair, is worth $1,100.00.

(continued) IPSWICH, NO. 1405

	Crystal	Sahara	Flamingo, Moongleam
Bowl, Finger	$18.00	$40.00	$45.00
Bowl, Floral, 11" *(Illus.)*	65.00	140.00	175.00
Candlesticks, 6" (1 Light), pr.	225.00	275.00	325.00
Candy Jar & Cover, ¼ lb.	100.00	245.00	275.00
Candy Jar & Cover, ¼ lb.	120.00	280.00	340.00
Centerpiece with Vase & Prisms, Footed, pr.	220.00	600.00	750.00
Cocktail Shaker, 1 qt.	275.00	800.00	
Cologne & Stopper	295.00		
Cream	35.00	48.00	65.00
Goblet, 10 oz.	22.00	50.00	75.00
Jug, ¼ Gal., Stuck Handle	200.00	250.00	500.00
Oil & Stopper, 2 oz.	100.00	225.00	265.00
Oyster Cocktail, 4 oz.	10.00	25.00	30.00
Plate, Square, 7"	14.00	30.00	35.00
Plate, Square, 8"	17.00	35.00	40.00
Saucer Champagne, 4 oz.	15.00	30.00	40.00
Schoppen, 12 oz.	22.00	35.00	40.00
Sherbet, 4 oz.	12.00	25.00	30.00
Soda, Footed, 5 oz.	22.00	40.00	45.00
Soda, Footed, 8 oz.	18.00	35.00	40.00
Soda, Footed, 12 oz.	18.00	35.00	40.00
Sugar	35.00	50.00	60.00
Tumbler, 10 oz	24.00	50.00	60.00

KING'S CROWN, NO. 4016

Date: 1950s. Later production in the 1970s by Indiana Glass

Manufacturer: Tiffin Glass Co., Tiffin, OH

Colors: Crystal. Decorated with ruby stain, cranberry, gold, platinum, yellow, green or blue.

This pattern is an early Victorian pattern made by Adams & Co. of Pittsburgh in the late 1800s and called XLCR (Excelsior). At the time it was made in crystal and crystal with ruby stain. Tiffin reintroduced the pattern in the 1950s and added pieces in modern shapes. Punch bowls were made in crimped and flared styles, and sets were available with a foot or with an underplate. After Tiffin closed, items in the pattern were continued by Indiana Glass with ruby stain, cranberry stain and eventually with other stains and colors such as avocado green and amber. Pieces made by Indiana include: 5" wedding bowl and cover, 7" wedding bowl, 7¼ oz. goblet, 4 oz. claret or wine, 3" low candlesticks, 2 oz. cordial, 2¼ oz. cocktail, 9" berry bowl, 4" dessert, 8¼" tall candlesticks with prisms, cup & saucer, 10¼" plate, sugar & cream, 13¼" plate, 8¼" salad plate, ice tea, salad bowl, tid-bit (2 tier). All descriptions are from a factory catalog and were available in cranberry or ruby stain. Platinum or gold bands were available on a limited number of these pieces. Prices below are for pieces with Ruby or Cranberry stain.

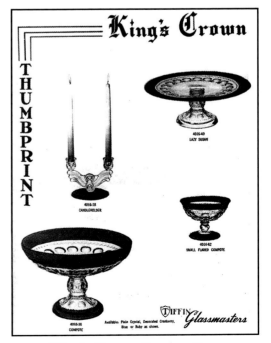

King's Crown Catalog Page

5

KING'S CROWN, NO 4016 *(continued)*

King's Crown Catalog Page

Ashtray, (Rectangular) 4" (No. 4016-56) $10.00
Ashtray, (Rectangular) 6" (No. 4016-54) 12.00
Ashtray, Square, 5¼" (No. 4016-17) 15.00
Bonbon, Crimped, 2 Handled, 8¾"
    (No. 4016-64) 45.00
Bowl, Cone Shape, 11¼" (No. 4016-37) 48.00
Bowl, Crimped, Footed (No. 4016-45) 40.00
Bowl, Crimped, 11¼" (No. 4016-24) 68.00
Bowl, Crimped, Footed, 12" (No. 4016-71) 45.00
Bowl, (Fruit Compote) Flared, Footed
    (No. 4016-26) 42.00
Bowl, Fruit, (Banana) Large Footed
    (No. 4016-70) 70.00
Bowl, Salad, 9¼" (No. 4016-25) 60.00
Bowl, Straight Edge (No. 4016-38) 48.00
Bowl, Wedding & Cover, Footed, 10¼"
    (No. 4016-35) 85.00
Candleholders, 2 Light, 5¼", pr. (No. 4016-18) 78.00

Candleholders, pr. 55.00
Candy Box & Cover, 6" (No. 4016-30) 45.00
Candy Box & Cover, Footed (No. 4016-44) 55.00
Cheese & Cracker Set (No. 4016-59) 60.00
Chip & Dip Set (No. 4016-60) 40.00
Cigarette Box & Cover (No. 4016-55) 55.00
Claret, 4 oz. (No. 4016-3) 10.00
Cocktail, 2¼ oz. (No. 4016-5) 10.00
Compote, Footed, Crimped (No. 4016-47) 50.00
Compote, Small (No. 4016-50) 24.00
Compote, Small, Crimped (No. 4016-68) 28.00
Compote, Small, Flared (No. 4016-62) 24.00
Compote, Small, Flat (No. 4016-63) 20.00
Cream (No. 4016-19) 23.00
Cup & Saucer (No. 4016-23) 22.00
Finger Bowl, 4" (No. 4016-16) 20.00
Flower Floater, 12¼" (No. 4016-27) 38.00
Goblet, 9 oz. (No. 4016-1) 10.00
Iced Tea, 11 oz. 15.00
Iced Tea, Footed, 12 oz. (No. 4016-11) 18.00
Juice, Footed, 4 oz. (No. 4016-8) 10.00
Juice, 4¼ oz. 12.00
Lazy Susan or Large Salver (No. 4016-40) 135.00
Mayonnaise Bowl, 2 Part (No. 4016-41) 20.00
Mayonnaise Bowl, 2 Part, 2 Handled, 8¼"
    (No. 4016-67) 22.00
Mayonnaise or Finger Bowl, 4", (No. 4016-41) 20.00
Nappy, Flared, 2 Handled, 8¼" (No. 4016-66) 17.00
Oyster Cocktail, 4 oz. 12.00
Party Server, Footed, 24" (No. 4016-39) 130.00
Pitcher, 48 oz. (No. 4016-53) 135.00
Plate, 2 Handled, 9¼" (No. 4016-65) 20.00
Plate, Bread & Butter, 5" 10.00
Plate, Dinner, 10" 38.00
Plate, Mayonnaise or Salad, 7¼" (No. 4016-13) 16.00
Plate, Torte, 14¼" (No. 4016-15) 45.00
Plate, With Indent, 9¾" 16.00
Punch Bowl, Flared or Cupped 195.00
Punch Bowl & Foot 195.00
Punch Cup 9.00
Relish, 5 Compartment, 14" (No. 4016-31) 62.00
Salver, 9¼" (No. 4016-42) 55.00
Salver, Cake, Footed, 12¼" (No. 4016-32) 65.00
Sugar (No. 4016-20) 20.00
Sundae, 5¼ oz. 8.00
Tumbler, 8¼ oz. 12.00
Vase, Bud, 12¼" (No. 4016-51) 50.00
Vase, Bud, 9" (No. 4016-52) 35.00
Wine, 2 oz. 8.00

MODERNTONE

Date: 1934 to 1942. Later production with fired-on colors.

Manufacturer: Hazel-Atlas Glass Co.

Colors: Amethyst, Deep Blue. Platonite with fired-on enamel colors.

Many collectors call the Deep Blue color Cobalt, but it is not a true cobalt glass, so we prefer the term Deep Blue to describe this. Platonite is Hazel-Atlas' milk glass. All-over enamel colors on Platonite include yellow, pink, blue, green, deep blue, orange, burgundy, chartreuse, gray, rust, and gold. Some pieces are found only with Platonite interiors, but other colors are found with colored interiors. Other decorations on Platonite include enamel stripes and the old fashioned Willow pattern in red and blue.

Moderntone Cup & Saucer

	Deep Blue	Amethyst	Platonite, Fired-on Colors
Ashtray/Match, 7¾"	$185.00	$	$
Bowl, Cream Soup, 5"	25.00	22.00	9.00
Bowl, 4¾"	25.00	25.00	6.00
Bowl, Crimped, 5"	58.00	36.00	
Bowl, 6¼"	105.00	85.00	10.00
Bowl, 7¼"	145.00	115.00	38.00
Bowl, 8¼"	60.00	48.00	24.00
Butter, With Metal Cover	115.00		
Cheese Dish With Metal Cover, 7" . .	375.00		
Cream	15.00	15.00	6.00
Cup & Saucer *(Illus.)*	15.00	15.00	6.00
Custard Cup.	20.00	18.00	
Iced Tea, 12 oz.	155.00	110.00	12.00
Juice, 5 oz.	47.00	42.00	8.00
Plate, 5¾"	7.00	6.00	4.00
Plate, 6¾"	12.00	9.00	5.00
Plate, 7¾"	15.00	13.00	5.00
Plate, 8¾"	20.00	18.00	7.00
Plate, Sandwich, 10¼"	67.00	50.00	15.00
Platter, Oval, 11"	55.00	50.00	18.00
Platter, Oval, 12"	105.00	75.00	22.00
Salt & Pepper, pr.	45.00	40.00	16.00
Sherbet.	16.00	14.00	5.00
Sugar, Metal Lid	50.00		
Sugar (no lid)	12.00	12.00	6.00
Tumbler, 9 oz.	47.00	35.00	10.00

"LITTLE HOSTESS PARTY SET"

These sets were offered in 14 and 16 piece sets of mixed colors, including pink, black, white, lemon, beige, aqua, gray, rust, gold, turquoise, green, chartreuse, burgundy, blue and yellow. While there is some price variation according to color, most pieces are valued in the following ranges:

Cup & Saucer	$ 17.00 to $30.00
Cream.	15.00 to 22.00
Plate	10.00 to 18.00
Sugar.	15.00 to 22.00
Teapot with Lid	120.00 to 160.00

MOONDROPS, NO. 37

Above: Moondrops 8¼" Relish, 3 Foot,
3 Compartment; ¾ oz. Cordial;
2 oz. Handled Bar Glass, Individual Cream

Date: 1932 to 1940s

Manufacturer: New Martinsville Glass Co., New Martinsville, WV

Colors: Amber, Amethyst, Black, Ritz Blue, Crystal, Dark Green, Green, Jade, Pale Blue, Pale Green, Ruby, Rose

Patented by Ira M. Clarke for New Martinsville Glass Co. in October of 1932. Patent No. 88,398 granted. The main motif of the pattern consists of the large raised lozenge shapes about the pieces. The decanters and wines which are now known as the "rocket" shape, were originally described as "tripod base." Goblets and wines may be found with metal stems—these should be valued at 75% of those listed below.

Right: Moondrops Decanter & Wines,
Rocket or Tripod Bases

	Ruby, Blue	All Other Colors
Ashtray, 4"	$28.00	$20.00
Ashtray, 6"	42.00	24.00
Bar Glass, 2 oz., with or without Handle *(Illus.)*	25.00	15.00
Bowl, 3 Footed, Console, 10"	115.00	80.00
Bowl, 3 Footed, Crimped, 10"	125.00	85.00
Bowl, 5¼"	34.00	18.00
Bowl, 6¾"	115.00	55.00
Bowl, Console, 13"	180.00	75.00
Bowl, Footed, 8¼"	80.00	35.00
Bowl, Oval Vegetable, 9¾"	100.00	74.00
Butter & Cover.	450.00	315.00
Candlesticks, 3 Light, pr.	150.00	80.00
Candlesticks, 5", pr.	110.00	55.00
Candlesticks, Crimped, 2", pr.	55.00	35.00
Candlesticks, Nappy Shape, 4¼", pr.	45.00	30.00
Candy Dish, 8"	45.00	26.00
Casserole & Cover, 9¾"	250.00	165.00
Celery, Boat Shape, 11¼"	50.00	30.00
Cocktail Shaker.	100.00	75.00

	Ruby, Blue	All Other Colors
Comport, 11¼"	78.00	54.00
Comport, 4".	35.00	24.00
Cordial, Footed, ¾ oz. *(Illus.)*	45.00	32.00
Cream	24.00	18.00
Cream, Individual *(Illus.)*.	26.00	17.00
Cup & Saucer.	24.00	15.00
Decanter, 7¾"	82.00	65.00
Decanter, 8¼"	110.00	75.00
Decanter, 10¼", Rocket or Tripod *(Illus.)*	375.00	270.00
Decanter, 11¼"	135.00	90.00
Goblet, 9 oz.	45.00	26.00
Gravy Boat	165.00	90.00
Iced Tea, 12 oz.	40.00	25.00
Juice, 5 oz.	26.00	20.00
Juice, Footed, 3 oz.	24.00	16.00
Juice, Footed, 5 oz.	26.00	18.00
Mug, 12 oz.	55.00	37.00
Oval, 2 Handled, 9¾"	95.00	72.00
Perfume & Stopper, Rocket or Tripod	260.00	160.00

(continued) MOONDROPS, NO. 37

	Ruby, Blue	All Other Colors		Ruby, Blue	All Other Colors
Pickle Dish, 7¼".	40.00	25.00	Sherbet, 2¼"	20.00	12.00
Pitcher, 24 oz..	190.00	120.00	Sherbet, 4¼"	27.00	18.00
Pitcher, 32 oz..	300.00	140.00	Sugar	20.00	14.00
Pitcher, 53 oz..	200.00	150.00	Sugar, Individual.	20.00	14.00
Pitcher with Ice Lip, 50 oz..	235.00	175.00	Tray, for Individual Sugar		
Plate, 5¾"	12.00	8.00	& Cream	45.00	25.00
Plate, 6"	9.00	6.00	Tumbler, 7 oz..	22.00	15.00
Plate, 7"	14.00	9.00	Tumbler, 8 oz..	22.00	15.00
Plate, 8¼"	15.00	12.00	Tumbler, 9 oz..	25.00	18.00
Plate, 9¼"	25.00	18.00	Tumbler, Handled, 9 oz.	34.00	24.00
Plate, Sandwich, 14"	50.00	25.00	Vase, 9¼" Rocket or Tripod.	240.00	140.00
Plate, Sandwich, Handled, 14" . . .	55.00	30.00	Vase, Crimped Top, 7¾"	90.00	70.00
Plate, with Indent, 6"	15.00	9.00	Vase, Bud, 8¼",		
Platter, 12"	40.00	25.00	Rocket or Tripod	260.00	165.00
Powder Jar & Cover, 3 Footed	185.00	120.00	Vase, 7"	90.00	70.00
Relish, 3 Footed, 3 Compartment,			Wine, Footed, 4 oz..	24.00	15.00
8¼" *(Illus.)*.	34.00	22.00	Wine, 4¾", Rocket or Tripod *(Illus.)*.	65.00	35.00

OLD ENGLISH, NO. 166

Date: 1930s

Manufacturer: Imperial Glass Corporation, Bellaire, OH

Colors: Crystal, Ruby

Prices are for pieces in crystal. For Ruby add 100%.

Old English Catalog Page

Baked Apple, 6".	$12.00	Iced Tea, 12 oz..	15.00
Bowl, Flower, 7"	32.00	Mug, 10 oz..	25.00
Cocktail, 5 oz..	10.00	Nappy, 6"	12.00
Comport or Pretzel Bowl, 9"	40.00	Plate, 7"	8.00
Compote, 4¼"	9.00	Water, 9 oz..	15.00
Finger Bowl.	12.00		

OLD SANDWICH, NO. 1404

Old Sandwich Large Beer Mug

Date: 1931 to 1956

Manufacturer: A. H. Heisey & Co., Newark, OH

Colors: Crystal, Sahara. Some pieces in Flamingo, Moongleam, Cobalt and Amber. A few very rare pieces are known in Tangerine and Zircon.

Reproductions: Imperial Glass Corp. made the stems and tumblers in crystal with the Diamond H intact.

Created as a copy of early Sandwich glass (Pillar) but in contemporary shapes. Originally called Early American Thumbprint, but changed to Old Sandwich within weeks. Some creams listed are made from the beer mugs. Most items are marked with the Diamond H. Imperial reissued most of the stemware and sodas in crystal only. Prices are for pieces in Crystal. For pieces in Moongleam, Flamingo or Sahara, add 100%.

Ashtray, Individual	$10.00
Bar, 1¼ oz.	22.00
Basket, Applied Handle (made from soda)	300.00+
Beer Mug, 12 oz.	35.00
Beer Mug, 16 oz.	50.00
Beer Mug, 18 oz. *(Illus.)*	60.00
Beer Mug, Sham, 10 oz.	110.00
Bowl, Finger	15.00
Bowl, Floral, Oval, Footed, 12"	40.00
Bowl, Floral, Round, Footed, 11"	50.00
Candlesticks, 1 Light, 6", pr.	90.00
Catsup Bottle & Stopper	50.00
Cigarette Holder, Square	100.00
Claret, 4 oz.	18.00
Cocktail, 3 oz.	15.00
Comport, 6"	40.00
Cream, 12 oz., (made from Beer Mug)	40.00
Cream, 14 oz., (made from Beer Mug)	45.00
Cream, 18 oz., (made from Beer Mug)	50.00
Cream, Oval	18.00
Cream, Round	40.00
Cup & Saucer	25.00
Decanter & Stopper, 1 pt., Oval	115.00
Goblet, Low Footed, 10 oz.	22.00
Jug, ¼ gal.	70.00

Jug, Ice, ¼ gal.	70.00
Oil & Stopper, 2¼ oz.	50.00
Oyster Cocktail, 4 oz.	15.00
Parfait, 4¼ oz.	22.00
Pilsner, 8 oz.	45.00
Plate, Square, 6"	12.00
Plate, Square, 7"	15.00
Plate, Square, 8"	15.00
Popcorn Bowl, Cupped, Footed	95.00
Salt & Pepper, pr.	40.00
Saucer Champagne, 5 oz.	18.00
Sherbet, 4 oz.	12.00
Soda or Iced Tea, 8 oz.	17.00
Soda or Iced Tea, Footed, 12 oz.	17.00
Soda, 5 oz. (cupped or straight)	17.00
Soda, 10 oz. (cupped or straight)	17.00
Soda, 12 oz. (cupped or straight)	17.00
Sugar, Oval	18.00
Sugar, Round	40.00
Sundae, 6 oz.	15.00
Toddy, 6¼ oz.	15.00
Tumbler, 8 oz.	15.00
Tumbler, Low Footed, 10 oz.	15.00
Wine, 2¼ oz.	22.00

PILGRIM, NO. 2400

Date: Ca. 1950s

Manufacturer: Jeannette Glass Co., Jeannette, PA

Colors: Crystal, pale blue, shell pink (opaque). Crystal sometimes decorated with 22k gold.

Jeannette also referred to this pattern by the name Thumbprint, so both names are original with the company. Prices are for pieces in Crystal. For pale blue pieces add 20% and for shell pink, add 50%.

Bowl, Fruit, 9¼" (No. 2459) *(Illus.)* . . . . $ 8.00
Cocktail Glass, 3 oz. (No. 2463) 4.00
Dish, Fruit, 5" (No. 2455) 3.00
Goblet, 8 oz. (No. 2428) 7.00
Juice Glass, 5 oz. (No. 2435) *(Illus.)* 4.00
Pitcher, Juice or Milk, 24 oz. (No. 2431) 10.00
Plate, Salad, 8¼" (No. 2408) 3.00
Sherbet, 5 oz. (No. 2412) 4.00
Tray, Oval, 10" (No. 2465) 8.00
Tumbler, Water, 10 oz. (No. 2440) *(Illus.)* 5.00

Pilgrim Bowl

Pilgrim Tumbler & Juice Glass

PLAZA, NO. 21

Date: 1931

Manufacturer: Duncan & Miller Glass Co., Washington, PA

Colors: Crystal, Amber, Rose, Green. Some items in Ruby.

This small table ware pattern was patented by William Reese and given patent number 84440. Note: Numbers and letters with listings indicate pieces shown in these ads.

Detail of Plaza Original Company Ad

Detail of Plaza Original Company Ad

PLAZA, NO. 21 *(continued)*

	Crystal	Colors		Crystal	Colors
Bowl, Flared, 16" (E)	$45.00	$85.00	Oil & Stopper (4)	40.00	95.00
Bowl, Regular, 10" (F).	30.00	50.00	Parfait.	14.00	30.00
Candlesticks, 2 Light, pr. (D)	50.00	80.00	Pitcher, Flip (15).	45.00	110.00
Cocktail (7)	8.00	17.00	Plate, 6" (H).	5.00	10.00
Cocktail, Footed (No. 21¼) (C, 2)	6.00	15.00	Plate, 7¼"	6.00	12.00
Cordial (10)	25.00	60.00	Plate, 8¼"	7.00	15.00
Cup & Saucer (G).	20.00	50.00	Plate, Finger Bowl	5.00	10.00
Goblet (A)	15.00	40.00	Plate, Handled, 10¼" (J).	24.00	45.00
Ice Cream (8)	8.00	15.00	Salt & Pepper, pr. (I)	30.00	55.00
Iced Tea, Flat (14)	10.00	22.00	Saucer Champagne (6)	8.00	16.00
Iced Tea, Footed (No. 21¼) (B, 1) .	12.00	25.00	Tumbler, Footed (No. 21¼).	7.00	14.00
Juice, Orange, Flat (12)	5.00	12.00	Tumbler, Table, Flat (13)	8.00	16.00
Juice, Orange, Footed (No. 21¼). .	6.00	17.00	Whiskey, Flat (11).	8.00	16.00
Mustard & Cover (3)	35.00	75.00	Wine (9).	12.00	35.00

PRISCILLA, NO. 2321

Priscilla Catalog Illustration

Date: 1925 to 1930

Manufacturer: Fostoria Glass Co., Moundsville, WV

Colors: Crystal, Amber, Blue, Green. The bouillon and cream were the only pieces made in Rose and Azure.

A very plain pattern relieved only by the interesting handles and the two raised bands around the tops of pieces. Blue is usually 10% to 20% higher than other colors. Fostoria made another Priscilla pattern earlier in pressed glass which is not similar to this one.

	Crystal	Colors		Crystal	Colors
Bouillon or Sugar	$12.00	$18.00	Mayonnaise	30.00	45.00
Cream	10.00	15.00	Iced Tea, Footed	15.00	22.00
Sugar	10.00	15.00	Jug, 3 Pint *(Illus.)*	75.00	110.00
Cup & Saucer.	15.00	22.00	Plate, Luncheon, 8"	10.00	15.00
Custard, Footed & Handled	10.00	15.00	Saucer Champagne *(Illus.)*	12.00	16.00
Goblet, 9 oz.	15.00	22.00	Sherbet	10.00	15.00
Goblet, Luncheon, 7 oz.	15.00	22.00	Tumbler, Footed & Handled	15.00	22.00

REEDED, NO. 701 (SPUN)

Date: 1935

Manufacturer: Imperial Glass Corporation, Bellaire, OH

Colors: Crystal, Ruby, Ritz Blue, Amber, Green

This pattern was patented by E. W. Newton in 1935. It was called "Reeded" by Imperial. Later researchers have applied the "Spun" name. Other companies made pieces similar to Reeded. Look closely and see that the reeded bands have 2 at one level and then 1 raised. This should help determine which pieces are truly Reeded and those which only appear to be part of the pattern. Pieces listed are from old catalog pages and factory information. All pieces may not be found in all colors. The prices are for crystal. For colored pieces, especially Ruby and Ritz Blue, add 100%.

Reeded Original Imperial Photograph

Ashtray, 2¼"	$6.00
Bitters & Tube, 3 oz.	18.00
Bowl & Cover *(Illus.)*	30.00
Bowl, Deep Salad, 10"	15.00
Bowl, Rose, 5"	25.00
Bowl, Rose, 6" (ball shape)	28.00
Bowl, 8" Fruit	12.00
Candleholders, 1 Light (ball shape), pr.	30.00
Cigarette Holder	12.00
Cocktail Shaker, 36 oz.	35.00
Cocktail, Footed, 3¼ oz.	10.00
Cologne & Stopper	35.00
Cream	15.00
Cup & Saucer	22.00
Fruit, 4¼"	8.00
Hi-ball, 12 oz. (straight sided)	15.00
Iced Tea, 12 oz. (No. 1701) *(Illus.)*	18.00
Ice Tub	28.00
Jar, Covered, Small	38.00

Jar, Covered, Medium	55.00
Juice, 5 oz. *(Illus.)*	10.00
Juice, 5 oz. (No. 1701)	12.00
Muddler	12.00
Nappy, 7"	11.00
Old Fashioned, 7 oz.	10.00
Pitcher, Ice Lip, 80 oz.	55.00
Plate, Cupped Edge, 13¼"	20.00
Plate, Flat Edge, 14"	20.00
Plate, Salad, 8" *(Illus.)*	8.00
Puff Box & Cover	30.00
Sherbet *(Illus.)*	12.00
Tumbler, 8 oz. (No. 1701) *(Illus.)*	15.00
Sugar	15.00
Vase, 9"	18.00
Vase, Ball, 2¼"	15.00
Vase, Ball, 4"	15.00
Vase, Bud, 5"	12.00

RING

Ring Ice Bucket with Colored Bands & Pitcher.

Date: 1927 to 1932

Manufacturer: Hocking Glass Co., Lancaster, OH

Colors: Crystal; Crystal decorated with many colored rings; Crystal decorated with platinum rims. Green. Limited production in Pink, Light Blue and Red.

Many variations in colored rings can be found. Some collectors add pieces which match exactly while others mix and match. Any pieces in Red, Pink or Blue are valued about 50% to 60% more than Green pieces.

	Crystal	Green, Crystal Decorated
Bar Glass, 1¼ oz.	$ 9.00	$18.00
Bowl, 5"	6.00	10.00
Bowl, 8"	15.00	25.00
Cocktail, Footed	12.00	17.00
Cocktail Shaker	25.00	42.00
Cup & Saucer	8.00	13.00
Cream	8.00	11.00
Decanter & Stopper	33.00	54.00
Goblet, 9 oz.	15.00	27.00
Ice Bucket *(Illus.)*	27.00	45.00
Iced Tea, Footed	16.00	27.00
Juice, 5 oz.	7.00	12.00
Pitcher, 60 oz.	24.00	35.00
Pitcher, 80 oz. *(Illus.)*	25.00	45.00
Plate, 6¼"	4.00	5.00
Plate, 6¼", (indent at edge)	7.00	10.00
Plate, 8"	3.50	7.50
Salt & Pepper, pr.	25.00	45.00
Sandwich, Center Handled	20.00	32.00
Sherbet, Low	7.00	21.00
Sherbet, Footed	7.50	12.00
Tumbler, 9 oz.	7.00	16.00

RIPPLE, NOS. 100, 101

Date: 1926

Manufacturer: Duncan & Miller Glass Co., Washington, PA

Colors: Crystal, Rose, Green, Cobalt, Amber, Ruby

Duncan & Miller advertised this pattern as a reproduction of Czechoslovakian glass. The ice cream dishes look like sherbets. For pieces in color, add 100%. No. 100 pieces are flat, not footed. Prices are for pieces in Crystal. For Amber add 10%, for pieces in Rose or Green, add 50%, for pieces in Ruby or Cobalt, add 150%.

Ripple Catalog Page

Bowl, Low Flower, Flared or Roll Edge $30.00	Oil & Stopper, 6 oz. 45.00
Candleblocks, 1 Light, pr. 25.00	Parfait, 5 oz. 15.00
Candlesticks, 1 Light, pr. 28.00	Pickle Tray, 8" 12.00
Celery Tray, 11" 15.00	Pitcher, ½ gal. 55.00
Cocktail, 3 oz. 10.00	Plate, 6" 5.00
Cream, Hotel, 6 oz. 12.00	Plate, 8" 7.00
Finger Bowl 12.00	Plate, 14" 20.00
Goblet, Luncheon, 9 oz. 12.00	Saucer Champagne, 5 oz. 8.00
Goblet, Tall, 9 oz. 14.00	Sugar & Cover, Hotel, 8 oz. 16.00
Honey Jar & Cover 45.00	Tumbler, 8 oz. (No. 100) 15.00
Ice Cocktail & Liner 20.00	Tumbler, 9 oz. (No. 100) 15.00
Ice Cream, Footed, 4 oz. or 5 oz. 10.00	Tumbler, Footed, 11 oz. 14.00
Iced Tea 15.00	Tumbler, Footed, 2 oz. 12.00
Iced Tea, Footed, 11 oz. 15.00	Tumbler, Footed, 9 oz. 12.00
Jello, Footed, 5 oz. 8.00	Vase. 30.00
Juice, Orange, Footed, 5 oz. 10.00	Water Bottle 25.00
Juice, Orange, 5 oz. (No. 100) 12.00	Wine, 3 oz. 12.00

SATURN, NO. 1485

Saturn Hostess Helper

Date: 1935 to 1957

Manufacturer: A. H. Heisey & Co., Newark, OH

Colors: Crystal, Zircon. Limited pieces in Sahara, Dawn and Limelight.

Reproductions: Imperial Glass Corp. made the stem ware and several serving pieces in crystal.

The name is derived from the heavy ringed optic in all pieces of the pattern. Tiffin and Duncan & Miller also made patterns using a Saturn optic. Most Saturn items are marked with the Diamond H. Imperial reproductions consist of about 25 items, all in crystal.

	Crystal	Zircon		Crystal	Zircon
Baked Apple	$25.00	$120.00	Parfait, 5 oz.	18.00	90.00
Bowl, Floral, 13"	45.00	160.00	Plate, 6"	15.00	45.00
Bowl, Fruit, 12"	50.00	190.00	Plate, 7"	18.00	50.00
Bowl, Salad, 11"	50.00	190.00	Plate, 8"	18.00	80.00
Candelabra with Ball Drops,			Plate, Rolled Edge, 6¼"	15.00	45.00
2 Light, pr.	350.00+	1,500.00+	Plate, Torte, 13"	37.00	150.00
Candleblocks, 2 Light, pr.	170.00	700.00+	Plate, Torte, 15"	45.00	170.00
Cocktail, 3 oz.	15.00	85.00	Relish, 2 Compartment,		
Comport, 7"	45.00	230.00	Handled, 7"	65.00	300.00+
Cream	30.00	170.00	Rose Bowl	55.00	185.00
Cup & Saucer	35.00	135.00	Saucer Champagne, 6 oz.	17.00	100.00
Finger Bowl	15.00	65.00	Sherbet, 4¼ oz.	10.00	75.00
Fruit Cocktail, 4 oz.	10.00	70.00	Soda, 5 oz.	15.00	75.00
Goblet, 10 oz.	22.00	130.00	Soda, 12 oz.	15.00	85.00
Hostess Helper, 2 pcs. *(Illus.)*	70.00		Sugar	30.00	170.00
Marmalade & Cover	48.00	285.00	Tray, Tid-Bit	25.00	110.00
Mayonnaise	25.00	120.00	Tumbler, Luncheon, 9 oz.	30.00	90.00
Mustard & Cover	35.00		Tumbler, 10 oz.	15.00	90.00
Mustard & Paddle Cover	85.00	400.00+	Vase, 8¼" (flared or straight)	45.00	275.00
Nappy, 5"	18.00	50.00	Vase, Violet	30.00	200.00
Oil & Stopper, 2 oz.	60.00	400.00+	Whipped Cream, 5"	30.00	135.00
Old Fashion, 8 oz.	20.00	80.00			

TALLY HO, NO. 1402

Date: Ca. 1932

Manufacturer: Cambridge Glass Co., Cambridge, OH

Colors: Crystal, Carmen, Royal Blue, Amethyst, and Windsor Blue (light opaque)

An extensive tableware and bar ware line with many interesting pieces. Other colors may have been made, but the entire line may not have been made in all listed colors. The design consists of plain wares with concentric rings usually about the lower part of the body. Stemware was made both with pressed and blown bowls.

Tally Ho Catalog Illustrations

	Crystal	Carmen & Blue		Crystal	Carmen & Blue
Ashtray, 4"	$12.00	$38.00	Cream	10.00	28.00
Ashtray, Center Handle, 4"	32.00	70.00	Cup & Saucer (*Illus.*)	18.00	35.00
Ash Well, 2 pcs.	38.00	75.00	Decanter, 34 oz. (No. 38)	35.00	80.00
Bowl, 10"	15.00	45.00	Decanter, 34 oz. (No. 39)	40.00	95.00
Bowl, 10¼"	18.00	50.00	Finger Bowl	8.00	18.00
Bowl, 11"	18.00	55.00	Frappe Cocktail & Liner, 5"	15.00	30.00
Bowl, 2 Handled, 10¼"	15.00	50.00	Frappe Cocktail & Liner, Tall,		
Bowl, 3 Compartment, 11"	35.00	75.00	Footed	18.00	34.00
Bowl, Low Footed, 10¼"	35.00	70.00	Fruit Saucer, Footed, 4¼"	8.00	20.00
Bowl, Pan, 12¼"	12.00	38.00	Goblet, 10 oz.	12.00	30.00
Bowl, Pan, 17"	24.00	55.00	Goblet, 14 oz.	14.00	35.00
Bowl, Pan, 9" or 10"	10.00	30.00	Goblet, 18 oz.	20.00	45.00
Candelabra with Prisms, 1 Light,			Goblet, Lunch, 10 oz.	10.00	24.00
6¼", pr.	75.00	135.00	Grape Fruit, 6¼"	7.00	18.00
Candlesticks, 1 Light, 5", pr.			Ice Pail	25.00	60.00
(*Illus. of one*)	32.00	70.00	Iced Fruit or Salad Service,		
Candlesticks, 1 Light, 6¼", pr.	40.00	75.00	6" or 7"	18.00	50.00
Celery, 12"	11.00	40.00	Jug, 88 oz.	40.00	110.00
Cereal, Footed, 6¼"	8.00	20.00	Jug, Tankard, 74 oz.	45.00	125.00
Cheese & Cracker, 2 pcs.,			Juice, Tomato or Orange,		
14" or 17"	30.00	75.00	Low Stem, 5 oz.	7.00	24.00
Cigarette Holder, Oval	30.00	48.00	Juice, Tomato or Orange,		
Claret, 4¼ oz.	9.00	26.00	Tall Stem, 6 oz. (*Illus.*)	7.00	24.00
Coaster, 4"	5.00	15.00	Mint, High Footed, 6"	12.00	30.00
Cocktail or Oyster Cocktail,			Mint, Low Footed	12.00	30.00
Low Stem, 4 oz.	8.00	24.00	Nappy, 2 Handled, 6"	7.00	18.00
Cocktail Shaker, Footed, 50 oz.	55.00		Nappy, 2 Handled, 6¼"	8.00	20.00
Cocktail Shaker, Handled	65.00		Plate, 2 Handled, 7"	8.00	17.00
Cocktail, 3 oz.	9.00	24.00	Plate, Bread & Butter, 6"	7.00	22.00
Comport, Low Footed, 4¼"	12.00	30.00	Plate, Buffet Lunch, 18"	28.00	65.00
Comport, Low Footed, 7"	16.00	38.00	Plate, Buffet, 18"	25.00	55.00
Comport, Tall, 4¼"	12.00	30.00	Plate, Cabaret, 17¼"	25.00	55.00
Comport, Tall, 6¼"	18.00	45.00	Plate, Dinner, 9¼"	18.00	45.00
Cookie Jar	65.00	185.00	Plate, Finger Bowl	4.00	10.00
Cordial, 1 oz.	18.00	55.00	Plate, Footed, 18"	27.00	65.00

TALLY HO, NO. 1402 *(continued)*

	Crystal	Carmen & Blue
Plate, Salad, 8" *(Illus.)*	7.00	22.00
Plate, Sandwich, 2 Handled, 11¼"	15.00	45.00
Plate, Service, 10¼"	22.00	55.00
Plate, Tea, 7"	7.00	22.00
Punch Bowl, Footed, 13"	70.00	275.00
Punch Cup, Footed	8.00	22.00
Punch Mug, 6 oz.	12.00	32.00
Punch Tray, 17¼"	25.00	55.00
Relish, 2 Compartment, 2 Handled, 6"	8.00	20.00
Relish, 3 Compartment, 8"	17.00	42.00
Relish, 4 Compartment, 2 Handled, 10"	18.00	42.00
Salad Dressing, Twin	18.00	45.00
Salad Dressing, Twin, Footed	20.00	55.00
Sauce Boat	18.00	45.00
Sherbet, Low, 6¼ oz.	7.00	20.00
Sherbet, Tall, 7¼ oz.	9.00	25.00
Stein, Handled, 12 oz. (straight sides)	18.00	55.00
Stein, Handled, 14 oz.	18.00	55.00
Sugar	10.00	28.00
Tumbler, 14 oz.	8.00	20.00
Tumbler, Tall, 15 oz.	9.00	26.00

	Crystal	Carmen & Blue
Tumbler, Handled, 2¼ oz.	15.00	30.00
Vase, Footed, 12"	34.00	150.00
Wine, 2¼ oz.	10.00	27.00

STEMWARE, NO. 1402/100

	Crystal	Carmen & Blue
Brandy Inhaler, Tall	$18.00	$40.00
Claret	15.00	35.00
Cocktail	15.00	32.00
Cordial	18.00	38.00
Goblet *(Illus.)*	18.00	45.00
Oyster Cocktail	9.00	25.00
Sherbet, Low	9.00	25.00
Sherbet, Tall	12.00	30.00
Wine	15.00	38.00

STEMWARE, NO. 1402/150

	Crystal	Carmen & Blue
Brandy Inhaler, Low	$15.00	$35.00
Tumbler, Footed, 3 oz.	11.00	25.00
Tumbler, Footed, 5 oz.	10.00	22.00
Tumbler, Footed, 12 oz.	10.00	24.00
Tumbler, Footed, 16 oz.	10.00	24.00

TRADITION

165. 10 ounce Goblet
6 dozen in No. 51 carton
Weight 60 pounds

165. 6 ounce Sherbet
6 dozen in No. 52 carton
Weight 45 pounds

165. 12 ounce Iced Tea
6 dozen in No. 29 carton
Weight 60 pounds

1654½ A. 4½ inch Finger Bowl
8 dozen in No. 1 carton
Weight 65 pounds

1654½ X. 6 inch Baked Apple
8 dozen in No. 1 carton
Weight 65 pounds

Tradition Catalog Illustration

Date: 1930s

Manufacturer: Imperial Glass Corporation, Bellaire, OH

Colors: Crystal, Green

Prices are for pieces in crystal, add 25% for color.

Baked Apple, 6"	$12.00
Cake Plate, Round, 72 holes (Birthday Cake)	110.00
Finger Bowl	12.00
Goblet, 10 oz.	15.00
Iced Tea, 12 oz.	12.00
Nappy, Flared, 6¾"	12.00
Nappy, Shallow, 7"	12.00
Pitcher, Ice Lipped	45.00
Plate, Salad, 8"	8.00
Sherbet, 6 oz.	8.00

WHIRLPOOL, NO.1506

Date: 1936 to 1957

Manufacturer: A. H. Heisey & Co., Newark, OH

Colors: Crystal, Zircon

Reproductions: Many items were made by Imperial Glass Corporation after they purchased the Heisey molds, still using the Diamond H during the 1960s. Any items occurring in colors other than crystal and zircon were made by Imperial. Imperial also made an ice lip jug which was never part of Heisey's production. In the Imperial pieces, the round Whirlpools are often hexagonal in shape. Heisey's were always round. Imperial colors include crystal, amber, heather, verde, azalea and a few items in red, nut brown, ultra blue and sunshine yellow.

Whirlpool was called Provincial in later years by the Heisey company. Most pieces are marked with the Diamond H, but some are never marked. Prices are for Crystal pieces. For pieces in Zircon, add 400% to 500%.

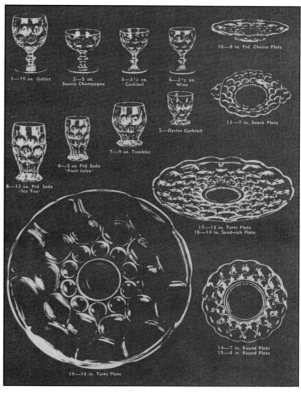

Whirlpool (Provincial) Catalog Page

Ashtray, Square	$8.00
Bonbon, 2 Handled, 7"	12.00
Bowl, 1000 Island Dressing	12.00
Bowl, Beverage, 12"	30.00
Bowl, Floral, Fruit or Salad, 12"	30.00
Bowl, Gardenia, 13"	30.00
Bowl, Nasturtium	18.00
Bowl, Orange, 15"	35.00
Bowl, Salad, 9"	22.00
Butter Dish & Cover (oblong)	45.00
Candleblocks, 1 Light, pr.	45.00
Candlesticks, 3 Light, pr.	100.00
Candy Box & Cover, 5¼"	65.00
Celery Tray, 13"	15.00
Cigarette Box & Cover	40.00
Coaster, 4"	8.00
Cream, Footed	15.00
Cream, Footed, Individual	40.00
Goblet, 10 oz.	15.00
Iced Tea, Footed, 12 oz.	20.00
Iced Tea, Regular (flat), 13 oz.	20.00
Jelly or Relish, 2 Handled, 5"	18.00
Juice, Footed, 5 oz.	18.00
Mayonnaise Bowl	20.00
Nappy, 4¼" or 5¼"	12.00

Nappy, Round or 3 Cornered, Stuck Handle, 5¼"	12.00
Nut or Jelly, Individual	20.00
Oil Bottle & Stopper, 4 oz.	85.00
Oyster Cocktail, 3¼ oz.	10.00
Plate, 7" or 8"	9.00
Plate, Cheese, Footed, 8"	12.00
Plate, Mayonnaise, 7"	9.00
Plate, Snack 7"	10.00
Plate, Torte, 13"	24.00
Plate, Sandwich, 14"	26.00
Punch Bowl Plate, 18"	60.00
Punch Bowl, 5 qt.	100.00
Punch Cup or Custard	9.00
Relish, 4 Compartment, 10"	25.00
Salt & Pepper, pr.	25.00
Sherbet or Saucer Champagne, 5 oz.	10.00
Sugar, Footed	15.00
Sugar, Footed, Individual	40.00
Tray, for Individual Sugar & Cream	30.00
Tumbler, Footed, 9 oz.	20.00
Tumbler, Regular (flat), 8 oz.	17.00
Vase, Pansy, 4"	15.00
Vase, Sweet Pea, 6"	20.00
Vase, Violet, 3¼"	15.00
Wine or Cocktail, 3¼ oz.	12.00

AMERICAN, No. 2056

TOAST TO CHRISTMAS..

THE *American* WAY

The spirit of '76 was toasted from a bowl like this. It is reminiscent of the glass your forefathers loved. Re-created years ago, and christened *American*, it is patriotically in keeping with these times . . . a pattern of cheer and charm and downright economical . . . a pattern from which you may select over 250 open stock gifts . . . from this gargantuan punch bowl to a dainty powder jar for your lady's dressing table.

P. S... For descriptive folder write to Dept. 4217.

FOSTORIA

GLASS COMPANY · · · MOUNDSVILLE · WEST VIRGINIA

American 1942 Ad

Gifts

to hear the angels sing

Snap off the lamps and burn the candles . . . listen to the heavenly music float. It's Christmas . . . a real old-fashioned family gathering with *American* crystal to keynote your fun . . . Fostoria's favorite pattern to give you a lift in winter, summer, or any season. And the nicest gift you can give or get . . . a lustrous, solid, rugged crystal for long life, prismic crystal for lasting beauty. But best of all you get so much for so little . . . over 180 inexpensive items in open stock at the better stores everywhere.

FOSTORIA

FOSTORIA GLASS COMPANY · · · MOUNDSVILLE · WEST VIRGINIA

American 1949 Ad

Date: 1915. Still in production by Indiana Glass Co. in only a few items.

Manufacturer: Fostoria Glass Co., Moundsville, WV

Colors: Crystal. Limited availability in Amber, Blue, Canary, Green and Ruby. A few pieces were made in the 1950s in Milk Glass.

Reproductions: Items followed by [R] are known to have been reproduced recently in crystal. There are probably more items than these reproduced and more may be made in the future by Indiana Glass, who has many of the molds.

Ruby pieces were made later by Viking Glass Co. for Fostoria. This pattern vies with Heisey's Old Williamsburg as being the longest made American glass pattern. Due to its lengthy production, many pieces were added and discontinued over the years, resulting in some very rare pieces. Pieces are well finished, fire polished and usually have ground bottoms. Prices are for pieces in Crystal. Some early colored pieces command large prices.

(continued) AMERICAN, No. 2056

Almond, Oval, 2¾", 3¾" & 4½" . . . . $ 20.00	Cheese & Cracker, 2 pc. 75.00
Ashtray & Match Stand 20.00	Cigarette Box & Cover. 40.00
Ashtray, Hat. 20.00	Claret, 7 oz.. . . . . 50.00
Ashtray, Oval, 5½" (match stand) 15.00	Coaster (2 styles) 10.00
Ashtray, Square, 3". 8.00	Cocktail, Footed, 3 oz. 15.00
Ashtray, Square, 5". 85.00	Cologne, 6 oz. 110.00
Banana Split Dish. . . . . 500.00+	Cologne, 8 oz. 135.00
Basket, Reed Handle 120.00	Comport, 5" 35.00
Beer Mug, 4½" 85.00	Comport, 8½" 45.00
Bell . . . . 350.00+	Comport, 9½" 55.00
Bitters Bottle with Tube 80.00	Cracked Ice, Hotel . . . . 3,000.00+
Boat, 8½" 20.00	Cracker Jar & Cover or Cookie Jar, Pretzel Jar [R] . . 285.00
Boat, 12" 25.00	Cream Soup. 50.00
Bon Bon, 3 Toed, 7" 15.00	Cream, 9½ oz. 22.00
Bottle, Cordial with Stopper. 110.00	Cream, Tea, 3 oz. (2056½) 22.00
Bottle, Water (carafe) . . . . 450.00+	Cream, Individual 12.00
Bowl & Cover, Square, Footed, 7" . . . . 200.00+	Crushed Fruit & Cover . . . . 1,500.00+
Bowl & Cover, Wedding, 6½" 110.00	Cup, Footed, & Saucer. 12.00
Bowl, 2 Handled, Footed, 8" (Trophy Shape) 125.00	Decanter & Stopper, 24 oz. 120.00
Bowl, 3 Toed, 10½" 45.00	Finger Bowl, 4½". 60.00
Bowl, Baby, 4½" (2 styles) . . . . 45.00+	Floating Garden, 10" & 11½" 75.00
Bowl, Cupped, 7" 55.00	Flower Pot & Cover. . . . . 1,400.00+
Bowl, Fruit, Footed, 12"(Tom & Jerry) [R] . . . . . . 200.00+	Goblet, Low, 9 oz. 12.00
Bowl, Fruit, Footed, 16" 200.00	Hair Receiver & Cover. . . . . 600.00+
Bowl, Fruit, Shallow, 13" 80.00	Hat, 2½" 22.00
Bowl, Handled, 8½" 65.00	Hat, 3" 28.00
Bowl, Rolled Edge, 11½" 60.00	Hat, 4" 55.00
Bowl, Salad, 10". 50.00	Ice Bucket 65.00
Bowl, Square, Footed, 7" 110.00	Ice Cream, 5½" 60.00
Bowl, Vegetable, 2 Part, 10" 45.00	Ice Cream, Square, 3½" 38.00
Bowl, Watercress 30.00	Ice Dish & Liner 55.00
Box & Cover, Glove. 350.00+	Iced Tea, 12 oz., Straight or Flared 17.00
Box & Cover, Handkerchief 275.00	Iced Tea, Flared, Footed 17.00
Box & Cover, Jewel . . . . 400.00+	Iced Tea, or Lemonade, Handled. . . . . 240.00+
Box & Cover, Match or Hairpin . . . . 400.00+	Ice Tub & Underplate, 5⅝" & 6½" 110.00
Box, Flower, Oblong (same as butter top) 20.00	Jam Jar & Cover 65.00
Butter & Cover, Oblong [R]. 35.00	Jelly & Cover, Footed 35.00
Butter & Cover, Round 125.00	Jelly, Footed, Straight or Flared 25.00
Candelabrum, 2 Light, Bell Shape. 175.00	Jug with Ice Lip, 2 qt.. . . . . 120.00
Candlestick, Chamber 35.00	Jug with Ice Lip, 3 pt., 6¼" 70.00
Candlesticks, 3", pr. 35.00	Jug, ½ gal. (69 oz.). 275.00
Candlesticks, 6", pr. 60.00	Jug, 1 qt., 7¼". 70.00
Candlesticks, 7", pr. 195.00	Jug, 2 qt., 8". 95.00
Candlesticks, Duo, Bell Shape, pr.. . . . . 200.00	Jug, 3 pt., 8". 85.00
Candlesticks, Twin, pr.. 85.00	Juice, Tumbler, 5 oz 12.00
Candy & Cover, 7" 45.00	Juice, Footed, 5 oz.. . . . . 15.00
Candy Box & Cover, 3 Part 85.00	Lamp, Candle, 3 pcs. 210.00
Catsup Bottle & Stopper 135.00	Lamp, Hurricane 200.00
Celery, 10" (tray) 25.00	Lemon Dish. 30.00
Celery, 6", Tall 50.00	Lemon Dish & Cover. 50.00
Centerpiece, 3 Cornered, 11" 60.00	Lily Pond. 70.00
Centerpiece, 9½" 55.00	Marmalade & Cover. 95.00

AMERICAN, NO. 2056 *(continued)*

Mayonnaise 25.00	Plate, Torte, 24" . . . . 300.00+
Mayonnaise, Divided, 6¼" 25.00	Plate, Torte, Oval, 13½" 68.00
Mayonnaise, Footed, 4½" 45.00	Plate, Watercress, 8" 35.00
Molasses Can, Large 350.00	Plate, Youth, 6" 65.00
Molasses Can, Small 300.00	Platter, Oval, 10½" or 12" 60.00
Mug, Tom & Jerry 45.00	Preserve & Cover, Handled. 70.00
Mustard & Cover. 40.00	Puff & Cover, Round 300.00
Napkin Ring, 2" 20.00	Puff & Cover, Square 200.00
Nappy & Cover, 5" 32.00	Punch Bowl with High Foot, 14" 275.00
Nappy, 3 Cornered, 5" 15.00	Punch Bowl with Low Foot, 18" 350.00
Nappy, 4¼", 4½", or 5" 12.00	Punch Cup, Flared or Straight. 12.00
Nappy, 6" 18.00	Relish, 2 Part 35.00
Nappy, 7" 25.00	Relish, 3 Part 40.00
Nappy, 8" 30.00	Relish, Oval, 4 Part 70.00
Nappy, Cupped, 7½" 45.00	Relish, Square, 4 Part 175.00
Nappy, Deep, 8" 62.00	Ring Holder. . . . . 350.00+
Nappy, Deep, 10" 40.00	Rose Bowl, 3½" 24.00
Nappy, Deep, Flared, 8½" 70.00	Rose Bowl, 5" 32.00
Nappy, Flared, 4½" 15.00	Salt & Pepper, 3½", pr. 25.00
Nappy, Flared, 6¼" 30.00	Salt & Pepper, Individual, with tray, pr. 35.00
Nappy, Flared, 7" 40.00	Salt, Individual. 12.00
Nappy, Flared, 8¼" 50.00	Salver, Cake, Round, Footed, 12" 65.00
Nappy, Flared, 9½" 60.00	Salver, Cake, Round, 10½". 75.00
Nappy, Flared, 10" 55.00	Salver, Cake, Square 95.00
Nappy, Fruit, 3¾" 18.00	Sauce Boat with Underplate 85.00
Nappy, Handled, 5" 15.00	Sherbet, 4½ oz. 10.00
Nappy, Round, Handled, 4½" 15.00	Sherbet, Footed & Handled, 4½ oz. 110.00
Nappy, Shallow, 7" 30.00	Sherbet, High, Flared or Straight, 4½ oz. 14.00
Nappy, Shallow, 8" 32.00	Sherbet, Low, Flared or Straight, 5 oz.. . . . . 12.00
Nappy, Shallow, 10" 50.00	Shrimp Bowl, 12¼" 375.00
Nappy, Square, Handled, 4½" 15.00	Spooner. 48.00
Oil, 5 oz. or 7 oz. (2 stopper styles). 50.00	Straw Jar & Cover [R] 290.00
Old Fashioned Cocktail, 6 oz.. . . . . 16.00	Sugar & Cover, 6¼". 65.00
Olive, 6" 16.00	Sugar & Cover, Handled, 5¼" 24.00
Oyster Cocktail, 4½" 14.00	Sugar or Cheese Shaker 65.00
Party Server, Divided, with Metal Spoon 40.00	Sugar, Individual, 2½" (No. 2056½). 15.00
Pickle & Cover 280.00	Sugar, Tea, 2¼" 22.00
Pickle, 8" 15.00	Sundae, 6 oz. 12.00
Picture Frame. 18.00	Syrup & Glass Top, 10 oz., with underplate. 150.00
Pitcher, 1 pt. 30.00	Syrup, 6 oz. (metal screw top). 240.00
Plate, Bread & Butter, 6" 10.00	Syrup, Dripcut, 6½ oz.. . . . . 45.00
Plate, Cake, 2 Handled. 35.00	Syrup, Sani-Server (No. 2056½) 100.00
Plate, Cake, 3 Footed, 12" 45.00	Tidbit with Metal Handle 65.00
Plate, Crescent Salad 55.00	Tidbit, 3 Toed 24.00
Plate, Dinner, 9½" 25.00	Toothpick Holder. 20.00
Plate, Finger Bowl 18.00	Tray, Appetizer, Square, with 6 inserts . . . . 250.00+
Plate, Salad, 7" or 8½" 12.00	Tray, Cake with metal handle 45.00
Plate, Sandwich, 10½", 11½". 35.00	Tray, Candy, 7" x 5" . . . . 275.00+
Plate, Sandwich, 9" 35.00	Tray, Cloverleaf Condiment 180.00
Plate, Torte, 14" 42.00	Tray, for Sugar & Cream 16.00
Plate, Torte, 18" 135.00	Tray, Ice Cream, 13½" 210.00
Plate, Torte, 20" 170.00	Tray, Lunch, Handled. 40.00

(continued)AMERICAN, NO. 2056

Tray, Muffin, Handled	36.00
Tray, Oblong, 10½"	125.00
Tray, Oblong, 10½"	125.00
Tray, Oblong, 5"	110.00
Tray, Oval, 6"	45.00
Tray, Oval, 10½"	58.00
Tray, Oval, 8½" x 12"	68.00
Tray, Pin, Oval, 5¼	165.00
Tray, Round, 12"	170.00
Tray, Square	160.00
Tray, Utility, Handled	45.00
Tumbler, Baby, 3"	300.00+
Tumbler, Footed, 9 oz.	15.00
Tumbler, Straight or Flared, 8 oz.	15.00
Urn, Square, 6" or 7½"	48.00
Vase, Bagged	1,000.00+
Vase, Bud, Footed, Cupped or Flared, 6"	22.00
Vase, Bud, Footed, Cupped or Flared, 8½"	30.00
Vase, Cupped, 10"	145.00

Vase, Flared, 6"	20.00
Vase, Flared, 7" (punch bowl base)	85.00
Vase, Flared or Straight, 8"	65.00
Vase, Flared, 9"	135.00
Vase, Flared, 10"	75.00
Vase, Porch, Small or Large	2,000.00+
Vase, Square, Footed, 9"	50.00
Vase, Straight	35.00
Vase, Straight, 10"	95.00
Vase, Straight, 12"	145.00
Vase, Straight, Footed	40.00
Vase, Sweet Pea, 4½" [R]	70.00
Vase, Swung, 9" to 12"	100.00 to 200.00
Vase, Swung, 14" to 16"	200.00 to 275.00
Vase, Swung, 18" to 20"	300.00 to 375.00
Vase, Swung, 23" to 26"	400.00+
Whiskey, 2 oz.	15.00
Wine, 2½ oz.	15.00

CUBE

Date: 1929 to 1933

Manufacturer: Jeannette Glass Co., Jeannette, PA

Colors: Pink, Green, Crystal

A pattern very similar to Fostoria's American, but without the finishing of elegant glass. Pieces have no fire polishing and do not have ground bottoms. Essentially, the pattern was made to compete with American, but in a cheaper glass. Also, most pieces do not have the jagged rims found on most American, but have plain rims.

Cube Sugar and Creamer

	Crystal	Pink	Green
Bowl, 4½"	$3.00	$6.00	$7.50
Bowl, Deep, 4½"	6.00	8.50	
Bowl, 6½"	8.00	12.00	20.00
Butter & Cover	35.00	75.00	75.00
Candy Jar & Cover, 6½"	15.00	30.00	35.00
Coaster, 3¼"	2.00	5.00	6.50
Cream, 2"	2.00	5.00	
Cream, 3" (Illus.)	4.00	9.00	11.00
Cup & Saucer	8.00	12.00	14.00

	Crystal	Pink	Green
Pitcher, 45 oz.	100.00	220.00	265.00
Plate, 6"	1.50	2.50	3.00
Plate, 8"	5.00	8.50	10.00
Powder Jar & Cover, 3 feet	14.00	22.00	24.00
Salt & Pepper, pr	18.00	35.00	35.00
Sherbet, Footed	3.50	7.00	9.00
Sugar, 2"	3.00	6.00	
Sugar & Cover, 3" (Illus.)	15.00	26.00	30.00
Tumbler, 9 oz.	25.00	65.00	78.00

Chapter 4
DIAMONDS

ASTAIRE, No. 22

Astaire Original Ad

Date: 1931

Manufacturer: Duncan & Miller Glass Co., Washington, PA

Colors: Crystal, Green, Rose

Duncan advertised this pattern as "a reproduction of old Waterford cutting combined with a band of diamond shapes." Later when the pattern in crystal was decorated with ruby it was called Kimberly; when decorated with Colony Blue it was called Hilton.

	Crystal	Colors, Decorated
Bonbon, Footed, 6".	$12.00	$22.00
Cocktail, 3 oz..	9.00	18.00
Cologne Bottle & Stopper	30.00	65.00
Cordial, 1 oz.	40.00	85.00
Finger Bowl	9.00	15.00
Goblet	12.00	25.00
Ice Cream, Footed, 5 oz.	7.00	14.00
Iced Tea, 12 oz., Flat	15.00	25.00
Juice, Orange, 5 oz., Flat	8.00	17.00
Old Fashioned Cocktail, 7 oz., Flat	9.00	18.00
Parfait, 5 oz.	10.00	22.00
Plate, 8½"	9.00	20.00
Powder Box & Cover	25.00	55.00
Saucer Champagne, 5 oz..	12.00	25.00
Tray, Oblong.	11.00	24.00
Tumbler, Flat, 2 oz..	10.00	22.00
Tumbler, Flat, 9 oz..	10.00	20.00
Wine, 3 oz..	9.00	18.00

AUNT POLLY

Date: 1920s

Manufacturer: U. S. Glass Co.

Colors: Medium Blue, Green. Iridized.

The attractiveness of the medium blue makes it highly desirable. As with many other patterns, sugar lids are hard to find. The pattern is relatively limited in pieces made and also is difficult to find.

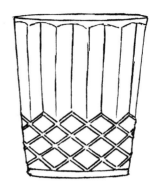

Aunt Polly Tumbler

	Blue	Green or Iridescent		Blue	Green or Iridescent
Bowl, 4¾"	$ 18.00	$ 12.00	Pitcher, 48 oz.	200.00	
Bowl, 7¾"	42.00	20.00	Plate, 6"	13.00	8.00
Bowl, Oval, 8¼"	92.00	45.00	Plate, 8"	18.00	
Butter & Cover.	215.00	275.00	Salt & Pepper	250.00	150.00
Candy & Cover, 2 Handled.	75.00	60.00	Sherbet	13.00	10.00
Cream	45.00	30.00	Sugar & Cover	200.00	120.00
Jelly, Handled, 5½".	25.00	15.00	Tumbler, 8 oz. *(Illus.)*	38.00	
Pickle, Handled, 7¼"	40.00	22.00	Vase, Footed, 6½".	38.00	28.00

CAPE COD, NO. 160

Date: 1931 to 1980s

Manufacturer: Imperial Glass Corp., Bellaire, OH

Colors: Crystal. Limited availability in the following colors: Ruby, Ritz Blue (Cobalt), Azalea, Verde Green, Amberglo, Sunshine Yellow, Fern Green, Ultra Blue, Nut Brown, Amber, Evergreen, Milk glass, Gold decoration on Crystal, Cranberry stain on Crystal

Cape Cod is second only to Candlewick as Imperial's most extensive line. It was a staple in their line for 50+ years, a remarkable length of time for a pattern to remain popular. Numbers following entries are original factory designations, as are the names of the pieces.

Cape Cod Square Cake Plate, Juice, Claret, Wine

CAPE COD, NO. 160 *(continued)*

Cape Cod 2 Oils with Original Stoppers

Ashtray, Double Rest, 5½" (160/150) $18.00
Ashtray, Single Rest, 4" (160/134/1) 12.00
Basket, 11" (160/40) 95.00
Basket, 11" (160/73/0) 125.00
Basket, Footed 11" (160/40) 90.00
Basket, Handled, 9" (160/221/0) 150.00
Bitter & Tube, 4 oz. (160/235) 35.00
Bottle, Bar & Stopper, 26 oz. (160/244) 100.00
Bottle, Cordial & Stopper, 16 oz. (160/82) 110.00
Bottle, Cordial & Stopper, 18 oz. (160/256) 110.00
Bowl, 11" (1608A) 40.00
Bowl, 2 Handled, 7½" (160/62B) 32.00
Bowl, 2 Handled, 9½" (160/145B) 40.00
Bowl, 7" (160/5F) 22.00
Bowl, 7" (160/5X) 20.00
Bowl, 7½"(160/7F) 22.00
Bowl, 8¾" (160/10F) 32.00
Bowl, Baked Apple, 6" (160/53X) 10.00
Bowl, Center, Rolled Edge, 13" (16010R) 50.00
Bowl, Crimped, 9½" (160/221C) 90.00
Bowl, Flanged Edge, 11" (Fruit, 1608X) 45.00
Bowl, Flared, 7" (160/5W) 25.00
Bowl, Float, 14" (160/92F) 65.00
Bowl, Float, 9½" (160/221F) 80.00
Bowl, Footed, 10" (160/137B) 70.00
Bowl, Fruit, 4½" (160/1W) 10.00
Bowl, Fruit, 5½" (160/23B) 15.00
Bowl, Fruit, 6" (160/3F) 15.00
Bowl, Fruit, 12½" (16010B) 65.00

Bowl, Fruit, Footed, 9" (160/67F) 62.00
Bowl, Oval Center, 12" (160/131B) 50.00
Bowl, Oval Crimped, 12" (160/131C) 80.00
Bowl, Oval Vegetable, 11" (160/124) 85.00
Bowl, Oval Vegetable, 2 Part, 11" (160/125) 85.00
Bowl, Salad, 11" (16010A) 45.00
Bowl, Salad, 11" (1608A) 45.00
Bowl, Salad, 12" (160/75B) 30.00
Bowl, Shallow Vegetable, 11¼" (1602) 75.00
Buffet Set: 16" Plate, Mayonnaise
   & Ladle, 3 pcs. (160/94) 80.00
Buffet Set: 17" Plate, Mayonnaise,
   & Ladle, 3 pcs.(16010D) 60.00
Butter & Cover, Spider, 5" (160/144) 35.00
Butter & Cover, Oblong (160/161) 40.00
Cake Server, Square, 4 Toed, 10" (160/220)
   (Illus. previous page) 95.00
Cake Stand, Footed, 10½" (160/67D) 55.00
Cake Stand, Plain Top, 11" (160/103D) 80.00
Candle Centerpiece, Flower, 6" (160/48BC) 60.00
Candleholders, 1 Light, 3" (160/170) pr. 35.00
Candleholders, 4" (160/81) pr. 50.00
Candleholders, 1 Light, 5" (160/80) pr. 40.00
Candleholders & Ornaments, 2 Light,
   (160/100) pr. 90.00
Candleholders, Aladdin, Handled, 4" (160/90) pr. . . 160.00
Candleholders, Flower, 5½" (160/45N) pr. 50.00
Candleholders, Flower, 5" (160/45B) pr. 110.00
Candleholders, Saucer, 1 Light (160/175) pr. 45.00
Candleholders, Spider, 4½" (16080) pr. 100.00
Candleholders, Twin, 2 Light (160/100) pr. 90.00
Candy Jar & Cover, 1 lb. (160/110) 60.00
Carafe, Wine & Stopper, 26 oz. (160/185) 120.00
Celery Dish, 8" (160/105) 35.00
Celery Tray, 10½" (160/189) 55.00
Cheese & Cover (160/123) 75.00
Cigarette Box & Cover, Handled (160/134) 35.00
Cigarette Lighter (1602) 30.00
Claret, 5 oz. (1602) *(Illus. previous page)* 8.00
Coaster with Spoon Rest (160/76) 5.00
Coaster (160/78) 10.00
Coaster, 4½" (1601R) 8.00
Coaster, Square, 3" (160/85) 14.00
Cocktail, 3½ oz. (1600) 15.00
Cocktail, 3½ oz. (1602) 8.00
Cocktail, Stem (160B) 9.00
Cologne & Stopper (1601) 50.00
Comport, Cupped, Footed, 5½" (160F) 30.00
Comport, Footed, 5¾" (160X) 30.00
Comport, Oval, Footed, 11¼" (1602) 45.00
Compote, Footed, 6" (160/45) 55.00
Compote & Cover, Footed, 6" (160/140) 60.00

(continued) **CAPE COD, NO. 160**

Compote, Footed, 7" (160/48B) 60.00	Mayonnaise Bowl, 12 oz. & Plate, Cupped,
Condiment Bottle & Tube or Hot Sauce, 6 oz.	7" (160/204) 80.00
(160/224) 40.00	Mayonnaise Set, 3 pc. (160/23) 25.00
Cookie/Pretzel Jar & Cover, Handled, 6¼ x 6½"	Mayonnaise Set, 3 pc. (160/52H) 35.00
(160/195) 85.00	Mayonnaise Set, 3 pc. (1604½B) 30.00
Cream (No. 160/30) 8.00	Mint, Handled, 6" (160/51H) 22.00
Cream, Footed (160/190) 15.00	Mint, Heart Shaped, 5" (160/49H) 22.00
Cream, Footed (160/31) 15.00	Mint, Round, Handled, 6" (160/51F) 22.00
Cream, Sugar & Tray Set, Square (160/25/26) 130.00	Mug, Tom & Jerry (160/200) 15.00
Cruet & Stopper, 4 oz. (160/119) *(Illus, right)* 22.00	Multi Server, 12" (160/93) 85.00
Cup & Saucer, Coffee (160/37) 10.00	Mustard & Cover (160/156) 25.00
Cup & Saucer, Tea (160/35) 8.00	Nut, Handled, 3" (160/183) 22.00
Cup, Bouillon (160/250) 35.00	Nut, Handled, 4" (160/184) 25.00
Decanter & Stopper, 24 oz. (160/212) 65.00	Oil & Stopper, 4 oz. (160/177) *(Illus. left)* 25.00
Decanter & Stopper, 30 oz. (160/163) 50.00	Oil or Vinegar & Stopper (160/70) 25.00
Dish, Individual Jelly (160/33) 10.00	Oil or Vinegar & Stopper, 6 oz. (160/241) 35.00
Dish, Vegetable, 10" (160/221) 75.00	Old Fashioned Cocktail, 7 oz 14.00
Egg Cup (No. 225) 22.00	Old Fashioned, 14 oz 14.00
Epergne, 2 pcs., 12" (160/196) 175.00	Oyster or Fruit Cocktail, 4 oz. (1602) 9.00
Finger Bowl (1602) 15.00	Oyster or Fruit Cocktail, 4 oz., Plain Stem (1602) . . . 12.00
Finger Bowl, 4½" (1604½A) 38.00	Parfait, 6 oz. (1602) 10.00
Goblet, 8 oz 8.00	Peanut & Mint Dish, 2 part, 8½" (160/192) 40.00
Goblet, 10 oz. (1600) 20.00	Peanut Jar & Cover, Handled, 12 oz. (160/210) . . . 50.00
Goblet, 11 oz. (1602) 8.00	Peanut Jar & Cover, Handled, 3½" x 4" (160/193) . . 70.00
Goblet, 14 oz 28.00	Peanut Jar & Cover, Handled, 4½" x 5" (160/194) . . 75.00
Goblet, Hoffman House, 14 oz 28.00	Pepper Mill (160/236) 22.00
Goblet, Luncheon, 9 oz. (1602) 8.00	Pitcher, Blown, 80 oz (160/176) 160.00
Gravy Bowl, 18 oz. & Plate, Cupped, 8" (160/201) . . 85.00	Pitcher, Ice Lipped, 16 oz. (160/239) 75.00
Heart, Handled, 6" (160/40H) 22.00	Pitcher, Ice Lipped, Footed, 40 oz. (160/19) 75.00
Horseradish Jar & Stopper (160/226) 60.00	Pitcher, Ice Lipped, Footed, 60 oz. (160/24) 75.00
Hurricane Lamps, 12" 2 pcs., pr 140.00	Pitcher, Martini, Blown, 40 oz. (160/178) 185.00
Hurricane Lamps, 2 pcs., (1604) pr 200.00	Pitcher, Milk, 16 oz. (160/240) 45.00
Hurricane Lamps, 9" 2 pcs (160/79) pr 145.00	Pitcher, Square, Tab Handle, 7 oz. (160/246) 95.00
Ice Bucket, 6½" (160/63) 120.00	Plate, 14" (for salad set) (160/75V) 40.00
Iced Tea or Hiball, 12 oz 10.00	Plate, 2 Handled, 8½" (160/62D) 30.00
Iced Tea, 12 oz. (1601) 15.00	Plate, 2 Handled, 9½" (160/62D) 35.00
Iced Tea, Footed, 12 oz. (1600) 15.00	Plate, 2 Handled, 11" (160/145D) 32.00
Iced Tea, Footed, 12 oz. (1602) 10.00	Plate, Birthday Cake, 72 Holes (160/72) 220.00
Iced Tea, Footed, 12 oz. Plain Stem (1602) 15.00	Plate, Bread & Butter, 6½" (160/1D) 7.00
Icer Set, 3 pcs. (160/53/3) 45.00	Plate, Bread, 12½" (160/222) 78.00
Jug, Refrigerator, 36 oz (160) 90.00	Plate, Crescent, Salad, 8" (160/12) 48.00
Juice Glass, Footed, 6 oz., Plain Stem (1602) 14.00	Plate, Cupped, 14" (160/75V) 45.00
Juice Tumbler, 6 oz. (1601) 15.00	Plate, Cupped, 16" (160/20V) 50.00
Juice Tumbler, Footed, 6 oz. (1600) 15.00	Plate, Dinner, 10" (160/10D) 25.00
Juice Tumbler, Footed, 6 oz. (1602)	Plate, Individual Butter or Coaster, 4½" (160/34) . . . 8.00
(Illus. with cake server) 8.00	Plate, Luncheon, 9" (160/7D) 15.00
Ketchup & Cover (160/252) 45.00	Plate, Regular Edge, 14" (160/75D) 32.00
Ketchup Bottle, 14 oz. (160/237) 90.00	Plate, Regular Edge, 18" (160/20D 45.00
Lug Bowl, 6½" (160/199) 30.00	Plate, Salad or Sherbet, 7" (160/3D) 7.00
Lug Dessert, 4½" (160/197) 25.00	Plate, Salad, 8" (160/5D) 7.00
Lug Soup, 5½" (160/198) 15.00	Platter, 13½" (160/124D) 45.00
Marmalade Set, 4 pcs. (160/89) 40.00	Pokal & Cover, 10" (160/133) 65.00

CAPE COD, No. 160 *(continued)*

Pokal & Cover, 11" (160/128) 65.00
Pokal & Cover, 15" (160/132) 65.00
Puff Box & Cover (1601) 45.00
Relish & Dressing Set, 4 pcs. (160/1112) 110.00
Relish, 2 part, 10½" (160/191) 45.00
Relish, 3 part, Oval, 11¼" (1602) 75.00
Relish, 4 part, 9½" (160/56) 30.00
Relish, 5 part, 11" (160/102) 60.00
Relish, Oval, 3 part, 9½" (160/55) 30.00
Salad Dressing Bowl, 6 oz. & Plate, 6" (160/207) . . . 60.00
Salad Fork & Spoon (160/701) 22.00
Salt & Pepper (160/116), pr. 22.00
Salt & Pepper (160/238), pr. 35.00
Salt & Pepper (160/96), pr. 20.00
Salt & Pepper, (160/109), pr. 20.00
Salt & Pepper, (160/117), pr. 22.00
Salt & Pepper, (1602), pr. 30.00
Salt & Pepper, Footed, (160/243), pr. 40.00
Salt & Pepper, Footed, (160/247), pr. 45.00
Salt & Pepper, Individual (160/251), pr. 20.00
Salt Dip & Pepper with Spoon, 3 pcs. (160/219) 40.00
Salt Dip (160/61) 16.00
Saucer Champagne or Tall Sherbet, 6 oz. (1602) 8.00
Server, 2 part, Handled, 8½" (160/233) 40.00
Sherbet 7.00
Sherbet, 6 oz. (1600) 15.00
Sherry, 2½ oz. (1602) 18.00
Spider, Handled, 4½" (160/180) 25.00
Spider, Handled, 5½" (160/181) 25.00
Spider, Handled, 6½" (160/182) 35.00
Spider, Handled, 2 part, 6½" (160/187) 40.00
Stein, Handled, 12 oz. (160/188) 27.00
Sugar (No. 160/30) 8.00
Sugar, Footed (160/190) 15.00
Sugar, Footed (160/31) 15.00
Sundae, 6 oz. (1602) 6.00
Tidbit Set, 2 Tier (160/2701) 60.00
Tray, Center Handled, 8" (160/149D) 60.00
Tray, Condiment, Square (160/455) 65.00
Tray for Cream & Sugar, 7" (No. 160/29) 15.00

Tray for Salt & Pepper, 5½" (160/242) 15.00
Tray, Handled, 6" (160/51T) 10.00
Tray, Pastry, 11" (160/68D) 70.00
Tumbler, 14 oz. 15.00
Tumbler, 16 oz. 22.00
Tumbler, Footed, 10 oz. (1602) 10.00
Tumbler, Juice, 6 oz. 8.00
Tumbler, Water, 9 oz. (1601) 15.00
Tumbler, Water, 10 oz. 10.00
Vase, Bud, Footed 7" (160/27) 25.00
Vase, Cylinder, 10" (160/192) 75.00
Vase, Fan, 8" (160/87F) 85.00
Vase, Flip, 8½" (160/143) 50.00
Vase, Flip, Footed, Flared, 11" (160/21) 25.00
Vase, Flip, Footed, Straight, 11" (1603) 35.00
Vase, Footed, 6¼" (160/22) 35.00
Vase, Footed, 6½" (160/110B) 65.00
Vase, Footed, 7½" (160/22) 40.00
Vase, Footed, 8½" (160/28) 30.00
Vase, Urn, 2 Handled, 10½" (160/186) 95.00
Whiskey, 2½ oz. 12.00
Wine, 2½ oz. 10.00
Wine, 3 oz. (1600) 15.00
Wine, 3 oz. (1602) *(Illus. with cake server)* 10.00

BLOWN STEMWARE, No. 3600

Cocktail, 4 oz. $15.00
Cordial, 1½ oz. 30.00
Goblet, 11 oz. 25.00
Iced Tea Tumbler, 12 oz. 20.00
Juice, 6 oz. 15.00
Sherbet, 6 oz. 15.00
Wine, 5 oz. 25.00

BLOWN TUMBLERS, No. 3611, 3612

Very hard to find.

Tumbler, 5 oz. (No. 3611) $48.00
Tumbler, 12 oz. (No. 3612) 45.00

DIAMOND, NO. 75

Date: 1940, as "Anniversary Special"

Manufacturer: Duncan & Miller Glass Co., Washington, PA

Colors: Crystal, Sienna (pale amber)

Reproductions: Much of the line was continued by U. S. Glass/Tiffin after they purchased the Duncan & Miller factory in 1955. These pieces were made in Glassport, PA.

Moderate table service including both pressed and blown stemware. Add 25% for items in color.

Diamond Divided Salad Dressing Bowl,
Iced Tea & Salad Plate

Bonbon, 2 Compartment, 2 Handled,
   Flared, 6½" $20.00
Bowl, 2 Compartment Salad Dressing, Footed,
   6" *(Illus.)* 35.00
Bowl, 2 Handled, Oval Centerpiece, 11" 35.00
Bowl, Crimped, 8" 20.00
Bowl, Crimped, 11½" 25.00
Bowl, Deep Salad, 9½" 35.00
Bowl, Flared, 9½" 25.00
Bowl, Flared, 11½" 25.00
Bowl, Oval, 10" 25.00
Bowl, Round, 9½" 25.00
Bowl, Shallow, Salad, 12" 20.00
Bowl, Sweet Pea, 8" 25.00
Candelabrum, 1 Light, 4", pr. 45.00
Candelabrum, 1 Light, 8", pr. 55.00
Candlestick, 1 Light, 4", pr. 25.00
Candy Basket, Oval, 2 Handled, 7½" 15.00
Candy Box & Cover, 6" 35.00
Celery & Relish, 3 Compartment, 2 Handled, 11" . . 22.00
Claret or Wine, 4 oz. 15.00
Cocktail, 3½ oz. 15.00
Cream, Individual, 3" 15.00
Finger Bowl, 4" 10.00
Flower Arranger, 5" t., 7¾" w. 24.00
Goblet, 9 oz. 12.00
Hors d'oeuvre, 4 Compartment, 2 Handled, 12" 3.00
Hurricane Lamp, 1 Light, 4" 35.00
Iced Tea, Footed, 12 oz. *(Illus.)* 15.00
Jelly, Oval, 2 Handled, 6" 15.00
Juice, Orange, Footed, 5 oz. 10.00
Mayonnaise, Flared, Handled, 5½" 20.00
Mint, Flared, 2 Handled, 6½" 10.00
Olive, Oval, 2 Handled, 6½" 10.00
Oyster Cocktail, 4½ oz. 15.00
Pickle, Oval, 2 Handled, 7" 15.00
Plate, 2 Handled, 6½" 10.00
Plate, Oval (lemon), 2 Handled, 8" 15.00
Plate, Rolled Edge, 13" 30.00

Plate, Round, 2 Handled, 6½" 10.00
Plate, Round, 2 Handled, 7½" 15.00
Plate, Salad, 8½" *(Illus.)* 15.00
Plate, Sandwich, Oblong, 2 Handled, 10"x12" 25.00
Plate, Torte, Flat Edge, 13" 30.00
Plate, Torte, Rolled Edge, 13" 30.00
Relish, 2 Compartment, 2 Handled, 6½" 20.00
Relish, Flared, 2 Compartment, 2 Handled, 6½" 20.00
Saucer Champagne or Tall Sherbet, 6 oz. 10.00
Sugar, Individual, 2½" 15.00
Sweetmeat, Crimped, 2 Handled, 6" 20.00
Tray, Muffin, 2 Handled, 11" 25.00
Tray, Oval, 8" 10.00
Vase or Ice Bucket, 6" 35.00
Vase, Violet, 2 Handled, 4½" 20.00
Wine, 3½ oz. 15.00

BLOWN STEMWARE, NO. 5375

For pieces with Ruby bowls & crystal stems add 75%.

Claret, 5 oz. $12.00
Cocktail, Liquor, 3½ oz. 10.00
Cordial, 1 oz. 20.00
Goblet, 9 oz. 15.00
Ice Cream, Sherbet, 6 oz. 8.00
Iced Tea, 12 oz. 10.00
Juice, Orange, 5 oz. 10.00
Oyster Cocktail, 4½ oz. 8.00
Saucer Champagne, 6 oz. 12.00
Tumbler, Footed, or Low Goblet, 9 oz. 12.00
Wine, 3 oz. 15.00

DIAMOND QUILTED

Diamond Quilted Plain Edge Bowl & Sugar

Diamond Quilted Punch Set

Diamond Quilted Covered Footed Bowl

Date: 1920s and 1930s

Manufacturer: Imperial Glass Corp., Bellaire, OH

Colors: Pink, Blue, Green, Crystal, Black. Limited production in Red and Amber.

	Crystal	Blue, Black	Pink, Green
Bar Glass, 1½ oz.	$10.00	$	$24.00
Bowl, Cream Soup, 4¾" . . .	15.00	22.00	15.00
Bowl, 5".	8.00	18.00	12.00
Bowl, Plain Edge or Crimped Top, 7" (Illus. of plain edge)	8.00	18.00	12.00
Bowl, Console	24.00	65.00	27.00
Bowl, Covered, Footed, 6½" (Illus.)	40.00	95.00	70.00
Bowl, Footed, 7¼"	30.00	70.00	55.00
Bowl, Footed, 7½"	30.00	70.00	55.00
Cake Salver, 10"	25.00		38.00
Candlesticks, pr.	25.00	55.00	30.00
Candy Jar & Cover, Footed	40.00	95.00	70.00
Compote & Cover, 1½" . . .	50.00		85.00
Cordial, 1 oz.	12.00		20.00
Cream	10.00	18.00	11.00
Cup & Saucer.	8.00	12.00	10.00
Goblet, 9 oz..	8.00		14.00
Ice Bucket	40.00	95.00	60.00
Iced Tea, 12 oz..	8.00		15.00

	Crystal	Blue, Black	Pink, Green
Iced Tea, Footed, 12 oz. . . .	12.00		24.00
Jelly, Handled, 5½"	10.00	18.00	12.00
Juice, Footed, 6 oz.	7.00		12.00
Mayonnaise Bowl & Plate . .	35.00		52.00
Pitcher, 64 oz..	35.00		60.00
Plate, 6"	6.00	11.00	5.00
Plate, 7"	7.00	14.00	8.00
Plate, 8"	8.00	16.00	10.00
Plate, Sandwich, 14"	15.00		20.00
Punch Bowl and Stand, 13½" (Illus.)	180.00		500.00+
Punch Cup (Illus.).	6.00		9.00
Sandwich, Center Handled .	22.00	60.00	30.00
Salver, 8¼"	30.00	70.00	55.00
Sherbet.	6.00	17.00	9.00
Sugar (Illus.)	10.00	18.00	11.00
Tumbler, 9 oz.	9.00		13.00
Tumbler, Footed, 9 oz.	11.00		205.00
Vase, Dolphin Handled. . . .	30.00	72.00	52.00
Wine, 2 oz..	10.00		16.00
Wine, 3 oz..	10.00		16.00

ENGLISH HOBNAIL

Date: 1925 through the 1970s

Manufacturer: Westmoreland Glass Co., Grapeville, PA

Colors: Crystal, Rose, Turquoise, Belgian Blue, Opal (1940s), Green, Cobalt, Milk (late), Amber (late), and Red (1980s.) Stemmed pieces were also made with crystal bowls and amber or black stems and bases.

English Hobnail is the original name for this pattern although the company also referred to it as Early American. Advertising by the company represented the pattern as a "reproduction of the old Sandwich glass." An original company price list from late 1940 lists pieces in crystal and opal—these are marked with an asterisk in the following list. The 555/2 and 555/3 listings were also from this price list. Asterisked pieces use the original company names for the pieces. Because of lack of information, the listings in this pattern are handled somewhat differently than others. The question marks indicate that it is now unknown if the pieces were made in colors. Much more study needs to be done by researchers and collectors alike to sort out the correct information about this pattern. Its long time of production has presented many problems in this area.

This pattern is often confused with Miss America. The stemware and tumblers of Miss America have three rings above the diamond pattern, while English Hobnail is plain there. The center design of English Hobnail is a hexagonal sunburst in which the rays are not all the same lengths. On Miss America pieces, the rays are of uniform length.

Only the items marked with + were listed in opal in 1940. No. 555—stemware has round bases, plates are round:

English Hobnail Table Setting—Original Ad

	Crystal	Pastels	Deep Colors
Ashtray, 3½"* or 4½"*+	$24.00	$36.00	$40.00
Basket, Crimped, 12" *+			
(listed in opal, not crystal) . .	50.00	?	?
Basket, Handled, 5" *+	20.00	35.00	85.00
Basket, Oblong, 7" *+			
(listed in opal, not crystal) . .	30.00	?	?
Basket, Oblong, 11" *+			
(listed in opal, not crystal) . .	40.00	?	?
Basket, Oblong, Handled,			
10" *+	40.00	?	?
Basket, Square, 8" *+			
(listed in opal, not crystal) . .	35.00	?	?
Basket, Tall, Handled, 6" *	40.00	80.00	175.00
Bitter Bottle, 2½ oz. *			
or 3½ oz *.	30.00	?	?
Bonbon, Handled, 6" *.	12.00	18.00	23.00

	Crystal	Pastels	Deep Colors
Bottle, Bathroom, 5 oz. *+			
(wide mouth).	30.00	50.00	75.00
Bottle, Toilet, 1 oz.			
(cologne) *+.	35.00	?	?
Bottle, Toilet, 2 oz. *+.	30.00	?	?
Bottle, Toilet, 3½ oz. *+	25.00	?	?
Bottle, Toilet, 5 oz. *+.	22.00	40.00	82.00
Bowl, 6 point, 6"*+, 7" *			
or 8"	25.00	?	?
Bowl, Bell, 11" *.	32.00	?	?
Bowl, Crimped, 9" * or 9½". . .	30.00	?	?
Bowl, Cupped, 8" *+	4.00	24.00	33.00
Bowl, Flange, 11" *.	32.00	40.00	65.00
Bowl, Flange, 12"	32.00	?	?
Bowl, Flared, 10" * or 12" *+ . .	30.00	40.00	?
Bowl, Footed, 2 Handled,			
8" *	50.00	75.00	200.00
Bowl, Oval, Crimped &			
Oblong, 12" *+	38.00	40.00	65.00
Bowl, Rolled Edge, 11" *	32.00	40.00	90.00
Candelabra, 7", *+ pr.			
(2 light candlestick)	45.00	?	?
Candlesticks, Large Cup, * pr. . .	50.00	?	?
Candlesticks, Low, 3½", *+ pr. .	24.00	45.00	78.00
Candlesticks, Tall, 9" *+ , pr . . .	50.00	70.00	120.00
Candy Box & Cover, 6" *+. . . .	30.00	75.00	135.00
Candy Jar & Cover, ½ lb. *+. . .	30.00	90.00	185.00
Celery, 12" *+.	25.00	45.00	85.00
Celery, Flat, 9" *+.	20.00	35.00	70.00
Cheese & Cracker, 2 Handled,			
Covered *	50.00	?	?

ENGLISH HOBNAIL *(continued)*

	Crystal	Pastels	Deep Colors
Cigarette Box & Cover, 4½" x 3½" *+	25.00	38.00	70.00
Cigarette Jar & Cover *+	25.00	35.00	70.00
Claret, 5½ oz. *	14.00	17.00	32.00
Coaster, 3" *+ or 5½" *	10.00	?	?
Cocktail Shaker, 40 oz *+	50.00	?	?
Cocktail, 3 oz. *	14.00	22.00	38.00
Comport, 2 Handled, 8" *+	25.00	?	?
Comport, Belled, 5½" *+	15.00	?	?
Comport, Rolled Edge, 6" *+	15.00	?	?
Comport, Round, 5" *+	15.00	30.00	?
Cordial, 1 oz. *	24.00	48.00	100.00
Cream Soup, 2 Handled *+	22.00	43.00	85.00
Cream, Footed *+	15.00	25.00	48.00
Cream, Individual *	20.00	?	?
Cream, Individual, Lip on Side *	30.00	?	?
Cream, Low *	12.00	30.00	52.00
Cup & Saucer *+ *(Illus.)*	18.00	25.00	50.00
Cup & Saucer, After Dinner *+	28.00	32.00	
Decanter & Stopper, 20 oz. *	55.00	?	?
Dish, Covered, 3 Footed, 6" *	55.00	75.00	135.00
Dish, Crimped, 6" *+	15.00	18.00	23.00
Dish, Vegetable, 6x8" *+ or 7x9" *+	20.00	22.00	35.00
Egg Cup *	18.00	40.00	
Finger Bowl, 4½" *+	9.00	14.00	?
Flip Jar & Cover *	35.00	90.00	?
Ginger Ale, 5 oz. (Juice) *+	114.00	20.00	
Goblet, 8 oz. *+	14.00	32.00	70.00
Goblet, Bridge, 5 oz. * (footed juice)	14.00	?	?
Grapefruit, 6½" *+	14.00	18.00	24.00
Hat, Colonial *+	15.00	?	?
Hat, Hi *+	15.00	?	?
Hat, Low *+	15.00	?	?
Hat, Puritan *	15.00	?	?
Honey, 6" *+	22.00	35.00	
Iced Tea, Footed, 12½ oz. *+	15.00	40.00	72.00
Iced Tea, Straight * or Bell *, 10 oz.	15.00	32.00	50.00
Iced Tea, Unfooted, 12 oz. *	16.00	32.00	50.00
Ice Tub, 2 Handled, 6" *	38.00	?	?
Ice Tub, 3" *, 4" *+, or 5½" *+	25.00	70.00	110.00
Ivy Ball, 3" *	30.00	?	?
Jug, Beer, 64 oz. *	85.00	110.00	
Jug, Straight Sided, ½ Gallon *+	200.00	320.00	500.00+
Jug, Straight Sided, Quart *	55.00	170.00	400.00
Jug, Stuck Handle, 23 oz *+	50.00	150.00	400.00
Jug, Stuck Handle, 38 oz. *	75.00	285.00	450.00+
Jug, Stuck Handle, 60 oz. *	120.00	360.00	550.00+
Juice Glass, Pineapple, 6 oz. *	15.00	?	?
Lamp, 6¼"	35.00	48.00	100.00
Lamp, 9¼"	48.00	60.00	150.00
Marmalade & Notched Cover *+	25.00	55.00	90.00
Mayonnaise, 6" *+	15.00	24.00	
Nappy, 3 Cornered, 4½" *	12.00	?	?
Nappy, 4½" *+	9.00	14.00	17.00
Nappy, Bell, 5½" *+	12.00	?	?
Nappy, Bell, 7½" *+ or 8" *	20.00	24.00	33.00
Nappy, Bell, 9" *	30.00	?	?
Nappy, Cupped, 8" *+	22.00	24.00	33.00
Nappy, Plain Edge, 6" *	12.00	18.00	24.00
Nappy, Round, 5" *+	11.00	16.00	20.00
Nappy, Round, 6½" *+ or 7" *+	15.00	?	?
Nappy, Round, 8" *+	22.00	24.00	33.00
Nappy, Square, 6½" *+	15.00	18.00	24.00
Nut and Card Holder *	18.00	?	?
Nut, Footed or Salt, Individual *	10.00	24.00	52.00
Oblong, 10" *	18.00	?	?
Oil & Stopper, 2 oz. *	22.00	?	?
Oil & Stopper, 6 oz. *	32.00	?	?
Oil or Vinegar & Stopper, 6 oz. *	40.00	?	?
Old Fashion Cocktail, 6 oz. *	12.00	?	?
Oval, Footed, 4½" *	8.00	?	?
Oval, Footed, Belled, 9" *+	20.00	?	?
Oval, Footed, Crimped, 8½" *+	20.00	?	?
Parfait, 5 oz. *+	18.00	?	?
Pickle, 8" *	20.00	?	?
Pilsner, 12 oz. *	35.00	?	?
Plate, 3 Footed, 8" *	15.00	?	?
Plate, 5½" *+	8.00	12.00	18.00
Plate, 8" *+ or 8½" *+	10.00	15.00	27.00
Plate, 10" *+ *(Illus.)*	18.00	35.00	75.00
Plate, Cream Soup *+	8.00	?	?
Plate, Finger Bowl, 6½" *+	8.00	12.00	18.00
Plate, Grill, 10½" *	24.00	?	?
Plate, Pie, 7" *	8.00	9.00	10.00
Plate, Plain Edge, 8½" *+	10.00	?	?
Plate, Salad with Depressed Center, 6½" *	12.00		
Plate, Torte, 14" *+	35.00	48.00	
Plate, Torte, 20½"	45.00		

(continued) ENGLISH HOBNAIL

	Crystal	Pastels	Deep Colors
Platter, Oval, 7½"x9" *	18.00	?	?
Platter, Oval, 9"x12" *	25.00	?	?
Preserve, 7" *+	15.00	?	?
Puff Box & Cover,			
3½" *+, 4½" *+ or 5" *+	20.00	?	?
Puff Box, Flat & Cover, 3½"*			
or 4½"* (also 5" and 6")	25.00	30.00	80.00
Punch Bowl & Foot	240.00		
Punch Cup	9.00		
Relish, 3 part, 8" *	16.00	?	?
Relish, 4 part (no cover),			
10½" *+	35.00	?	?
Relish, 4 part with Cover,			
10½" *+	45.00	?	?
Relish, 5 part with			
Marmalade, 12½" *	75.00	?	?
Rose Bowl, 4" *+	20.00	50.00	
Rose Bowl, 6" *	25.00	?	?
Salt & Pepper, pr *+	60.00	95.00	160.00
Salve Box & Cover, 2¼" *+	35.00	?	?
Salver, Cake, 12" *+	50.00	?	?
Shade for Lamp, 17"	190.00		
Sherbet, Low Foot *+			
or High Foot *+	8.00	12.00	18.00
Spoon, Oblong, 7" *+	15.00	?	?
Sugar, Footed *+	15.00	25.00	48.00
Sugar, Low *	12.00	30.00	50.00
Sweetmeat, Ball Stem, Belled,			
8" (comport) *+	45.00	60.00	95.00
Sweetmeat, Ball Stem, Round,			
5½" (comport) *+	22.00	55.00	85.00
Tray, 2 Handled, 12½" *	25.00	?	?
Tray, Roll, 12" *+	20.00	?	?
Tray, Round, 4½" *	10.00	?	?
Tumbler, 8 oz. *+	22.00	25.00	48.00
Tumbler, Footed, 7 oz. *	12.00	27.00	48.00
Tumbler, Footed, 9 oz. *+	15.00	30.00	55.00
Vase or Straw Jar, 10" *	60.00	90.00	
Vase, 3 Handled, 8½",			
Plain or Crimped *	60.00	?	?
Vase, 5½" *	20.00	?	?
Vase, 11" *	50.00	?	?
Vase, Flip, 7½" *+	30.00	70.00	?
Vase, Flower, 8½" *+	40.00	120.00	235.00
Vase, Swung, 9" to 12"*	45.00	?	?
Vase, Swung, 12" to 16"*+	90.00	?	?
Whiskey, 2½ oz. *+	14.00	20.00	30.00
Whiskey, Sham, 1½ oz. *	14.00	20.00	30.00
Wine, 2 oz. *+	15.00	35.00	72.00

No. 555/2—stemware has square bases and plates are square. Only the pieces with a + were listed in opal in 1940.

	Crystal	Pastels	Deep Colors
Ashtray, Square, 4½" *	$9.00	$28.00	$
Bowl, 8" *	24.00	?	?
Bowl, Cupped, 9" *	30.00	?	?
Bowl, Square, 12" *	32.00	?	?
Butter & Cover,			
Individual, 4½" *	25.00	?	?
Candlesticks, 5½", pr. *+	40.00	?	?
Cheese & Cover, 6" *+	40.00	?	?
Cheese & Cover, 8¾" *	55.00	?	?
Claret, 5½ oz. *	12.00	?	?
Claret, Footed, 5½ oz. *	15.00	?	?
Coaster, 4½" *+	10.00	?	?
Coaster, 6" *	15.00	?	?
Cocktail, Liquor, 3 oz.,			
Footed *+	10.00	?	?
Cocktail, Oyster, 4 oz.,			
Footed *+	10.00	17.00	
Comport, Belled *+,			
Crimped *+ or Round *+, 9"		30.00	?
?			
Comport, Belled, 5½" *+	17.00	?	?
Comport, Rolled Edge, 6" *+	18.00	?	?
Comport, Round, 5" *+	15.00	?	?
Cordial *	18.00	?	?
Cream *+	15.00	50.00	
Cup & Saucer, After Dinner,			
Square *	28.00	?	?
Cup, Tea & Saucer, Square *+	16.00	?	?
Finger Bowl, Footed, 4" *+	12.00	20.00	38.00
Flower Holder, Footed, 6½" *	25.00	?	?
French Brandy *	20.00	?	?
Fruit Icer, 2 piece *	50.00	?	?
Ginger Ale, 5 oz.,			
Footed (juice) *+	14.00	?	?
Goblet, 8 oz., Footed *+	15.00	35.00	60.00
Goblet, Jumbo, 24 oz. *	40.00	?	?
Grapefruit, 6" *	15.00	25.00	
Honey, Footed, 6" *+	15.00	?	?
Iced Tea, 11 oz., Footed *+	14.00	?	?
Ivy Ball, Plain or Crimped,			
6½" *+	35.00	?	?
Jelly, Covered, 4"	25.00	?	?
Mustard, Footed,			
with Notched Cover *	30.00	?	?
Nappy, Footed, 4½" *	9.00	?	?
Nappy, Low, Square, 4½" *	9.00	14.00	17.00
Nut, Low, Square, 3½" *	10.00	?	?

ENGLISH HOBNAIL (continued)

	Crystal	Pastels	Deep Colors
Plate, 1 Roll, 15½" *	40.00	?	?
Plate, 4 Roll, 13" *	45.00	?	?
Plate, Square, 10" *+	18.00	?	?
Plate, Square, 15½" *+	40.00	?	?
Plate, Square, 6" *+	9.00	11.00	
Plate, Square, 8¾" *+	10.00	15.00	27.00
Salt & Pepper, pr. *+	50.00	?	?
Sherbet, Low Foot *+ or High Foot *+	9.00	12.00	
Sugar *+	15.00	50.00	
Tumbler, Footed, 7 oz. *+	14.00	?	?
Tumbler, Footed, 9 oz. *+	14.00	?	?
Wine, Footed, 2 oz. *+	15.00	35.00	70.00

No. 555/3—stemware has round base, barrel shape. Only the goblet and low footed sherbet were listed in opal in 1940.

	Crystal	Pastels	Deep Colors
Champagne *	$22.00	$?	$?
Cocktail, 3½ oz. *	20.00	?	?
Cordial, 1 oz. *	25.00	?	?
Ginger Ale, 5 oz. (juice) *	16.00	?	?
Goblet, 8 oz. *	20.00	?	?
Iced Tea, Footed, 11 oz. *	28.00	?	?
Sherbet, Low Foot * or High Foot *	9.00	?	?
Tumbler, Footed, 9 oz. *	20.00	?	?
Urn & Cover, 11" *	40.00	360.00	
Wine, 2½ oz. *	28.00	?	?

HOLIDAY

Holiday Sherbet

Date: 1947 to 1949

Manufacturer: Jeannette Glass Co., Jeannette, PA

Colors: Pink. Iridescent on Crystal. Limited production in Pink opaque (Shell Pink) and Crystal.

A very busy, geometric pattern. Once called Buttons & Bows. Prices given are for pink, all others are 50% less.

Bowl, 5"	$14.00
Bowl, 7¾"	60.00
Bowl, 8½"	35.00
Bowl, Oval Vegetable, 9½"	35.00
Bowl, Console, 10¾"	120.00
Butter & Cover	45.00
Cake Plate, 3 Footed, 10½"	90.00
Candlesticks, 3" pr	85.00
Cream	15.00
Cup & Saucer	14.00
Iced Tea, Footed	150.00

Juice, Footed	60.00
Pitcher, 16 oz.	70.00
Pitcher, 52 oz.	45.00
Plate, 6"	6.00
Plate, 9"	17.00
Plate, 13¾"	95.00
Platter, Oval, 11¼"	27.00
Sandwich Tray, 10½"	25.00
Sherbet *(Illus.)*	6.00
Sugar & Cover	28.00
Tumbler, 10 oz.	25.00

MISS AMERICA

Date: 1933 to 1937

Manufacturer: Hocking Glass Co., Lancaster, OH

Colors: Crystal, Pink. Limited production in Green, Medium Blue and Red.

Reproductions have been done of several pieces. Some reproductions include the butter and cover, pitchers, salt and pepper shakers and tumblers. Again, be wary of unusual colors. The new butter dishes are difficult to tell from old, especially in the newer repros. The best way to tell a reproduction is to study one (look for a color never made originally), and become familiar with its characteristics. Learn the old colors so you can eliminate all colors not originally made. Miss America repros are better than some others, and this makes telling old from new more difficult. Old water pitchers, plain not ice lip, have a bulge at the handle attachment which is absent in the new. Also, the diamonds near the base in the old pitchers gradually decrease in size while in the new the diamonds are pushed together. The salt and pepper shakers are noticeably heavier, having extra glass filling the interior. New tumblers also are much heavier than the old due to extra glass in the bases. Old tumblers have 4 mold lines while new have only 2.

This pattern is often confused with English Hobnail by Westmoreland. The stemware and tumblers of Miss America have three rings above the diamond pattern, while English Hobnail is plain there. The center design of English Hobnail is a hexagonal sunburst, in which the rays are not all the same lengths. On Miss America pieces, the rays are of uniform length.

Miss America Plate, Cup & Saucer

	Crystal	Pink
Bowl, 4½" (Green only--$15.00) . .	$	$
Bowl, 6¼"	2.00	27.00
Bowl, Cupped, 8"	45.00	85.00
Bowl, Straight, 8¾"	40.00	70.00
Bowl, Oval Vegetable, 10"	20.00	35.00
Butter & Cover.	200.00	500.00+
Cake Plate, Footed, 12"	30.00	58.00
Candy Jar & Cover, 11½"	65.00	150.00
Celery, 10½"	18.00	34.00
Coaster, 5¾".	16.00	28.00

	Crystal	Pink
Comport, 5"	18.00	30.00
Cream, Footed	9.00	22.00
Cup & Saucer *(Illus.)*.	12.00	27.00
Goblet, 10 oz..	28.00	55.00
Iced Tea, 14 oz..	32.00	90.00
Juice, 5 oz.	20.00	58.00
Juice, Footed, 5 oz.	28.00	85.00
Pitcher, 65 oz..	55.00	115.00
Pitcher, Ice Lip, 65 oz..	75.00	130.00
Plate, 5¾"	6.00	10.00
Plate, 6¾" (Green only--$9.00) . . .		
Plate, 8½" *(Illus.)*	8.00	25.00
Plate, 10¼"	18.00	35.00
Plate, Grill, 10¼"	12.00	27.00
Platter, Oval, 12¼"	22.00	32.00
Relish, 4 Part, 8¾"	14.00	28.00
Relish, 5 Part, 11¾"	18.00	700.00+
Salt and Pepper, pr	35.00	72.00
Sherbet.	10.00	18.00
Sugar	10.00	20.00
Tumbler, 10 oz..	18.00	38.00

MOUNT VERNON

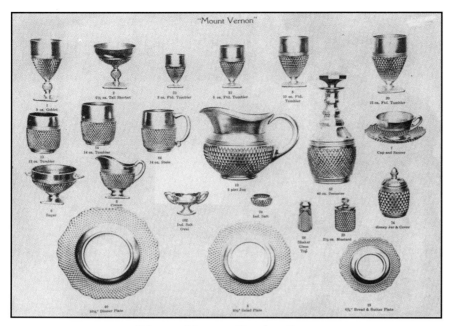

Mount Vernon Catalog Page

Date: Ca. 1931

Manufacturer: Cambridge Glass Co., Cambridge, OH

Colors: Crystal, Carmen, Royal Blue, Amber, Emerald (light green), Heatherbloom, Milk, Gold Krystol, Crown Tuscan, Forest Green (deep yellow green)

This pattern was made in an extensive tableware service. Because it was made over a relatively long period of time, not all pieces were made in all colors. Pieces in Heatherbloom are the same value as Carmen, for other colors add 100% to Crystal prices.

	Crystal	Carmen, Royal Blue
Bonbon, 7"	$15.00	$35.00
Bonbon, Footed, Shallow, 7"	14.00	35.00
Bottle, Toilet, Cologne, 7 oz.	22.00	75.00
Bowl, 10"	15.00	45.00
Bowl, 10½"	18.00	50.00
Bowl, 12" and 12½"	18.00	60.00
Bowl, Belled, 10"	14.00	45.00
Bowl, Belled, 11½"	15.00	45.00
Bowl, Oval, 11"	15.00	40.00
Bowl, Shallow Cupped, 10"	14.00	40.00
Bowl, Shallow Cupped, 11½"	12.00	35.00
Box, Toilet & Cover, Square, 4"	18.00	75.00
Box, Toilet & Cover, 4½" (puff box)	25.00	
Box, Vanity & Cover (toilet box), 3"	15.00	
Butter Tub & Cover	28.00	125.00
Candelabra, 13½", pr.	260.00	
Candlesticks, 4", pr.	25.00	50.00
Candlesticks, 8", pr.	45.00	200.00
Candy Jar & Cover, 1 lb.	27.00	85.00
Celery & Relish, 6"	17.00	40.00
Celery & Relish, 5 Compartment, 12"	20.00	50.00
Celery Tray, 10½"	15.00	40.00
Celery Tray, 12"	15.00	40.00
Cereal, 6"	8.00	17.00
Cologne, 2½ oz.	24.00	

	Crystal	Carmen, Royal Blue
Comport, Tall, 4½"	24.00	55.00
Comport, 2 Handled, 6"	30.00	75.00
Comport, Tall, 6"	24.00	55.00
Comport, 2 Styles, 6½"	18.00	45.00
Comport, 9½"	40.00	95.00
Comport, 2 Handled, 5½"	28.00	85.00
Comport, Footed, 7½"	16.00	40.00
Comport, Oval, 2 Handled, 9"	30.00	125.00
Coupe Salad or Jug Coaster, 7½"	8.00	22.00
Cream	10.00	25.00
Cup & Saucer	12.00	28.00
Decanter & Stopper, 11 oz.	30.00	
Decanter & Stopper, 40 oz.	40.00	115.00
Finger Bowl	8.00	22.00
Fruit Saucer, 5 1/4"	5.00	15.00
Goblet, 9 oz.	12.00	35.00
Honey Jar & Cover	18.00	125.00
Jug, 1½ Pint	25.00	80.00
Jug, 3 Pint	35.00	100.00
Jug, 50 oz.	45.00	125.00
Jug, 86 oz.	50.00	150.00
Mustard & Cover, 2½ oz.	20.00	48.00
Old Fashion Cocktail, 7 oz.	8.00	
Pickle, 8"	10.00	25.00
Pickle, 1 Handled, (jelly) 6"	15.00	30.00
Plate, 11½"	14.00	35.00
Plate, Bread & Butter, 6"	5.00	12.00

(continued) MOUNT VERNON

	Crystal	Carmen, Royal Blue		Crystal	Carmen, Royal Blue
Plate, Dinner, 10½"	15.00	50.00	Sweetmeat, 4 Compartment, 2 Handled, 8½"	18.00	45.00
Plate, Finger Bowl	6.00	14.00	Tumbler, 12 oz.	8.00	18.00
Plate, Salad, 8½"	7.00	16.00	Tumbler, 14 oz.	9.00	20.00
Preserve, 6"	7.00	17.00	Tumbler, Footed, 3 oz.	8.00	20.00
Relish, 3 Compartment, 8"	15.00	40.00	Tumbler, Footed, 5 oz.	8.00	20.00
Relish, 2 part, 12"	15.00	40.00	Tumbler, Footed, 10 oz.	9.00	22.00
Relish, Center Handled, 2 Compartment, 6"	17.00	40.00	Tumbler, Footed, 12 oz.	9.00	22.00
Rose Bowl, 6½"	17.00	50.00	Tumbler, Tall, 2 oz.	7.00	
Rose Bowl, Footed, 4½"	18.00	50.00	Tumbler, Tall, 5 oz.	7.00	
Salt & Pepper, Glass Tops, pr.	18.00	75.00	Tumbler, Tall, 10 oz.	9.00	
Salt Dip, Oval, 2 Handled	12.00	35.00	Tumbler, Tall, 14 oz.	10.00	
Salt, Round, Individual	6.00	18.00	Tumbler, Tall, Table, 10 oz.	8.00	
Sauce Boat, Footed	17.00	35.00	Urn, 8"	30.00	90.00
Sherbet, Tall, 6½ oz.	9.00	22.00	Vase, 5"	12.00	40.00
Stein, 14 oz.	20.00	55.00	Vase, 6"	14.00	50.00
Sugar	10.00	25.00	Vase, 7"	14.00	50.00
Sweetmeat or Relish, 2 Handled, 2 Compartment, 8½"	18.00	45.00	Vase, 10"	22.00	75.00
			Vase, Squat, 6½"	22.00	55.00

NORMANDIE

Date: 1933 to 1940

Manufacturer: Federal Glass Co., Columbus, OH

Colors: Crystal, Amber, Pink, Iridescent Crystal

	Crystal	Pink	Amber	Iridescent
Bowl, 5"	$4.00	$9.00	$8.00	$6.00
Bowl, 6½"	10.00	35.00	30.00	10.00
Bowl, 8½"	20.00	28.00	25.00	16.00
Bowl, Oval Vegetable, 10".	18.00	42.00	24.00	20.00
Cream, Footed	6.00	15.00	9.00	9.00
Cup & Saucer (Illus. of cup)	9.00	16.00	14.00	12.00
Iced Tea, 12 oz.	30.00	85.00	40.00	
Juice, 5 oz.	20.00	52.00	27.00	
Pitcher, 80 oz.	55.00	145.00	90.00	
Plate, 6"	2.00	4.00	4.00	4.00
Plate, 8"	8.00	13.00	11.00	55.00
Plate, 9¼"	10.00	17.00	10.00	18.00
Plate, 11"	12.00	110.00	35.00	14.00
Plate, Grill, 11"	10.00	22.00	16.00	12.00
Platter, 11¾"	15.00	36.00	26.00	18.00
Salt & Pepper, pr.	30.00	85.00	50.00	
Sherbet	4.00	10.00	6.00	5.00
Sugar & Cover	60.00	195.00	110.00 (no lid) 8.00	
Tumbler, 9 oz.	15.00	45.00	22.00	

Normandie Cup

PRETZEL, NO. 622

Pretzel Sugar

Date: 1920s to 1970s

Manufacturer: Indiana Glass Co.

Colors: Crystal. Teal Blue/Green

Motif is comprised of raised ribs in a lattice effect which result in large diamonds on all pieces. Prices are for Crystal; for Teal, add at least 100%.

Bowl, 7½"	$9.00
Bowl, 9¼"	18.00
Celery, 10¼"	5.00
Cream	6.00
Cup & Saucer	6.00
Iced Tea, 12 oz.	38.00
Juice, 5 oz.	25.00
Olive Dish, Leaf Shape, 7"	5.00
Pickle, 2 Handled, 8½"	7.00
Pitcher, 40 oz.	200.00+

Plate, 6"	3.00
Plate, Square with Ring, 7¼"	10.00
Plate, Square, 3 Compartment, 7¼"	10.00
Plate, 8¼"	6.00
Plate, 9¼"	10.00
Plate, Sandwich, 11½"	14.00
Sherbet	5.00
Sugar *(Illus.)*	6.00
Tumbler, 9 oz.	30.00

STARLIGHT

Starlight Plate

Date: 1938 to 1940

Manufacturer: Hazel-Atlas Glass Co.

Colors: Crystal, Pink. Limited production in Deep Blue (Cobalt) and White.

For pieces in Blue, add 25% to the Pink prices.

	Crystal	Pink
Bowl, 5½"	$5.00	$10.00
Bowl, 11½"	24.00	30.00
Bowl, Handled, 8½"	15.00	20.00
Bowl, Shallow, 12"	24.00	30.00
Cream	9.00	
Cup & Saucer	8.00	12.00
Plate, 6"	3.00	3.00
Plate, 8½"	6.00	7.00
Plate, 9" *(Illus.)*	10.00	14.00
Plate, Sandwich, 13"	20.00	20.00
Relish	14.00	20.00
Salt & Pepper, pr.	26.00	
Sherbet	14.00	
Sugar	8.00	

WAKEFIELD, NO. 1932

Date: 1932

Manufacturer: Westmoreland Glass Co., Grapeville, PA

Colors: Crystal

In the late 1940s the pattern was available with red stain, but possibly all pieces did not come with this decoration. In later years its name was also changed to Waterford. (A name previously used by Westmoreland for another pattern similar to English Hobnail.)

Wakefield Table Setting—Original Ad

Bowl, Bell, Footed, Console, 12". $25.00	Mint, Footed, Shallow Comport 10.00
Bowl, Cupped, 10". 18.00	Nappy, Cupped, 6" 8.00
Bowl, Lipped, Crimped, 12" 20.00	Nappy, Heart, 1 handled Jelly, 5" 12.00
Bowl, Turned Edge, 13" 18.00	Nappy, Heart, 1 Handled, 8" 15.00
Candlesticks, 1 Light, 6", pr. 35.00	Plate, 8½" 8.00
Candy & Cover 20.00	Plate, 14" 18.00
Candy, Crimped (small low footed comport) 8.00	Plate, Bread & Butter 6.00
Celery, 12". 12.00	Salver, Cake, 12" 25.00
Compote, Crimped 18.00	Sherbet 8.00
Cream, Footed. 12.00	Sugar, Footed. 12.00
Cup & Saucer 18.00	Urn & Cover, 12½" 60.00
Goblet, 10 oz. 15.00	Wine, 2 oz. 15.00
Iced Tea, Footed, 12 oz. 15.00	

WATERFORD

Waterford Tumbler, Cup & Saucer

Date: 1938 to 1944

Manufacturer: Hocking Glass Co., Lancaster, OH

Colors: Crystal, Pink. Limited production in White and Yellow. In the 1950s it was made in Forest Green, a deep green.

Depending on how you look at this pattern, it is composed of either diamonds or squares. We have placed it in Diamonds as the usual orientation of the motif suggests diamonds even though the motif is composed of squares.

	Crystal	Pink
Ashtray, 4"	$8.00	$11.00
Bowl, 4¾"	6.00	15.00
Bowl, 5½"	20.00	28.00
Bowl, 8¼"	16.00	20.00
Butter & Cover.	30.00	200.00+
Coaster, 4"	3.50	8.00
Cream	6.00	12.00
Cup & Saucer *(Illus.)*.	9.00	16.00
Goblet	17.00	
Juice, 5 oz.	38.00	
Lamp, 4" Round Base	30.00	
Pitcher, Ice Lip, 42 oz..	27.00	

	Crystal	Pink
Pitcher, Ice Lip, 80 oz..	35.00	150.00
Plate, 6"	3.00	14.00
Plate, 7"	7.00	10.00
Plate, 9½"	15.00	24.00
Plate, Handled, 10¼"	11.00	21.00
Plate, Sandwich, 13¾"	22.00	35.00
Relish, 5 Compartment, 13¾". . . .	18.00	
Salt & Pepper, pr (2 sizes)	14.00	
Sherbet.	3.50	6.00
Sugar & Cover	16.00	45.00
Tumbler, Footed, 10 oz. *(Illus.)* . . .	18.00	27.00

WINDSOR

Date: 1936 to 1946

Manufacturer: Jeannette Glass Co., Jeannette, PA

Colors: Pink, Green, Crystal. Limited production in Delphite Blue, Orange Red and Pale Blue.

A Depression pattern which is more extensive than most. The pattern apparently was popular for a longer period of time than usual, allowing the company to add extra pieces to the line.

Windsor Platter

	Crystal	Pink	Green
Ashtray, 5¾"	$15.00	$36.00	$55.00
Bowl, 4¾"	5.00	11.00	15.00
Bowl, 5¼"	10.00	22.00	24.00
Bowl, 8"	12.00	42.00	
Bowl, 8½"	9.00	25.00	30.00
Bowl, 3 Footed, 7"	9.00	32.00	
Bowl, Boat, 11¾"	22.00	38.00	40.00
Bowl, Console, 12½"	35.00	115.00	
Bowl, Cream Soup, 5"	12.00	26.00	40.00
Bowl, Handled, 8"	8.00	18.00	24.00
Bowl, Notched Rim, 5"	6.00	20.00	
Bowl, Notched Rim,10½"	27.00	125.00	
Bowl, Oval Vegetable, 9½"	10.00	28.00	37.00
Bowl, Smooth Rim, 10½	15.00		
Butter & Cover	28.00	55.00	95.00
Cake Plate, Footed, 10¾"	12.00	32.00	34.00
Cake Plate, 13½"	12.00	50.00	50.00
Candlesticks, 3", pr	27.00	100.00	
Candy Jar & Cover	20.00	110.00	
Coaster, 3¼"	4.50	16.00	18.00
Comport	12.00	35.00	
Cream (2 styles)	8.50	15.00	18.00
Cup & Saucer	7.00	12.00	20.00
Iced Tea	16.00	40.00	55.00
Iced Tea, Footed	22.00		

	Crystal	Pink	Green
Juice, 5 oz.	12.00	21.00	37.00
Juice, Footed	10.00		
Pitcher, 16 oz.	22.00	135.00	
Pitcher, 20 oz.	22.00		
Pitcher, 52 oz.	21.00	32.00	55.00
Plate, 6"	4.00	5.00	8.00
Plate, 7"	5.00	16.00	18.00
Plate, 9"	7.00	25.00	24.00
Plate, 13½"	18.00	55.00	57.00
Plate, Sandwich, Handled, 10¼"	10.00	25.00	27.00
Platter, 11½" *(Illus.)*	12.00	30.00	32.00
Relish Plate, Divided, Oval, 11½"	22.00	210.00	
Salt & Pepper, pr.	22.00	42.00	55.00
Sherbet	4.50	11.00	15.00
Sugar & Cover	20.00	32.00	32.00
Tray, Handled, 4" x 9"	8.00	24.00	32.00
Tray, Handled, Square, 4"	8.00	20.00	21.00
Tray, No Handles, Square, 4"	8.00	42.00	
Tray, Square, Divided, 8½"	11.00	95.00	
Tray, With or Without Handles, 8½" x 9¾"	11.00	37.00	52.00
Tumbler, 9 oz.	10.00	26.00	40.00

Chapter 5

FANCY RIMS

CANDLEWICK, No. 400

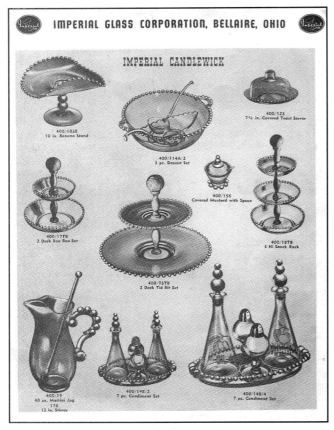

Candlewick Catalog Page

Date: 1936 to 1982

Manufacturer: Imperial Glass Corporation, Bellaire, OH

Colors: Crystal. Limited production in Ritz Blue, Evergreen, Black, Ruby, Amethyst. Many other late Imperial Colors.

Reproductions of many pieces exist. Several pieces of Candlewick are currently being made by Dalzell-Viking in crystal and many colors including ruby, cobalt, evergreen (deep green), ebony (black), and pink. Many pieces/colors have gold painted beads. Be careful of all colors of Candlewick, they may be new.

Imperial's most popular pattern made for many years. It is very extensive and contains many, many unusual and difficult to find pieces. Imperial held several patents on Candlewick (original name). For detailed information on this pattern please refer to Candlewick The Jewel of Imperial, Book II by Mary M. Wetzel-Tomalka. Prices are for pieces in crystal. For early Imperial colors, add 100% to 150%. For late Imperial colors, add 75% to 100%.

Ashtray, 2¾" (No. 400/19) . . . . $ 9.00	Baked Apple, 6½" 25.00
Ashtray, Heart Shape, 4½" or 5½" 12.00	Banana Stand (No. 400/67D) 1,600.00
Ashtray, Heart Shape, 6½" 17.00	Banana Stand, 10" (No. 400/103E) 1,250.00
Ashtray, Matchbook Center, 6" 100.00	Basket, Handled, 5" (various shapes)
Ashtray, Oblong, 4½" (No. 400/134/1) 7.00	(No. 400/273) 195.00
Ashtray, Round 4" (No. 400/440) 7.00	Basket, Handled, 6½" (various styles) 40.00
Ashtray, Round, 5" (No. 400/133) 8.00	Basket, Handled, 11" or 12" 170.00
Ashtray, Round, 6" (various styles) (No. 400/150) . . 12.00	Bell, Dinner (No. 400/108) 60.00
Ashtray, Square, 3¼" (No. 400/651) 32.00	Bell, Dinner, 4" (No. 400/179) 70.00
Ashtray, Square, 3½" 20.00	Bonbon Set, 2 Tier 145.00
Ashtray, Square, 4½" (No. 400/652) 32.00	Bonbon, Handled, Cupped Base, 7½"
Ashtray, Square, 5¾" (No. 400/653) 35.00	(No. 400/149F) 200.00

Bonbon, Heart, Handled, 5" 25.00
Bonbon, Heart, Handled, 6" 25.00
Bottle & Stopper, Cordial, 18 oz. (No. 400/18) . . . 400.00
Bottle & Stopper, Salad Dressing (No. 400/277) . . 105.00
Bottle, Bitters, 4 oz. 50.00
Bottle, Cordial, 15 oz. (No. 400/82/2) 280.00
Bottle, Cordial, Handled, 15 oz. (No. 400/82) 300.00
Bouillon Cup, 2 Handled 40.00
Bowl or Jelly, Divided, 2 Handled, 8½" 85.00
Bowl with Base (No. 400/92F/150) 85.00
Bowl, 7" 25.00
Bowl, 8" 30.00
Bowl, 9" 40.00
Bowl, 10" 40.00
Bowl, 12" 45.00
Bowl, 2 Handled, 8½" 25.00
Bowl, 3 Toed, 6" (No. 400/183) 50.00
Bowl, 3 Toed, 8½" (No. 400/182) 100.00
Bowl, 3 Toed, 10" (No. 400/205) 145.00
Bowl, 4 Toed (No. 400/74) 70.00
Bowl, 4 Toed, Crimped, Square 70.00
Bowl, 4 Toed, Ribbed, Round, 8" or 8½" 75.00
Bowl, Belled, 7½" (No. 400/127B) 100.00
Bowl, Belled, 10½" 50.00
Bowl, Belled, 12" (No. 400/106B) 60.00
Bowl, Belled, Shallow, 14" or 14½" 75.00
Bowl, Center, 11" 55.00
Bowl, Center, Mushroom Shape, 13" 55.00
Bowl, Center, Mushroom Shape, Rolled Edge, 12" . . 65.00
Bowl, Cottage Cheese, 6" 30.00
Bowl, Crimped, 9" (No. 400/67C) 100.00
Bowl, Crimped, Footed, 7½" (No. 400/132C) 500.00
Bowl, Deep, 2 Handled, 10" (No. 400/113A) 140.00
Bowl, Divided, 2 Handled (No. 400/114B) 150.00
Bowl, Divided, Deep, Handled, 10"
    (No. 400/114A) 175.00
Bowl, Float, 12" 45.00
Bowl, Float, Cupped Rim, 10" or 11" 40.00
Bowl, Float, Straight Sides, 13" 70.00
Bowl, Fluted (beaded top rim), 5½" 45.00
Bowl, Fruit (No. 400/103F) 175.00
Bowl, Fruit, 6" 12.00
Bowl, Fruit, 9" (No. 400/67B) 90.00
Bowl, Fruit, 10½" (No. 400/68F) 110.00
Bowl, Handled, 12" (No. 400/113B) 150.00
Bowl, Heart Shaped, 5" 22.00
Bowl, Heart Shaped, 5½" 16.00
Bowl, Heart Shaped, 9" 105.00
Bowl, Jelly, Divided, 2 Handled, 6" 22.00
Bowl, Lily, 4 Toed, 7" 175.00
Bowl, Lily, Plain Base, 7½" 325.00
Bowl, Nappy, 2 Handled, 6½" 22.00
Bowl, Oval, 11" 170.00

Candlewick Catalog Page

Bowl, Oval, 2 part, 11" 175.00
Bowl, Oval, Center, 14" 225.00
Bowl, Round, 2 Handled, 10" (No. 400/145B) 45.00
Bowl, Salad, 10" 37.00
Bowl, Square Base, 5" 32.00
Bowl, Vegetable, Round, 8½" 35.00
Butter & Cover, California (No. 400/276) 145.00
Butter & Cover, Oblong, ¼ lb. 45.00
Butter & Cover, Round, Handled, 5½"
    (No. 400/144) 35.00
Cake Stand, Low, 10" (No. 400/67) 60.00
Cake Stand, Tall, 11" (No. 400/103D) 75.00
Candle/flower Centerpiece, 9" (No. 400/196FC) . . 165.00
Candleholders, 3 Light, pr. (No. 400/115) 250.00
Candleholders, 3 Light, pr. (No. 400/147) 50.00
Candleholders, 3 Toed, 4½", pr. (No. 400/207) . . . 120.00
Candleholders, 3½", pr. (No. 400/79R) 35.00
Candleholders, 3½", pr. (No. 400/80) 30.00
Candleholders, 3½", pr. (No. 400/280) 125.00
Candleholders, 3 Part Stem, 5½", pr.
    (No. 400/224) 175.00
Candleholders, 4", pr. (No. 400/66F) 100.00

CANDLEWICK, NO. 400 *(continued)*

Candleholders, Eagle (2), 3 Light, pr.
(No. 400/115/1) 600.00
Candleholders, Eagle, 2 pcs., 9½", pr.
(No. 400/155) . . . . 1,000.00+
Candleholders, Eagle, 3 Light, pr.
(No. 400/147/2) 325.00
Candleholders, Eagle, Handled, pr. 325.00
Candleholders, Flower with Vase, pr. 160.00
Candleholders, Flower, 4½", pr. (No. 400/66C) . . . 140.00
Candleholders, Flower, Crimped, 5", pr. 80.00
Candleholders, Flower, Heart, 5", pr. 140.00
Candleholders, Flower, Round, 6", pr. 65.00
Candleholders, Flower, Square, 6½", pr. 100.00
Candleholders, Handled, 3½", pr. (No. 400/81) . . . 100.00
Candleholders, Handled, 5", pr. (No. 400/90) 90.00
Candleholders, Flat, pr. (No. 400/79B) 100.00
Candleholders, Low, 3½", pr. (No. 400/170) 35.00
Candleholders, Mushroom, Flat Edge, pr.
(No. 400/86) 60.00
Candleholders, Prism, pr. (No. 400/1752) 425.00
Candleholders, Twin, pr. (No. 400/100) 40.00
Candleholders, Twin Eagle, pr.
(No. 400/100/2-2) 600.00
Candleholders, Urn, 6", pr. (No. 400/129R) 200.00
Candy & Cover or Vegetable, 8" 155.00
Candy Box & Cover, 3 part, 7" (No. 400/158) . . . 150.00
Candy Box & Cover, Deep, 7" (No. 400/260) 135.00
Candy Box & Cover, Divided, 8" 110.00
Candy Box & Cover, Footed (variations)
(No. 400/140) 225.00
Candy Box & Cover, Round, 3 part, 7"
(No. 400/110) 70.00
Candy Box & Cover, Round, 5½" or 6½" 40.00
Candy Box & Cover, Round, 6½"
(No. 400/245) 225.00
Candy Box & Cover, Round, Shallow, 7"
(No. 400/259) 120.00
Candy, Crimped, Handled, 6" 30.00
Celery, 2 Handled, 13½" (No. 400/105) 45.00
Celery, Oval, 11" 70.00
Cheese & Cracker Set, 2 pcs., 10" 45.00
Chip & Dip, Divided, 1 pc., 14" (No. 400/228) . . 625.00
Cigarette Box & Cover, Oblong, 5¼"
(No. 400/134) 45.00
Cigarette Holder, 3" 27.00
Coaster or Ashtray, 4½" (No. 400/34) 8.00
Coaster with Spoon Rest 18.00
Coaster, 4" or 4½" (No. 400/78) 7.00
Cocktail Set, Tray & Glass, 2 pc. (No. 400/97) 40.00
Cocktail, 3½ oz. (No. 400/18) 40.00
Cocktail, 3½ oz. (No. 400/19) 20.00
Cocktail, 3½ to 4 oz. (No. 400/190) 20.00
Cocktail, Hollow Stem, 4 oz. (No. 400/195) 85.00

Compote, 3 part Stem, 5" (No. 400/220) 80.00
Compote, 4½" 50.00
Compote, 5½" (No. 400/45) 75.00
Compote, 5½" (various types) 26.00
Compote, 8" (No. 400/48F) 85.00
Compote, Fruit, Crimped, 10" (No. 400/103C) . . . 150.00
Compote, Oval, Footed (No. 400/137) . . . . 1,000.00+
Cordial, 1 oz. (No. 400/190) 95.00
Cream (No. 400/18) 70.00
Cream (No. 400/30) 10.00
Cream (No. 400/31) 20.00
Cream, Individual (No. 400/122) 9.00
Cream Soup, 2 Handled, 5½" 47.00
Cruet & Stopper, 2 oz. or 4 oz. (No. 400/177) 45.00
Cruet & Stopper, 3 or 4 oz. (No. 400/70) 50.00
Cruet & Stopper, 6 oz. (No. 400/119) 32.00
Cruet & Stopper, 6 oz. (No. 400/71) 70.00
Cruet & Stopper, Handled 4 oz. (No. 400/278) 60.00
Cruet & Stopper, Handled 6 oz. (No. 400/279) 65.00
Cruet & Stopper, Oil, 4 oz. (No. 400/164) 30.00
Cruet & Stopper, Oil, No Handle, 4 oz.
(No. 400/274) 38.00
Cruet & Stopper, Vinegar, 6 oz. (No. 400/166) . . . 55.00
Cruet & Stopper, No Handle, 6 oz. (No. 400/275) . 40.00
Cup & Saucer, After Dinner 23.00
Cup & Saucer, Coffee 14.00
Cup & Saucer, Tea 12.00
Decanter & Stopper, 26 oz. (No. 400/163) 225.00
Dessert, Hollow Stem, 6 oz. (No. 400/195) 70.00
Deviled Egg Server, Heart Center Handle,
11½" or 12" 155.00
Dish & Cover, Oblong, Divided, 10"
(No. 400/216) 240.00
Dish, Covered, 10" (No. 400/214) 285.00
Dish, Sauce, 5½" (No. 400/243) 40.00
Egg Cup, 6 oz.—2 Styles 35.00
Epergne Set, 2 Pc. (No. 400/196) 180.00
Finger Bowl or Mayonnaise, 5½" 16.00
Fork & Spoon, pr. 30.00
Fruit, Heart Shaped, 5" 18.00
Goblet, 10 oz. (No. 400/190) 20.00
Goblet, 3 Part Stem, 6½" (No. 400/225) 180.00
Heart, Handled, 4½", 5½", or 6½" 45.00
Heart, Handled, 9" or 10" 105.00
Ice Bucket, 7" (No. 400/168) 170.00
Ice Tub, 7" or 8" 100.00
Iced Drink, Hollow Stem, 14 oz. (No. 400/195) . . . 65.00
Icer (beaded top rim) 55.00
Jelly & Cover, 4¾" (No. 400/157) 65.00
Jelly or Ashtray, 4" (No. 400/33) 11.00
Jug, 80 oz. 225.00
Jug, Martini, 40 oz. (No. 400/19) 235.00
Juice, Hollow Stem, 6 oz. (No. 400/195) 85.00

(continued) CANDLEWICK, NO. 400

Ladle, Marmalade, 4¾" (No. 400/130) 16.00
Ladle, Mayonnaise (No. 400/165) 12.00
Ladle, Mayonnaise, 6½" (No. 400/135) 14.00
Ladle, Small (No. 400/139) 40.00
Lamp, Hurricane (No. 400/142-K/HL) 450.00
Lamp, Hurricane Candlelamp, 2 pcs.
    (No. 400/79) 100.00
Lamp, Hurricane with Prisms, 3 pcs.
    (No. 400/1753) 270.00
Lamp, Hurricane, 16" (No. 400/32) 225.00
Lamp, Hurricane, 2 pcs. (No. 400/178) 240.00
Lamp, Hurricane, 2 pcs. (No. 400/264) 140.00
Lamp, Hurricane, 2 pcs. (No. 400/76) 125.00
Lamp, Hurricane, 3 pcs. (No. 400/152) 175.00
Lamp, Hurricane, 3 pcs. (No. 400/155) 500.00
Lamp, Hurricane, 3 pcs. 14" (No. 400/152R) 150.00
Lamp, Hurricane, 3 pcs. (No. 400/26) 700.00
Lamp, Hurricane, Twin, 5 pcs. (No. 400/680) . . . 1,000.00
Marmalade & Cover (No. 400/289) 30.00
Marmalade & Cover, Low Foot (No. 400/1989) 45.00
Marmalade Bowl & Cover (various styles)
    (No. 400/89) 25.00
Marmalade, (No. 400/19) 30.00
Mayonnaise, 5¼" (No. 44/23) 12.00
Mayonnaise, Divided, 6½" 35.00
Muddler, 4½ 25.00
Mustard & Cover, Low, Footed (No. 400/156) 45.00
Nappy or Bowl, Divided, 6½" (No. 400/84) 40.00
Nappy or Fruit, 4 3/4" 12.00
Nappy or Mint, Center Handle, 6" 22.00
Nappy, 10" 40.00
Nappy, 3 Toed, 4½" 55.00
Nappy, Bowl, 2 Handled, 7" 14.00
Nappy, Divided, 6½" (No. 400/181) 65.00
Nappy, Fruit, 5" 12.00
Nappy, Peg, 7" (No. 400/240D) 26.00
Nappy, Peg, Divided (No. 400/241) 35.00
Nappy, Square, 5" (No. 400/231) 90.00
Nappy, Square, 6" (No. 400/232) 110.00
Nappy, Square, 7" (No. 400/233) 135.00
Nut Cup or Ashtray (No. 400/64) 10.00
Old Fashioned, Hollow Stem, 9 oz. (No. 400/195) . . 70.00
Old Fashioned, 7 oz. (No. 400/18) 35.00
Old Fashioned, 7 oz. (No. 400/19) 25.00
Parfait, 7 oz. (No. 400/18) 40.00
Party Set, Tray & Cup, 2 pc. (No. 400/98) 20.00
Pickle or Celery, Oval, 6" or 7½" 30.00
Pickle or Celery, Oval, 8" or 8½" 20.00
Pickle, Oval, Handled, 10" (No. 400/217) 28.00
Pitcher, 1 pt. 165.00
Pitcher, 20 oz. (No. 400/416) 40.00
Pitcher, 40 oz. (No. 400/419) 50.00

Pitcher, 40 oz. 190.00
Pitcher, 80 oz. (No. 400/424) 65.00
Pitcher, Ice Lip, 80 oz. 150.00
Pitcher, Lilliputian, 16 oz. 250.00
Pitcher, round, 13 or 14 oz. (No. 400/330) 100.00
Plate, 2 Handled, 7½" 15.00
Plate, 2 Handled, 8½" 14.00
Plate, 2 Handled, 10" 23.00
Plate, Birthday Cake, 13" or 14" 450.00
Plate, Bread & Butter, 6" 8.00
Plate, Canape, 6" 18.00
Plate, Cocktail, 2½" (off center seat) 16.00
Plate, Crescent, 8½" 55.00
Plate, Crimped, 2 Handled, 12" (No. 400/145C) . . . 40.00
Plate, Crimped, 2 Handled, 14" (No. 400/113C) . . . 50.00
Plate, dinner, 10½" 45.00
Plate, Flat, 13½" 50.00
Plate, Luncheon, 9" 15.00
Plate, Open Handled, 5½" 11.00
Plate, Oval, 8" (No. 400/169) 35.00
Plate, Oval, 12½" 80.00
Plate, Round, 14" 40.00
Plate, Round, 2 Handled, 12" or 12½"
    (No. 400/145C) 25.00
Plate, Round, 2 Handled, 14" (No. 400/113D) 50.00
Plate, Salad, 7" 10.00
Plate, Salad, 8" 10.00
Plate, Salad, Oval, 9" 32.00
Plate, Service, 12" 35.00
Plate, Slanted Sides, 7½" 20.00
Plate, Torte, 14" 42.00
Plate, Torte, Cupped Edge, 13½" 45.00
Plate, Torte, Cupped Edge, 17" 55.00
Plate, Torte, Cupped Rim, 12½" or 13" 30.00
Plate, Torte, Flat Edge, 17" 65.00
Platter, Oval, 12½" or 13" 90.00
Platter, Oval, 16" 190.00
Punch Bowl & Base, 10 Qt. (No. 400/210) 175.00
Punch Bowl & Cover with Ladle 475.00
Punch Bowl, 13" 85.00
Punch Cup, 5 oz. (No. 400/211) 30.00
Relish, 3 or 4 part, Oblong, 10" (No. 400/213) 58.00
Relish, 3 part, 3 Toed (No. 400/208) 95.00
Relish, 4 part, Oblong, Handled, 12"
    (No. 400/215) 55.00
Relish, 5 part, 13" (No. 400/209) 65.00
Relish, Oval, 2 part, 8" (No. 400/268) 20.00
Relish, Oval, 2 part, Handled 10½"
    (No. 400/256) 28.00
Relish, Oval, 3 part, 10½" (No. 400/262) 150.00
Relish, Square, 2 part, 7" (No. 400/234) 130.00
Rose Bowl with Flower Holder Insert
    (No. 400/242) 170.00

CANDLEWICK, NO. 400 *(continued)*

Rose Bowl, Beaded Edge, 7"	260.00
Rose Bowl, Footed, 7½"	425.00
Salt & Pepper, pr. (No. 400/190)	55.00
Salt & Pepper, pr. (No. 400/96)	12.00
Salt & Pepper, 4½", pr. (No. 400/167)	25.00
Salt & Pepper, Footed, pr. (No. 400/116)	90.00
Salt & Pepper, Individual, pr. (No. 400/109)	16.00
Salt & Pepper, Straight Side, pr. (No. 400/247)	35.00
Salt Dip, 2"	12.00
Salt Dip, 2¼"	6.00
Sauce Boat (No. 400/169)	110.00
Saucer Champagne, 5 oz. (No. 400/190)	16.00
Server, Individual, 6½" (No. 400/269)	150.00
Shades, Lamp—(various styles)	150.00+
Sherbet, 6 oz. (No. 400/18)	35.00
Sherbet, Dessert, 5 oz. (No. 400/19)	15.00
Snack Jar & Cover, Tall, 6¼"	370.00
Snack Set, Oval Tray & Tumbler, 2 pcs. (No. 400/99)	40.00
Stein, 14 oz. Applied Handle, (No. 400/19)	175.00
Sugar (No. 400/18)	70.00
Sugar (No. 400/30)	10.00
Sugar(No. 400/31)	20.00
Sugar, Individual (No. 400/122)	9.00
Tête-ā-Tête, Tray, Cup & Brandy (No. 400/111)	80.00
Toast & Cover, Round, 7¾"	300.00
Tray, 2 Handled, 11½" (No. 400/145E)	45.00
Tray, 5" (No. 400/96T)	20.00
Tray, 8" (No. 400/171)	40.00
Tray, Bon Bon, Center Handled, 8" (No. 400/222)	300.00
Tray, Cake, 3 part Stem, 12" (No. 400/223)	1,500.00+
Tray, Card, Handled, 6"	135.00
Tray, Condiment, 5¼" x 9¼" (No. 400/148)	70.00
Tray, Crimped, 2 Handled, 6¾" or 8½"	27.00
Tray, Crimped, 2 Handled, 10"	30.00
Tray, Handled, 5½"	17.00
Tray, Handled, 8½"	22.00
Tray, Handled, 10" (No. 400/72E)	40.00
Tray, Heart Shaped (No. 400/204)	210.00
Tray, Lemon, Center Handled, 5½" (No. 400/221)	45.00
Tray, Mint, Heart Center Hdl., 8" or 9" (No. 400/149D)	25.00
Tray, Muffin, 2 Handled, 11½" (No. 400/145H)	340.00
Tray, Oblong, 7" (various types)	15.00
Tray, Pastry, Center Heart Handled, 11½" or 12½"	45.00
Tray, Plain or Mirrored, 9" (No. 400/159)	28.00
Tray, Relish, 10½" (various styles)	60.00
Tray, Relish, 4 part, 4 Handled, 8½"	26.00
Tray, Relish, 5 part, 13" or 13½"	70.00
Tray, Relish, 5 part, 5 Handled, 10½"	55.00

Tray, Relish, Divided, 2 Handled, 6½"	17.00
Tray, Relish, Round, Slanted Sides, 7"	16.00
Tray, Round, 10" (various styles) (No. 400/151)	50.00
Tray, Round, 2 Handled, 14" (No. 400/113E)	50.00
Tray, Wafer, Heart Shaped, Center Handled, 6"	25.00
Tumbler, 6 oz. (No. 400/15)	130.00
Tumbler, 10 oz. (No. 400/15)	145.00
Tumbler, 13 oz. (No. 400/15)	160.00
Tumbler, Beaded Flat Base, 8 oz. (No. 400/195)	45.00
Tumbler, Beaded Flat Base, 12 oz. (No. 400/195)	40.00
Tumbler, Beaded Flat Base, 16 oz. (No. 400/195)	45.00
Tumbler, Iced Tea, 12 oz. (No. 400/18)	45.00
Tumbler, Iced Tea, 14 oz. (No. 400/19)	20.00
Tumbler, Juice, 3½ oz. (No. 400/142)	20.00
Tumbler, Juice, 5 oz. (No. 400/18)	30.00
Tumbler, Juice, 5 oz. (No. 400/19)	15.00
Tumbler, Water, 9 oz. (No. 400/18)	35.00
Tumbler, Water, 10 oz. (No. 400/19)	15.00
Vase, 8¼" (No. 400/27)	200.00
Vase, 8½" (No. 400/28)	75.00
Vase, Beaded Top, 6" (No. 400/198)	250.00
Vase, Bud (3 Styles)	200.00+
Vase, Bud, Ball, 4"	45.00
Vase, Bud, 8½"	75.00
Vase, Bud, 9" (No. 400/189)	200.00
Vase, Bud, Low Foot, 5¾" (2 styles) (No. 400/107)	65.00
Vase, Crimped, 6" (No. 400/287C)	45.00
Vase, Crimped, 8" (various styles)	30.00
Vase, Dome Foot, 10" (3 styles)	150.00
Vase, Fan Shaped, 6" (No. 400/287F)	48.00
Vase, Fan Shaped, 8" or 8½" (various styles)	32.00
Vase, Flip, 8" (No. 400/143A)	130.00
Vase, Flip, Crimped, 8" (No. 400/143C)	75.00
Vase, Footed, 6" (No. 400/138B)	110.00
Vase, Handled, 7" (No. 400/87R)	36.00
Vase, Handled, 9" (No. 400/87)	45.00
Vase, Handled, Flat, 8½" (No. 400/227)	190.00
Vase, Ivy Bowl or Brandy, 7" (No. 400/188)	160.00
Vase, Miniature, 4 Shapes	42.00
Vase, Straight, 10"	125.00
Water, Hollow Stem, 11 or 12 oz. (No. 400/195)	60.00
Wine, 2 oz. (No. 400/19)	90.00
Wine, 3 oz. (No. 400/19)	22.00
Wine, 5 oz. (No. 400/190)	28.00
Wine, Hollow Stem, 2 oz., (No. 400/195)	85.00

BLOWN STEMWARE NO. 3400

Claret, 5 oz.	$50.00
Cocktail, 4 oz.	18.00
Cordial, 1 oz.	42.00
Finger Bowl, Footed	30.00
Goblet, 9 oz. (4 bead stem)	25.00

(continued) CANDLEWICK, NO. 400

Oyster Cocktail, 4 oz. (1 bead stem) 18.00
Parfait, 6 oz (1 bead stem). 42.00
Saucer Champagne or Sherbet, 6 oz. 16.00
Seafood Icer or Fruit Cocktail with Insert
    (1 bead stem) 75.00
Sherbet, Low, 5 oz. (1 bead stem) 14.00
Tumbler, Footed, 9 oz. (1 bead stem) 22.00
Tumbler, Iced Tea, Footed, 12 oz. (1 bead stem) 17.00
Tumbler, Juice, Footed, 5 oz.(1 bead stem) 23.00
Tumbler, Water, Footed, 10 oz. (1 bead stem). 17.00
Wine, 4 oz. 24.00

BLOWN STEMWARE NO. 3800

Brandy (2 bead stem) $45.00
Champagne, or Tall Sherbet, 4 oz. 30.00
Claret 30.00
Cocktail, 4 oz. 22.00

Cordial, 1 oz. 40.00
Finger Bowl, 8 oz. 30.00
Goblet, 10 oz. (2 bead stem) 35.00
Icer, 2 pcs. (1 bead stem) 75.00
Sherbet, Low (1 bead stem) 30.00
Tumbler, Footed, 5 oz. (1 bead stem) 30.00
Tumbler, Footed, 9 oz. (1 bead stem) 30.00
Tumbler, Footed, 12 oz. (1 bead stem) 30.00
Wine, 2 oz. 30.00

BLOWN STEMWARE NO. 4000

Cocktail, 4 oz. $24.00
Cordial, 1¼ oz. (2 bead stem) 30.00
Goblet, 11 oz. (3 bead stem) 37.00
Iced Tea, or Hi-ball, Footed, 12 oz. (1 bead stem) . . . 30.00
Sherbet, Tall, 6 oz. 35.00
Wine, 5 oz. 30.00

CENTURY, NO. 2630

Dates: 1949 to 1985

Manufacturer: Fostoria Glass Co., Moundsville, WV

Colors: Crystal

One of Fostoria's most popular patterns with many pieces. Due to the length of production, many pieces were added and discontinued in the line over the years, resulting in some hard to find pieces. Century is the original pattern name, and the following list uses Fostoria's original piece names.

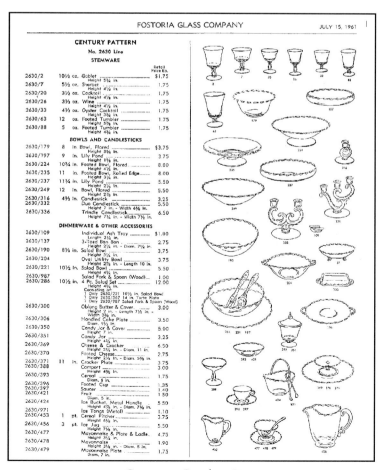

Century Catalog Page

CENTURY, NO. 2630 *(continued)*

Century Footed Comport

Ashtray, Individual, 2¾" $12.00
Basket, 10½" 110.00
Bonbon, 3 Toed, 7¼" 22.00
Bowl, Flared, 8" 58.00
Bowl, Flared, 12" 46.00
Bowl, Flared, Footed, 10¾" 65.00
Bowl, Nappy, Handled, 4½" 12.00
Bowl, Oval Utility, 10" 45.00
Bowl, Oval Vegetable, 9½" 40.00
Bowl, Rolled Edge, Footed, 11" 65.00
Bowl, Salad, 8½" 48.00
Bowl, Salad, 10½" 55.00
Bowl, Snack, 3½" 20.00
Butter & Cover. 50.00
Cake Plate, Handled, 9½" 50.00
Candlesticks, 4½", pr. 35.00
Candlesticks, Duo, 7", pr. 68.00
Candlesticks, Trindle, 7¾", pr. 85.00
Candy Jar, 4¾" 38.00
Candy Jar & Cover, 7" 65.00
Cereal, 6" 15.00
Cheese & Cracker, 11" 75.00
Cocktail, 3½ oz. 15.00
Comport, 4¼" *(Illus.)* 24.00
Cream, Footed 11.00
Cream, Individual, 3½" 15.00
Cup & Saucer. 18.00
Dish, Serving, Handled, 10½". 45.00
Fruit, 5" 13.00

Goblet, 10½ oz. 22.00
Goblet, Luncheon (iced tea), 12 oz. 24.00
Ice Bucket, 4¾" 65.00
Iced Tea Tumbler, Footed, 12 oz. 24.00
Juice Tumbler, Footed, 5 oz. 15.00
Lily Pond, 9" 55.00
Lily Pond, 11¼" 65.00
Mayonnaise 35.00
Mayonnaise, 2 part 35.00
Mustard & Cover 45.00
Oil & Stopper, 5 oz. 35.00
Oyster Cocktail, 4½ oz. 15.00
Party Plate & Cup. 40.00
Pickle, 8¾". 22.00
Pitcher, Cereal, Pint, ... 58.00
Pitcher, Ice Lip, 3 Pint. 165.00
Plate, 6" 11.00
Plate, 7" 15.00
Plate, 8" 18.00
Plate, 9" 22.00
Plate, Dinner, 10½" 55.00
Plate, Torte, 14" 32.00
Plate, Torte, 16" 36.00
Platter, Oval, 12" 45.00
Preserve & Cover, Footed, 6". 45.00
Preserve, Footed, 3¾". 26.00
Relish, 2 Part, 7¼" 23.00
Relish, 3 Part, 11¼" 26.00
Salad, Crescent, 7½". 45.00
Salt & Pepper, 3¼", pr. 24.00
Salt & Pepper, Individual, 2¼", pr. 28.00
Salver, 12¼". 95.00
Sherbet, 5½ oz.. . . . . 9.00
Sugar, Footed 12.00
Sugar, Individual, 3¼" 12.00
Tidbit, 3 Toed, 8". 24.00
Tidbit, Two Tier, 10¼" 50.00
Tray, for Cream & Sugar, 7" 25.00
Tray, for Salt & Pepper, 4½" 18.00
Tray, Lunch, Handled, 11¼" 37.00
Tray, Muffin, Handled, 9½" 40.00
Tray, Snack, 10½". 25.00
Tray, Utility, Handled, 9" 38.00
Tricorne, 3 Toed, 7" 24.00
Vase, Bud, Footed, 6" 22.00
Vase, Handled, 7½" 95.00
Vase, Oval, 8½" 95.00
Wine, 3½ oz. 28.00

CORONET, No. 2560

Date: 1938 to 1960

Manufacturer: Fostoria Glass Co., Moundsville, WV

Colors: Crystal

A very good seller for Fostoria for many years. Many pieces are found with decorations. Coronet is the original name, and the following list uses Fostoria's original piece names.

Bonbon, 5¼" $9.00
Bonbon, 3 Toed, 7¼" 15.00
Bowl, Cereal, 6" 8.00
Bowl, Crimped, 11½" 25.00
Bowl, Cupped, 8½" 35.00
Bowl, Flared, 12" 25.00
Bowl, Fruit, 13" 24.00
Bowl, Handled, 8½" 18.00
Bowl, Handled, 11" 25.00
Bowl, Nut, 3 Toed, Cupped. 11.00
Bowl, Salad, 10" 24.00
Bowl, Salad, 2 part 30.00
Bowl, Serving, Handled. 24.00
Bowl, Sweetmeat, 5½" 12.00
Cake Plate, Handled, 10½" 25.00
Candlesticks, 4", pr. 25.00
Candlesticks, 4½", pr. 35.00
Candlesticks, Duo, 5¼", pr. 40.00
Celery Tray, 11" 18.00
Cheese & Cracker, 2 pcs.. . . . . 35.00
Compote, 6". 15.00
Cream, Footed, 4" 9.00
Cream, Individual. 12.00
Cup & Saucer. 15.00
Fruit, Individual, 5" 5.00
Ice Bucket with handle 32.00
Mayonnaise Set, 2 compartment, 3 pcs. 55.00
Mayonnaise Set, 3 pcs. 45.00
Oil & Stopper, Footed. 35.00
Olive, 6¾" 12.00
Pickle, 8¾". 16.00
Plate, 6" or 7". 6.00
Plate, 8" 10.00
Plate, 9" 20.00
Plate, Lemon, 6¼" 9.00
Plate, Torte, 13" or 14" 25.00

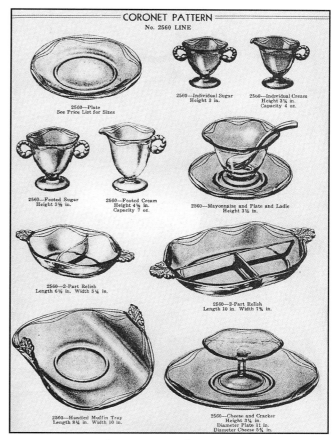

Coronet Catalog Page

Relish, 2 part, 6½" 15.00
Relish, 3 part, 10". 22.00
Relish, 4 part 25.00
Relish, 5 part 30.00
Salt & Pepper, pr. 20.00
Sugar, Footed 9.00
Sugar, Individual. 12.00
Tid-Bit, Flat, 3 Toed 15.00
Tray, for Sugar & Cream 15.00
Tray, Lunch, Handled, 11½" 32.00
Tray, Muffin, Handled, 8½" 20.00
Vase, Handled, 6" 35.00
Vase, Pansy, 3¾" 20.00
Whipped Cream, 5" 12.00

EMPRESS, NO. 1401

Empress Dinner Plate; Mayonnaise, Dolphin
Footed (cut); Individual Nut,
Dolphin Footed; Nappy

Date: 1930 to 1938

Manufacturer: A. H. Heisey & Co., Newark, OH

Colors: Crystal, Flamingo, Moongleam, Sahara. Many pieces
in Alexandrite. Limited production in Tangerine and Cobalt.

Reproductions: Imperial Glass made the dolphin footed 3
toed candlestick in sunshine yellow in 1981. (See Queen Ann
for further discussion).

*Extensive tableware line. Empress is the original company name,
and the piece names are also original with the company. Plates
and several serving pieces were made in round and square styles.
Several pieces have 3 dolphin feet—designated d.f. in the
following list. The lemon dish has a dolphin finial. There is a
floral bowl in the pattern with 4 lions' heads around the bowl
and it also has 4 paw feet. Many pieces of the pattern were
reworked with an internal optic and became pattern No. 1509
Queen Ann. (see page 56). Prices are for items in Sahara
(yellow). Moongleam pieces are approximately the same as
Sahara. Flamingo prices are slightly less by 5% or 10%. Crystal
prices are 20% less. Unusual colors such as Alexandrite,
Tangerine and Cobalt are valued at 100% more. Some rare
pieces command up to 500% over Sahara prices.*

Ashtray	$135.00
Bonbon, 6"	24.00
Bouillon, 2 Handled	32.00
Bowl, Floral, 10" (Lion)	475.00
Bowl, Floral, 2 Handled, Footed, 8½"	55.00
Bowl, Floral, d.f., 11"	85.00
Bowl, Floral, Flared, 9" (Leaf design on bowl)	120.00
Bowl, Floral, Rolled Edge, 9"	40.00
Bowl, Frappe and Center	60.00
Bowl, Nasturtium, d.f., 7½"	120.00
Bowl, Salad, 2 Handled, 10"	55.00
Bowl, Salad, Square, 2 Handled, 10"	55.00
Candlestick, d.f., 6" 3 toed, pr	275.00
Candlestick, Handled, Footed, 2", pr	85.00
Candy Box & Cover, d.f., 6"	115.00
Celery, 13"	35.00
Comport, Footed, 6" Round	60.00
Comport, Oval, 7"	70.00
Comport, Square, 6"	75.00
Compotier, d.f., 6"	175.00
Cream Soup, 2 Handled	32.00
Cream, d.f.	40.00
Cream, Individual	35.00
Cup & Saucer	40.00
Cup & Saucer, After Dinner Coffee	60.00
Cup & Saucer, plain rim (1401½)	38.00
Custard, 4 oz.	35.00
Dessert, Oval, 2 Handled, 10"	60.00

Dish, Vegetable, Oval, 10"	40.00
Goblet, 9 oz.	72.00
Grapefruit, Square, 6"	22.00
Hors d'oeuvre, 2 Handled, 13"	50.00
Hors d'oeuvre, 7 Compartment, 10"	90.00
Ice Tub, d.f.	125.00
Jelly, Footed, 2 Handled, 6"	20.00
Jug, d.f., 3 pt.	175.00
Lemon & Cover, Oval, 6½"	85.00
Marmalade & Cover, d.f.	110.00
Mayonnaise, d.f., 5½" (*Illus.*)	42.00
Mint, d.f., 6"	42.00
Mint, Footed, 8"	45.00
Mustard & Cover	80.00
Nappy, 8" (*Illus.*)	30.00
Nappy, d.f., 7½"	32.00
Nut, Individual, d.f. (*Illus.*)	27.00
Oil & Stopper, 4 oz.	125.00
Oyster Cocktail, 2½ oz.	18.00
Pickle & Olive, 2 Compartment, Handled, 12"	27.00
Plate, Muffin, 2 Handled, 12"	48.00
Plate, Round, 4½"	12.00
Plate, Round, 6"	15.00
Plate, Round, 7"	15.00
Plate, Round, 8"	22.00
Plate, Round, 9"	22.00
Plate, Round, 10½"	165.00
Plate, Round, 12"	65.00

(continued) EMPRESS, NO. 1401

Plate, Round, 15" 75.00
Plate, Sandwich, 2 Handled, 12" 65.00
Plate, Sandwich, 2 Handled, 13" 48.00
Plate, Sandwich, 2 Handled, Square, 12" 48.00
Plate, Square, 6" 12.00
Plate, Square, 7" 15.00
Plate, Square, 8" 32.00
Plate, Square, 8" (1401½) 50.00
Plate, Square, 10½" *(Illus.)* 175.00
Platter, 14" 48.00
Preserve, Footed, 2 Handled, 5" 25.00
Punch Bowl, d.f., 15" 1,200.00
Relish Buffet, 4 Compartment, 16" 110.00
Relish, Combination, 3 Compartment, 10" 70.00
Relish, Triplex, 7" 38.00

Relish, Triplex, 10" 55.00
Relish, Triplex, Center Handled, 7" 75.00
Salt & Pepper, pr. 115.00
Saucer Champagne, 4 oz. 50.00
Sherbet, 4 oz. 22.00
Soda, 5 oz. 22.00
Soda, 12 oz. 40.00
Sugar, d.f. 40.00
Sugar, Individual 35.00
Tray, Condiment (for individual cream and sugar) . . 40.00
Tray, Sandwich, Center Handled, 12" 70.00
Tumbler, 8 oz. 40.00
Tumbler, d.f., 8 oz. 130.00
Vase, d.f., 9" 165.00
Vase, Flared, 8" 80.00

GADROON, NO. 3500

Date: Ca. 1933

Manufacturer: Cambridge Glass Co., Cambridge, OH

Colors: Crystal, Crown Tuscan, Carmen, Royal Blue, Amber, Forest Green, Amethyst

An extensive tableware pattern by Cambridge and used for many of their popular etchings. Gadroon is the original company name. The following piece names are taken from company catalogs. Other pieces may have been made. All pieces were not made in all colors. For pieces in colors other than listed, add 100% to Crystal prices.

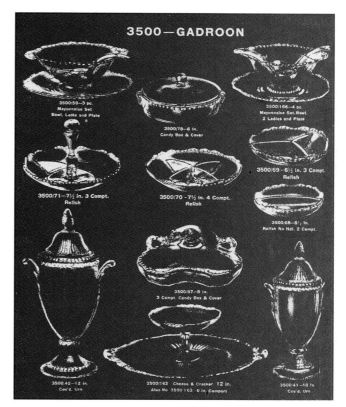

Gadroon Catalog Illustrations

GADROON, NO. 3500 *(continued)*

	Crystal	Carmen & Royal Blue		Crystal	Carmen & Royal Blue
Basket, 2 Handled, 6" or 7"	$ 12.00	$22.00	Plate, Torte, 13"	18.00	
Basket, Fruit, Ram's Head, 12"	115.00	350.00	Punch Bowl, Ram's Head, 13"	125.00	
Basket, Fruit, 12"	35.00	85.00	Relish Set, 6 part	45.00	
Basket, Handled, 5" or 6"	30.00	60.00	Relish, 1 Handle,		
Bonbon, 5"	9.00	18.00	2 Compartment, 5½"	8.00	20.00
Bowl, 10"	24.00	45.00	Relish, 2 Compartment, 5½"	8.00	22.00
Bowl, Crimped, 11"	24.00	50.00	Relish, 1 Handle,		
Bowl, 11"	24.00	50.00	3 Compartment, 6½"	10.00	30.00
Bowl, 12"	24.00	50.00	Relish, 3 Compartment,		
Bowl, Ram's Head, Square, 8"	115.00	350.00	Round, 6½"	12.00	30.00
Bowl, Ram's Head, 9"	135.00	400.00	Relish, 2 Handled,		
Bowl, Oval, 12"	40.00	100.00	4 Compartment, 7½"	10.00	24.00
Bowl, Oval, Handled &			Relish, 4 Compartment, 7½"	15.00	40.00
Footed, 12"	55.00	135.00	Relish, Oval, 10"	12.00	30.00
Candelabra, 6½", pr.	70.00	160.00	Sugar Basket with Metal Bail	20.00	40.00
Candlesticks, 2 Light, pr.	75.00		Sugar	10.00	25.00
Candlesticks, 4", pr.	55.00	110.00	Sugar, Individual	12.00	30.00
Candlesticks, 6½", pr.	30.00	75.00	Tray, 12"	22.00	
Candy Box & Cover,			Urn or Candy Jar & Cover, 10"	65.00	175.00
3 Compartment, 8"	50.00	120.00	Urn or Candy Jar & Cover, 12"	80.00	250.00
Celery & Relish, 3 or 4			Vase, Footed, 10" (urn)	45.00	120.00
Compartment, 10" (oblong)	18.00	45.00	Vase, Footed, 8" (urn)	30.00	85.00
Cereal, 6"	7.00				
Comport, Low, 6½"	10.00	20.00	**BLOWN STEMWARE, NO. 3500**		
Comport, Tall, 6" or 7"	30.00	85.00	Cocktail	9.00	28.00
Cream Soup	9.00		Finger Bowl	8.00	20.00
Cream	10.00	25.00	Finger Bowl, Footed	10.00	22.00
Cream, Individual	12.00	30.00	Goblet, Long Bowl	10.00	30.00
Cup & Saucer	10.00		Goblet, Short Bowl	10.00	35.00
Fruit Saucer, Nappy, 5"	4.00		Oyster Cocktail	8.00	22.00
Mayonnaise, 2 Handled	15.00		Sherbet, Low	8.00	22.00
Nappy, 1 Handled, 5" or 6"	9.00	18.00	Sherbet, Tall	9.00	25.00
Plate, Bread & Butter, 6"	5.00		Tumbler, Footed, 2½ oz.	8.00	22.00
Plate, Dessert, 7½"	5.00		Tumbler, Footed, 5 oz.	8.00	22.00
Plate, Finger Bowl	6.00	10.00	Tumbler, Footed, 10 oz.	8.00	24.00
Plate, Salad, 8½"	8.00		Tumbler, Footed, 13 oz.	9.00	25.00
Plate, Sandwich, Footed			Wine	10.00	30.00
2 Handled, 12"	20.00				

LACED EDGE (KATY BLUE), NO. 7498 (and others)

Date: 1935 to 1949

Manufacturer: Imperial Glass Corporation, Bellaire, OH

Colors: Crystal, Stiegel Green, Ritz Blue, Rose Pink, Green, Amber, Moonstone (blue opalescent), Sea Green (green opalescent)

Laced Edge is the original factory name. This line is also sometimes called "Crocheted." Many bowls were made with Intaglio etched fruit centers. Prices are for blue opalescent. Due to its rarity, green opalescent may sell for slightly more. Crystal items should sell for at least 50% less. Transparent colors should sell for 25% less. It is possible that not all items were made in opalescent colors.

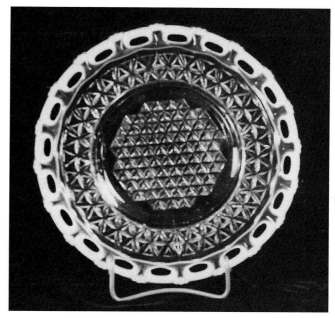

Laced Edge Plate

Bowl, 4½"	$16.00
Bowl, 5"	16.00
Bowl, 5½"	17.00
Bowl, 9"	40.00
Bowl, 9½"	40.00
Bowl, 10"	45.00
Bowl, 11"	45.00
Bowl, Basket, 9½"	45.00
Bowl, Console, 9" (straight)	50.00
Bowl, Console, 9½" (cupped)	50.00
Bowl, Console, 10" (straight	60.00
Bowl, Console, 11" (cupped)	60.00
Bowl, Console, 12" (flared)	60.00
Bowl, Console, 13" (cupped)	60.00
Bowl, Flower with Wire Holder, 6½", 7½"	50.00
Bowl, Flower, 6½"	40.00
Bowl, Flower, 7½" or 8½"	45.00
Bowl, Fruit, 13"	55.00
Bowl, Orange, 12"	55.00

Bowl, Oval, 11"	45.00
Bowl, Oval, Divided, 11"	45.00
Bowl, Rose with Wire Holder, 6½", 7½"	50.00
Candlesticks, 2 Light, pr.	95.00
Cream	22.00
Cup & Saucer	32.00
Mayonnaise Set, 3 pcs.	40.00
Nappy, 8"	35.00
Plate, 6½"	15.00
Plate, 8"	18.00
Plate, 9½"	24.00
Plate, 11" (*Illus.*)	40.00
Plate, 12"	40.00
Plate, 14"	50.00
Platter, 13"	60.00
Sugar	22.00
Tid Bit Set, 2 Tier (2 styles)	70.00
Tumbler, 9 oz.	40.00
Vase, 5½"	40.00

LARIAT, NO. 1540

Lariat Torte Plate, 3 Light Candlestick,
Oil/Cologne

Date: 1941 to 1957

Manufacturer: A. H. Heisey & Co., Newark, OH

Colors: Crystal

Reproductions: Imperial Glass Corp. made the blown stem ware for about 6 years in crystal.

Extensive tableware line. Lariat is the original name and the piece listing uses original catalog descriptions. Very plain except for the looped edge. Made to compete with Imperial's Candlewick. "Heavy Edge" pieces have very heavy, large loops on edges compared with the loops on regular pieces.

Ashtray, 4"	$10.00
Basket, Handled, Footed, 8½ "	175.00
Basket, Handled, Footed, 10"	325.00
Bonbon, 7"	28.00
Bonbon, Handled, 7" (basket)	115.00
Bowl, Baked Apple, 7"	22.00
Bowl, Camellia, 9½ "	32.00
Bowl, Centerpiece, Rolled Edge, 12"	38.00
Bowl, Cereal, 7"	22.00
Bowl, Crimped, 13"	55.00
Bowl, Dressing, 2 Compartment, 7"	30.00
Bowl, Flared, 13"	45.00
Bowl, Floating Flower, 10"	40.00
Bowl, Floral, 9"	32.00
Bowl, Floral, 12"	40.00
Bowl, Shallow, Heavy Edge 13"	85.00
Bowl, Floral, Heavy Edge, 14"	95.00
Bowl, Floral, Oval, Shallow, 13"	50.00
Bowl, Gardenia, 13"	45.00
Bowl, Gardenia, Heavy Edge, 15"	95.00
Bowl, Party Salad, 2 Handled, 10½"	58.00
Bowl, Salad, 10½"	45.00
Candleblocks, 1 Light (nappy candle), pr.	40.00
Candleblocks, 3 Light, pr. (No. 1540½)	300.00
Candlesticks, 2 Light, pr.	75.00
Candlesticks, 3 Light, pr. *(Illus. of one)*	90.00
Candy Box & Cover, 7"	85.00
Candy Box & Cover, 2 Compartment, 7"	85.00
Candy Box & Cover, Footed	115.00
Candy Box & Cover, Small, 5"	70.00
Candy Box & Cover with Horse Head Finial, 8"	2,500.00+
Candy Box & Cover with Plume Finial, 8"	160.00
Celery & Olive, 13"	28.00

Celery Heart, Handled	50.00
Celery, 13"	25.00
Cheese & Cover, Footed, 6"	55.00
Cigarette Box & Cover, 4"	50.00
Coaster, 4"	10.00
Cocktail, 3½ oz.	22.00
Comport & Cover, 10"	125.00
Confection, Handled, 7" (basket)	115.00
Cream	22.00
Cream Soup, 2 Handled	45.00
Cup & Saucer	35.00
Dish, Applesauce, 5"	16.00
Dish, Candy, 7"	22.00
Dish, Caramel, 7"	22.00
Dish, Caramel & Cover, 7"	55.00
Dish, Nut, Individual, 4"	22.00
Dish, Sauce, 6"	15.00
Goblet, 9 oz.	20.00
Iced Tea, Footed, 12 oz.	20.00
Ice Tub, Medium, 7"	65.00
Jelly, Handled, 7"	35.00
Juice, Footed, 5 oz.	18.00
Lamp, Black Out, with 5" Globe, pr	800.00
Lamp, Hurricane, with 7" Globe, pr	375.00
Marshmallow, Rolled Edge, 8"	24.00
Mayonnaise, 5"	28.00
Mayonnaise, Footed, Rolled Edge, 5"	35.00
Nappy, 7"	18.00
Nappy, 8"	22.00
Nougat, Flat, 8"	18.00
Oil & Stopper, (cologne), 4 oz. *(Illus.)*	95.00
Oil & Stopper, Handled, 4 oz.	115.00
Oyster Cocktail, 4½ oz.	12.00

(continued) LARIAT, NO. 1540

Plate, 6"	10.00
Plate, 7"	18.00
Plate, 8"	18.00
Plate, Baked Apple, 8"	18.00
Plate, Buffet, 21"	180.00
Plate, Cookie, 11"	30.00
Plate, Cream Soup, 7"	12.00
Plate, Egg, 14"	200.00
Plate, Egg, Oval, 14"	230.00
Plate, Mayonnaise, 6", 7" or 8"	12.00
Plate, Sandwich, 14"	35.00
Plate, Sandwich, 2 Handled, 14"	65.00
Plate, Sandwich, Center Handled, 14"	85.00
Plate, Sandwich, with Cheese & Cover, 14"	85.00
Plate, Service, 10½"	90.00
Plate, Toast or Cheese with Dome Cover, 8"	65.00
Plate, Torte, 16" *(Illus.)*	45.00
Plate, Torte, Demi, Rolled Edge, 10"	28.00
Plate, Torte, Rolled Edge, 13"	35.00
Punch Bowl, 7½ qt.	150.00
Punch Cup, 4 oz.	16.00
Relish, 2 Compartment	35.00
Relish, 3 Compartment, Round, 10"	45.00
Relish, 4 Compartment, 8½"	55.00
Relish, Oblong, 3 Compartment, 11"	40.00
Salt & Pepper, Footed, pr	425.00
Saucer Champagne, 6 oz.	16.00
Sherbet, Low, 6 oz.	15.00

Shrimp Cocktail, Footed	35.00
Sugar	22.00
Sweetmeat, Handled, 7" (basket)	115.00
Tray for Cream & Sugar, 8"	25.00
Tray, Oval, 14"	40.00
Urn Jar & Cover, 12"	185.00
Vase, Crimped Top, Footed, 5"	55.00
Vase, Crimped, Footed, 7"	55.00
Vase, Fan, Footed, 6½"	45.00
Vase, Fan, Footed, 7"	45.00
Vase, Square Top, Footed, 7"	55.00
Vase, Straight, Footed, 7"	45.00
Vase, Swing, 10 to 12"	60.00
Vase, Swing, 12 to 15"	90.00
Wine, 3½ oz.	22.00

BLOWN WARE: (ALL NO. 5040)

Claret, 4 oz.	$20.00
Cocktail, 3½ oz.	20.00
Cordial, Low Stem, 1 oz.	120.00
Cordial, Tall Stem, 1 oz.	180.00
Goblet, 10 oz.	25.00
Iced Tea, Footed, 12 oz.	25.00
Juice, Footed, 5 oz.	22.00
Oyster Cocktail, 4½ oz.	18.00
Saucer Champagne, 5½ oz.	22.00
Wine, 2½ oz.	32.00

OLD COLONY

Date: 1935 to 1938

Manufacturer: Hocking Glass Co., Lancaster, OH

Colors: Pink. Limited in Crystal.

This is still often called Lace Edge or Open Lace, but Old Colony was the original name. Prices are for pieces in Pink. This pattern is found with satin finish, but most collectors do not consider this as desirable. On the 13" plates, the edge is solid rather than open.

Grill Plate, Sugar & Cream, Cup & Saucer

OLD COLONY *(continued)*

Covered Butter, Covered Cookie Jar

Bowl, 6¼" $20.00
Bowl, 8¼" (crystal only) 14.00
Bowl, Plain or Ribbed, 9½". 28.00
Bowl, Ribbed, 7¾" 48.00
Bowl, 3 Footed, 10½" 220.00
Butter & Cover *(Illus.)* 75.00
Candlesticks, pr 265.00
Candy Jar & Cover, Ribbed. 48.00
Comport & Cover, Footed, 7". 48.00

Comport, 7" 28.00
Comport, 9" (rayed base) . . . . 750.00+
Cookie Jar & Cover *(Illus.)* 85.00
Cream *(Illus.)* 24.00
Cup & Saucer *(Illus.)* 38.00
Fish Bowl, (crystal only) 25.00
Flower Container with Crystal Frog 27.00
Juice, 5 oz. 95.00
Plate, 7¼" 24.00
Plate, 8¾" 18.00
Plate, 10½" 32.00
Plate, 13" 35.00
Plate, Grill, 10½" *(Illus.)*. 22.00
Platter, 12¾" 37.00
Platter, 5 Compartment, 12¾" 37.00
Relish, 3 Compartment, 7½" 70.00
Relish, 3 Compartment, 10½". 27.00
Sherbet. 70.00
Sugar *(Illus.)* 24.00
Tumbler, 9 oz.. . . . . 26.00
Tumbler, Footed, 10½ oz.. . . . . 68.00
Vase, 7" . . . . 400.00+

QUEEN ANN, NO. 1509

Queen Ann Catalog Page

Date: 1939 to 1957

Manufacturer: A. H. Heisey & Co., Newark, OH

Colors: Crystal only

Reproductions: Imperial Glass Corp. made the dolphin footed console bowl in sunshine yellow, which can be confused with No. 1401 Empress pieces in Sahara.

Queen Ann (original name) is a reissued pattern made up mostly from old No. 1401 Empress molds. Identifying items in Queen Ann becomes simpler when you realize that Queen Ann was made only in crystal. Almost all pieces of Queen Ann also have had a wide, swirl optic added to the pattern which is easily felt on the interiors of pieces. Empress pieces are smooth and the same thickness throughout with no optic. Some pieces in Queen Ann were entirely new, with new shapes never before used in Heisey's other patterns. Many pieces also have the dolphin feet of the Empress pieces. These are designated as "d.f." in the following list.

QUEEN ANN, NO. 1509

Bowl, Combination Dressing, 7" $35.00
Bowl, Flared, 8½" 35.00
Bowl, Floral, d.f., 8½" 45.00
Bowl, Floral, d.f., 11" 50.00
Bowl, Floral, 12½" 50.00
Bowl, Floral, 2 Handled, Footed, 8½" 35.00
Bowl, Gardenia, 9" 30.00
Bowl, Lily, 7" 30.00
Bowl, Sauce, d.f., 7½" 45.00
Bowl, Sunburst, 9" 30.00
Bowl, Sunburst Floral, 10" 30.00
Bowl, Swing, 13" 50.00
Candelabra & Prisms, 1 Light, 7½", pr. 220.00
Candlesticks, Footed, 2 Handled (nappy), pr. 65.00
Cheese & Cracker, 2 pc. 45.00
Celery Tray, 13" 22.00
Comport, Oval, 7" 40.00
Cream, d.f. 22.00
Cream, Individual 25.00
Cream Soup 25.00
Cup & Saucer 30.00
Grape Fruit, 6" 22.00
Ice Cube Bucket, d.f. 80.00
Jelly, Footed, 2 Handled, 6" 18.00
Jug, 3 pt., d.f. 110.00
Lemon & Cover, Dolphin Finial, 6½" 45.00
Mayonnaise, d.f., 5½" 28.00

Mint, d.f., 5½" 18.00
Mint, Footed, 6" 18.00
Mint, Footed, 8" 45.00
Mustard & Cover 65.00
Nappy, 4½" 8.00
Nappy, 8" 25.00
Oil Bottle & Stopper 55.00
Pickle & Olive, 13" 18.00
Plate, Round, 4½" 10.00
Plate, Round or Square, 6" 10.00
Plate, Round or Square, 7" 10.00
Plate, Round or Square, 8" 15.00
Plate, Round, 10½" 95.00
Plate, Demi-torte, 11" 30.00
Plate, Sandwich, 10" 30.00
Plate, Sandwich, 2 Handled, Round or Square, 12" . . . 28.00
Plate, Sandwich, Center Handled, 12" 32.00
Plate, Service, 10½" 110.00
Plate, Snack Rack & Center, 16" 50.00
Plate, Torte, Social Hour Tray, 15" 50.00
Relish, 3 Compartment, 11" (5 o'clock) 30.00
Relish, Triplex, 7" 22.00
Salad Dressing, Combination, 2 part, 7" 30.00
Salt & Pepper, pr. 45.00
Sugar, d.f. 22.00
Sugar, Individual 25.00
Tray, for Individual Cream & Sugar 25.00

RIPPLE

Date: 1960s

Manufacturer: Hazel-Atlas Glass Co., Clarksburg, WV

Colors: Milky White, Jewel Turquoise, Princess Pink

This late tableware pattern is made in a luncheon set with a few extra pieces. The colors listed are as the company described in its catalogs and Ripple is its original name. The turquoise and pink colors are applied to the white glass. Plates have colored edges and the cups and bowls are solid color on the exterior. No. 6091 referred to the Jewel Turquoise and No. 6040 to the Princess Pink. Luncheon sets were sold in 16 or 18 piece sets and a 30 piece dinner set was available (serving 6). Names of pieces are from the original catalog listing.

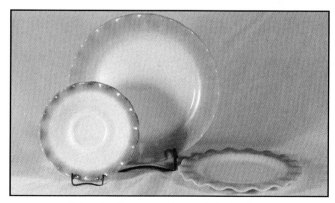

Ripple Saucer, Plate, Salad Plate

Cereal-Soup $5.00
Cream, 7 oz. 6.00
Cup & Saucer (*Illus. of saucer*) 10.00
Dish, Dessert 4.50

Plate, 7" (*Illus.*) 5.00
Plate, 9" (*Illus.*) 8.00
Plate, Chop-Steak, 10½" 10.00
Sugar, 7 oz. 6.00

WAVERLY, NO. 1519

Factory Photo, Waverly Sugar & Cream, Triplex Relish, Footed Honey

Date: 1940 to 1957

Manufacturer: A. H. Heisey & Co., Newark, OH

Colors: Clear. Limited items in light amber.

Reproductions: Imperial Glass Corp. continued the production of Waverly in a limited number of pieces for several years. Imperial also reproduced the Lion covered trinket box in amber with a few known in crystal also. Candy boxes were made in caramel slag and a few other Imperial colors.

A major pattern line used for many cuttings and etchings by Heisey, but also available plain. The pattern was designed by Horace King, Heisey's designer at the time. Many pieces have a sea motif, with finials shaped like waves, sea horse feet on the floral bowl, sea horse handles and others. The small, graduated balls in groups about the rim add to the water motif.

Bowl, Crimped, 10" or 12" $25.00	Oil & Stopper, Footed, 3 oz. 80.00
Bowl, Dressing, Oval, 2 Compartment, 6½" 20.00	Plate, Demi-Torte, 11" 32.00
Bowl, Floral, 3 Sea horse Feet, 11" 60.00	Plate, Dinner, 10½" 90.00
Bowl, Fruit or Salad, Footed, 9" 50.00	Plate, Mayonnaise, 7" 9.00
Bowl, Gardenia, 10" or 13" 25.00	Plate, Salad, 7" or 8" 9.00
Bowl, Salad, 7" 35.00	Plate, Sandwich, 11" 32.00
Bowl, Salad, 9" 35.00	Plate, Sandwich, 14" 37.00
Butter Dish & Cover, Square, 6" 55.00	Plate, Sandwich, Center Handled, 14" 48.00
Candlesticks, 2 Light, pr. 65.00	Plate, Torte, 14" 37.00
Candlesticks, 3 Light, pr. 75.00	Relish, Oblong, 3 Compartment, 11" 18.00
Candy Box & Cover, 6" 45.00	Relish, Round, 3 Compartment, 7" *(Illus.)* 20.00
Candy Box & Cover, Tall, Footed, 5" 50.00	Relish, Round, 4 Compartment, 9" 22.00
Celery Tray, 12" 15.00	Salt & Pepper, Footed, pr 48.00
Cheese & Cracker, 11", 2 pc. 35.00	Salver, Footed, 13½" 60.00
Cheese or Honey, Footed *(Illus.)* 18.00	Sugar, Footed *(Illus.)* 20.00
Chocolate & Cover, 5" (No. 1559) 40.00	Sugar, Individual, Footed. 25.00
Cigarette Holder & Cover. 85.00	Tray, for Individual Cream & Sugar 22.00
Comport, Low Footed, 6" 18.00	Vase, Fan, Footed, 7". 20.00
Comport, Oval, Footed, 7" 20.00	Vase, Footed, 7" 20.00
Cream, Footed *(Illus.)* 20.00	Vase, Violet, 3½" 28.00
Cream, Individual, Footed. 25.00	
Cup & Saucer. 30.00	**BLOWN STEMWARE: (ALL NO. 5019)**
Dish & Cover, Lemon, Oval, 6" 38.00	Cocktail, 3½ oz. $12.00
Epergnette Candleholder, 5" 18.00	Cordial, 1 oz. 45.00
Epergnette Candleholder, Cupped, 6½" 18.00	Goblet, 10 oz. 17.00
Epergnette Candleholder, Deep, 6" 18.00	Iced Tea, Footed, 13 oz. 15.00
Ice Bowl, 2 Handled, 6½" 48.00	Juice, Footed, 5 oz. 15.00
Jelly, Footed, 6½" 18.00	Sherbet or Saucer Champagne, 5½ oz. 12.00
Mayonnaise, Footed, 5½" 20.00	Wine or Claret, 3 oz. 15.00

Chapter 6
FLOWERS, FRUITS & LEAVES

ALICE

Date: Ca. 1940

Manufacturer: Anchor Hocking Glass Corporation, Lancaster, OH

Colors: Anchorwhite with decorated enamel rims; Jade-ite

Marketed under the Fire-King brand of table and kitchenware. Mainly made as a promotional pattern, making the dinner plates very difficult to find.

Alice Saucer

	Jade-ite	White Decorated
Cup & Saucer *(Illus. of Saucer)*	$8.00	$24.00
Plate, 9½"	25.00	25.00

AVOCADO, NO. 601

Date: 1923 to 1933

Manufacturer: Indiana Glass Co., Dunkirk, IN

Colors: Crystal, Pink, Green. Later made in Milk Glass.

Reproductions: They include the pitcher, tumblers, sherbet, 8" pickle, sugar and cream, 6" and 8" plates, and 3 footed nappy. In later years, Indiana made most of these pieces in their old molds, some for Tiara Party Plan. Avoid all colors other than those mentioned above such as pink frosted, green frosted, amethyst, deep blue, red and yellow. For pitchers and tumblers in pink or green, the new colors are darker than the original ones. Also they are heavier than the originals.

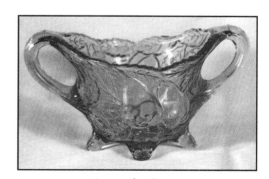

Avocado Sugar

	Crystal	Green	Pink		Crystal	Green	Pink
Bowl, Salad, 9"	$26.00	$145.00	$115.00	Plate, Cheese, 6½"	8.00	20.00	15.00
Cream, Handled, Berry	17.00	45.00	38.00	Plate, Salad, 8¼"	12.00	22.00	20.00
Cup & Saucer		65.00	60.00	Preserve, Shallow, 7¼"	16.00	45.00	35.00
Jelly, Handled, 7"	12.00	30.00	26.00	Relish, Footed, 6"	15.00	35.00	30.00
Jug, ½ gal.	36.00	1,000.00+	850.00+	Sugar, Handled Berry *(Illus.)*.	17.00	40.00	38.00
Olive, 2 Handled, 5¼"	14.00	35.00	35.00	Sundae, Footed (sherbet) . . .		60.00	60.00
Pickle, 2 Handled, 8"	16.00	45.00	35.00	Tumbler, Footed	30.00	260.00	185.00
Plate, 2 Handled, 10"	18.00	62.00	45.00				

CHERRY, NO. 15, 339

Cherry 7½" Bowl

Date: Late 1927

Manufacturer: U. S. Glass Co., Gas City, IN

Colors: Crystal, Green, Pink. Crystal Iridized.

[See also Strawberry] Collectors call this pattern Cherryberry, but the original company name is simply Cherry. The pattern was made at the Gas City, Indiana, plant of U. S. Glass Co. Items made in Cherry were also made in Strawberry.

	Crystal	Pink, Green
Bowl, 4"	$7.00	$12.00
Bowl, 6⅜"	18.00	24.00
Bowl, 7½" *(Illus.)*	20.00	32.00
Bowl, Deep, 6¼"	42.00	70.00
Butter & Cover.	110.00	155.00
Comport, 5¾"	10.00	15.00
Cream	17.00	25.00
Cream, Large	16.00	20.00

	Crystal	Pink, Green
Jug, 7¾"	155.00	145.00
Nappy, Handled, 5"	9.00	17.00
Pickle, Oval, 8¼"	10.00	18.00
Plate, 6"	5.00	8.00
Plate, 7½"	9.00	12.00
Sugar	17.00	25.00
Sugar & Cover, Large	75.00	120.00
Sundae (sherbet)	8.00	12.00
Tumbler, 8 oz..	22.00	38.00

CHERRY BLOSSOM

Cherry Blossom Cake Plate,
Cup & Saucer, Bowls, Sherbet

Date: 1930 to 1939

Manufacturer: Jeannette Glass Co., Jeannette, PA

Colors: Clear, Pink, Green, Red, Delphite, Jadite

Reproductions: They abound in this pattern. Some were made several years ago and had crude designs with poor detail. Recent reproductions have improved somewhat. Pieces known to have been reproduced include the cereal bowl, 8½" bowl, cake plate, child's cup, cup and saucer, plate, divided platter, pitcher, salt and pepper shakers, 2 handled tray and tumblers. Be cautious when buying Cherry Blossom. Look for weak or poor pattern detail, unusual colors such as cobalt and red, and generally heavy and poorly finished glass. The child's butter is completely new as old ones were never made.

One of the most popular patterns in Depression Glass, at least until the multitude of reproductions began and made many collectors wary of investing in and collecting this pattern. Most pieces are still safe, but care must be taken about several pieces.

(continued) CHERRY BLOSSOM

	Green	Pink	Delphite
Bowl, 4¾" *(Illus.)*	$20.00	$19.00	$13.00
Bowl, 5¾" *(Illus.)*	45.00	45.00	
Bowl, Soup, 7¾"	85.00	85.00	
Bowl, 8½"	48.00	45.00	40.00
Bowl, Fruit, 3 Footed, 10½".	95.00	95.00	
Bowl, Handled, 9"	60.00	57.00	24.00
Bowl, Oval Vegetable, 9" . . .	55.00	52.00	44.00
Butter & Cover	125.00	110.00	
Cake Plate, 10" *(Illus.)*	45.00	38.00	
Coaster	16.00	18.00	
Cream	20.00	20.00	20.00
Cup & Saucer *(Illus.)*	25.00	25.00	22.00
Ice Tea, 12 oz.			
(pattern at top)	75.00	65.00	
Juice, 4 oz.	32.00	25.00	
Juice, Footed, 5 oz.			
(pattern at top)	26.00	24.00	20.00
Mug, 7 oz.	220.00	300.00	
Pitcher, 36 oz. (all-over			
pattern)	75.00	68.00	
Pitcher, Footed, 36 oz. (pattern			
at top, cone shape)	120.00	105.00	100.00
Pitcher, Straight Sided,			
42 oz. (pattern at top) . . .	85.00	85.00	

	Green	Pink	Delphite
Plate, 6"	9.00	10.00	12.00
Plate, 7"	22.00	20.00	
Plate, 9"	25.00	22.00	20.00
Plate, Grill, 9"	34.00	28.00	
Platter, 9"	750.00+	800.00+	
Platter, 11"	55.00	48.00	40.00
Platter, 13"	85.00	90.00	
Platter, Divided, 13"	80.00	85.00	
Salt & Pepper, pr	1,500.00+	1,700.00+	
Sherbet *(Illus.)*	15.00	17.00	15.00
Sugar & Cover	40.00	45.00	
Tray, Sandwich, Handled,			
10½"	38.00	35.00	24.00
Tumbler, Round or Scalloped			
Foot, 8 oz., ...	27.00	22.00	20.00
Tumbler, 9 oz.			
(pattern at top)	32.00	24.00	

CHILDREN'S DISHES:

	Green	Pink	
Cream		$50.00	$55.00
Cup & Saucer		58.00	58.00
Plate, 6"		12.00	12.00
Sugar		50.00	55.00

CLOVERLEAF

Date: 1930 to 1936

Manufacturer: Hazel-Atlas Glass Co.

Colors: Green, Yellow, Clear. Luncheon sets in Black. Limited availability in Pink.

	Green	Yellow	Black
Ashtray & Match Holder,			
4"	$	$	$90.00
Ashtray & Match Holder,			
5¾"			110.00
Bowl, 4"	24.00	34.00	
Bowl, 5"	38.00	35.00	
Bowl, 7"	50.00	60.00	
Bowl, 8"	85.00		
Candy & Cover	80.00	140.00	
Cream, Footed	15.00	18.00	25.00
Cup & Saucer	10.00	15.00	22.00
Plate, 6"	5.00	7.00	36.00
Plate, 8" *(Illus.)*	9.00	15.00	17.00
Plate, Grill, 10¼"	28.00	25.00	

Cloverleaf Plate

	Green	Yellow	Black
Salt & Pepper, pr	40.00	125.00	100.00
Sherbet	9.00	14.00	25.00
Sugar, Footed	10.00	15.00	24.00
Tumbler, 8 oz.		55.00	
Tumbler, Flared, 9 oz.	55.00		
Tumbler, Footed, 10 oz	30.00	35.00	

61

DAISY, NO. 620

Daisy Catalog Page

Date: Various times from 1933 to 1940. Late production in 1960+

Manufacturer: Indiana Glass Co., Dunkirk, IN

Colors: Clear, Amber. Later in Dark Green and Milk Glass

	Crystal	Amber
Bowl, 4½"	$4.00	$9.00
Bowl, 6"	12.00	24.00
Bowl, Berry, 7¼"	8.00	16.00
Bowl, Berry, 9¼"	14.00	28.00
Bowl, Cream Soup, 4½"	8.00	12.00
Bowl, Oval, 10"	9.00	18.00
Cream	5.00	9.00
Cup & Saucer	5.00	10.00
Ice Tea, Footed, 12 oz.	20.00	45.00
Plate, 6"	2.50	4.50

	Crystal	Amber
Plate, 7¼"	3.00	7.00
Plate, 8¼"	4.00	8.00
Plate, 9¼"	5.00	10.00
Plate, Grill, 10¼"	5.00	11.00
Plate, Sandwich, 11½"	7.00	14.00
Platter, 10¾"	7.00	15.00
Relish, 3 part, 6¼"	10.00	20.00
Sherbet	4.00	9.00
Sugar	5.00	9.00
Tumbler, Footed, 9 oz.	12.00	24.00

DELLA ROBBIA, NO. 1058

Date: 1920s to late 1940s

Manufacturer: Westmoreland Glass Co., Grapeville, PA

Colors: Crystal. Milk glass. Fruits on crystal may have applied natural colors in both light and dark shades.

Prices are for crystal with applied colors. R. E. is Westmoreland's designation for what otherwise is called a rolled edge on bowls.

Della Robbia Table Setting, Original Ad

Basket, Handled, 12"	$300.00
Basket, Handled, 16"	400.00
Basket, Round, Handled, 8½"	200.00
Basket, Round, Handled, 9"	250.00
Bowl, Bell, 12"	120.00
Bowl, Bell, 15"	195.00
Bowl, Flange, Oval or Straight Edge, 14"	175.00
Bowl, R. E., 13"	120.00
Candelabra, 2 Light, pr.	125.00
Candlesticks, 4", pr.	55.00
Champagne, High Footed	25.00
Chocolate Box & Cover	75.00
Cocktail or Claret, 3¼ oz.	25.00
Comport or Mint Dish, 6½"	30.00
Comport, Footed, 12"	120.00
Comport, R. E., 11½"	120.00
Comport, R. E., 13"	120.00
Cream	18.00
Cream, Individual	20.00
Cup & Saucer	35.00
Finger Bowl	35.00
Ginger Ale, Tumbler, 5 oz.	28.00
Goblet, 8 oz.	35.00
Iced Tea, Bell or Straight, 12 oz.	38.00
Jug, 32 oz (sometimes listed as 36 oz.).	210.00
Nappy, 6"	38.00
Nappy, 7½"	42.00
Nappy, Bell, Handled, 8"	65.00

Nappy, Cupped, Handled, 6½"	35.00
Nappy, Heart, Handled, 8"	110.00
Nappy, Round, 4¼"	30.00
Nappy, Round, 9"	70.00
Nappy, R. E., 8"	50.00
Plate, 7½"	22.00
Plate, 9"	35.00
Plate, 10½"	90.00
Plate, 14"	90.00
Plate, 18"	180.00
Plate, Bread & Butter, 6"	12.00
Plate, Cupped Edge, 9"	35.00
Plate, Cupped Edge, 14"	90.00
Plate, Handled, 9"	40.00
Plate, R. E., 18"	180.00
Platter, Oval, 14"	150.00
Punch Bowl	210.00
Punch Cup	18.00
Salt & Pepper, pr.	60.00
Salver, Cake, 14"	130.00
Sherbet, High Footed	25.00
Sherbet, Low Footed	20.00
Sugar	18.00
Sweetmeat, High Footed, 8"	110.00
Tray, for Cream & Sugar, 5" x 7"	30.00
Tumbler, 8 oz.	25.00
Tumbler, Footed, 8 oz.	35.00

DOGWOOD

Dogwood Plate, Cup & Saucer

Dogwood Pitcher, Applied Design

Date: 1929 to 1932

Manufacturer: MacBeth-Evans Glass Co., Charleroi, PA

Colors: Pink, Green, Monax, Cremax, Yellow. Limited amount in Clear.

Water set made with an applied, not molded, design.

	Pink	Green
Bowl, 5½"	$30.00	$30.00
Bowl, 8½"	70.00	140.00
Bowl, Fruit, 10¼"	385.00	220.00
Cake Plate, Footed, 11"	700.00	
Cake Plate, Footed, 13"	125.00	100.00
Cream (2 varieties)	25.00	47.00
Cup & Saucer *(Illus.)*	24.00	35.00
Juice, 5 oz. (applied design)	330.00	
Pitcher, 80 oz. (applied design)		
(Illus.)	200.00	525.00
Pitcher, 80 oz.	625.00	
Plate, 6"	10.00	12.00
Plate, 8"	10.00	12.00
Plate, 9¼" *(Illus.)*	38.00	
Plate, Grill, 10½"	24.00	20.00
Plate, 12"	36.00	
Platter, 12"	600.00+	
Sherbet	40.00	100.00
Sugar, 2½" or 3¼"	20.00	46.00
Tumbler, 10 oz.	45.00	90.00
Tumbler, 10 oz. (applied design) . .	62.00	95.00
Tumbler, 12 oz. (applied design) . .	72.00	110.00

DORIC

Date: 1935 to 1938

Manufacturer: Jeannette Glass Co., Jeannette, PA

Colors: Pink, Green, Yellow. Limited production in Delphite.

	Pink	Green
Bowl, 4½"	$12.00	$12.00
Bowl, 8"	14.00	18.00
Bowl, Cereal, 5½"	60.00	72.00
Bowl, Cream Soup, 5"		395.00
Bowl, Handled, 9"	32.00	32.00
Bowl, Oval Vegetable, 9"	35.00	15.00
Butter & Cover	95.00	115.00
Cake Plate, Footed, 10"	35.00	38.00
Candy & Cover, 8"	48.00	55.00
Candy, 3 part	8.00	10.00
Coaster, 3"	24.00	24.00
Cream *(Illus.)*	20.00	22.00
Cup & Saucer	16.00	20.00
Iced Tea, Footed, 12 oz.	78.00	100.00
Pitcher, 36 oz.	55.00	60.00
Pitcher, Footed, 48 oz.	525.00+	1,000.00+
Plate, 6"	5.00	7.00
Plate, 7"	24.00	27.00
Plate, 9"	17.00	21.00
Plate, Grill, 9"	17.00	21.00
Platter, 12"	36.00	38.00

Doric Cream

	Pink	Green
Relish Tray, 4" x 4"	12.00	16.00
Relish Tray, 4" x 8"	20.00	25.00
Salt & Pepper, pr.	45.00	50.00
Sherbet	12.00	15.00
Sugar & Cover	30.00	40.00
Tray, 8" x 8"	24.00	30.00
Tray, Sandwich, Handled, 10"	24.00	28.00
Tumbler, 9 oz.	78.00	110.00
Tumbler, Footed, 10 oz.	67.00	90.00

DORIC AND PANSY

Date: 1937 to 1938

Manufacturer: Jeannette Glass Co., Jeannette, PA

Colors: Crystal, Pink, Teal

	Crystal	Pink	Teal
Bowl, Berry, 4½"	$7.00	$12.00	$24.00
Bowl, Berry, 8"	25.00	50.00	75.00
Bowl, Handled, 9"	18.00	32.00	48.00
Butter & Cover			460.00+
Cup & Saucer	10.00		25.00
Cream	60.00		120.00
Plate, 6"	7.00	12.00	16.00
Plate, 7"			50.00
Plate, 9"	9.00		38.00
Salt & Pepper, pr			400.00+
Sugar	60.00		110.00
Tray, Handled, 10"			40.00
Tumbler, 9 oz. *(Illus.)*			74.00

Doric & Pansy Tumbler

CHILDREN'S DISHES

	Crystal	Pink	Teal
Cream	$	$36.00	$47.00
Cup & Saucer		45.00	65.00
Plate		9.00	11.00
Sugar		36.00	47.00

EARLY AMERICAN SANDWICH

Early American Sandwich Tumbler, Plate, Cup & Saucer

Date: 1924 to 1955

Manufacturer: Duncan & Miller Glass Co., Washington, PA

Colors: Crystal, Green, Amber, Rose. Chartreuse in 1949. Ruby in 1932. Some Cobalt.

Reproductions: Fairly extensive line produced by U. S. Glass/Tiffin in Milk Glass and Crystal after 1955 at their Glassport, PA, factory. Several items were made by Colony in Dunkirk, Indiana, in deep amber, red-yellow, green and blue. These items do not have ground and polished bottoms.

Very extensive tableware service. In addition to individual pieces listed, the company also offered many sets such as mayonnaise sets, salad sets, smoking sets and others utilizing several pieces. Compare this pattern with Sandwich patterns made by Indiana Glass and Hocking Glass, both in this chapter and Westmoreland's Princess Feather in Stylized Patterns chapter. These patterns are much less detailed and lack the fine finishing of Duncan & Miller's pattern. Prices are for pieces in crystal, for amber, chartreuse or green pieces add 40%, for ruby or cobalt pieces add 150%.

Ashtray, Individual, Square, 2¾"	$10.00
Ashtray, Rectangular, 3½"	35.00
Ashtray, Rectangular, 5"	55.00
Basket, Crimped, Handled, 10"	250.00
Basket, Handled Candy, 5½"	95.00
Basket, Handled Candy, 6½"	95.00
Basket, Oval Fruit, Footed, 12"	250.00
Basket, Oval, Handled, 10"	250.00
Basket, Tall Handled, 11"	125.00
Bonbon & Cover, Footed, 5" wide	55.00
Bonbon, Heart Shaped, Handled, 5½"	35.00
Bonbon, Heart Shaped, Handled, 6"	40.00
Bowl, Flower, Crimped, 11½"	45.00
Bowl, Fruit, 3 Compartment, 10"	150.00
Bowl, Fruit, Crimped, Footed, 11"	225.00
Bowl, Fruit, Flared, 12"	55.00
Bowl, Fruit, Footed, Flared, 11"	225.00
Bowl, Gardenia, 11½"	85.00
Bowl, Lily, 10"	95.00
Bowl, Nut, Cupped, 11"	95.00
Bowl, Oblong, 12"	250.00
Bowl, Salad, 10"	75.00
Bowl, Salad, Shallow, 12"	125.00
Bowl, Salad, Shallow, 15"	75.00
Bowl, Square Flower, 7"	65.00
Butter & Cover, ¼ lb.	85.00
Butter or Cheese & Cover, 1 lb. (round)	125.00
Camellia Flower Pan, 10½" x 6¼"	50.00

Candelabra, 1 Light, 4", pr.	125.00
Candelabra, 1 Light, 10", pr.	195.00
Candelabra, 2 Light, 5", pr.	175.00
Candelabra, 2 Light, 7", pr.	195.00
Candelabra, 2 Light, 10", pr.	225.00
Candelabra, 3 Light, 7", pr.	250.00
Candelabra, 3 Light, 10", pr.	600.00
Candelabra, 3 Light, 16", pr.	800.00+
Candelabra, Hurricane Lamp, 15", pr.	425.00+
Candlesticks, 1 Light, 4", pr.	55.00
Candlesticks, 2 Light, 5", pr.	95.00
Candlesticks, 2 Light, 6", pr.	110.00
Candlesticks, 3 Light, 7", pr.	125.00
Candy Box and Cover, 3 Compartment, Square, 7"	395.00
Candy Box and Cover, 7"	375.00
Candy Box and Cover, Round, 5"	45.00
Candy Jar and Cover, 8½"	65.00
Celery and Relish, 3 Compartment, 10½"	45.00
Celery, 10"	40.00
Cheese and Cracker Set, 2 pcs., 13"	75.00
Cigarette Box and Cover, 3½" x 2¾"	45.00
Cigarette Box and Cover, Rectangular, 5"	135.00
Cigarette Box and Cover, Square, 3½"	45.00
Coaster, 5"	9.00
Cocktail, 3 oz.	16.00
Comport, Low, Candy, Flared, 7"	40.00
Comport, Low, Crimped, 5½" w	30.00

(continued) EARLY AMERICAN SANDWICH

Comport, Low Foot, 6" w 35.00
Comport, Low Foot, 7" 40.00
Comport, Low Foot, Flared, 6" w 35.00
Comport, Tall, 6" w 35.00
Condiment Set: Vinegar, Oil, Salt, Pepper,
   8" Tray, 5 pcs. 115.00
Cream, Footed, 5 oz. 12.00
Cream, Footed, 9 oz. 18.00
Cup & Saucer *(Illus.)* 16.00
Epergne Garden, 9" 125.00
Epergne Garden, 13" h 275.00
Epergne, Fruit and Flower, Footed, 12" 275.00
Epergne, Fruit and Flower, Footed, 14" 275.00
Finger Bowl, 4" 15.00
Fruit Cup or Jello, 6 oz. 15.00
Fruit or Nut, 3½" 14.00
Fruit Salad, 6" w 30.00
Goblet, 9 oz. 18.00
Grapefruit or Cereal, 6" 22.00
Grapefruit with Fruit Cup Liner, 5½" 150.00
Grapefruit with Rim Liner
   or Large Frozen Fruit Server, 5½" 150.00
Grapefruit, Footed, 5½" 65.00
Ice Cream 5 oz. (sherbet) 12.00
Iced Tea, Footed, 12 oz. 17.00
Iced Tea, Straight, 13 oz. 20.00
Ivy Bowl, Footed, 5" 75.00
Jelly, Individual, 3" 10.00
Juice, Orange, Footed, 5 oz. 12.00
Juice, Straight, 5 oz. 15.00
Mayonnaise, Footed, 5" 20.00
Mayonnaise, Footed, 6" 20.00
Nappy, 2 Compartment (round), 5" 20.00
Nappy, 2 Compartment (round), 6" 20.00
Nappy, Dessert, 6" 15.00
Nappy, Fruit, 3½" 15.00
Nappy, Fruit, 5" 15.00
Nappy, Handled, Regular, 5" 25.00
Nappy, Handled, Regular, 5½" 25.00
Nappy, Handled, Regular, 6" 35.00
Oil, 3 oz. 28.00
Old Fashioned, Straight, 7 oz. 22.00
Parfait, 4 oz. 35.00
Pickle Tray, 7" 18.00
Pitcher, Ice Lip, ½ gal. 135.00
Pitcher, Water, 64 oz. 135.00
Plate, 15" 115.00
Plate, 2 Handled, 11½" 45.00
Plate, Bread and Butter, 6" 8.00
Plate, Dessert, 7" 10.00
Plate, Deviled Egg, 12" 75.00
Plate, Finger Bowl, 6½" 15.00
Plate, Hostess or Torte, 16" 125.00

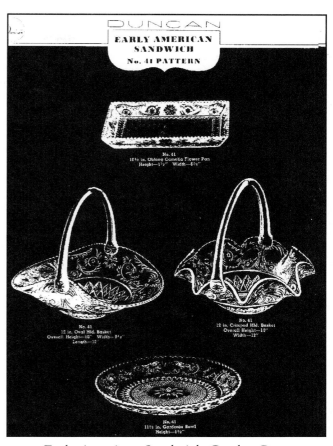

Early American Sandwich Catalog Page

Plate, Salad, 8" 12.00
Plate, Service or Dinner, 9½" *(Illus.)* 65.00
Plate, Torte, 12" 65.00
Plate, Torte, Flat Edge, 13" 65.00
Plate, Torte, Rolled Edge, 13" 65.00
Plate, with Ring, 7" 15.00
Plate, with Ring, 8" 18.00
Relish, 2 Compartment, 1 Handle, 5½" 25.00
Relish, 2 Compartment, Handled, 5" 25.00
Relish, 2 Compartment, Handled, 6" 25.00
Relish, 2 Compartment, 7" 25.00
Relish, 3 Compartment (oblong), 10" 40.00
Relish, 3 Compartment, 12" 45.00
Relish, 4 Compartment, 2 Handled, 10" 45.00
Relish, Square, 5" 35.00
Salad Dressing Bowl, 2 Compartment, 4" 40.00
Salad Dressing Bowl, Twin, 6" 40.00
Salt & Pepper, Large, 3¾", pr. 36.00
Salt & Pepper, Small, 2½", pr. 45.00
Salt or Nut, Individual, 2½" (almond) 15.00
Salver, Cake, Flat Edge, Footed, 13" 95.00

EARLY AMERICAN SANDWICH *(continued)*

Salver, Cake, Footed, 11½"	125.00
Salver, Cake, Rolled Edge, Footed, 12"	95.00
Saucer Champagne, 5 oz.	20.00
Sea Food Cocktail, 5 oz.	15.00
Sherbet (Champagne), 5 oz.	20.00
Shrimp or Crabmeat Service, 2 pcs., 6"	65.00
Sugar or Grated Cheese Shaker, 13 oz.	75.00
Sugar, Footed, 5 oz.	12.00
Sugar, Footed, 9 oz.	20.00
Sundae, Flared, 5 oz.	15.00
Syrup Pitcher, 13 oz.	85.00
Tray, Ice Cream, 12"	65.00
Tray, Mint, Handled, 6"	35.00
Tray, Mint, Handled, 7"	35.00

Tray, Oval, 8"	22.00
Tumbler, Footed, 9 oz.	14.00
Tumbler, Table, Straight, 9 oz. *(Illus.)*	20.00
Urn and Cover, 12"	165.00
Vase, Crimped, 4½"	55.00
Vase, Crimped, Footed, 3"	48.00
Vase, Crimped, Footed, 5"	55.00
Vase, Fan Shape, Footed, 3"	48.00
Vase, Fan Shape, Footed, 5"	55.00
Vase, Flared, Footed, 3"	48.00
Vase, Flared, Footed, 5"	55.00
Vase, Footed, 10"	95.00
Wine, 3 oz.	15.00

EVERGLADE

Everglade Designs: a–Berry & Leaf; b–Buffalo Hunt; c–Daffodil;
d–Flower & Leaf; e–Paneled Floral; f–Swan; g–Tulip

Date: Ca. 1933

Manufacturer: Cambridge Glass Co., Cambridge, OH

Colors: Crystal, Violet, Willow Blue, Milk, Forest Green, Royal Blue, Carmen, Amber. Crown Tuscan

Reproductions: The Fenton Art Glass Co. has made some of the vases in Fenton colors and finishes.

Pieces were made in satin finish and with buffed highlights. Also called Leaf Line or Arcadia. We have attempted to describe the motif of each piece since the designs vary widely from item to item. All items were not made in all colors. Prices are for pieces in Crystal. For pieces in colors, add 50% to 200%. As with the wide variety in design, the various colors vary widely in value.

Beer Mug, 12 oz. (No. 43) Leaf	$30.00
Bowl, 10" (No. 1) Leaf	35.00
Bowl, 10" (No. 61) Leaf	40.00
Bowl, 10" (Nos. 48, 49) Paneled Floral	35.00
Bowl, 10½" (No. 11) Crimped Edge, Tulip	50.00
Bowl, 11" or 12" (Nos. 7, 8) Paneled Floral	35.00
Bowl, 12" (No. 12) Tulip	50.00
Bowl, 13" (No. 13) Rolled Edge, Tulip	50.00
Bowl, 13" (No. 17) Rolled Edge, Swan	55.00
Bowl, 14" (No. 14) Shallow, Tulip	50.00

Bowl, 7½" (No. 27) Leaf	15.00
Bowl, Belled, 3 Footed, 11", 12" (Nos. 7, 8) Paneled Floral	35.00
Bowl, Crimped, 3 Footed, 11" or 12" (Nos. 15, 16) Swan	55.00
Bowl, Cupped, 16" (No. 28) Buffalo Hunt	70.00
Bowl, Cupped, Shallow, 14" (No. 18) Swan	55.00
Bowl, Oval, 12" (No. 36) Tulip	35.00
Bowl, Oval, Footed, 12", (No. 19) Leaf	40.00
Candlesticks, 1 Light (Nos. 32 or 33) pr., Leaf	50.00

(continued) EVERGLADE

Candlesticks, 1 Light, 3½", (No. 62) pr., Leaf 70.00
Candlesticks, 1 Light, 3½", (No. 10) pr., Leaf 50.00
Candlesticks, 1 Light, 5", (No. 2) pr., Leaf 50.00
Candlesticks, 2 Light, 6", (No. 3) pr., Leaf 90.00
Cheese & Cracker, 2 pcs., 16" (No. 60) Tulip 65.00
Comport, 6", 2 Styles (Nos. 40, 42) 22.00
Comport, 7" (No. 41) 22.00
Cream (No. 26) Leaf 18.00
Epergne, 2 pcs. (No. 51) Paneled Floral 70.00
Epergne, 2 pcs. (No. 53) Paneled Floral 70.00
Epergne, Oval, Footed, 2 pcs., 13" (No. 37) 70.00
Epergne, Oval, Footed, 2 pcs., 14½" (No. 55) 85.00
Flower Holder, 2 pcs. (No. 45) 55.00
Flower Holder, 3 pcs. (No. 58) 100.00
Goblet, Low, Footed, 10 oz. 20.00
Plate, 16" (No. 30) Swan 50.00
Plate, 16" (No. 31) Tulip 45.00
Plate, Oval, Footed, 14½" (No. 39) Leaf 30.00
Plate, Salad, 8" or 8½" (No. 25) Leaf 12.00
Plate, Sandwich, Footed, 13" (No. 56)
　　Paneled Floral 25.00
Plate, Sandwich, Footed, 15" (No. 57)
　　Paneled Floral 28.00
Sherbet (No. 24) Leaf 15.00
Sugar (No. 26) Leaf 18.00
Tumbler, Footed, 12 oz. (No. 34) 20.00
Vase, 5" (No. 23) Berry & Leaf 20.00
Vase, 6" (No. 22) Flower & Leaf 25.00
Vase, 6" (No. 29) Floral 22.00
Vase, 7½" (No. 21) Daffodil 30.00
Vase, 10½" (No. 20) Tulip 35.00
Vase, Footed, 11½" (No. 38) 35.00

Everglade Original Ad Using
the Company Name of Arcadia, 1943

FLORAGOLD

Date: Ca. 1950

Manufacturer: Jeannette Glass Co., Jeannette, PA

Colors: Crystal iridized. Limited production in clear, shell pink, and pale blue.

Salt and pepper originally had plastic lids. Prices are for iridized crystal.

Floragold Covered Butter, Covered Sugar
& Cream, Salt & Pepper

FLORAGOLD *(continued)*

Floragold Water Set: Tumblers & Pitcher

Bowl, Square, 4½"	$8.00
Bowl, 5½"	32.00
Bowl, Crimped Edge, 5½"	10.00

Bowl, Crimped Edge, 8½"	10.00
Bowl, Crimped Edge, 12"	14.00
Bowl, Salad, 9½"	52.00
Butter & Cover, Oblong	32.00
Butter & Cover, Round *(Illus. previous page)*	55.00
Candlesticks, 2 Light, pr.	75.00
Candy Dish & Cover	55.00
Candy Dish, 4 Footed, 5¼"	10.00
Coaster, 4"	8.00
Cream *(Illus. previous page)*	12.00
Cup & Saucer (5¾" plate)	18.00
Iced Tea, Footed, 15 oz.	135.00
Jelly, Handled, 5"	11.00
Pitcher, 64 oz. *(Illus.)*	42.00
Plate, 5¾"	12.00
Plate, 8½"	50.00
Platter, 11¼"	28.00
Salt & Pepper, pr. *(Illus. previous page)*	60.00
Sherbet	15.00
Sugar & Cover *(Illus. previous page)*	28.00
Tray, 13½"	30.00
Tray with Indent, 13½"	60.00
Tumbler, Footed, 10 or 11 oz. *(Illus.)*	30.00
Vase	400.00+

FLORAL

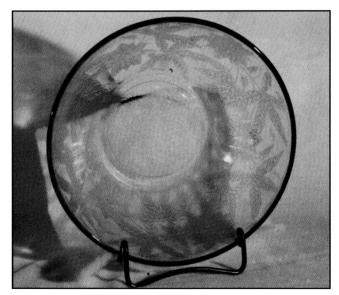

Floral 8" Bowl

Date: 1931 to 1935

Manufacturer: Jeannette Glass Co., Jeannette, PA

Colors: Pink, Green. Limited production in Delphite, Jadite, Crystal, Amber, Red, Yellow.

This pattern includes some unusual pieces not usually found in other DG patterns such as a refrigerator dish with a floral patterned cover and a dresser set.

	Pink	Green
Bar Glass, Footed, 3 oz.	$	$165.00
Bowl, 7½"	30.00	36.00
Bowl, 8" *(Illus.)*	27.00	34.00
Bowl, Berry, 4"	28.00	28.00
Bowl, Berry, Crimped Edge, 4"	85.00	
Bowl, Cream Soup, 5½"		500.00+
Bowl, Crimped Edge, 7½"	170.00	
Bowl, Oval, 9"	28.00	32.00
Bowl & Cover, Vegetable, 8"	50.00	60.00
Butter & Cover	95.00	115.00
Candlesticks, 4", pr.	75.00	85.00

(continued) FLORAL

	Pink	Green
Candy Jar & Cover	50.00	50.00
Cream	15.00	15.00
Coaster, 3¼".	18.00	16.00
Comport, 9".	525.00+	575.00+
Cup & Saucer.	23.00	23.00
Dresser Set, 7 pcs.		1,100.00+
Ice Tub, Oval, 3½" tall	800.00+	800.00+
Juice, Footed, 5 oz.	22.00	30.00
Lamp	215.00	215.00
Lemonade, Footed, 9 oz.	55.00	60.00
Pitcher, 24 oz.		450.00+
Pitcher, 48 oz.	250.00	300.00
Pitcher, Footed, Cone Shape,		
32 oz.	45.00	50.00
Plate, 6"	6.00	8.00
Plate, 8"	12.00	15.00
Plate, 9"	24.00	30.00
Plate, Grill, 9".		175.00
Platter, 10¾"	22.00	30.00
Platter with Inner Rim, 10¾"	78.00	
Refrigerator Dish & Cover,		
Square, 5"		75.00
Relish, Oval, 2 Compartment	28.00	32.00
Rose Bowl, 3 Footed.	26.00	35.00

Floral Covered Sugar

	Pink	Green
Salt & Pepper, Footed, 4", pr.	450.00+	450.00+
Salt & Pepper, 6", pr	55.00	
Sherbet.	55.00	65.00
Sugar & Cover (Illus.)	22.00	22.00
Tray, Square, Handled, 6"	38.00	38.00
Tumbler, 9 oz.		210.00
Tumbler, Footed, 7 oz.	27.00	32.00
Vase, Octagon, 7"	400.00+	400.00+
Vase with Frog, 3 Footed.	850.00+	850.00+

FLORAL & DIAMOND BAND

Date: 1920s

Manufacturer: U. S. Glass Co.

Colors: Black, Crystal, Green, Pink. Limited in Crystal Iridescent.

An attractive pattern, but many pieces are poorly finished with prominent mold seams and roughness. However, some pieces are finished with ground bottoms. Black is difficult to find. For Black items, add at least 50% to Green prices.

Floral & Diamond Band Sherbet

	Crystal	Green	Pink
Bowl, 4½".	$ 5.00	$10.00	$8.00
Bowl, 8"	10.00	20.00	22.00
Bowl, Handled, 5¾"	4.00	12.00	12.00
Butter & Cover	70.00	150.00	150.00
Compote, 5½"	10.00	18.00	18.00
Cream	9.00	20.00	25.00
Cream, Small.	8.00	18.00	22.00

	Crystal	Green	Pink
Iced Tea.	22.00	45.00	38.00
Pitcher, 42 oz.	75.00	150.00	100.00
Plate, 8"	15.00	42.00	42.00
Sherbet (Illus.)	5.00	10.00	10.00
Sugar & Cover.	50.00	100.00	90.00
Sugar, Small.	9.00	18.00	22.00
Tumbler	14.00	25.00	22.00

FLORENTINE 1

Florentine 1 Cream

Date: 1932 to 1935

Manufacturer: Hazel-Atlas Glass Co.

Colors: Crystal, Deep Blue, Green, Pink, Yellow

This is very similar to Florentine 2. This pattern occurs on blanks with notched edges on the feet, while Florentine 2 is plain. Crystal pieces are valued at 75% of green.

	Green	Yellow	Pink
Ashtray, 5½"	$25.00	$32.00	$32.00
Bowl, 5"	15.00	20.00	15.00
Bowl, 6"	24.00	24.00	24.00
Bowl, 8½"	24.00	32.00	34.00
Bowl & Cover, Oval Vegetable, 9½"	55.00	62.00	55.00
Butter & Cover	150.00	165.00	185.00
Coaster, 3¾"	18.00	20.00	30.00
Cream *(Illus.)*.	15.00	20.00	20.00
Cream, Crimped Top	60.00		65.00
Cup & Saucer	10.00	15.00	15.00
Iced Tea, Footed, 9 oz.			95.00
Iced Tea, Footed, 12 oz.	28.00	25.00	28.00
Juice, Footed, 5 oz..	22.00	27.00	25.00

	Green	Yellow	Pink
Pitcher, Footed, 36 oz.	50.00	65.00	58.00
Pitcher, with or without Ice Lip, 48 oz.	80.00	220.00	150.00
Plate, 6"	6.00	8.00	8.00
Plate, 8½"	8.00	7.00	12.00
Plate, 10"	21.00	27.00	25.00
Plate, Grill, 10"	14.00	17.00	17.00
Platter, 11½"	20.00	25.00	30.00
Salt & Pepper, pr	45.00	58.00	60.00
Sherbet, 3 oz..	10.00	12.00	15.00
Sugar & Cover.	36.00	42.00	40.00
Sugar, Crimped Top	47.00		50.00
Tumbler, Footed, 10 oz.	20.00	25.00	25.00

FLORENTINE 2

Florentine 2 Sherbet & Pitcher

Date: 1934 to 1937

Manufacturer: Hazel-Atlas Glass Co.

Colors: Crystal, Green, Yellow. Limited availability in Pink, Medium Blue and Deep Blue.

Reproductions: These have recently been done of the pitcher and tumblers with poor pattern detail in dark pink unlike the original color and in dark green and dark blue (cobalt).

Prices for crystal are 50% of green. The design of this pattern is very similar to Florentine 1, but it is on different blanks. Florentine 2 is found on blanks with smooth edges.

	Green	Yellow	Pink
Bowl, 4½"	$15.00	$18.00	$22.00
Bowl, 5½"	15.00	18.00	20.00
Bowl, 6"	42.00	38.00	
Bowl, 7½"		225.00	
Bowl, 8"	26.00	30.00	35.00
Bowl, Cream Soup, 4¾"	20.00	25.00	20.00
Bowl, Crimped, 5"	58.00		25.00
Bowl, Oval Vegetable & Cover, 9"	40.00	67.00	
Butter & Cover	125.00	145.00	
Candlesticks, 2¾", pr.	65.00	85.00	
Candy Dish & Cover	110.00	165.00	140.00
Coaster or Ashtray, 3¾"	20.00	27.00	
Coaster or Ashtray, 5½"	45.00	45.00	
Coaster, 3¼"	18.00	20.00	24.00
Comport, 3½"	28.00		20.00
Cream	10.00	15.00	10.00
Cup & Saucer	12.00	12.00	
Gravy Boat		65.00	
Iced Tea, 12 oz.	42.00	48.00	35.00
Iced Tea, Blown, 12 oz.	85.00		
Jello Dish, Individual	11.00	10.00	
Juice, 5 oz.	17.00	27.00	18.00
Juice, Blown, 6 oz.	25.00		

	Green	Yellow	Pink
Juice, Footed, 5 oz.	18.00	15.00	
Pitcher, 48 oz.	75.00	145.00	120.00
Pitcher, 72 oz.	110.00	400.00+	240.00
Pitcher, Footed, Cone Shape, 24 oz. *(Illus.)*		145.00	
Pitcher, Footed, Cone Shape, 28 oz.	38.00	34.00	
Plate with Indent, 6¼"	20.00	26.00	
Plate, 6"	5.00	7.00	5.00
Plate, 8½"	8.00	11.00	14.00
Plate, 10"	22.00	15.00	25.00
Plate, for under Gravy, 11½"		50.00	
Plate, Grill, 10¼"	14.00	14.00	
Platter, 11"	24.00	22.00	
Relish, 10"	22.00	20.00	25.00
Relish, 3 Compartment, 10"	22.00	20.00	25.00
Salt & Pepper, pr.	48.00	48.00	
Sherbet *(Illus.)*	10.00	12.00	
Sugar & Cover	32.00	38.00	25.00
Tray, for Salt & Pepper		85.00	
Tumbler, 9 oz.	18.00	24.00	16.00
Tumbler, Footed, 9 oz.	28.00	32.00	
Vase, 6"	37.00	60.00	

FLOWER AND LEAF BAND

Date: 1930s and later in 1950s

Manufacturer: Indiana Glass Co., Dunkirk, IN

Colors: Custard (Ivory) in the 1930s. White in the 1950s.

	White	Custard
Bowl, 5½"	$5.00	$9.00
Bowl, 6½"	14.00	22.00
Bowl, Soup, 7½"	22.00	32.00
Bowl, 9"	22.00	32.00
Bowl, Oval Vegetable, 9½"	20.00	30.00
Butter & Cover	45.00	65.00
Cup & Saucer	35.00	48.00
Cream	12.00	18.00
Plate, 5¾"	4.00	8.00
Plate, 7½"	10.00	18.00
Plate, 9"	10.00	18.00
Plate, 9¾"	18.00	28.00
Platter, 11½"	22.00	35.00
Sherbet *(Illus.)*	60.00	85.00
Sugar & Cover	20.00	32.00

Flower and Leaf Band Sherbet

FRUITS

Fruits Plate

Date: 1931 to 1933

Manufacturer: Hazel-Atlas Glass Co.

Colors: Green, Pink. Limited availability in Crystal and Crystal Iridized.

Tumblers may be found with one or a variety of fruits in the design. Crystal or Crystal Iridized is valued at 50% to 75% of Green.

	Green	Pink
Bowl, 5"	$27.00	$24.00
Bowl, 8"	65.00	40.00
Cup & Saucer	16.00	14.00
Juice, 3½"	28.00	22.00
Pitcher, 7"	95.00	
Plate, 8" *(Illus.)*	8.00	8.00
Sherbet	10.00	8.00
Tumbler, 12 oz	135.00	100.00
Tumbler, 1 Fruit, 4"	20.00	17.00
Tumbler, Variety of Fruits, 4"	27.00	22.00

IRIS

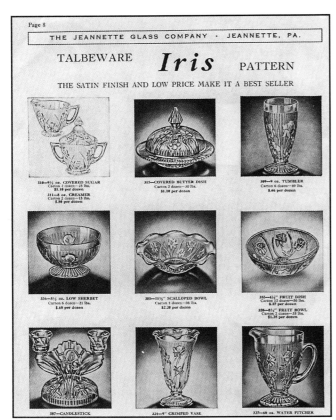

Iris Catalog Page

Date: 1928 to 1932. Later in 1950s and 1970s

Manufacturer: Jeannette Glass Co., Jeannette, PA

Colors: Old: Crystal, Golden Iridescent, limited amount in Pink. Newer: White and two colored combinations.

Also called Iris & Herringbone.

	Crystal	Golden Iridescent
Bowl, 7½"	$200.00	$75.00
Bowl, 11"	65.00	
Bowl, Beaded Rim, 8"	135.00	35.00
Bowl, Crimped Rim, 5"	15.00	28.00
Bowl, Ruffled Rim, 9½"	18.00	18.00
Bowl, Ruffled Rim, 11½"	22.00	20.00
Butter & Cover	65.00	65.00
Candlesticks, 2 Light, pr.	37.50	45.00
Candy Jar & Cover	225.00	
Coaster	100.00	
Cocktail, Footed, 3 oz.	25.00	
Cream	22.00	28.00
Cup & Saucer	32.00	32.00
Cup & Saucer, Demitasse	200.00+	325.00+
Dish, Fruit, Beaded Rim, 4½"	55.00	15.00
Goblet, Footed, 8 oz.	35.00	
Iced Tea, Footed, 6½"	45.00	

	Crystal	Golden Iridescent		Crystal	Golden Iridescent
Lamp Shade (several colors)	120.00		Sherbet, 4"	27.00	
Nut Set	90.00		Sherbet, Low, 5½ oz	35.00	18.00
Pitcher, Footed, 9½"	50.00	60.00	Sugar & Cover	40.00	45.00
Plate, 5½"	16.00	15.00	Tumbler, 4"	135.00	
Plate, 8"	105.00		Tumbler, Footed, 6"	28.00	22.00
Plate, Dinner, 9"	70.00	55.00	Vase, Crimped Top, 9"	35.00	40.00
Plate, Sandwich, 11¾"	48.00	42.00	Wine, Footed, 3 oz	14.00	40.00

LAUREL

Date: 1935 to 1940+

Manufacturer: McKee Glass Co.

Colors: French Ivory, Jade Green, White Opal, and Poudre Blue—all opaque colors.

Poudre Blue is scarce but very desirable.

	White Opal Jade Green	French Ivory	Poudre Blue
Bowl, 11"	$35.00	$40.00	$70.00
Bowl, Soup, 7⅞"	35.00	35.00	
Bowl, Utility, Round, 10½"	30.00	35.00	70.00
Candlesticks, 1 Light, 4", pr.	40.00	35.00	
Cheese & Cover	55.00	60.00	
Cream, Footed, No. 1, (tall)	12.00	12.00	32.00
Cream, No. 2, (short)	12.00	12.00	
Cup & Saucer *(Illus.)*	12.00	11.00	30.00
Dish, Cereal, 6"	9.00	11.00	22.00
Dish, Fruit, 4¾"	8.00	9.00	15.00
Dish, Oval Vegetable, 9¾"	22.00	22.00	48.00
Dish, Round Vegetable, 9"	20.00	22.00	48.00
Iced Tea, 12 oz.		45.00	
Jelly, 3 Toed, 6"	15.00	18.00	
Plate, 6"	6.00	6.00	12.00
Plate, 7½"	11.00	10.00	15.00
Plate, 9" *(Illus.)*	16.00	14.00	22.00
Plate, Grill, 9"	14.00	14.00	
Platter, Oval, 10¾"	24.00	28.00	40.00
Salt & Pepper, pr	65.00	50.00	
Sherbet, Footed *(Illus.)*	10.00	12.00	
Sugar, No. 1 (tall)	10.00	10.00	32.00
Sugar, No. 2 (short)	10.00	10.00	
Tumbler, 9 oz.	45.00	32.00	

Laurel Plate, Sherbet, Cup & Saucer

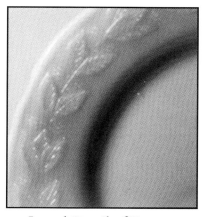

Laurel Detail of Pattern

LAUREL (continued)

CHILDREN'S TEA SET

These sets also come with enamel colored rims and Scotty Dog decorations which are quite difficult to find. Jade Green or pieces with enameled rims are valued about 150% of French Ivory. Scotty Dog on French Ivory pieces are valued about 65% of Jade Green.

	French Ivory	Scotty Dog, Jade Green
Cream	$25.00	$120.00
Cup & Saucer	30.00	130.00
Plate	12.00	60.00
Sugar	25.00	120.00

LAUREL LEAF

Laurel Leaf Cups & Saucers, Cream & Sugar

Date: 1952 to 1963

Manufacturer: Anchor Hocking Glass Corporation, Lancaster, OH

Colors: Decorated "Gray Laurel" and Decorated "Peach Lustre"

We have given the name Laurel Leaf to this pattern since it comes in both decorations, and referring to it by the name of the decoration is misleading. Gray Laurel is much more scarce, having been in production for a very short time. Names and numbers of pieces are taken from company literature.

	Gray Laurel	Peach Lustre		Gray Laurel	Peach Lustre
Bowl, Vegetable, 8¼" (No. 4378)	$11.00	$9.00	Plate, Dinner, 9⅛" (No. 4341)	9.00	6.00
Cream (No. 4354) *(Illus.)*	6.00	5.00	Plate, Salad, 7¾" (No. 4338)	5.00	4.00
Cup & Saucer (No. 4379) *(Illus.)*	7.00	5.50	Soup Plate, 7⅝" (No. 4367)	6.00	7.00
Dessert, 4⅞" (No. 4374)	5.00	4.00	Sugar (No. 4353) *(Illus.)*	6.00	5.00

MARTELÉ—FIVE FRUITS

Martelé Five Fruits Catalog Illustration

Date: 1926

Manufacturer: Consolidated Lamp & Glass Co., Coraopolis, PA

Colors: Crystal

Martelé was a term used by Consolidated for many of their handmade lines of glassware—not for just one specific pattern. Five Fruits was made in a tableware line, and also tableware was made in a flower motif. Often crystal pieces are found with various colored washes which allow part of the crystal to show through, but also highlight the depressed areas with a faint coat of color. For detailed information about Consolidated's patterns, we recommend the book Phoenix & Consolidated Art Glass 1926 to 1980 *by Jack D. Wilson.*

(continued) MARTELÉ—FIVE FRUITS

	Crystal Various Color Washes
Berry Dish	$40.00
Box & Cover, 1 lb.	125.00
Cocktail	20.00
Goblet, 9 oz.	30.00
Jug, Footed, ½ gal.	275.00
Plate, 12"	120.00
Plate, 14"	125.00

	Crystal Various Color Washes
Plate, Bread & Butter	25.00
Plate, Salad, 8"	40.00
Sundae (No. 2579)	20.00
Sundae (No. 508)	35.00
Tray (For No. 2579 Sundae)	20.00
Tray, Plate for Berry	25.00
Tumbler, Footed	35.00

MARTELÉ—NO. 700 VINE

Date: 1929

Manufacturer: Consolidated Lamp & Glass Co., Coraopolis, PA

Colors: Jade, Powder Blue, Honey, Crystal, Fiery Milk, Gray, Reuben Blue, Red

This line is most often found in French crystal which is crystal glass with satin (acid etched) highlights. For colors add 25%. For Reuben Blue add 50 to 75%. For Red add 100% or more.

	French Crystal
Ashtray (No. 720)	$175.00
Bowl, Flared, 10½" (No. 704)	220.00
Bowl, Flared, 13" (No. 706)	225.00
Bowl, Flared, 15" (No. 707)	225.00
Bowl, Flared, 7" *(Illus.)*	75.00
Bowl, Fruit, 10" (No. 705)	175.00
Bowl, Salad, 8" (No. 703)	95.00
Candlesticks, 1 Light, pr. (No. 708)	160.00
Cigarette Box & Cover (No. 719)	275.00
Comport, 5½" (No. 716)	85.00
Comport, Flared, 5½" (No. 715)	85.00
Finger Bowl (No. 713)	40.00
Goblet, 10 oz. (No. 712) *(Illus.)*	125.00
Plate, 8"	75.00
Plate, Bread & Butter, 6"	80.00
Plate, Service, 10" *(Illus.)*	155.00
Sundae (No. 714)	35.00
Vase, 8" (No. 700)	210.00
Vase, 10" (No. 701)	450.00
Vase, Fan, 6½" (No. 702)	135.00

Martelé Vine Bowl & Goblet

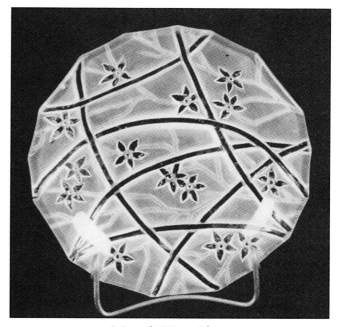

Martelé Vine Plate

MAYFAIR (FEDERAL)

Mayfair (Federal) Plate & Cup

Date: 1934

Manufacturer: Federal Glass Co., Columbus, OH

Colors: Amber, Crystal, Green

Compare this to Federal's Rosemary pattern, which lacks the Diamond motif. The pattern is somewhat hard to find. The footed, handleless sugar is often mistaken for a sherbet.

	Crystal	Amber	Green
Bowl, 5"	$8.00	$12.00	$15.00
Bowl, 6"	11.00	18.00	21.00
Bowl, Cream Soup	12.00	20.00	20.00
Bowl, Oval Vegetable, 10" . . .	18.00	30.00	32.00
Cream	12.00	15.00	18.00
Cup & Saucer *(Illus. of cup)* . .	7.00	10.00	10.00
Plate, 6¾"	6.00	9.00	10.00
Plate, 9½" *(Illus.)*	10.00	17.00	17.00
Plate, Grill, 9½"	10.00	17.00	17.00
Platter, 12"	18.00	28.00	30.00
Sugar	12.00	15.00	18.00
Tumbler, 9 oz.	12.00	30.00	32.00

MAYFAIR (HOCKING)

Mayfair (Hocking) Pitcher & Tumblers

Date: 1931 to 1937

Manufacturer: Hocking Glass Co., Lancaster, OH

Colors: Pink, Medium Blue. Limited in Crystal, Green and Yellow.

Reproductions: Consist of the cookie jars in pink, green, amethyst, red and cobalt blue. Old jars have a distinct circle in the middle of the base. Old juice pitchers have a distinct circle in the middle of the bottom also. There are some pattern differences in the salt and peppers in that ridges on the new shakers are heavy and go from top to bottom. Also the new shakers are slightly smaller than the old in all dimensions. The bar or shot glasses were originally never made in any color but pink, so all other colors are reproductions. The pink color is either lighter or more orange than the original. Be aware of the colors originally made in all pieces, and be suspicious of any unusual or odd shades of color.

Sugar covers are so scarce that they alone sell for $1,500.00 or more when found. Footed salts were made in pink, but are so rare that no price can be set.

(continued) MAYFAIR (HOCKING)

	Pink	Blue
Bar Glass, 1½ oz.	$90.00	$
Bowl & Cover, 10"	150.00	175.00
Bowl, Vegetable, 7"	30.00	65.00
Bowl, Vegetable, 10"	35.00	50.00
Bowl, Cereal, 5½"	30.00	58.00
Bowl, Console, 3 Feet, 9"	6,000.00+	
Bowl, Cream Soup	60.00	
Bowl, Deep Scalloped, 12"	72.00	115.00
Bowl, Low, 11¾""	68.00	95.00
Butter & Cover	85.00	295.00
Cake Plate, Footed, 10"	36.00	78.00
Cake Plate, Handled, 11½"	65.00	75.00
Candy Dish & Cover	55.00	300.00
Celery, 10"	50.00	70.00
Celery & Olive, 2 Compartment	200.00	65.00
Claret, Footed, 4½ oz.	900.00+	
Cocktail, Footed, 3½ oz.	80.00	
Cookie Jar & Cover	58.00	285.00
Cordial, Footed, 1 oz.	900.00+	
Cream	35.00	85.00
Cup & Saucer	40.00	85.00
Cup & Ringed Saucer	55.00	
Decanter & Stopper, 32 oz.	215.00	
Goblet, Footed, 9 oz. (blown)	250.00	310.00
Goblet, Footed, 9 oz. (pressed)	78.00	
Iced Tea, 13½ oz.	60.00	185.00
Iced Tea, Footed, 15 oz.	58.00	210.00
Juice, 5 oz.	52.00	150.00
Juice, Footed, 3 oz.	90.00	
Pickle & Olive, 2 Compartment, 8½"	200.00	
Pitcher, 37 oz.	65.00	125.00
Pitcher, 60 oz.	75.00	200.00
Pitcher, 80 oz. *(Illus.)*	145.00	215.00
Plate, 6"	16.00	27.00
Plate, 6½"	15.00	
Plate, 8½" *(Illus.)*	32.00	58.00
Plate, 9½"	62.00	95.00
Plate, Grill, 9½"	48.00	65.00
Plate, Grill, Handled, 11½" (yellow only)	115.00	
Plate, with Indent, 6½"	35.00	38.00
Platter, Closed Handled, 12½" (green & yellow only)	235.00	

Mayfair (Hocking) Plate

	Pink	Blue
Platter, Open Handled, 12"	38.00	78.00
Relish, 8¼"	220.00	
Relish, 4 Compartment, 8¼"	40.00	72.00
Salt & Pepper, Flat Base, pr	75.00	325.00
Sandwich, Center Handle	40.00	85.00
Sherbet, 2¼" (blown)	225.00	155.00
Sherbet, Footed, 3"	20.00	
Sherbet, Footed, 4¾" (blown)	92.00	84.00
Sugar	28.00	85.00
Tumbler, 9 oz. *(Illus.)*	38.00	120.00
Tumbler, 11 oz.	250.00	225.00
Tumbler, Footed, 10 oz.	45.00	145.00
Vase, Sweet Pea	225.00	160.00
Wine, Footed, 2½ oz.	900.00+	
Wine, Footed, 3 oz.	110.00	

PINEAPPLE & FLORAL, NO. 618

Pineapple & Floral Plate

Date: 1932 through 1937

Manufacturer: Indiana Glass Co., Dunkirk, IN

Colors: Crystal, Amber. Late colors include Avocado green, pink and blue.

Prices are for pieces in Crystal. Amber is valued about 25% more than Crystal. Crystal with fired red color is valued about the same as Amber. Since Indiana Glass is still in business and still owns molds for this pattern, they are able at any time to reissue some pieces. Be alert for unusual colors in case this occurs. The names of the pieces in the list were taken from an old catalog except for a few pieces.

Ashtray	$22.00
Berry, 4½"	30.00
Berry, Deep, 7"	5.00
Cereal or Oatmeal, 6"	30.00
Comport, Footed (diamond shaped)	3.00
Cream Soup, 2 Handled	24.00
Cream, Handled (diamond shaped)	10.00
Cup & Saucer	20.00
Iced Tea, 12 oz.	52.00
Plate, Cake or Sandwich, 11½"	20.00
Plate, Dinner, 9⅜" *(Illus.)*	20.00
Plate, Salad, 8⅜"	10.00
Plate, Sherbet, 6"	7.00
Platter, 10¾"	20.00
Relish, 3 Compartment, 11½"	22.00
Sherbet, Footed	24.00
Sugar, Handled (diamond shaped)	10.00
Tumbler, 9 oz.	40.00
Vase	50.00
Vegetable Bowl, 10"	30.00

PLANTATION, NO. 1567

Plantation Oil & Stopper

Date: 1948-1957

Manufacturer: A. H. Heisey & Co., Newark, OH

Colors: Crystal

Reproductions: Imperial Glass Corp. made the pineapple shaped covered marmalade in milk glass, marked with the Diamond H. Imperial also made the oval 5 part relish in crystal.

Made in an extensive table ware service. Designed by Horace King, Heisey's designer, from an old pressed glass pattern resembling pineapples. Pineapples are a symbol of hospitality and are prominently featured on most pieces of Plantation. Most pieces are marked with the Diamond H.

(continued) PLANTATION, NO. 1567

Ashtray, 3½" $22.00
Bowl, Dressing, 2 Compartment, 8½" 40.00
Bowl, Floral, 12" 80.00
Bowl, Fruit or Flower, Crimped, 9½" 45.00
Bowl, Fruit or Flower, Crimped, 12" 80.00
Bowl, Gardenia, 9½" 40.00
Bowl, Gardenia, 13" 75.00
Bowl, Gardenia, Footed, 11½" 85.00
Bowl, Salad, 9" 55.00
Butter & Cover, Oblong (¼ lb.) 115.00
Butter or Candy & Cover, Round 125.00
Candelabra, 3 Light, pr. 350.00
Candleblocks, 1 Light, pr. (pineapple shape) 190.00
Candleholder, Epergne, Footed, 5" pr. 250.00
Candlesticks, 1 Light, pr. 200.00
Candlesticks, 2 Light, pr. 200.00
Candlesticks, 3 Light, pr. 230.00
Candy Box & Cover, 7" 275.00
Candy Jar & Cover, Tall, Footed, 5" 225.00
Celery & Olive, 13" 45.00
Celery Tray, 13" 40.00
Cheese & Cracker, 14", 2 pcs. 115.00
Cheese & Cracker & Cover, 14", 3 pcs. 175.00
Claret, 4 oz. 30.00
Coaster, 4" 15.00
Cocktail, 3½ oz. 25.00
Comport & Cover, Deep, 5" 80.00
Cream, Footed 40.00
Cup & Saucer, Tea 35.00
Goblet, 10 oz. 35.00
Honey, Cupped, Footed, 6½" 45.00
Iced Tea, Footed, 12 oz. 35.00
Jelly, 2 Handled, 6½" 28.00
Jelly, Flared, 6½" 25.00
Jug, Ice Lip, ½ gal. (blown) 425.00
Juice, Footed, 5 oz. 30.00
Lamps, Hurricane, 13" Globe, pr. *(Illus.)* 1,400.00
Marmalade Jar & Cover (pineapple shape) 150.00
Mayonnaise, 5¼" 45.00
Mayonnaise, Rolled Foot, 4½" 60.00
Nappy, 5" or 5½" 20.00
Oil Bottle & Stopper, 3 oz. *(Illus.)* 150.00
Oyster Cocktail, 3½ oz. 35.00
Plate, Buffet, 18" 125.00
Plate, Demi-Torte, 10½" 50.00
Plate, Mayonnaise, 7" 25.00
Plate, Punch Bowl, 18" 125.00
Plate, Salad, 7" or 8" 45.00
Plate, Sandwich, 14" 55.00
Plate, Torte, 14" 55.00
Punch Bowl, Dr. Johnson Shape, 9 qt. 400.00
Punch Cup 25.00

Plantation Hurricane Lamps

Relish, 3 Compartment, 11" 45.00
Relish, Oval, 5 Compartment, 13" (No. 1567½) 85.00
Relish, Round, 4 Compartment, 8" 45.00
Salt & Pepper, pr. 120.00
Salver, Footed, 13" 170.00
Sherbet or Saucer Champagne, 5 oz. 25.00
Sugar, Footed 40.00
Syrup Bottle with Drip Cut Top 125.00
Tray, Condiment, 8½" 80.00
Tumbler, 10 oz. 125.00
Vase, Flared, 5" 60.00
Vase, Flared, 8" 85.00

BLOWN STEMWARE (ALL NO. 5067)
Claret, 4½ oz. $35.00
Cocktail, 4½ oz. 25.00
Cordial, 1 oz. 140.00
Goblet, 10 oz. 35.00
Iced Tea, Footed, 12 oz. 35.00
Juice, Footed, 5 oz. 30.00
Oyster or Fruit Cocktail, 4 oz. 20.00
Sherbet or Saucer Champagne, 6½ oz. 25.00

ROCK CRYSTAL

Rock Crystal Catalog Page

Rock Crystal Catalog Page

Date: 1904. Some production into the 1940s and possibly later.

Manufacturer: McKee Glass Co., Jeannette, PA

Colors: Several shades of Green, Turquoise, Vaseline, Yellow, Amber, Pink, Red Slag, Red, Amethyst, Milk Glass and Cobalt Blue. Rarely found with an all-over red stain with platinum flowers. Also satin finish according to a 1922 ad.

The true name of this pattern is Early American Rock Crystal. This is an example of early pressed glass which continued to be popular into the depression years and beyond. Because of this long production, not all pieces were made for the entire length of time. Pieces in color were primarily made in the Depression era, so only the pieces made during this period will be found in colors. We do not have exact catalog reference indicating all of the pieces made in colors. There may be other pieces available in colors and also in the pattern. Most names of pieces are from original catalogs. Many bowls and plates were available with a plain edge or a scalloped edge (S. E.)

	Crystal	Cobalt, Red	Other Colors
Bonbon, High Foot, S.E. 7½"	$50.00	$140.00	$75.00
Bonbon, Small, Handled	32.00		
Bowl, 10½"	40.00	120.00	55.00
Bowl, Console, 12½"	75.00	300.00	125.00
Bowl, Round, S. E. 10½"	35.00	135.00	70.00
Bowl, Round, S. E., 7"	25.00	70.00	40.00
Bowl, Round, S. E., 8"	30.00	75.00	45.00
Bowl, Round, S. E., 9"	30.00	125.00	60.00
Butter & Cover	350.00		
Cake Stand, Salver, 11"	50.00	165.00	65.00
Candelabra, 2 Light, pr.	50.00	275.00	125.00
Candelabra, 3 Light, pr.	60.00	360.00	150.00
Candlesticks, 5½", pr.	85.00	245.00	160.00
Candlesticks, 8½", pr.	145.00	325.00	135.00
Candy Box & Cover, 7"	60.00	210.00	85.00
Candy Jar & Cover, 16 oz.	75.00	250.00	100.00
Celery Tray, Oblong, or Comb & Brush Tray, 12"	75.00		
Champagne or Tall Sundae, Footed, 6 oz.	22.00	60.00	30.00
Cocktail, Footed, 3½ oz.	16.00	45.00	22.00
Comport, 7"	40.00	110.00	58.00
Comport, Footed, 7"	50.00		
Cordial, Footed, 1 oz.	30.00	120.00	55.00
Cream	42.00		
Cream, Berry, Footed	40.00	95.00	45.00
Cup & Saucer	30.00	95.00	35.00
Custard or Punch Cup	12.00		

(continued) ROCK CRYSTAL

	Crystal	Cobalt, Red	Other Colors
Finger Bowl, Plain Edge 5"...	15.00	60.00	27.00
Goblet, Large, 8 oz. (Footed) .	27.00	98.00	37.00
Goblet, Low Footed, 7½ oz. or 8 oz.	22.00	85.00	30.00
Goblet, Low Footed, 8 oz	25.00		
Goblet, Tall Footed, Small ...	25.00		
Iced Tea or High Ball, No. 1 Straight, 12 oz......	27.00	90.00	37.00
Iced Tea, Straight or Concave, 12 oz........	34.00	65.00	45.00
Iced Tea, Low Footed, 11 oz. .	27.00	90.00	37.00
Jelly, Footed.............	50.00	110.00	75.00
Jelly, Footed, S. E. 5"	22.00	58.00	30.00
Jug & Cover, 46 oz........	210.00	650.00+	375.00
Jug, Squat, 1 qt...........	200.00		280.00
Jug, Squat, ½ gal..........	130.00		260.00
Jug, Tankard, Fancy, 52 oz ...	210.00	1,000.00+	600.00
Juice, Tomato, 5 oz.	20.00	75.00	30.00
Lamp..................	210.00	850.00+	425.00+
Mayonnaise Bowl..........	20.00		
Molasses Can, Syrup........	100.00		170.00
Nappy, 7"	25.00	85.00	40.00
Nappy, 8"	30.00	85.00	40.00
Nappy, 9"	35.00	110.00	48.00
Nappy, Handled, 5" (jelly) ...	24.00	75.00	
Nappy, S. E., 4"	14.00	40.00	187.00
Nappy, S. E., 4½" or 5"	15.00	42.00	20.00
Nappy, Shallow, 10½"	40.00	110.00	55.00
Nappy, Shallow, 5"........	18.00	58.00	27.00
Nappy, Shallow, 6"........	20.00	60.00	30.00
Nappy, Shallow, 8"........	30.00	85.00	40.00
Nappy, Shallow, 9"........	35.00	110.00	48.00
Nut Bowl, Handled, Large (same shape as Bonbon)...	45.00		
Oil & Stopper, 6 oz........	120.00	450.00	350.00
Old Fashioned Whiskey, 5 oz..	22.00	85.00	35.00
Parfait, Low, Footed, 3½ oz...	25.00	120.00	52.00
Pickle Tray or Spoon Tray	25.00	68.00	32.00
Plate, Bread & Butter, S. E. 5½" or 6"	8.00	20.00	10.00
Plate, Plain or S. E, 7" or 7½"	10.00	26.00	12.00
Plate, Plain or S. E., 8½"	11.00	36.00	15.00
Plate, Cake, 9"...........	20.00	68.00	30.00
Plate, Cake, 10½"	22.00	72.00	32.00
Plate, Cake, 11½"	22.00	72.00	32.00
Plate, Dinner, S. E., 10½" ...	50.00	200.00	85.00
Plate, Finger Bowl	11.00	20.00	12.00
Plate, S. E., 11½"..........	22.00	62.00	30.00
Punch Bowl & Stand, 12" or 14".............	525.00		
Relish, 2 Compartment, Plain Edge, 11½"	21.00	75.00	42.00
Relish, 6 Compartment, 14" (hexagonal)	42.00		75.00
Salt & Pepper (2 types), pr ...	120.00		150.00
Salt, Individual Open.......	40.00		
Sandwich, Center Handle....	28.00	135.00	40.00
Saucer Champagne, 6 oz.....	20.00	40.00	25.00
Saucer, Round, Shallow Bowl, 5"........	18.00	45.00	22.00
Saucer, Round, Shallow Bowl, 8"........	30.00	80.00	40.00
Sherbet or Egg, Footed, 3½ oz.	22.00	70.00	32.00
Spoon	50.00		
Spoon Tray..............	65.00		
Sugar & Cover, Berry, Footed...........	45.00	140.00	55.00
Sugar & Cover, Large.......	100.00		
Sundae, Low Footed, 6 oz. (sherbet)	15.00	60.00	24.00
Tray, Ice Cream, Oblong, 12".	48.00	130.00	60.00
Tray, Roll, Plain Edge, 13" ..	32.00	115.00	48.00
Tumbler, Champagne or Grape Juice	20.00	75.00	30.00
Tumbler, Concave Bell, No. 2, 9 oz.............	27.00	65.00	37.00
Tumbler, Concave Cupped, No. 2, 9 oz.............	30.00		
Tumbler, No. 1 Straight, 9 oz. .	25.00	62.00	25.00
Tumbler, Taper, No. 1	27.00		
Tumbler, Whiskey, Bell, Crimp or Toothpick, 2½ oz......	25.00	72.00	32.00
Vase, Cornucopia	75.00		
Vase, Footed, 11" or 12".....	75.00	315.00	150.00
Wine, Large, Footed, 3 oz. ...	24.00	60.00	32.00
Wine, Small, Footed, 2 oz. ...	20.00	55.00	28.00

ROSEMARY

Rosemary Cup & Saucer, Plate & Small Bowl

Date: 1935 to 1937

Manufacturer: Federal Glass Co., Columbus, OH

Colors: Amber, Green, Pink. Limited in Crystal Iridized.

Compare this pattern with Federal's Mayfair, which has a diamond band on the interior of plates and other pieces.

	Amber	Pink	Green
Bowl, 5" *(Illus.)*	$9.00	$16.00	$15.00
Bowl, Cream Soup, 5"	18.00	28.00	25.00
Bowl, 6"	32.00	42.00	38.00
Bowl, Oval Vegetable, 10"	22.00	38.00	40.00
Cream	12.00	22.00	20.00
Cup & Saucer *(Illus.)*	11.00	17.00	16.00
Plate, 6¾"	7.00	10.00	9.00
Plate, Dinner *(Illus.)*	16.00	25.00	20.00
Plate, Grill	10.00	24.00	16.00
Platter, 12"	26.00	40.00	34.00
Sugar	11.00	22.00	20.00
Tumbler, 9 oz.	38.00	52.00	36.00

SANDWICH, NO. 170

Sandwich (Indiana) Catalog Page

Date: Ca. 1925. Many items made in late years.

Manufacturer: Indiana Glass Co., Dunkirk, IN

Colors: Originally made in crystal, pink, green and amber. Blue green (Teal) was made during the 1950s and milk glass in the 1950s through the 1960s. Since Indiana is still using the Sandwich molds, some late pieces are available in red and amber/gold.

Compare with the Sandwich pattern made by Hocking Glass, Early American Sandwich made by Duncan & Miller in this chapter and Princess Feather by Westmoreland in the Stylized Patterns chapter. Duncan's pattern will have greater detail and will be more carefully finished than the others, and often pieces will have ground and polished bottoms.

Sandwich Candlesticks & Saucer

	Crystal	Pink, Green	Teal	Red
Ashtray, Card Suit Shapes, set of 4...	$12.00	$16.00	$	$
Bowl, Berry, 4½"	2.50	4.50		
Bowl, Berry, 8½"	9.00	10.00		18.00
Bowl, Console, Deep, Flat or Crimped Top, 9"	17.00	42.00		
Bowl, Console, Rolled Edge, 11½" . .	20.00	5.00		
Butter & Cover	65.00	165.00	160.00	
Candlesticks, Low, 1 Light, 3½", pr. *(Illus.)*.	15.00	25.00		
Candlesticks, Tall, 1 Light, 7", pr. . . .	20.00	45.00		
Celery Tray.	18.00			
Cocktail, Footed, 3 oz.	9.00	16.00		
Cream	9.00	10.00	12.00	45.00
Cup & Saucer, cup only in red (*Illus. of saucer*).	6.00	9.00	12.00	30.00
Decanter & Stopper	25.00	120.00		90.00
Goblet, 9 oz.	20.00	18.00		40.00
Iced Tea, Footed, 12 oz.	16.00	27.00		
Jug, 68 oz.	40.00	110.00		145.00
Mayonnaise Bowl	15.00	35.00		
Nappy, Deep, 6".	4.00	6.00		
Nappy, Hexagon, 6"	5.00		15.00	
Oil & Stopper, 6 oz.	32.00	170.00	140.00	
Plate, 6" or 7"	4.00	8.00	8.00	
Plate, 10½"	10.00	20.00	17.00	
Plate, Salad, 8¼"	5.00	9.00	9.00	
Plate, Sandwich, 13".	20.00	25.00	27.00	
Puff Box & Cover.	20.00			
Sandwich, Center Handled, 11"	20.00	27.00		
Sherbet, Footed	4.00	6.00	10.00	
Sugar	9.00	10.00	12.00	45.00
Tray, for Sugar & Cream.	12.00	15.00	27.00	18.00
Tumbler, Footed, 8 oz.	11.00	16.00		

SANDWICH

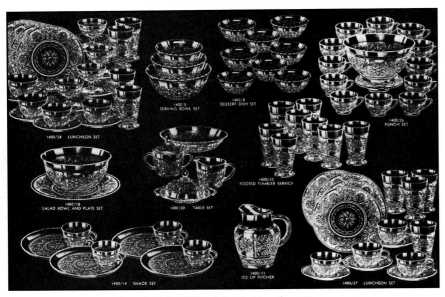

Sandwich (Hocking) Catalog Page

Date: 1939 to 1940; 1956 to 1964. Limited production in Crystal in 1977.

Manufacturer: Hocking Glass Co., Lancaster, OH

Colors: Early: (1939-early 1940s) Crystal, Pink, Royal Ruby. Late: (Late 1950s) Desert Gold (Amber), Crystal, Forest Green, Opaque White.

Compare this pattern with the Sandwich design made by Indiana Glass, Early American Sandwich made by Duncan & Miller and Princess Feather by Westmoreland in the Stylized Patterns chapter. Duncan & Miller's pieces are more detailed and better finished, including ground bottoms on many pieces.

	Crystal	Desert Gold	Forest Green		Crystal	Desert Gold	Forest Green
Bowl, 4¾", or 5", Plain Edge	$5.00	$	$4.00	Custard Cup Underplate . . .	18.00		2.00
Bowl, Crimped, 5"	16.00			Juice, 3 oz.	15.00		
Bowl, 5¼", Scalloped Edge .	8.00	7.00		Juice, 5 oz.	7.00		5.00
Bowl, 6½", Plain or Scalloped Edge	8.00	7.00	42.00	Pitcher, 6"	65.00		140.00
Bowl, 6¾", Plain Edge	35.00	14.00		Pitcher, Ice Lip, ½ gal.	80.00		375.00
Bowl, 7"	8.00			Plate, 7"	11.00		
Bowl, 7½" or 8¼", Scalloped Edge	9.00		65.00	Plate, 8"	5.00		
Bowl, 9"	24.00	28.00		Plate, 9"	20.00	10.00	100.00
Bowl, Oval, 8¼"	8.00			Plate, Oval, Indent for Cup, 9"	7.00		
Butter & Cover	50.00			Plate, Sandwich, 12"	14.00	15.00	
Cookie Jar & Cover (No Forest Green Cover) .	38.00	38.00	20.00	Punch Bowl	24.00		
Cream	8.00		30.00	Punch Bowl Stand	28.00		
Cup & Saucer	5.00	8.00	40.00	Punch Cup	3.00		
Custard Cup	4.00		2.00	Sherbet	8.00		
Custard Cup, Crimped Edge	14.00			Sugar & Cover (No Forest Green Cover)	30.00		30.00
				Tumbler, 9 oz.	10.00		6.00
				Tumbler, Footed, 9 oz.	30.00	130.00	

SHARON

"SHARON" FLORAL SPRAY DESIGN . . . In Topaz-Golden Glow Glass
Deep process-etched pattern, pressed (except blown jug and tumbler), brilliant fire polished, smooth edges, beautiful topaz-golden glow color.

Sharon Catalog Ad

Date: 1935 to 1939

Manufacturer: Federal Glass Co., Columbus, OH

Colors: Amber, Green, Pink. Limited availability in Crystal.

Reproductions: These are done in many new colors in addition to pink and green. The butter and cover varies from the original in that the finial is much easier to grasp on the new butter and the base has a well defined rim to hold the lid in place. The cheese underplate is shaped almost like a bowl rather than the flat plate of the original. The lid of the old candy and cover has a 2" ring under the finial while the new has only about a ½" ring. The mold line on the old cream goes up the center of the spout but is offset on the new. The handle of the sugar at the attachment to the body appears V-shaped on the old but is round on the new. The salt and pepper shakers have poorly defined pattern, especially the rosebuds which appear to be only rather crude leaves on the new.

	Amber	Pink	Green
Bowl, 5"	$8.00	$12.00	$14.00
Bowl, 6"	18.00	24.00	24.00
Bowl, 8½"	7.00	32.00	32.00
Bowl, 10½"	24.00	40.00	40.00

	Amber	Pink	Green
Bowl, Cream Soup, 5"	25.00	48.00	54.00
Bowl, Oval Vegetable, 9½"..	18.00	30.00	34.00
Bowl, Soup, 7½"	45.00	55.00	
Butter & Cover	50.00	55.00	90.00
Cake Plate, Footed, 11½". . .	22.00	45.00	55.00
Candy Jar & Cover	40.00	55.00	150.00
Cheese & Cover.	200.00	800.00+	
Cream.	15.00	18.00	22.00
Cup & Saucer	16.00	28.00	30.00
Iced Tea, 12 oz.	55.00	60.00	85.00
Iced Tea, Footed, 15 oz.	110.00	45.00	
Jam Dish, 7½".	35.00	200.00	45.00
Pitcher, 80 oz. (with or without ice lip)	130.00	145.00	400.00+
Plate, 6"	6.00	8.00	10.00
Plate, 7½"	14.00	20.00	22.00
Plate, 9½"	12.00	20.00	22.00
Platter, 12½"	15.00	32.00	32.00
Salt & Pepper, pr..	45.00	55.00	65.00
Sherbet	10.00	16.00	32.00
Sugar & Cover.	30.00	48.00	55.00
Tumbler, 9 oz.	25.00	40.00	65.00

STRAWBERRY, NO. 15,340

Strawberry Large Bowl

Date: Late 1927

Manufacturer: U. S. Glass Co.. Gas City, IN

Colors: Crystal, Green, Pink. Crystal Iridized.

(See also Cherry) This pattern was made at the Gas City, Indiana plant of U. S. Glass. Strawberry is the original name of the pattern according to company literature. All items made in Strawberry were also made in Cherry (Cherryberry).

	Crystal	Pink, Green		Crystal	Pink, Green
Bowl, 4"	$7.00	$12.00	Nappy, Handled, 5"	9.00	17.00
Bowl, 6⅜"	18.00	24.00	Pickle, Oval, 8½"	10.00	18.00
Bowl, 7½"	20.00	32.00	Plate, 6"	5.00	8.00
Bowl, Deep, 6½" *(Illus.)*	42.00	70.00	Plate, 7½"	9.00	12.00
Butter & Cover..............	110.00	155.00	Sugar	17.00	25.00
Comport, 5¾"	10.00	15.00	Sugar & Cover, Large	75.00	120.00
Cream	17.00	25.00	Sundae (Sherbet).............	8.00	12.00
Cream, Large	16.00	20.00	Tumbler, 8 oz................	22.00	38.00
Jug, 7¾"...................	155.00	145.00			

SUNFLOWER

Sunflower Cake Plate

Date: 1930s

Manufacturer: Jeannette Glass Co., Jeannette, PA

Colors: Green, Pink. Limited availability in Delphite and opaque colors.

	Pink	Green
Ashtray, 5"	$10.00	$12.00
Cake Plate, 3 Footed, 10" *(Illus.)*..	16.00	16.00
Cream	17.00	18.00
Cup & Saucer................	22.00	25.00
Plate, 9"	15.00	20.00
Sugar	20.00	20.00
Trivet, 3 Footed, 7"	250.00+	285.00+
Tumbler, Footed, 8 oz.	27.00	32.00

THISTLE

Date: 1929 to 1930

Manufacturer: MacBeth-Evans Glass Co., Charleroi, PA

Colors: Green, Pink. Limited availability in Crystal and Yellow. Difficult to find in any color.

	Pink	Green
Bowl, 5½"	$25.00	$27.00
Bowl, 10¼" *(Illus.)*	275.00	200.00
Cake Plate, 13"	125.00	150.00
Cup & Saucer	35.00	45.00
Plate, 8"	17.00	21.00
Plate, Grill, 10¼"	24.00	28.00

Thistle Bowl

WISTAR, NO. 2620

Date: 1941 to 1944

Manufacturer: Fostoria Glass Co., Moundsville, WV

Colors: Crystal

Bonbon, 3 Toed, 6⅝"	$16.00
Bowl, Fruit, 13"	24.00
Bowl, Nut, 3 Toed, 5½"	20.00
Bowl, Salad, 10"	24.00
Candlesticks, 1 Light, 4", pr.	35.00
Celery, 9½"	15.00
Cream, Footed	15.00
Goblet, 9 oz.	20.00
Lily Pond, 12"	35.00
Mayonnaise	24.00
Nappy, 3 Cornered, Handled, 4½"	10.00
Nappy, Flared, Handled, 5"	10.00
Nappy, Regular, Handled, 4¼"	10.00
Nappy, Square, Handled, 4"	10.00
Plate, 7"	7.00
Plate, Mayonnaise	8.00
Plate, Torte, 14"	22.00
Sherbet, High Foot, 6½ oz.	8.00
Sugar, Footed	15.00
Tricorne, 3 Toed, 6¾"	16.00
Tumbler (juice), 5 oz.	12.00
Tumbler (iced tea), 12 oz.	15.00

Wistar Catalog Page

Chapter 7
FLUTES & PANELS

ARGUS, NO. 2770

Argus Catalog Illustration

Date: 1960

Manufacturer: Fostoria Glass Co., Moundsville, WV

Colors: Crystal, Olive, Cobalt, Ruby. Late production in Gray.

Fostoria produced this for the Henry Ford Museum, Dearborn, MI. This is a copy of early Victorian pressed glass. Prices are for items in Crystal. For Ruby add 50%. For Olive and Cobalt add 25%.

Compote & Cover, 8"	$45.00
Cream, 6"	25.00
Dessert, 5"	10.00
Goblet, 6½ oz.	12.00
Goblet, 10½ oz.	14.00
Hi-ball/Tumbler, 12 oz.	15.00
Ice Tea or Luncheon Goblet, 13 oz.	15.00
Juice or Cocktail, 4½ oz.	8.00
Old Fashioned, 10 oz.	12.00
Plate, Dessert, 8"	5.00
Sherbet, 8 oz.	8.00
Sugar & Cover	30.00
Wine, 4½ oz.	12.00

BAROQUE, NO. 2496

Date: 1936 to 1966

Manufacturer: Fostoria Glass Co., Moundsville, WV

Colors: Crystal. Topaz/Gold Tint, Azure

One of Fostoria's most popular collectible tableware patterns. Made in a great variety of pieces. Topaz is valued slightly less than Azure/Gold Tint. Only the Trindle Candlestick was made in Ruby, Amber, Burgundy, Empire Green, Ebony, and Regal Blue.

Baroque Goblet, Plate, Cup & Saucer

	Crystal	Azure
Ashtray, Oblong	$10.00	$18.00
Bonbon, 3 Toed, 7¼"	15.00	30.00
Bowl, Cupped, 7"	25.00	42.00
Bowl, Flared, 12"	30.00	48.00
Bowl, Handled, 10"	24.00	55.00
Bowl, Rolled Edge, 11"	24.00	60.00
Bowl, Salad, 10½"	22.00	50.00
Bowl, Vegetable, 9½"	38.00	110.00
Candelabrum, 2 Light, 8¼"	75.00	135.00
Candelabrum, 3 Light, 9½"	125.00	195.00
Candlesticks, 4", pr.	32.00	75.00
Candlesticks, 5½", pr.	35.00	70.00
Candlesticks, Duo, 4½", pr.	35.00	120.00
Candlesticks, Trindle, 6", pr.	55.00	100.00
Candy Box & Cover, 3 part	40.00	110.00
Celery, 11"	18.00	55.00
Cheese & Cracker, 2 pcs.	40.00	95.00
Cigarette Box & Cover	50.00	110.00
Cocktail, Footed	15.00	22.00
Comport, 5½"	20.00	35.00
Comport, 6½"	25.00	40.00
Cream Soup	25.00	70.00
Cream, Footed, 3¾"	10.00	28.00
Cream, Individual	15.00	35.00
Cup & Saucer *(Illus.)*.	15.00	35.00
Dish, Mint, Handled.	20.00	35.00.
Dish, Sauce, Oblong, 6½"	20.00	45.00.
Dish, Serving, 2 Handled, 8½" . . .	22.00	48.00
Floating Garden, 10"	40.00	90.00
Fruit, 5"	15.00	27.00
Goblet *(Illus.)*	15.00	32.00
Ice Bucket.	40.00	135.00
Iced Tea, 14 oz.	30.00	85.00
Iced Tea, Footed, 12 oz.	15.00	35.00
Jelly & Cover	35.00	75.00
Jug, 3 pt.	160.00	900.00+
Juice, 5 oz.	15.00	32.00
Mayonnaise	30.00	60.00
Mayonnaise, 2 part, 6½"	30.00	60.00
Mustard & Cover	30.00	70.00.
Nappy, 3 Cornered, 4½"	16.00	30.00
Nappy, Flared	16.00	30.00

	Crystal	Azure
Nappy, Flared, Handled, 5"	18.00	34.00
Nappy, Square.	16.00	32.00
Oil & Stopper, 3½ oz.	75.00	450.00
Old Fashioned Cocktail, 7 oz.	20.00	80.00
Pickle, 8"	15.00	32.00
Plate, 6" or 7" *(Illus.)*	8.00	16.00
Plate, 8"	12.00	25.00
Plate, 9"	30.00	75.00
Plate, Cake, 2 Handled, 10"	25.00	42.00
Plate, Torte, 14"	25.00	55.00
Platter, Oval, 12"	35.00	75.00
Preserve & Cover	30.00	125.00
Punch Bowl, Footed, 1½ gal.	300.00	700.00+
Punch Cup	10.00	16.00
Relish, 3 part, 10"	20.00	38.00
Relish, 4 part	24.00	45.00
Relish, Square, 2 part, 6"	16.00	32.00
Rose Bowl, 3½"	30.00	65.00
Salt & Pepper, pr.	45.00	135.00
Salt & Pepper, Individual, pr.	60.00	200.00
Sherbet, 5 oz.	12.00	25.00
Sugar, Footed	15.00	35.00
Sugar, Individual	15.00	35.00
Sweetmeat, Square, 6"	20.00	35.00
Tid Bit, 3 Toed, Flat, 8¼"	18.00	40.00
Tray, for Individual Sugar & Cream	18.00	30.00
Tray, Oblong, 8"	20.00	35.00
Tray, Oval, 11"	30.00	65.00
Tray, for Sugar & Cream, 6½"	16.00	32.00
Tumbler, 9 oz.	24.00	55.00
Tumbler, Footed, 9 oz.	15.00	32.00
Vase, 7" or 8"	38.00	110.00

COLONIAL

Colonial Cream

Date: 1935 to 1936

Manufacturer: Hocking Glass Co., Lancaster, OH

Colors: Crystal, Pink, Pale Green. Milk White

This was once called Knife and Fork, but Colonial is the original name.

	Crystal	Green	Pink
Bar Glass, 1½ oz.	$25.00	$30.00	$16.00
Bowl, 3¾"			25.00
Bowl, 4½"	6.00	20.00	10.00
Bowl, 5½"	35.00	110.00	50.00
Bowl, 7"	25.00	75.00	47.00
Bowl, 9"	14.00	38.00	17.00
Bowl, Cream Soup, 4½"	40.00	68.00	47.00
Bowl, Oval Vegetable, 10"	23.00	42.00	38.00
Butter & Cover	40.00	72.00	500.00+
Cheese & Cover		170.00	
Claret, 4 oz.	21.00	35.00	
Cocktail, 3 oz.	15.00	27.00	
Cordial, 1 oz.	21.00	40.00	
Cream (*Illus.*)	12.00	23.00	50.00
Cup & Saucer	9.00	13.00	13.00
Goblet, 8½ oz.	25.00	42.00	55.00
Iced Tea, 12 oz.	30.00	62.00	55.00
Iced Tea, 15 oz. (Lemonade)	48.00	90.00	75.00
Juice, 5 oz.	15.00	32.00	24.00

	Crystal	Green	Pink
Juice, Footed, 5 oz.	20.00	45.00	38.00
Mug, 4½"		800.00+	450.00+
Pitcher, with or without Ice Lip, 54 oz.	35.00	60.00	55.00
Pitcher, with or without Ice Lip, 68 oz.	35.00	82.00	68.00
Plate, 6"	4.00	7.00	7.00
Plate, 8½"	6.00	10.00	10.00
Plate, 10"	25.00	67.00	55.00
Plate, Grill, 10"	15.00	30.00	26.00
Platter, 12"	18.00	35.00	42.00
Salt & Pepper, pr	55.00	145.00	155.00
Sherbet, 2 sizes	6.00	14.00	10.00
Spooner	75.00	125.00	110.00
Sugar & Cover	28.00	47.00	85.00
Tumbler, 9 oz.	15.00	32.00	32.00
Tumbler, 10 oz.	27.00	52.00	52.00
Tumbler, Footed, 10 oz.	30.00	52.00	52.00
Wine, 2½ oz.	17.00	35.00	

COLONIAL FLUTED

Date: 1928 to 1933

Manufacturer: Federal Glass Co., Columbus, OH

Colors: Crystal, Green

Prices are for pieces in Green; Crystal items are valued 50% less.

Bowl, 4" *(Illus.)*	$6.00
Bowl, 6"	8.00
Bowl, 7½"	18.00
Bowl, Deep, 6½"	22.00
Cream	8.00
Cup & Saucer	8.00
Plate, 6" *(Illus.)*	3.00
Plate, 8"	6.00
Sherbet	7.00
Sugar & Cover	24.00

Colonial Fluted Small Plate, Bowl

CORINTH, NO. 3900

Date: Ca. 1940s

Manufacturer: Cambridge Glass Co., Cambridge, OH

Colors: Crystal

A pressed tableware pattern which was used for many decorations by Cambridge. Stemware in the pattern was blown, not pressed. The jugs and tumblers were made in a wide optic and gyro (wide swirl) optic, and were made in Midnight Blue, Emerald Green, Mandarin Gold, Amber, and Amethyst.

Bitter Bottle & Tube, 4 oz.	$18.00
Bonbon Plate, 2 Handled, 8"	10.00
Bonbon, Footed, 2 Handled, 7"	12.00
Bowl, 2 Handled, 11"	20.00
Bowl, Flared, 4 Footed, 10"	18.00
Bowl, Flared, 4 Footed, 12"	22.00
Bowl, Footed, 11½"	20.00
Bowl, Oval, 4 Footed, 12"	20.00
Candlesticks, 1 Light, 3", pr.	28.00
Candlesticks, 1 Light, 5", pr.	28.00
Candlesticks, 2 Light, 6", pr.	55.00
Candlesticks, 3 Light, 6", pr.	55.00
Candy Box & Cover.	28.00
Celery & Relish, 3 Part, 9"	15.00
Celery & Relish, 3 Part, 12"	20.00
Celery & Relish, 5 Part, 12"	20.00
Cheese & Cracker, 2 pcs.	28.00
Claret, 4½ oz.	8.00
Cocktail Icer, 2 pcs.	17.00
Cocktail, 3 oz.	8.00

Corinth 1949 Ad

CORINTH, NO. 3900 *(continued)*

Comport, 5" (low) 12.00	Plate, Bread & Butter, 6½" 5.00
Comport, 5½" 20.00	Plate, Cake, 2 Handled, 13½" 20.00
Comport, Blown, 5" 18.00	Plate, Dinner, 10½" 25.00
Cordial, 1 oz. 30.00	Plate, Rolled Edge, 14" 24.00
Cream 10.00	Plate, Salad, 8" 8.00
Cream, Individual 15.00	Plate, Torte, Rolled Edge, 4 Footed, 13" 24.00
Cup & Saucer 15.00	Relish or Pickle, 7" 12.00
Goblet, 9 oz. 12.00	Relish, 2 Part, 7" (2 styles) 12.00
Ice Bucket 25.00	Salt & Pepper, pr. 20.00
Iced Tea, Footed, 12 oz. 10.00	Sherbet, Low, 6 oz. 8.00
Jug, 20 oz. 25.00	Sherbet, Tall, 6 oz. 8.00
Jug, 32 oz. 30.00	Sugar 10.00
Jug, 76 oz. 35.00	Sugar, Individual 15.00
Jug, Ball, 80 oz. 50.00	Tray for Cream & Sugar 8.00
Jug, Martini, 32 oz. 40.00	Tumbler, 5 oz. 8.00
Mayonnaise, 2 Part 20.00	Tumbler, 13 oz. 10.00
Mayonnaise, Flared 16.00	Tumbler, Footed, 5 oz. (juice) 9.00
Mayonnaise, Footed 16.00	Tumbler, Footed, 10 oz. 10.00
Oil & Stopper, 6 oz. 22.00	Vase, Cornucopia, 10" 30.00
Oyster Cocktail, 4½ oz. 7.00	Wine, 2½ oz. 9.00
Plate, 4 Footed, 12" 25.00	

DECAGON

Decagon Small Plate, Cup & Saucer

Date: Ca. 1930s

Manufacturer: Cambridge Glass Co., Cambridge, OH

Colors: Crystal, Emerald, Amber, Peach-Blo or Dianthus Pink, Ritz Blue, Willow Blue, Royal Blue, Ebony

A plain, paneled dinnerware line used for many decorations by Cambridge. It comes in a wide variety of colors, but not all pieces may be found in all colors.

	Crystal	Colors		Crystal	Colors
Almond, Footed, 6"	$14.00	$22.00	Celery Tray, 11"	9.00	18.00
Almond, Footed, Individual,			Cereal, Flat Rim or Belled, 6"	6.00	10.00
2½"	20.00	25.00	Cheese & Cracker, 2 pcs.	25.00	45.00
Basket, 2 handled, 7"	11.00	18.00	Comport, 11½"	18.00	35.00
Bonbon, 2 handled, 5½"	9.00	15.00	Comport, 5¾" or 6½"	10.00	18.00
Bonbon, 2 handled, 6¼"	9.00	15.00	Comport, Tall, 7"	18.00	40.00
Bouillon Cup	8.00	18.00	Cranberry, Flat Rim or Belled,		
Bowl, 11" (console)	20.00	38.00	3¾" (Nappy)	5.00	15.00
Bowl, Berry, 10"	10.00	22.00	Cream, Footed (No. 867)	10.00	22.00
Candlesticks, 4", pr.	20.00	40.00	Cream, Flat (No. 979)	8.00	18.00

(continued) DECAGON

	Crystal	Colors
Cream (No. 1094).	8.00	17.00
Cream, Cone Shape (No. 1096). . .	9.00	18.00
Cream Soup	6.00	15.00
Cup & Saucer *(Illus.)*.	10.00	18.00.
Dish, Oval Vegetable, 9½" or 10½"	8.00	35.00
Dish, Round Vegetable, 9".	10.00	30.00
Dish, Round Vegetable, 11".	12.00	35.00
French Dressing & Stopper	30.00	50.00
French Dressing & Stopper, Footed	35.00	55.00
Fruit, Flat Rim or Belled, 5¾" (nappy)	5.00	10.00
Gravy Boat & Stand (underplate). .	35.00	60.00
Ice Pail	22.00	45.00
Ice Tub	15.00	40.00
Mayonnaise, 2 Handled (flat)	10.00	22.00
Mayonnaise, Footed	12.00	25.00
Mayonnaise, Footed, 2 Handled . .	12.00	28.00
Oil & Stopper, 6 oz. (No. 193) . . .	20.00	45.00
Oil & Stopper, Tall, 6 oz. (No. 197).	24.00	55.00
Pickle Tray, 2 Handled, 8"	9.00	20.00
Pickle Tray, 9"	7.00	15.00

	Crystal	Colors
Plate, 12½"	10.00	35.00
Plate, 2 Handled, 7"	9.00	15.00.
Plate, 7½"	6.00	8.00
Plate, Bread & Butter, 6¼" *(Illus.)*. .	5.00	8.00
Plate, Club Luncheon (grill), 10". . .	12.00	30.00
Plate, Dinner, 9½"	15.00	40.00
Plate, Salad, 8⅜".	6.00	12.00
Plate, Service, 10½"	10.00	35.00
Relish, 2 part, 9"	8.00	18.00
Relish, 2 part, 11"	9.00	20.00
Salt Dip, Footed, 1½"	22.00	38.00
Sauce Bowl & Stand (underplate) .	35.00	60.00
Soup Plate, 8½" (bowl)	8.00	22.00
Soup Plate, Flat Rim, 8½" (bowl) . .	8.00	18.00
Sugar, Footed (No. 867)	10.00	22.00
Sugar, Flat (No. 979).	8.00	18.00
Sugar (No. 1094)	8.00	17.00
Sugar, Cone Shape (No. 1096). . . .	9.00	18.00
Tray, Center Handled for Cream & Sugar	12.00	30.00
Tray, Oval Service, 11" or 12 ". . . .	10.00	45.00
Tray, Oval Service, 15"	15.00	65.00
Tray, Service, 2 Handled, 13".	20.00	50.00

FAIRFAX, No. 2375

Date: 1927 to 1960

Manufacturer: Fostoria Glass Co., Moundsville, WV

Colors: Crystal, Amber, Green, Orchid, Rose, Azure, Topaz. A few items in Ebony and Ruby.

Covered by design patents Nos. 76852 and 76913. One of Fostoria's early extensive tableware lines. Used for etchings by Fostoria.

	Crystal, Amber	Rose, Green, Topaz	Orchid, Azure
Ashtray	$10.00	$12.00	$16.00
Baker, Oval, 9".	20.00	25.00	35.00
Baker, Oval, 10½"	22.00	28.00	40.00
Bonbon, 2 Handled	10.00	12.00	14.00
Bottle, Salad Dressing.	85.00	110.00	180.00
Bouillon, Footed.	10.00	15.00	18.00
Bowl, 12".	22.00	30.00	40.00

Fairfax Catalog Page

FAIRFAX, NO. 2375 *(continued)*

	Crystal, Amber	Rose, Green, Topaz	Orchid, Azure
Bowl, Dessert, Two Handled, 8½"	22.00	28.00	35.00
Bowl, Whipped Cream	12.00	16.00	20.00
Butter & Cover	85.00	110.00	155.00
Cake Plate, 2 Handled, 10"	16.00	20.00	25.00
Candlesticks, 1 Light, 3", pr.	24.00	30.00	35.00
Candlesticks, 1 Light, Mushroom, (No. 2375½), pr.	25.00	35.00	50.00
Celery, 11½"	14.00	18.00	25.00
Centerpiece, 12" or 15"	28.00	35.00	45.00
Centerpiece, Oval, 13" (No. 2375½), complete	28.00	65.00	120.00
Cereal, 6"	12.00	16.00	24.00
Cheese & Cracker, 2 pcs.	30.00	40.00	50.00
Comport, 7"	18.00	27.00	35.00
Cream Soup, Footed	15.00	20.00	25.00
Cream	10.00	15.00	20.00
Cream, Footed (No. 2375½)	12.00	15.00	18.00
Cream, Tea, Footed (No. 2375½")	15.00	20.00	25.00
Cream, Tea, Footed	15.00	20.00	25.00
Cup & Saucer	12.00	15.00	20.00
Cup & Saucer, After Dinner	20.00	28.00	35.00
Flower Holder, Oval, 2 piece (No. 2371)	35.00	55.00	165.00
Fruit, 5"	10.00	14.00	18.00
Ice Bucket	40.00	50.00	60.00
Lemon Dish, 2 Handled	14.00	18.00	20.00
Lunch Tray, Center Handled (Fleur de lis), 11"	25.00	38.00	50.00
Mayonnaise, Footed	20.00	25.00	30.00
Nappy, Round, 7"	20.00	25.00	30.00
Nappy, Round, 8"	20.00	25.00	30.00
Nut Dish, Individual (No. 2374)	18.00	20.00	24.00
Oil & Stopper, Footed	90.00	120.00	150.00
Pickle, 8½"	12.00	16.00	22.00
Plate, 6"	5.00	6.00	8.00
Plate, 13"	20.00	28.00	35.00
Plate, Canape	7.00	8.00	10.00
Plate, Cream Soup or Mayonnaise	7.00	8.00	10.00
Plate, Dinner, 10"	28.00	35.00	50.00
Plate, Grill, 10"	24.00	32.00	45.00
Plate, Salad, 7" or 8"	8.00	10.00	12.00
Plate, Sauce Boat	8.00	10.00	18.00
Platter, Oval, 10½"	15.00	24.00	32.00
Platter, Oval, 12"	20.00	28.00	38.00
Platter, Oval, 15"	45.00	60.00	80.00
Relish, 2 Compartment, 8½"	15.00	20.00	26.00
Relish, 3 Compartment, 11½"	18.00	24.00	30.00
Salt & Pepper, Footed, pr.	40.00	58.00	75.00
Sauce Boat	30.00	45.00	45.00
Soup, 7"	8.00	12.00	16.00
Sugar & Cover, Footed (No. 2375½)	25.00	32.00	40.00
Sugar	10.00	15.00	20.00
Sugar, Footed	15.00	20.00	25.00
Sugar, Tea	15.00	20.00	25.00
Sugar, Tea, Footed (No. 2375½)	15.00	20.00	25.00
Sweetmeat, 2 Handled	12.00	16.00	20.00

FANCY COLONIAL, NO. 582

Date: 1920s

Manufacturer: Imperial Glass Corporation, Bellaire, OH

Colors: Crystal, Rose Marie (pink), Rubigold, Green, Blue-green

A fairly extensive tableware line with a rather complete stem line included. To help identify the bowls, nappies are shown as having flat bottoms while berries and nut bowls have a small ring foot. Catalog illustrations indicate that all tumblers have ground bottoms. Other colors are priced the same as Rose Marie.

Fancy Colonial Catalog Page

	Crystal	Rose Marie
Berry, 2 Handled, 7½"	$12.00	$25.00
Berry, 4½" or 5"	6.00	9.00
Berry, 7"	8.00	15.00
Berry, 9"	10.00	20.00
Bonbon, Handled, 5½"		
(1 handled jelly)	10.00	18.00
Bowl, Footed, 2 Handled, 5"	14.00	20.00
Bowl, Footed, 4" or 5¼"	15.00	22.00
Bowl, Footed, 6½"	17.00	24.00
Bowl, Nut or Lily, 5" or 6"	6.00	20.00
Bowl, Nut or Lily, 7"	8.00	18.00
Bowl, Nut or Lily, 8"	9.00	18.00
Burgundy, 4 oz.	12.00	45.00
Butter & Cover.	35.00	95.00
Butter, Table, & Cover, 5¼"		
(small)	25.00	35.00
Café Parfait.	12.00	17.00
Celery Tray, 12"	15.00	25.00
Champagne, 6 oz.	14.00	45.00
Claret, 5 oz.	12.00	20.00
Cocktail or Tall Ice Cream, 4½ oz. .	10.00	15.00
Cocktail, 3 oz.	10.00	15.00
Cordial, 1 oz.	15.00	50.00
Cream (for table set—flat)	20.00	40.00
Cream, Footed	15.00	22.00
Custard (low punch cup)	7.00	15.00
Egg Cup	10.00	15.00
Goblet, 8 oz.	14.00	22.00
Goblet, 10 oz.	14.00	40.00
Iced Tea, 12 oz.	10.00	18.00
Iced Tea, 14 oz.	10.00	18.00
Jelly, Footed, 4¾"	15.00	22.00
Jug, 3 Pint	40.00	80.00
Mayonnaise, 5" (tapered sides)	8.00	15.00
Nappy, 3½"	5.00	8.00
Nappy, 4½" or 5"	6.00	12.00
Nappy, 6" or 7"	8.00	15.00
Nappy, 8"	10.00	18.00
Oil & Stopper, 5½ oz.		
(tall tapered)	25.00	50.00

	Crystal	Rose Marie
Oil & Stopper, 6¼ oz.		
(round base)	25.00	50.00
Olive, Handled, 5"		
(1 handled jelly)	10.00	15.00
Pickle Tray, Oval, 8"	10.00	18.00
Plate, 5¾"	5.00	8.00
Plate, Cake, 10½"	15.00	35.00
Plate, Mayonnaise	6.00	12.00
Plate, Salad, 7½"	6.00	18.00
Port, 3 oz.	12.00	20.00.
Punch Cup	7.00	15.00
Salad, 8" (tapered sides)	10.00	18.00
Salt & Pepper, pr.	25.00	38.00
Salt, Handled Table (salt dip)	15.00	25.00
Saucer Champagne or		
Tall Ice Cream, 6 oz.	10.00	45.00
Sherbet (3 sizes)	8.00	40.00
Spoon Tray, Oval, 8"	12.00	20.00
Spoon.	20.00	40.00
Sugar & Cover		
(for table set—flat)	30.00	48.00
Sugar, Footed	15.00	22.00
Tumbler, 4 oz. or 5 oz.	7.00	11.00
Tumbler, 6 oz.	8.00	15.00
Tumbler, 10 oz.	8.00	20.00
Tumbler, Bell, 8 oz.	8.00	15.00
Tumbler, Table	8.00	15.00
Vase, 8"	20.00	40.00
Vase, Rose, 10" (ruffled top)	20.00	40.00
Water Bottle	24.00	50.00
Whiskey, 2 oz.	7.00	11.00
Wine, 2 oz.	12.00	20.00

HERMITAGE, NO. 2449

THE GLASS OF FASHION

8 A. M. JUNE MORNING

Nothing so befits a fresh spring morning as a breakfast service of sparkling Fostoria. This quaint pattern, the "Hermitage," is derived from the "thumb-print" designs of our colonial days. It is *particularly* in vogue just at the minute. As smart for luncheon as it is for breakfast, and it comes in 6 lovely colors. The flower-bowl (shown above) lends a gay touch to the table, but may be used separately to add new beauty to *any* room. You'll be pleasantly surprised to learn how modestly "Hermitage" is priced.

8 P. M. JUNE EVENING

And on those balmy spring evenings, when the tinkle of ice is music to the ears, you'll want to serve drinks in the glasses shown above. It's the same delightful "Hermitage" pattern. In high-ball size, cocktail size, "old-fashion" cocktail size, and liquor "ponies." In 6 different colors ... and *so* inexpensive you have no worries even when the party is gayer than usual. You will find Fostoria Glassware at all the better shops.

•

Hermitage 1932 Ad

Date: 1932 to 1945

Manufacturer: Fostoria Glass Co., Moundsville, WV

Colors: Crystal, Wisteria, Green, Azure, Amber, Topaz/Gold Tint. The ashtray is the only piece in Ebony.

Moderate tableware line, but made for a number of years and in several colors, adding to its interest to collectors. For items in Wisteria, add 100%.

	Crystal	Colors
Ashtray	$10.00	$15.00
Bar Bottle & Stopper, 27 oz.	35.00	
Beer Mug, Footed, 9 oz.	30.00	45.00
Beer Mug, Footed, 12 oz.	35.00	50.00
Bowl, Deep, 8"	22.00	32.00
Bowl, Flared, 10"	30.00	45.00
Bowl, Shallow, 10"	30.00	45.00
Candlesticks, 1 Light, 6", pr.	40.00	60.00
Celery, 11"	17.00	25.00
Cereal, 6"	12.00	18.00
Claret, 4 oz.	15.00	22.00
Coaster, 5⅝"	10.00	15.00
Cocktail, 4 oz.	12.00	18.00
Comport, 6"	15.00	22.00
Coupe Salad, 6½", 7½"	20.00	30.00
Cream	15.00	22.00
Cup & Saucer	17.00	25.00
Decanter & Stopper, 28 oz.	75.00	110.00
Finger Bowl, 4½"	10.00	15.00
Fruit Cocktail, 5 oz.	8.00	12.00
Fruit, 5"	8.00	12.00
Goblet	18.00	27.00
Grapefruit	28.00	40.00
Grapefruit Liner	8.00	
Ice Dish, Plate & Liner	35.00	55.00
Iced Tea, Footed, 12 oz.	18.00	27.00
Ice Tub, 6"	30.00	45.00
Jug, 3 pt.	50.00	75.00
Jug, Hall Boy	75.00	110.00
Jug, qt., Ice Lip	60.00	90.00
Mayonnaise, 5⅞"	24.00	36.00
Mustard & Cover, 3½"	32.00	48.00
Nappy, 7"	14.00	21.00
Oil & Stopper, 3 oz.	50.00	75.00
Old Fashioned Cocktail, 6 oz.	12.00	18.00
Pickle, 8"	15.00	22.00
Pitcher, 1 pt.	30.00	52.00
Plate, 6" or 7"	8.00	12.00
Plate, 8"	10.00	15.00
Plate, 9"	16.00	24.00
Plate, Mayonnaise, 7"	8.00	12.00
Plate, Salad, Crescent, 7⅜"	24.00	45.00

(continued) HERMITAGE, No. 2449

	Crystal	Colors
Plate, Sandwich, 12"	20.00	30.00
Relish, 2 part, 6"	15.00	22.00
Relish, 3 part, 7¼"	18.00	27.00
Salt & Pepper, 3¾", pr.	35.00	50.00
Salt, Individual (salt dip)	10.00	15.00
Salver, 11"	40.00	85.00
Sherbet, High Footed, 5½ oz.	10.00	15.00
Sherbet, Low, 7 oz.	9.00	12.00
Soup, 7"	15.00	22.00
Sugar	15.00	22.00

	Crystal	Colors
Tray, Condiment, 6½"	20.00	28.00
Tumbler, 5 oz.	12.00	18.00
Tumbler, 9 oz.	14.00	21.00
Tumbler, 13 oz.	16.00	24.00
Tumbler, Bar, 2 oz.	15.00	22.00.
Tumbler, Bar, Footed, 2 oz.	18.00	27.00
Tumbler, Footed, 5 oz.	15.00	22.00
Tumbler, Footed, 12 oz.	20.00	30.00
Vase, 6"	35.00	50.00

LAFAYETTE, No. 2440

Date: 1931 to 1960

Manufacturer: Fostoria Glass Co., Moundsville, WV

Colors: Crystal, Wisteria, Rose, Green, Amber, Topaz/Gold Tint in the 1930s and early 1940s. Some pieces in Regal Blue, Burgundy, Empire Green and Ruby.

A moderate length line of tableware, but made for a long period of time. For Wisteria add 100% + to crystal prices.

	Crystal	Colors
Almond, Individual	$10.00	$15.00
Baker, Oval, 10"	15.00	25.00
Bonbon, Handled, 5"	12.00	15.00
Bowl, "B", 10"	15.00	28.00
Bowl, "D", 7"	15.00	28.00
Bowl, Salad, 12"	22.00	35.00
Celery, 11½"	18.00	22.00
Cereal, 6"	9.00	15.00
Cream	15.00	18.00
Cream Soup	15.00	22.00
Cup & Saucer	15.00	18.00
Cup & Saucer, After Dinner	18.00	22.00
Dish, Sauce, Oval, 2 Handled, 6½"	16.00	20.00
Fruit, 5"	8.00	10.00
Lemon, Handled, 5"	15.00	18.00
Mayonnaise, 2 part, Handled, 6½"	18.00	22.00
Olive, 6½"	12.00	15.00
Pickle, 8½"	12.00	15.00
Plate, 6" or 7"	7.00	9.00
Plate, 8"	10.00	12.00
Plate, 9"	18.00	22.00
Plate, 10"	20.00	30.00

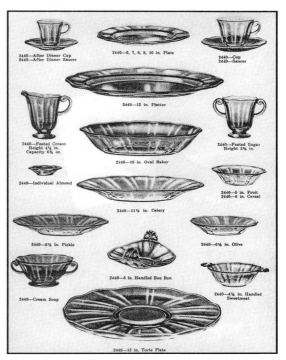

Lafayette Catalog Page

	Crystal	Colors
Plate, Oval, Cake, 2 Handled, 10½"	22.00	37.00
Plate, Torte, 13"	25.00	32.00
Platter, 12"	24.00	30.00
Relish, Handled, 2 part, 6½"	18.00	22.00
Relish, Handled, 3 part, 7½"	20.00	25.00
Sugar	15.00	18.00
Sweetmeat, Handled, 4½"	15.00	18.00
Tray, Oval, 2 Handled, 8½"	20.00	25.00

MARTHA WASHINGTON

Date: Ca. 1930s

Manufacturer: Cambridge Glass Co., Cambridge, OH

Colors: Crystal, Carmen, Royal Blue. Some items in Milk Glass, Heatherbloom, Forest Green (deep yellow green) and Emerald (light green).

Some pieces were made from the 1930s until the factory closed. Because of this, not all pieces were made in colors. Extensive variety of pieces made with several types of tumblers and stemware. The factory used at least two other names for this pattern: Victorian and Heirloom.

Martha Washington Ad
Ca. 1953 When It Was Called Heirloom

	Crystal	Carmen, Royal Blue
Bowl, 8½" (No. 27)	$12.00	$42.00
Bowl, 9" (No. 4)	18.00	45.00
Bowl, 2 Handled, 9½" (No. 12) . .	18.00	45.00
Bowl, 10" (No. 28)	18.00	45.00
Bowl, 10" (No. 6)	18.00	45.00
Bowl, 10½" (No. 25)	15.00	50.00
Bowl, 10½" (No. 5)	18.00	55.00
Bowl, Low Console, 12½" (No. 7) . .	18.00	45.00
Bowl, 12½" (No. 8)	18.00	45.00
Bowl, Low Console, 13" (No. 11) . .	18.00	45.00
Bowl, 13½" (No. 26)	15.00	50.00
Bowl, 7½" (No. 13)	15.00	40.00
Bowl, Cupped, 10" (No. 6)	15.00	45.00
Candlesticks, 3½", pr. (No. 5000/67)	45.00	
Candlesticks, 4", pr.	30.00	65.00
Candlesticks, 10", pr. (No. 3)	60.00	150.00

	Crystal	Carmen, Royal Blue
Candy Box & Cover (No. 5000/165)	30.00	
Candy Box & Cover, 3 Compartment, 7½" (No. 43)	27.00	90.00
Candy Jar & Cover, 1 lb., also Urn & Cover (No. 41)	40.00	110.00
Celery & Relish, Oval, 3 Compartment, 10" (No. 5000/126)	18.00	
Cheese & Cracker, 11", 2 pcs. (No. 66)	28.00	60.00
Cocktail, 3½ oz. (No. 61)	7.00	22.00
Comport (No. 5000/136)	16.00	
Comport, 5½" (No. 10)	9.00	30.00
Comport, 5½" (No. 15)	10.00	28.00
Comport, 6" (No. 1400)	10.00	27.00
Coupe Salad or Jug Coaster, 7½" (No. 22)	8.00	24.00

(continued) MARTHA WASHINGTON

	Crystal	Carmen, Royal Blue
Cream, Footed, Tall (No. 1).	12.00	35.00
Cream, Low (No. 14)	10.00	28.00
Cream, Low Footed (No. 19).	15.00	40.00
Cream (No. 5000/41)	12.00	
Cream, Individual	10.00	
Cup & Saucer.	10.00	25.00
Finger Bowl (No. 52)	5.00	18.00
Fruit Salad, Sherbet, 7 oz. (No. 47).	7.00	17.00
Fruit Saucer, Nappy, 5¼" (No. 57).	5.00	14.00
Goblet, 9 oz. (No. 34).	8.00	28.00
Goblet, 10 oz. (No. 51).	9.00	25.00
Ice Tub, Tab Handles, 6½" (No. 58).	20.00	75.00
Jug, 32 oz. (No. 5000/79)	45.00	
Jug, 80 oz. (No. 30)	48.00	130.00
Juice, Tomato or Orange, Footed, 5 oz. (No. 46)	7.00	17.00
Lustre & Prisms, 10", pr. (10" Candlesticks) (No. 1269). .	65.00	225.00
Mayonnaise or Low Footed Comport (No. 5000/127)	15.00	
Oil or Vinegar & Stopper (No. 5000/100)	25.00	
Oyster Cocktail, 4½ oz. (No. 60) .	7.00	20.00
Plate, 12½" (No. 23).	15.00	35.00
Plate, Bread & Butter, 6⅜" (No. 20).	4.00	12.00
Plate, Dinner, 9½"	12.00	
Plate, Finger Bowl (No. 53)	5.00	10.00
Plate, Rolled Edge, 13" (No. 5000/32)	20.00	
Plate, Salad, 8¼" (No. 21).	7.00	18.00
Plate, Sandwich, 11½" (No. 44) . .	18.00	45.00
Relish, 3 Compartment, 7" (No. 5000/124)	14.00	
Salt & Pepper, pr. (No. 5000/76). .	18.00	
Sherbet, Footed, 5 oz. (No. 59) . . .	6.00	18.00
Sherbet, Tall, 7 oz. (No. 45).	8.00	25.00
Stein, 8 oz. (No. 54)	18.00	45.00
Stein, 10 oz. (No. 55)	18.00	45.00
Stein, 12 oz. (No. 56)	20.00	45.00
Sugar, Footed, Tall (No. 1).	12.00	35.00
Sugar, Low (No. 14)	10.00	28.00
Sugar, Low Footed (No. 19).	15.00	40.00
Sugar (No. 5000/41)	12.00	
Sugar, Individual.	10.00	
Tumbler, Barrel Shape, Footed, 8 oz. (No. 48)	9.00	18.00

	Crystal	Carmen, Royal Blue
Tumbler, Tall, Footed, 10 oz. (No. 35).	8.00	24.00
Tumbler, Barrel Shape, Footed, 10 oz. (No. 49).	9.00	18.00
Tumbler, Barrel Shape, Footed, 12 oz. (No. 50).	9.00	20.00
Urn & Cover, 9½" (No. 41)	35.00	130.00
Urn & Cover, 10" (No. 39)	35.00	130.00
Urn & Cover, 14½" (No. 40)	45.00	175.00
Vase, Fan, 7½" (No. 17)	16.00	75.00
Vase, Footed, 11" or 12" (No. 18).	38.00	100.00
Vase, Sweet Pea, 10" (No. 16)	38.00	100.00

STEMWARE AND TUMBLERS:

No. 1400 stems have barrel-shaped bowls while No. 1401 have cone-shaped bowls. No. 1203 and 1204 tumblers are flat, not footed.

	Crystal	Carmen, Royal Blue
Cocktail, 3½ oz. (No. 1400)	$6.00	$24.00
Cordial, 1 oz. (No. 1400)	16.00	50.00
Goblet, 10 oz. (No. 1400).	8.00	25.00
Sherbet, 5½ oz. (No. 1400)	6.00	20.00
Sherbet, Low, 7 oz. (No. 1400) . . .	6.00	24.00
Sherbet, Tall, 7 oz. (No. 1400). . . .	6.00	20.00
Tumbler, Footed, 5 oz. (No. 1400).	6.00	20.00
Tumbler, Footed, 12 oz. (No. 1400).	8.00	22.00
Wine, 2 oz. (No. 1400).	8.00	24.00
Claret, 4½ oz. (No. 1401).	8.00	22.00
Cocktail, 3 oz. (No. 1401).	7.00	20.00
Cordial, 1 oz. (No. 1401)	17.00	55.00
Finger Bowl, (No. 1401)	5.00	18.00
Goblet, 10 oz. (No. 1401	8.00	25.00.
Sherbet, Tall 6 oz. (No. 1401)	8.00	20.00
Tumbler, Footed, 5 oz. (No. 1401).	7.00	20.00
Tumbler, Footed, 10 oz. (No. 1401)	8.00	20.00
Wine, 3 oz. (No. 1401).	9.00	22.00
Old Fashioned Cocktail, 7 oz. (No. 1203).	5.00	15.00
Tumbler, 2½ oz. (No. 1203)	5.00	15.00
Tumbler, 5 oz. (No. 1203).	5.00	15.00
Tumbler, 8 oz. (No. 1203).	5.00	15.00
Tumbler, 10 oz. (No. 1203).	5.00	15.00
Tumbler, 12 oz. (No. 1203).	5.00	15.00
Tumbler, 14 oz. (No. 1203).	5.00	15.00
Ginger Ale, Hollow Stem, 6 oz. (No. 1204).	8.00	
Tumbler, 14 oz. (No. 1204).	5.00	15.00

OCTAGON, NO. 1231

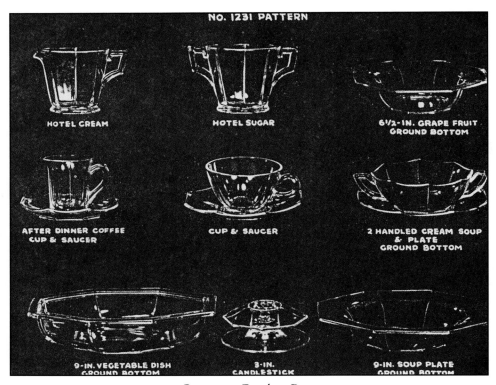

NO. 1231 PATTERN

HOTEL CREAM | HOTEL SUGAR | 6½-IN. GRAPE FRUIT GROUND BOTTOM

AFTER DINNER COFFEE CUP & SAUCER | CUP & SAUCER | 2 HANDLED CREAM SOUP & PLATE GROUND BOTTOM

9-IN. VEGETABLE DISH GROUND BOTTOM | 3-IN. CANDLESTICK | 9-IN. SOUP PLATE GROUND BOTTOM

Octagon Catalog Page

Date: 1925 to 1936

Manufacturer: A. H. Heisey & Co., Newark, OH

Colors: Crystal, Flamingo, Moongleam, Hawthorne

Some, but not all, pieces are marked with the Diamond H. The rum pot is found in Crystal, Moongleam, Flamingo, Sahara ($1,600.00+) and Cobalt ($1,800.00+). If complete with stoppers, values are greater. Heisey made patterns called No. 500 Octagon and No. 1229 Octagon, but they do not include a luncheon set and are not included in No. 1231 Octagon.

	Crystal	Moongleam, Flamingo		Crystal	Moongleam, Flamingo
Bowl, Salad, 12½"	$27.00	$35.00	Plate, 6"	10.00	18.00
Candlesticks, 3", pr.	40.00	75.00	Plate, 7"	10.00	18.00
Celery Tray, 9"	14.00	25.00	Plate, 8"	12.00	22.00
Celery Tray, 12"	16.00	30.00	Plate, 10½"	45.00	70.00
Cream Soup, 2 Handled	16.00	27.00	Plate 14"	35.00	50.00
Cream, Hotel	17.00	32.00	Plate, Soup, 9" (bowl)	17.00	28.00
Cup & Saucer	18.00	32.00	Platter, Oval, 12¾"	20.00	38.00
Cup & Saucer, After Dinner Coffee	24.00	45.00	Rum Pot	500.00+	1,400.00+
Dish, Vegetable, 9"	17.00	26.00	Sandwich Plate, Center Handled, 10½"	27.00	45.00
Grapefruit, 6½"	12.00	17.00	Sugar, Hotel	17.00	32.00

OCTAGON

Date: 1930s

Manufacturer: Imperial Glass Corporation, Bellaire, OH

Colors: Crystal, Rose Pink, Green

Called Molly by Hazel Marie Weatherman. The primary pattern number was No. 725, but Imperial grouped many pieces with other numbers together in this pattern, especially No. 727. Prices are for pieces in crystal, add 50% to 75% for colors.

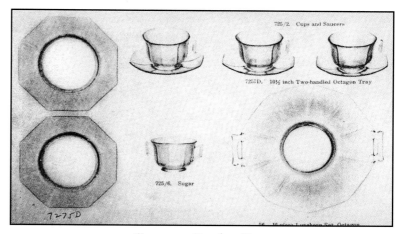

Octagon Catalog Page

Bell, (metal clapper) $15.00	Dish, Preserve, 3 Legs, 7½" 16.00
Bouillon Cup & Plate 18.00	Dish, Muffin, 12" 12.00
Bowl, Bulb, Round, 8" 10.00	Goblet, 9 oz. 8.00
Bowl, Fruit, 8½" 12.00	Ice Tub 24.00
Bowl, Oval, 8" or 10" 15.00	Ladle, Mayonnaise 10.00
Bowl, Nut, 8½" 12.00	Marmalade & Cover. 12.00
Bowl, Console, 11" 15.00	Mayonnaise, Footed, Flared 12.00
Bowl, Console, Cupped (with base) 22.00	Mayonnaise, Footed, Rolled Edge 12.00
Bowl, Flower, 11" 12.00	Mayonnaise, Oval 10.00
Bowl, Center, 13" (2 styles) 20.00	Mayonnaise, Round 10.00
Cake Plate, 12" 12.00	Mayonnaise, 2 Handled (flat) 10.00
Candlesticks, pr. (top flange, 2 styles) 20.00	Nut Box & Cover, 6¼" 18.00
Candlesticks, (Footed) pr. 15.00	Nut Box, 3 Compartment, & Cover, 6¼" 18.00
Candy Box & Cover, 5¾" 15.00	Pitcher, ½ gal. 25.00
Candy Box & Cover, Footed, 5¾" (hexagonal) 18.00	Plate, Mayonnaise (2 styles) 8.00
Casserole & Cover, 8" 15.00	Plate, Salad, 8" 8.00
Cheese & Cracker, 2 pcs., 10" Oval 20.00	Plate, Oval, 9½" 12.00
Cheese & Cracker, 2 pcs., Handled. 20.00	Plate, Oval, 11" 15.00
Comport, 10½" 12.00	Rose Bowl, 7" 15.00
Comport & Cover, 6¼" 16.00	Salt & Pepper, pr. 12.00
Coupe Soup, 7" 8.00	Sugar 10.00
Cream 10.00	Sugar, Tall 10.00
Cream Soup, Covered, with Underplate 25.00	Tray for Cream & Sugar 10.00
Cream, Tall 10.00	Tray, Bonbon, 7½" (center handled—heart) 15.00
Cup & Saucer 15.00	Tray, Mint, 8½" (center handled—heart) 16.00
Cup & Saucer, After Dinner. 18.00	Tray, 2 Handled, 10½" 15.00
Dish, 3 Legs, 8" 16.00	Tray, Fruit, 11" (center handled—heart) 17.00
Dish & Cover, 3 Legs, 6½" 20.00	Tray, Sandwich, 12" (center handled—heart). 17.00
Dish, Olive, 2 Handled, 4¾" 10.00	

PETALWARE

Petalware Large Plate, Salad Plate, Cup & Saucer,
Sugar & Cream, Gold Trim

Date: 1930 to 1940

Manufacturer: MacBeth-Evans Glass Co., Charleroi, PA

Colors: Monax, Cremax, Pink, Deep Blue, Crystal. Various enameled colors as decoration.

Crystal is 50% of pink. Cremax is 75% of Monax. For decorated Monax or Cremax, add 50% to plain prices.

Petalware Plates
with Handpainted Cherries and Plums

	Pink	Monax
Bowl, Cream Soup, 4½"	$20.00	$12.00
Bowl, 5¾"	15.00	10.00
Bowl, 7"		75.00
Bowl, 8¾"	25.00	27.00
Cup & Saucer *(Illus.)*.	14.00	9.00
Cream *(Illus.)*	18.00	12.00
Lamp Shade (various sizes).	15.00 to	28.00
Plate, 6" *(Illus.)*	6.00	3.00
Plate, 8"	9.00	6.00
Plate, 9" *(Illus.)*	21.00	10.00
Plate, 11"	24.00	12.00
Plate, 12"		20.00
Platter, 13"	30.00	20.00
Sherbet	12.00	9.00
Sugar *(Illus.)*	15.00	11.00

RALEIGH, NO. 2574

Date: 1939 to 1966

Manufacturer: Fostoria Glass Co., Moundsville, WV

Colors: Crystal

A moderate length pattern, but popular for a long period of time.

Bonbon, 2 Handled, 5"	$15.00
Bowl, Flared, 12"	24.00
Bowl, Fruit, 13"	24.00
Bowl, Handled, 9½"	18.00
Cake Plate, 10"	17.00
Candlesticks, 1 Light, 4", pr.	20.00
Candlesticks, Duo, 2 Light, 5¼" pr.	25.00
Celery, 10½"	15.00
Comport, 5"	10.00
Cream	12.00
Cream, Individual	15.00
Cup & Saucer	15.00
Dish, Serving, 2 Handled, 8½"	20.00
Ice Tub	20.00
Lemon, 2 Handled, 6½"	10.00
Mayonnaise, 4¾"	25.00
Oil & Stopper, 4¼ oz.	20.00
Olive, 6"	9.00
Pickle, 8"	12.00
Plate, 6" or 7"	7.00
Plate, 8"	9.00
Plate, Mayonnaise, 7¼"	9.00
Plate, Torte, 14"	22.00
Relish, 3 Part, 7" x 10"	18.00
Salt & Pepper, 2⅝", pr.	25.00
Sugar	12.00
Sugar, Individual	15.00
Sweetmeat, 2 Handled, 5¼"	10.00
Tray for Cream & Sugar	12.00
Tray, Muffin, Handled	18.00
Whipped Cream, 2 Handled, 5"	10.00

Raleigh Catalog Page

RIBBON

Ribbon Candy & Cover

Date: Early 1930s

Manufacturer: Hazel-Atlas Glass Co.,

Colors: Green. Limited production in Black, Crystal and Pink.

For Black add 25%. Prices for Pink are the same as Green; for Crystal, deduct 25%.

	Green
Bowl, 4"	$22.00
Bowl, 8"	32.00
Candy & Cover *(Illus.)*	40.00
Cream	17.00
Cup & Saucer	10.00
Plate, 6¼"	4.00
Plate, 8"	7.00
Salt & Pepper, pr	35.00
Sherbet	7.00
Sugar	17.00
Tumbler, 10 oz.	30.00

SIERRA

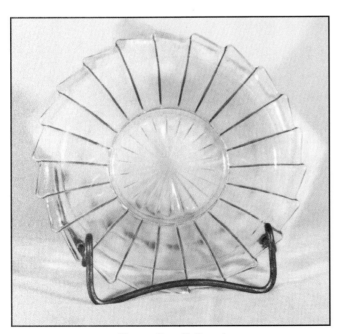

Sierra Small Bowl

Date: 1931 to 1933

Manufacturer: Jeannette Glass Co., Jeannette, PA

Colors: Green, Pink

	Green	Pink
Bowl, 5½" *(Illus.)*	$17.00	$15.00
Bowl, 8½"	70.00	65.00
Bowl, Oval, Vegetable, 9¼"	100.00	95.00.
Butter & Cover	90.00	85.00
Cup & Saucer	24.00	20.00
Pitcher, 32 oz.	135.00	115.00
Plate, 9"	27.00	22.00
Platter, 11"	57.00	48.00
Salt & Pepper, pr.	58.00	55.00
Sugar & Cover	52.00	42.00
Tray, 2 Handled, 10¼"	27.00	25.00
Tumbler, Footed, 9 oz.	82.00	67.00

SQUARE, NO. 760

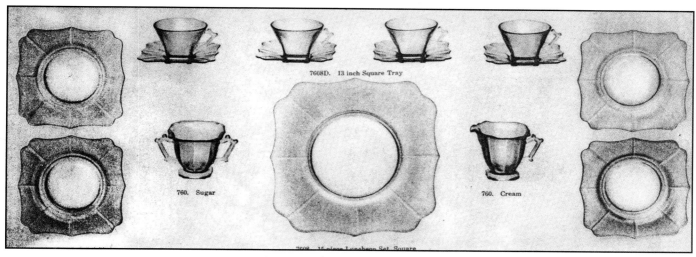

Square Catalog Page

Date: 1930s

Manufacturer: Imperial Glass Corporation, Bellaire, OH

Colors: Crystal

Made in a luncheon set.

Cream	$10.00
Cup & Saucer	15.00
Plate, Salad, 8"	8.00
Sugar	10.00
Tray, 13"	15.00

TEA ROOM, NO. 600

Date: 1926 to 1931

Manufacturer: Indiana Glass Co.,

Colors: Amber, Green, Pink. Limited production in Crystal.

Because of its Art Deco motif, there is considerable collector interest in this pattern. A rather extensive pattern for true Depression Glass. Design patent 76986 granted to this pattern.

Tea Room Catalog Page

107

TEA ROOM, No. 600 *(continued)*

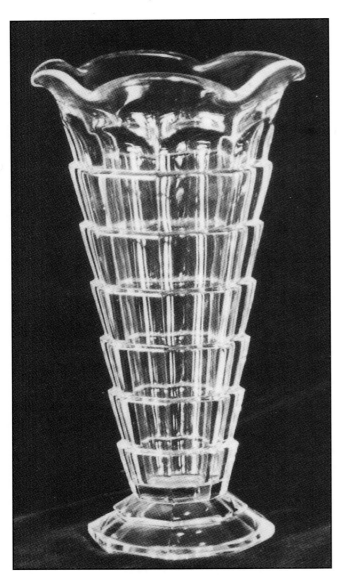

Tea Room Vase with Ruffled Top

	Crystal	Green	Pink
Banana Split Dish, 7½" (2 styles)	$34.00	$95.00	$90.00
Bowl, 8¾"	70.00	90.00	85.00
Bowl, Oval, Vegetable, 9½"	50.00	78.00	67.00
Candlesticks, pr	80.00	100.00	100.00
Celery, 8½"	24.00	38.00	38.00
Cream, 3¼"	20.00	25.00	25.00
Cream, 4½"	20.00	25.00	25.00
Cream, Rectangular	22.00	32.00	32.00
Cup & Saucer	48.00	90.00	65.00
Finger Bowl	40.00	57.00	65.00
Goblet, 9 oz.	50.00	90.00	80.00
Ice Bucket	55.00	85.00	85.00
Iced Tea, Footed, 11 oz.	42.00	70.00	65.00
Iced Tea, Footed, 12 oz.		80.00	75.00
Juice, Footed, 6 oz.	27.00	55.00	50.00
Lamp, 9"	50.00	85.00	85.00
Mustard & Cover	105.00	170.00	185.00
Parfait	55.00	85.00	85.00
Pitcher, 64 oz.	500.00+	180.00	180.00
Plate, 6½"	25.00	30.00	30.00
Plate, 8¼"	30.00	38.00	36.00
Plate, Handled, 10½"	45.00	75.00	70.00
Relish, Divided	20.00	27.00	27.00
Salt & Pepper, pr	45.00	85.00	70.00
Sherbet	24.00	30.00	27.00
Sherbet, Flared	22.00	30.00	28.00
Sherbet, Tall	32.00	40.00	40.00
Sugar & Cover	130.00	200.00	170.00
Sugar & Cover, Footed, 3"	90.00	165.00	135.00
Sugar, Footed, 4½"	14.00	20.00	18.00
Sugar, Rectangular	20.00	30.00	30.00
Sundae, Footed, Crimped	55.00	100.00	95.00
Tray, Center Handle		210.00	200.00
Tray, Rectangular, for Cream and Sugar		77.00	65.00
Tumbler, 8½ oz.	175.00+	150.00	125.00
Tumbler, Footed, 9 oz.	35.00	55.00	55.00
Vase, 9½"	35.00	77.00	70.00
Vase, 11"	95.00	135.00	125.00
Vase, Ruffled Top, 5"			250.00
Vase, Ruffled Top, 6½"		125.00	155.00
Vase, Ruffled Top, 9½" *(Illus.)*	45.00	80.00	90.00
Vase, Ruffled Top, 11"	110.00	215.00	300.00

VICTORY

Date: 1929 to 1932

Manufacturer: Diamond Glass-Ware Co. Indiana, PA

Colors: Amber, Pink, Black, Green, Ritz Blue, Amethyst

	Pastels	Black, Cobalt Blue
Bonbon, 7"	$12.00	$22.00
Bowl, 6½"	12.00	28.00
Bowl, 8½"	22.00	48.00
Bowl, 12½"	32.00	70.00
Bowl, Console, 12"	35.00	70.00
Bowl, Oval, Vegetable, 9"	35.00	90.00
Bowl, Rolled Edge, 11"	30.00	55.00
Candlesticks, 3", pr.	32.00	100.00
Cheese & Cracker, 2 pcs.	42.00	
Comport, 6"	18.00	
Cream	18.00	48.00
Cup & Saucer	15.00	50.00
Goblet, 7 oz.	20.00	
Gravy Boat & Underplate	180.00	330.00
Mayonnaise Set, 3 pcs.	45.00	110.00
Plate, 6"	6.00	15.00
Plate, 7"	7.00	20.00
Plate, 8"	8.00	32.00
Plate, 9"	20.00	45.00
Platter, 12"	30.00	75.00
Sandwich, Center Handle	30.00	75.00
Sherbet	15.00	28.00
Sugar	18.00	48.00

Victory 1929 Ad

Chapter 8
HOBNAILS & BEADS

AMERICAN PIONEER

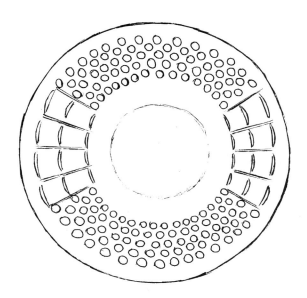

American Pioneer Plate

Date: 1931 to 1934

Manufacturer: Liberty Glass Works, Egg Harbor, NJ

Colors: Pink, Green, Crystal. Limited availability in Amber.

This pattern differs from most Hobnail patterns in that it has panels of plain ribs between sections of hobnails.

	Crystal	Green	Pink
Bar Glass (whiskey), 2 oz.	$35.00	$45.00	$55.00
Bowl, Handled, 5"	12.00	18.00	15.00
Bowl, Handled, 9"	20.00	35.00	22.00
Bowl & Cover, 8¾"	42.00	110.00	90.00
Candlesticks, pr., 6½"	60.00	90.00	70.00
Candy Jar & Cover, 1 lb.	60.00	95.00	70.00
Candy Jar & Cover, 1½ lb.	70.00	120.00	90.00
Coaster, 3½"	20.00	25.00	28.00
Cream, 2¾"	20.00	20.00	20.00
Cream, 3½"	20.00	20.00	20.00
Cup & Saucer	15.00	20.00	16.00
Dresser set: Tray, 7½",			
Powder Box, 2 Colognes		300.00	270.00
Goblet, 8 oz.	30.00	45.00	40.00
Ice Bucket, 6"	35.00	55.00	45.00
Iced Tea, 12 oz.	30.00	45.00	38.00
Juice, 5 oz.	20.00	30.00	28.00
Lamp, Low Round Style, 5½".	60.00	110.00	95.00
Lamp, Tall, 8½"	95.00	145.00	120.00
Mayonnaise, Footed, 4"	40.00	90.00	70.00
Pitcher & Cover, 5"	135.00	165.00	150.00
Pitcher & Cover, 7"	135.00	210.00	170.00
Plate, 6"	10.00	15.00	12.00
Plate, 8" *(Illus.)*	8.00	12.00	10.00
Plate, Handled, 6"	10.00	15.00	12.00
Plate, Handled, 11½"	17.00	20.00	20.00
Sherbet, 3½" (low)	12.00	18.00	16.00
Sherbet, 4½" (tall)	15.00	40.00	30.00
Sugar, 2¾"	20.00	23.00	22.00
Sugar, 3½"	20.00	23.00	22.00
Tumbler, 8 oz.	20.00	40.00	25.00
Vase, 7" (3 types)	47.00	110.00	70.00
Wine, 3 oz.	25.00	38.00	48.00

COLUMBIA

Date: 1938

Manufacturer: Federal Glass Co., Columbus, OH

Colors: Crystal. Limited items in pink.

Columbia is the original name used by Federal Glass for this pattern. Prices listed are for pieces in Crystal. For Pink, add 100% to 150%.

Bowl, Cereal, 5"	$20.00
Bowl, Soup, 8"	24.00
Bowl, Salad, 8½"	24.00
Bowl, Crimped Rim, 10½" *(Illus.)*	25.00
Butter & Cover	24.00
Cup & Saucer	12.00
Plate, 11½"	12.00
Plate, Bread & Butter, 6"	3.50
Plate, Luncheon, 9½"	9.00
Tumbler, 4"	30.00

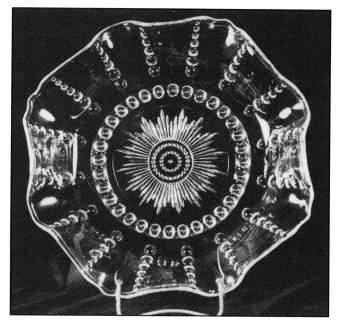

Columbia 10½" Bowl, Crimped Rim

EARLY AMERICAN HOBNAIL, NO. 741, 742

Date: 1931

Manufacturer: Imperial Glass Corporation, Bellaire, OH

Colors: Crystal, Ruby, Ritz Blue, Stiegel, Amber, Imperial Green, Rose Pink, Moonstone (Crystal Opalescent at edges), Harding Blue (Opalescent Blue). Not all items were listed in all colors in catalogs. For opalescent colors, add 10%.

Early American Hobnail is the original Imperial name for this pattern and piece names are taken from original factory material. Prices are for items in color. Crystal items are from 25% to 50% less.

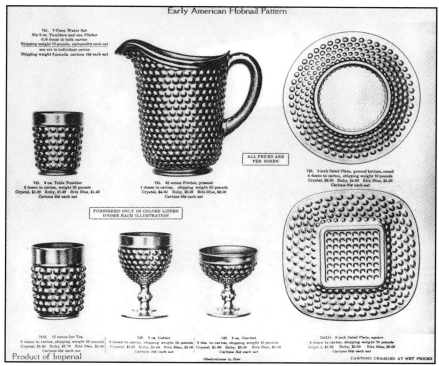

Early American Hobnail Catalog Page

EARLY AMERICAN HOBNAIL, NO. 741, 742 (continued)

Early American Hobnail Powder Box

Cologne & Stopper $45.00
Compote, 7" 20.00
Goblet, 9 oz. 15.00
Iced Tea, 12 oz. 12.00
Ivy Ball, Blown, with Chain 40.00
Ivy Ball, Footed 30.00
Nappy, Square, 7" 20.00
Pitcher, 55 oz. 45.00
Pitcher, Blown, ½ Gal. 70.00
Pitcher, Square Top 55.00
Plate, Salad, Round or Square, 8" 15.00
Powder Box & Cover (*Illus.*) 40.00
Salver, Square, 4 Toed, 10" 45.00
Sherbet, 9 oz. 15.00
Tumbler, Table, 9 oz. 20.00
Tumbler, Table, 10 oz. 23.00
Vase, Flip, 8" 35.00

HOBNAIL, NO. 118, NO. 118½

Hobnail Catalog Page

Date: 1930

Manufacturer: Duncan & Miller Glass Co., Washington, PA

Colors: Clear, Amber, Green, Rose, Ruby, Cape Cod Blue (Opalescent Blue), Cranberry Pink (Opalescent Pink)

Reproductions: U. S. Glass/Tiffin continued to make many items in Hobnail at their Glassport, PA factory in Milk Glass, Wisteria and other colors.

Extensive tableware line. Duncan & Miller made Hobnail (original name) until they closed their plant in 1955. Piece names are taken from original factory material. Prices given are for Crystal pieces. For Green & Rose add 25%. For Ruby add 50%. For Opalescent colors add 100% or more.

Ashtray, 3" $5.00
Basket, Candy, Handled, 5" 22.00
Basket, Candy, Handled, 7" 25.00
Basket, Crimped, Handled, 10" 45.00
Basket, Oval, Footed, 2 Handled, 6" 15.00
Basket, Oval, Handled, 12" 65.00
Basket, Square, 10" 65.00
Basket, Tall, Handled, 10" tall 35.00
Bonbon, Heart Shape, Handled, 5" 12.00
Bonbon, Heart Shape, Handled, 6" 15.00
Bonbon, Diamond Shape, Footed, Handled, 6" 10.00
Bowl, Center Piece, Crimped, 12" 25.00
Bowl, Center Piece, Flared, 11½" 25.00
Bowl, Crimped, 9" 20.00

(continued) HOBNAIL, NO. 118, NO. 118½

Bowl, Crimped, 2 Handled, 10"	25.00
Bowl, Fruit, Oval, 2 Handled, 10"	25.00
Bowl, Fruit, Square, 10"	30.00
Bowl, Oval, 10"	20.00
Bowl, Oval, 12"	25.00
Bowl, Oval, Crimped, 12"	25.00
Bowl, Salad, Deep, 9"	20.00
Bowl, Salad, Deep, 13"	25.00
Bowl, Salad, Shallow, 12"	22.00
Candelabra, with Prisms, 4", pr.	40.00
Candlesticks, 1 Light, 4", pr.	25.00
Celery & Relish, Oval, 2 Handled, 12"	20.00
Cheese & Cracker, 11"	30.00
Cigarette Jar & Cover, 3½"	30.00
Coaster, 3"	5.00
Cocktail, 3½ oz.	8.00
Cologne, 8 oz., 6½" tall	30.00
Comport, Crimped, 6"	15.00
Comport, Flared, 6"	10.00
Comport, Flared, Footed, Handled, 6"	15.00
Comport, Low, 6½"	15.00
Comport, Low, 8"	20.00
Comport, Low, Crimped, 6½"	15.00
Comport, Low, Crimped, 8"	20.00
Cream, Individual, 5 oz.	8.00
Cup & Saucer, Tea	12.00
Decanter & Stopper, 12 oz.	75.00
Finger Bowl, 4"	10.00
Goblet, 9 oz.	10.00
Iced Tea, Footed, 13 oz.	10.00
Iced Tea, Straight, 13 oz.	10.00
Ivy Ball, Footed, 4"	20.00
Ivy Ball, Footed, 5"	25.00
Jam Jar & Cover, 5"	25.00
Jello, Footed, 5 oz.	10.00
Jug	40.00
Jug, Flip, ½ gal.	40.00
Juice, Orange, Footed, 5 oz.	10.00
Juice, Straight, 5 oz.	8.00
Mayonnaise, Flared, Footed, 2 Handled, 5"	10.00
Mint Box & Cover, Low, ½" d.	30.00
Mint Tray, Handled, 6"	10.00
Mint Tray, Handled, 7"	15.00
Nappy Dessert, 6"	6.00
Nappy Dessert, Handled, 7"	10.00
Nappy, 2 Handled, 9"	18.00
Nappy, 2 Handled, Diamond Shape, 10"	22.00
Nappy, 6"	5.00
Nappy, 7"	6.00
Nappy, Dessert, Handled, 5"	10.00
Nappy, Dessert, Handled, 6"	12.00
Nappy, Fruit, 5"	6.00
Nappy, Handled, 5"	8.00
Nappy, Handled, 6"	10.00
Oil & Stopper, 6 oz.	25.00
Olive, Oval, Footed, Handled, 6"	10.00
Oyster Cocktail, Footed, 4 oz.	8.00
Plate, Bread & Butter, 6"	5.00
Plate, Dessert, 7½"	8.00
Plate, Finger Bowl, 6"	6.00
Plate, Flat Edge, 13"	20.00
Plate, Mayonnaise, with Ring, 6"	10.00
Plate, Rolled Edge, 13"	20.00
Plate, Rolled Edge, 16"	40.00
Plate, Salad, 8½"	8.00
Plate, Sandwich, 2 Handled, 11"	25.00
Puff Box & Cover, 4"	25.00
Punch Bowl, 10½", 1 gal.	75.00
Punch Bowl Plate, 16½"	50.00
Punch Cup, Handled, 5 oz.	8.00
Punch Ladle, 5 oz.	35.00
Relish, 2 Compartment, Handled, 6"	15.00
Relish, 3 Compartment, 2 Handled, 10"	20.00
Salt & Pepper, Small, 3", pr.	25.00
Salver, Footed, 10"	85.00
Saucer Champagne, 5 oz.	8.00
Sherbet, Footed, 5 oz.	8.00
Sherbet, Low, 6 oz.	8.00
Sugar, Individual, 5 oz.	5.00
Sweetmeat, Crimped, Footed, Handled, 6"	8.00
Top Hat, 2½"	10.00
Top Hat, 3½"	15.00
Top Hat, 6"	15.00
Top Hat, 10"	110.00
Tray, Footed, 6½"	10.00
Tray, Oval, 8"	10.00
Tumbler, Footed, 10 oz.	10.00
Tumbler, Table, 10 oz.	8.00
Vase, Crimped, 4"	15.00
Vase, Crimped, 6"	18.00
Vase, Flared, 8"	25.00
Vase, Flared, 12"	35.00
Vase, Flip, 8"	25.00
Vase, Flip, 12"	35.00
Vase, Flip, Crimped, 8"	25.00
Vase, Oval, 4½"	15.00
Vase, Violet, Footed, #1, 4"	20.00
Vase, Violet, Footed, 5"	25.00
Whiskey, 2 oz.	8.00
Wine, 3 oz.	10.00

HOBNAIL

Hobnail Cup

Date: 1934 to 1936

Manufacturer: Hocking Glass Co., Lancaster, OH

Colors: Crystal. Limited production in Pink.

Crystal pieces are sometimes decorated with red. Later some molds were reused in the Moonstone pattern.

	Crystal	Pink
Bar Glass, 1½ oz.	$9.00	$
Bowl, Cereal, 5½"	8.00	
Bowl, Salad, 7"	8.00	
Cordial, 5 oz.	10.00	
Cup & Saucer *(Illus. of cup)*	10.00	12.00
Cream, Footed	7.00	
Decanter & Ground Stopper,		
32 oz.	32.00	
Goblet, 10 oz.	10.00	

	Crystal	Pink
Iced Tea, Footed, 13 oz.	12.00	
Iced Tea, 15 oz.	12.00	
Juice, 5 oz.	7.00	
Pitcher, Milk, 18 oz.	24.00	
Pitcher, Water, 67 oz.	27.00	
Plate, Sherbet, 6" (saucer)	4.00	4.00
Plate, Luncheon, 8½"	6.00	6.00
Sherbet	4.00	6.00
Sugar, Footed	5.00	
Tumbler, 9 or 10 oz.	8.00	

HOBNAIL, NO. 250

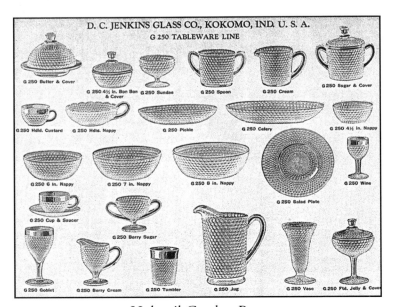

Hobnail Catalog Page

Date: Ca. 1930

Manufacturer: D. C. Jenkins Glass Co., Kokomo, IN

Colors: Crystal, Green

Jenkins referred to this pattern only by the line number. Old catalogs indicate that the design was patented. Names of pieces are taken from original factory material.

(continued) HOBNAIL, No. 250

	Crystal	Green		Crystal	Green
Bonbon & Cover, 4½"	$10.00	$15.00	Nappy, 6" or 7".	8.00	10.00
Butter & Cover.	30.00	45.00	Nappy, 8"	9.00	12.00
Celery.	22.00	36.00	Nappy, Handled (jelly)	8.00	12.00
Cream	10.00	15.00	Pickle	8.00	12.00
Cream, Berry (footed & handled) .	12.00	18.00	Plate, Salad	6.00	9.00
Cup & Saucer.	10.00	15.00	Spoon, Handled	24.00	35.00
Custard, Handled	8.00	12.00	Sugar & Cover	25.00	38.00
Goblet	8.00	12.00	Sugar, Berry (footed & handled) . .	24.00	35.00
Jelly & Cover, Footed	10.00	15.00	Sundae (sherbet)	6.00	8.00
Jug.	35.00	55.00	Vase	12.00	27.00
Nappy, 4½"	6.00	8.00	Wine	7.00	12.00

MOONSTONE

Date: 1942 to 1946

Manufacturer: Anchor Hocking Glass Corp., Lancaster, OH

Colors: Crystal opalescent. A few items in Green.

Do not confuse this pattern with Fenton's Hobnail. If you have a piece not listed here, check the Fenton listings in William Heacock's books on Fenton glass. For pieces in Green, add 50% to Crystal opalescent prices listed below.

Bonbon, Heart, 1 Handled *(Illus.)*.	$16.00
Bowl, Berry, 5½"	20.00
Bowl, Dessert, Crimped Edge, 5½".	12.00
Bowl, Handled, Crimped Edge, 6½".	16.00
Bowl, 7¾"	15.00
Bowl, Crimped Edge, 9½"	27.00
Bowl, Clover Leaf, Divided, 3 part	15.00
Candlesticks, pr..	22.00
Candy Dish & Cover	28.00
Cigarette Box & Cover.	25.00
Cream.	9.00
Cup & Saucer	18.00
Goblet, 10 oz.	25.00
Plate, Sherbet, 6¼" (saucer)	7.00
Plate, Luncheon, 8" *(Illus.)*	16.00
Plate, Sandwich, 10"	32.00
Puff Box & Cover, 4¾"	30.00
Relish, 2 part, 7¾".	12.00
Sherbet, Footed.	8.00
Sugar.	10.00
Vase, 5½"	14.00

Moonstone Plate & Heart Bonbon

RADIANCE, NO. 42

Radiance Plate, Crimped & Etched Compote,
Etched Cream

Radiance Punch
Bowl or Ball Vase

Date: Late 1936 until about 1944

Manufacturer: New Martinsville Glass Co., New Martinsville, WV

Colors: Crystal, Ruby, Amber, Ritz Blue, Ice Blue, Rose, Green. Limited availability in Canary.

Radiance was the original name of this pattern. Likewise, the following list uses original catalog names for pieces. Other pieces may have been made in the line. New Martinsville decorated Radiance blanks with etchings.

	Crystal	Pastels	Blues & Ruby
Ball Vase, 9" (punch bowl) (Illus.)	$60.00	$125.00	$210.00
Bonbon, Covered, 6"	25.00	50.00	100.00
Bonbon, Crimped, 6" (2 styles)	10.00	18.00	32.00
Bonbon, Flared, 6"	10.00	18.00	32.00
Bonbon, Footed, 6" (low footed, crimped)	11.00	20.00	35.00
Bowl, Footed (center pedestal)	22.00	32.00	55.00
Bowl, Footed, Crimped, 10"	20.00	30.00	50.00
Bowl, Footed, Crimped Edge	20.00	30.00	50.00
Bowl, Footed, Flared, 10"	20.00	30.00	50.00
Bowl, Footed, Flared Edge, 11"	15.00	25.00	45.00
Bowl, Round, Crimped, 9½"	16.00	22.00	40.00
Bowl, Round, Crimped, Deep or Shallow, 12"	22.00	32.00	55.00
Bowl, Straight, Flared or Crimped, 10"	15.00	25.00	45.00
Butter & Cover	125.00	210.00	500.00
Candlesticks, 1 light, 5¼", pr.	48.00	90.00	185.00
Candlesticks, 2 light, pr.	38.00	75.00	125.00
Candy Box & Cover, 3 Compartment	32.00	60.00	120.00
Candy Dish & Cover, 7½"	24.00	55.00	115.00
Celery, 10"	11.00	20.00	32.00
Centerpiece, Shallow Fruit or Flower, 13"	24.00	35.00	60.00
Cheese & Cracker, 2 pcs.	24.00	35.00	60.00
Comport, Footed, 5"	11.00	20.00	32.00
Compote, 6" (low footed)	15.00	24.00	37.00
Compote, Crimped, 6" (low footed) (Illus.)	15.00	24.00	37.00
Cordial, 1 oz.	20.00	30.00	45.00
Cream (Illus.)	10.00	18.00	30.00
Cup & Saucer	10.00	18.00	28.00
Jug, 4 Pint	110.00	165.00	240.00
Mayonnaise	12.00	22.00	50.00
Mint or Compote, Footed, 5"	11.00	20.00	32.00
Oil & Stopper	28.00	40.00	80.00
Pickle, 7"	10.00	18.00	28.00
Plate, 14"	22.00	50.00	95.00
Plate, Cake or Sandwich, 11"	15.00	25.00	40.00
Plate, Mayonnaise	8.00	11.00	18.00
Plate, Salad, 8¼" (Illus.)	8.00	11.00	18.00
Relish Dish, 3 Compartment, 8" x 11"	18.00	28.00	38.00
Relish, 3 Compartment (large)	18.00	28.00	38.00
Relish, 3 Compartment (small)	12.00	22.00	30.00
Salt & Pepper, pr.	32.00	60.00	100.00
Salver	20.00	30.00	45.00
Salver, Footed, 8" (low)	15.00	25.00	38.00
Sugar	10.00	18.00	30.00
Tray, for Cream & Sugar	15.00	25.00	32.00
Tumbler, 9 oz.	14.00	22.00	30.00
Vase, Crimped or Flared, 10"	22.00	50.00	70.00
Vase, Crimped or Flared, 12"	32.00	60.00	85.00

TEARDROP, NO. 301, 5301, 5300

Date: 1935 to 1955

Manufacturer: Duncan & Miller Glass Co., Washington, PA

Colors: Clear. Punch cups are available with Amber, Royal Blue (Cobalt), and Ruby handles. Rare pieces have been found in Royal Blue.

Reproductions: Many items in crystal were continued by U. S. Glass/Tiffin after its purchase of the Duncan & Miller factory in 1955. These items were made in Crystal at the Tiffin, OH, factory.

Teardrop is an extensive tableware line due to its long life. It is easily found but as with all patterns made over a long period of time, it does have its hard-to-find pieces. Teardrop is the original name, and the piece names following are from original company material.

Teardrop Plate, Champagne, Marmalade & Cover

PRESSED ITEMS, NO. 301:

Ashtray, 5"	$8.00
Ashtray, Individual, 3"	5.00
Bar Bottle with Stopper, 12"	120.00
Basket, Crimped, Handled, 10"	65.00
Basket, Crimped, Handled, 12"	75.00
Basket, Oval, Candy, 2 Handled, 5½"	15.00
Basket, Oval, Handled, 12"	65.00
Bonbon, 4 Handled, 6"	15.00
Bowl, 4 Handled, 12"	30.00
Bowl, Crimped, Low Footed, 12"	75.00
Bowl, Flower, Crimped, 11½"	35.00
Bowl, Flower, Flared, 11½"	35.00
Bowl, Flower, Oval, Handled, 12"	40.00
Bowl, Flower, Round, 12"	35.00
Bowl, Fruit, Flared, 10"	35.00
Bowl, Gardenia, 13"	40.00
Bowl, Salad, 9"	35.00
Bowl, Salad, Deep, Footed, 11"	45.00
Bowl, Salad, Shallow, 12"	30.00
Bowl, Shallow, 15"	35.00
Butter & Cover, ¼ lb.	25.00
Candelabra, 2 Light with Prisms, 7", pr.	75.00
Candlesticks, 1 Light, 4", pr.	25.00
Candlesticks, 2 Light, pr.	45.00
Candlesticks, 2 Light, 6", pr.	50.00
Candy Box & Cover, 7"	55.00
Candy Box & Cover, 2 Compartment, 7"	55.00
Candy Box & Cover, 3 Compartment, 3 Handled, 8"	55.00
Candy Dish, Heart Shape, 5" x 7½"	15.00
Celery, Handled, 11"	15.00

Celery & Relish, 2 Compartment, 11"	20.00
Celery & Relish Tray, Oblong, 6" x 12"	20.00
Celery & Relish, Oblong, 3 Compartment, 12"	25.00
Celery & Relish Tray, 5 Compartment, 12"	35.00
Center Piece, Star Shape, 2 Handled, 10"	35.00
Cheese & Cracker Set, 11", 2 pcs.	35.00
Coaster or Ashtray, 3"	5.00
Comport, Footed,	10.00
Comport, Low Footed, 6"	15.00
Cream, 6 oz.	10.00
Cream, Individual, 3 oz.	15.00
Cup & Saucer, Demitasse, 2½ oz.	25.00
Cup & Saucer, Tea, 6 oz.	20.00
Finger Bowl	10.00
Ice Bucket or Vase, 6½"	65.00
Ice Cream, 5 oz.	5.00
Marmalade & Cover *(Illus.)*	35.00
Mayonnaise, Flared, Handled, 4½"	15.00
Mayonnaise, Footed, 4½"	25.00
Mint, 2 Compartment, 6"	15.00
Mustard or Horseradish & Cover, 4¼"	25.00
Nappy, 7"	15.00
Nappy, Dessert, 6"	10.00
Nappy, Fruit, 5"	8.00
Nappy, Handled, 5"	10.00
Nappy, Handled, 7"	10.00
Nappy, Handled, 9½"	20.00
Nut Dish, 2 Compartment, Handled, 6"	15.00
Oil & Stopper, 3 oz.	25.00
Olive, 2 Compartment, Handled, 6"	10.00
Olive, Oval, 2 Handled, 5"	10.00
Pickle & Olive, 2 Handled, 7"	10.00

TEARDROP, NO. 301, 5301, 5300 *(continued)*

Teardrop Catalog Page

Pickle Dish, Handled, 3" x 6" 8.00
Pitcher, Stuck Handle, pt., 5" 75.00
Plate, 2 Handled, 11" 35.00
Plate, 4 Handled, 13" 40.00
Plate, 6" 5.00
Plate, 7½" 5.00
Plate, 8½" *(Illus. previous page)* 8.00
Plate, 10½" 45.00
Plate, Canape with Ring, 6" 15.00
Plate, Handled, 6" 8.00
Plate, Handled, 8" 10.00
Plate, Lemon, 4 Handled, 7" 15.00
Plate, Marmalade, 2 Handled, 6" 10.00
Plate, Torte, Flat Edge, 13" 35.00
Plate, Torte, Flat Edge, 14" 40.00
Plate, Torte, Flat Edge, 16½" 55.00
Plate, Torte, Rolled Edge, 13" 35.00
Plate, Torte, Rolled Edge, 14" 40.00
Plate, Torte, Rolled Edge, 16½" 55.00
Preserve, Handled, 7" 20.00
Preserve, Handled, 2 Compartment, 7" 25.00
Relish, 2 Compartment, 2 Handled, 7" 15.00
Relish, 2 Compartment, 2 Handled, Star Shape, 7" . . 15.00
Relish, 2 Compartment, Heart Shape, 7½" 15.00
Relish, 3 Compartment, 3 Handled, 8" 15.00
Relish, 3 Compartment, 3 Handled, 9" 20.00
Relish, 3 Compartment, Handled, 11" 25.00
Relish, 4 Compartment, 2 Handled, 9" 25.00
Relish, 5 Compartment, 10" 25.00
Relish, 5 Compartment, 10" (No. 301½) 35.00
Relish, 5 Compartment, 12" (No. 301½) 45.00
Relish, 6 Compartment, 10" 35.00
Relish, 6 Compartment, 12" 45.00

Relish, Oval, 3 Compartment, 12" 35.00
Relish Tray, 4 Compartment, 4 Handled, 12" 35.00
Salt & Pepper, 3", pr. 25.00
Salt & Pepper, 5", pr. 30.00
Salver, Cake, Footed, 13" 85.00
Sugar, 8 oz. 15.00
Sugar, Individual, 3 oz. 15.00
Sweetmeat, Handled, 6½" 15.00
Sweetmeat, Star Shape, 2 Handled, 7" 15.00
Tray for Salt & Pepper, 6" 15.00
Tray for Sugar & Cream, 10" 10.00
Urn & Cover, 9" 125.00
Vase, Fan, 9" 25.00
Vase, Regular, 9" 25.00
Vase, Regular, 10" 35.00

BLOWN ITEMS, NO. 5301, 5300:

Ale Goblet, Footed, 8 or 9 oz. $20.00
Claret, Footed, 4 oz. 15.00
Cocktail or Liquor, Footed, 3½ oz. 15.00
Cordial, Footed, 1 oz. 25.00
Finger Bowl, 4½" 12.00
Goblet, 9 oz. 10.00
Goblet, Luncheon, 9 oz. 10.00
Hi-ball or Iced Tea, Flat, 12 oz. (No. 5300) 20.00
Hi-ball, Flat, 10 oz. (No. 5300) 15.00
Ice Cream, 4 oz. 8.00
Ice Cream, 5 oz. 8.00
Iced Tea or Hi-ball, Flat, 14 oz. (No. 5300) 10.00
Iced Tea or Hi-ball, Footed, 12 oz. 10.00
Iced Tea or Hi-ball, Footed, 14 oz. 10.00
Juice, Orange, Footed, 4½ oz. 9.00
Old Fashioned or Whiskey & Soda, Double, Flat
    10 oz. 12.00
Old Fashioned, Flat, 7 oz. 12.00
Orange Juice, Flat, 3½ oz. (No. 5300) 8.00
Orange Juice, Flat, 5 oz. (flat) (No. 5300) 8.00
Oyster Cocktail, Footed, 3½ oz. 10.00
Pitcher, Ice Lip, ½ gal. 85.00
Saucer Champagne or Tall Sherbet,
    5 oz. *(Illus. previous page)* 10.00
Scotch & Soda or Split, Flat, 8 oz. 10.00
Sherbet, Footed, 5 oz. 8.00
Sherry, Footed, 1¾ oz. 25.00
Split or Party Glass, Footed, 8 oz. (No. 5300) 20.00
Tumbler, Flat, 9 oz. (No. 5300) 10.00
Tumbler, Flat, 10 oz. (No. 5300) 10.00
Tumbler, Footed, 9 oz. 10.00
Tumbler, Table, Flat, 9 oz. (No. 5300) 10.00
Whiskey, Footed, 2 oz. 15.00
Whiskey, Straight, Flat, 2 oz. (No. 5300) 15.00
Whiskey or Cocktail, Footed, 3 oz. 12.00
Wine, Footed, 3 oz. 15.00

Below: Ruba Rombic toilet bottle.

Right: Duncan & Miller Terrace covered urn, blue.

Bottom: Duncan & Miller Teardrop console bowl, blue. Rare in this color.

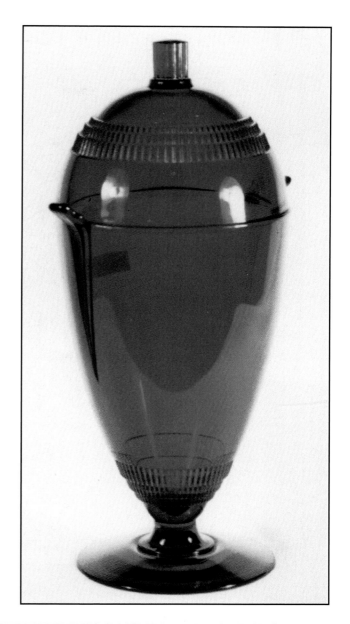

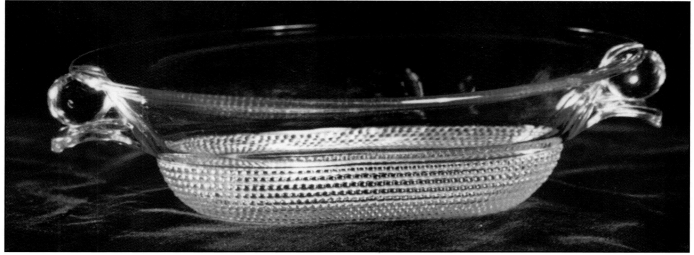

Left: Duncan & Miller Terrace divided mayonaise, plate, ruby; pitcher with silver overlay crystal.

Below: Duncan & Miller Colonial Spiral (Spiral Flutes) compote, plate, luncheon goblet, pink.

Right: Miss America divided relish plate, sherbet, pink.

Below: Duncan & Miller Hobnail Ice Tea, pink; relish & vase, green; cocktail, crystal; & cologne, amber.

Left: Swirl (Jeannette) plate, cup & saucer, ultramarine.

Below: Mayfair (Hocking) covered candy, plate, salt & pepper, sherbet & plate, blue.

Right: Duncan & Miller
Plaza salt & pepper, pink;
salt & pepper, goblet, green;
vase, cup, pink.

Below: Fostoria Baroque,
Azure.

Left: Heisey, Yeoman oils, Flamingo and Moongleam.

Below: Duncan & Miller Canterbury ruby bowl, crystal condiments, green vase.

Right: Iris tumbler and pitcher, Golden Iridescent.

Below: Cherry Blossom, 2 handled bowl, Delphite.

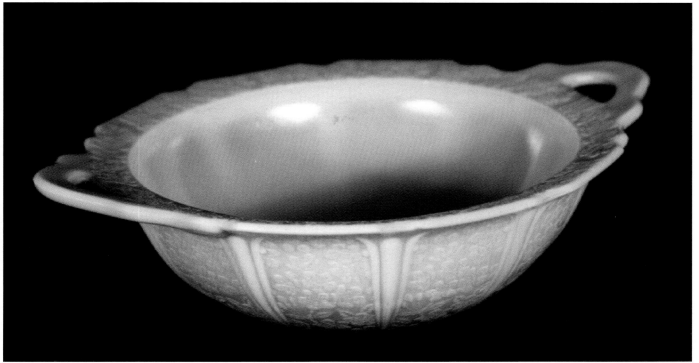

Left: Moderntone, plate, sugar, blue.

Below: Snack Set, turquoise blue with 22k gold decoration.

Right: Pyrex Assortment, 1954 advertisement.

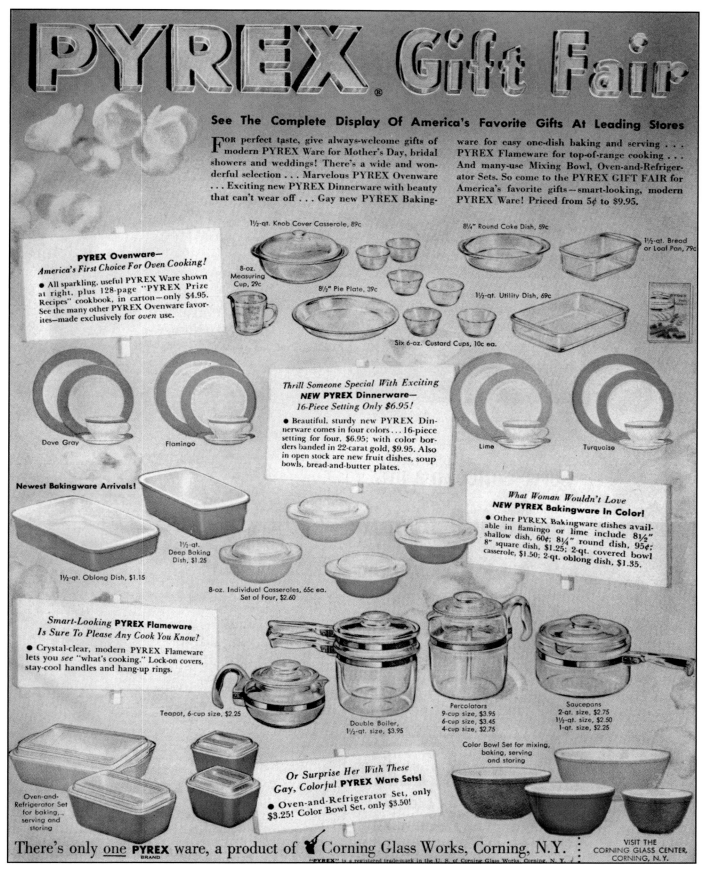

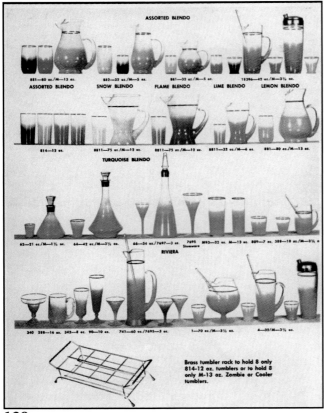

Above right: Iris in Golden Iridescent. Jeannette Glass, 1951 catalog.

Above left: Golden Iridescent Water & Juice Sets. Jeannette Glass, 1951 catalog.

Left: Blendo assortments. West Virginia Glass Specialty, 1958 catalog.

Right: Various decorated tumblers. Libbey Glass, 1955.

129

Galaxy of Gifts
in Libbey glass
each a sparkling new idea!

"Golden Foliage" Caddy Set. 8 on-the-rocks glasses* and matching ice-bowl shine with golden leaves on a frosted background. And each strikingly gift-boxed set comes complete with brass caddy for only about **$8.95**

"Caribbean Cruise" Caddy Set. Each frosted pilsner* is gay with colorful calypso figures in brilliant orange and shining 22K gold. (Or you can have the set in Golden Foliage pattern—see caddy set at left for design.) Either beautifully gift-boxed set with its own brass caddy is only about **$9.95**

"Cocktails for Two" Set. So elegant with its distinctive "Drum" cutting! In every set are 2 bright and shining little glasses*, a just-the-right-amount server, and a slim and sparkly stirrer. All beautifully gift-boxed—and the whole handsome set is only about **$2.50**

"Continental Cups." A 22K gold Grecian Key design bands each sparkling glass and is repeated in the handsome golden holder—made detachable for easy wash-ups. Beautiful—yet practical*—and the stunningly gift-boxed set of 8 is only about **$7.50**

*If the rim of a Libbey "Safedge" glass ever chips, Libbey will replace the glass. At all leading stores. Prices slightly higher in South, West and Canada.

LIBBEY SAFEDGE GLASSWARE
AN Ⓘ PRODUCT

OWENS-ILLINOIS
GENERAL OFFICES · TOLEDO 1, OHIO

1959

130

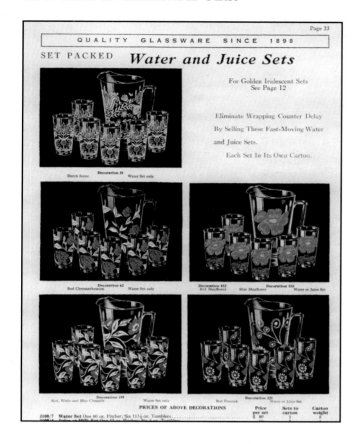

Left: Assortments of Barware. Libbey Glass, 1959.

Above left: Decorated Water & Juice Sets. Jeannette Glass, 1951 catalog.

Above right: Decorated Water Sets. Jeannette Glass, 1951 catalog.

Right: Swirl dinnerware, pink.

MARTIN BRUEHL

Sportsman's Favorite

Culmination of a day in the field—pleasant prospect, bright memory. Genuine Imperial Cape Cod Crystal is the resplendent example of hand-crafted crystal chosen for male hospitality, because it has an affinity with his other mellow favorites. A compatible crystal, its practical sturdiness wins his applause while his eye approves its scintillating 18th century design . . . Bringing home prize pieces of Imperial Cape Cod Crystal is as thrilling to a woman as the bagging of prize game is to the sportsman. Sold in fine stores everywhere; hand-crafted by The Imperial Glass Corporation, Bellaire, Ohio.

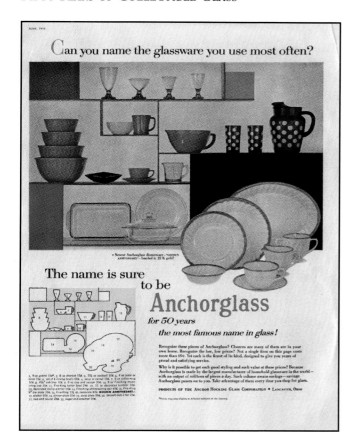

Left: Cape Cod. Imperial Glass, 1947 advertisement.

Above left: Examples of Anchor Hocking (Fire King) glass. 1955 advertisement.

Above right: Mixing Bowls and refrigerator jars. Jeannette Glass, 1951 catalog.

Right: Tangerine Blendo. West Virginia Glass Specialty, 1958 catalog.

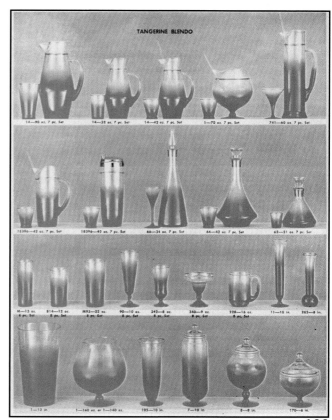

Extra Smart! PYREX WARE in COLOR!

you'll use each dish a dozen ways!

IMAGINE THESE beautiful dishes on *your* table . . . they're strikingly designed, vibrant with color, real "show-off" pieces when you're entertaining.

And think of what a joy they are to own . . . for they're honest-to-goodness *Pyrex Ware!*

All of these sturdy beauties go in the oven, then right to the table! Any leftovers? Put your Pyrex Ware dish in the refrigerator, ready to heat up again.

Illustrated above: the new Pyrex *Color* Ware Casserole Set . . . a 1½-quart casserole complete with cover and four individual dishes (7-ounce size). In gay red or sunny yellow.

Pyrex Color Ware Casserole Set, complete **$2.95**

Additional individual dishes **29¢ each**

2½-quart bowl with four 12-ounce dishes. Red or yellow.
Oven-and-Table Set,
$2.95

4 gay-colored dishes with clear glass covers. For baking, serving, storing.
Oven-and-Refrigerator Set,
$2.95

Wonderful mixing bowls to use a dozen ways. A size for every use.
Color Bowl Set,
$2.95

2½-quart size for buffet suppers. Bake in it, serve in it. Red or yellow.
Covered Casserole,
$2.25

PYREX WARE A PRODUCT OF **CORNING GLASS WORKS**

"Pyrex" is a registered trade-mark in the U. S. of Corning Glass Works, Corning, N. Y.

Above: Pyrex Color Ware. 1951 advertisement.

Chapter 9
HONEYCOMB

HEX OPTIC

Date: 1928 to 1932. Later in the 1950s.

Manufacturer: Jeannette Glass Co., Jeannette, PA

Colors: Green, Pink. Iridescent Crystal later in the 1950s.

This pattern is unusual in that it includes mixing bowls and refrigerator dishes as part of the pattern. Prices for Green and Pink are about equal. Iridescent Crystal is valued at 50% to 75% of colored pieces.

Bar Glass, 1 oz. (whiskey) $12.00
Bowl, 7½" 9.00
Bowl, Crimped Edge, 4¼" 8.00
Bowl, Mixing, 7¼" 18.00
Bowl, Mixing, 8¼" 22.00
Bowl, Mixing, 9" 25.00
Bowl, Mixing, 10" 27.00
Butter & Cover (rectangular) 75.00
Cream *(Illus.)* 8.00
Cup & Saucer 10.00
Ice Bucket 22.00
Iced Tea, 12 oz. 10.00
Pitcher, 32 oz., Flowered Bottom *(Illus.)* 27.00
Pitcher, 96 oz. . . . . 200.00+
Pitcher, Footed, 48 oz. 45.00
Plate, 6" 4.00
Plate, 8" 8.00
Platter, Round, 11" 17.00
Reamer 55.00
Refrigerator Dish, 4" x 4" 12.00
Refrigerator Stack Set, Round, 4 pcs. 75.00
Salt & Pepper, pr. 32.00
Sugar Shaker . . . . 175.00+
Sugar 8.00
Tumbler, 9 oz. 8.00
Tumbler, Footed, 5¾" 12.00
Tumbler, Footed, 7 oz. 10.00
Tumbler, Footed, 7" 15.00

Hex Optic Cream

Hex Optic Pitcher, 32 oz., Flowered Bottom

GEORGIAN, NO. 103

THE DUNCAN & MILLER GLASS CO.
WASHINGTON, PENNA.

No. 103—Georgian Pattern
Among the several lines of quality tableware, the Georgian Pattern is of timely interest. Can be had in Crystal, Green, Amber and Rose.

Georgian 1928 Advertisement

Date: 1925

Manufacturer: Duncan & Miller Glass Co., Washington, PA

Colors: Crystal, Ruby, Cobalt, Green, Amber, Rose (pink)

Duncan & Miller's Georgian is very well finished and has ground bottoms. The pieces are well fire-polished and no mold lines are visible since the mold joint follows the design of the honeycombs. Tumblers are non-stacking. Georgian tumblers were made by many companies and are very difficult to properly identify. Prices given are for crystal pieces, for those in color add 100%.

Cream, Oval, Berry	$8.00
Cup & Saucer, Tea	12.00
Finger Bowl	7.00
Goblet, 9 oz.	9.00
Grapefruit	8.00
Ice Bucket, 6"	24.00
Ice Cream, Footed, 5 oz.	6.00
Iced Tea, 12 oz.	12.00
Jello, 5 oz.	6.00
Jug, ½ gal.	32.00
Juice, Orange, 5 oz.	6.00
Nappy, 5"	5.00
Parfait	7.00
Plate, 6"	5.00
Plate, 7½"	7.00
Plate, 8½"	7.00
Plate, 9½"	12.00
Plate, Chop, 14"	15.00
Plate, Finger Bowl	5.00
Saucer Champagne, or Footed Ice Cream, 6 oz.	8.00
Sugar, Oval, Berry	8.00
Tumbler, Table, 9 oz.	7.00
Vase, #2 Shape, 8"	15.00
Vase, Crimped, 8"	15.00
Whiskey, 2 oz.	9.00
Wine	7.00

GEORGIAN, NO. 1611

Date: 1931 to 1942

Manufacturer: Fenton Art Glass Co., Williamstown, WV

Colors: Crystal, Amber, Ebony, Aquamarine, Jade Green, Rose, Green, Milk Glass, Ruby and Royal Blue

Very similar to other Georgian or Honeycomb patterns, especially in the tumblers. Note that Fenton made many pieces and colors not made by other companies, so these are clues when you are trying to identify Georgian pieces. Georgian is the original name, but it was first introduced as Agua Caliente.

Georgian Catalog Illustrations

	Crystal, Amber, Green, Rose, Milk Glass	Black, Ruby, Aquamarine, Jade Green, Royal Blue		Crystal, Amber, Green, Rose, Milk Glass	Black, Ruby, Aquamarine, Jade Green, Royal Blue
Bonbon, 5"	$7.00	$14.00	Mug, Beer, 8 oz.	20.00	32.00
Bowl, Cupped	7.00	12.00	Mug, Beer, 10 oz.	22.00	35.00
Bowl, Cupped, 9"	12.00	25.00	Mug, Beer, 12 oz.	24.00	40.00
Bowl, Flared, 7½"	9.00	15.00	Nut Cup	7.00	10.00
Candlesticks, pr.	60.00	120.00	Plate, 12"	10.00	25.00
Candy Jar	22.00	80.00	Plate, Bread & Butter, 6"	4.00	7.00
Claret, 4½ oz.	8.00	16.00	Plate, Compartment, 11"	10.00	30.00
Cocktail, 2½ oz.	10.00	18.00	Plate, Salad, 8"	5.00	9.00
Cocktail Shaker, 24 oz.	48.00	100.00	Plate, Service, 10"	15.00	35.00
Cordial, Footed, 1 oz.	15.00	28.00	Salt & Pepper, pr.	40.00	85.00
Cream	10.00	15.00	Sherbet, Cupped or		
Cup & Saucer	12.00	18.00	Flared (low)	6.00	12.00
Decanter & Stopper, 21 oz.	45.00	120.00	Sherbet, High Footed	8.00	14.00
Finger Bowl	7.00	15.00	Sugar	10.00	15.00
Goblet, 10 oz.	10.00	20.00	Tumbler, Flat (bar), 2½ oz.	6.00	12.00
Ice Pail		100.00	Tumbler, Flat (juice), 5 oz.	5.00	10.00
Iced Tea, Flat, 12 oz.	7.00	15.00	Tumbler, Flat, 9 oz.	5.00	10.00
Jug, 54 oz., with or			Tumbler, Footed, 9 oz.	10.00	12.00
without ice lip	60.00	120.00			

GEORGIAN, NO. 69, 69½

Georgian Catalog Illustrations

Date: 1934

Manufacturer: Paden City Glass Manufacturing Co., Paden City, WV

Colors: Crystal and "all Paden City colors." Paden City made the following colors: Green, Cheriglo (Pink), Yellow, Forest Green, Ruby, Amber, Light Blue, Light Green Royal Blue and Mulberry. At this point we do not know if Georgian was made in all these colors or not.

Paden City's Georgian pieces should have ground bottoms. Most items are pressed, but a few blown items were also made. Prices are for Crystal pieces. For items in colors, add 100% to 200% depending on piece and color. The Peach Melba is shaped like a sherbet with flared bowl, but the volume of a goblet.

Cocktail, Low Foot, 3½ oz. (No. 69½) $6.00	Salt & Pepper, pr. (No. 69½) 18.00
Finger Bowl 6.00	Sherbet (No. 69½) 5.00
Goblet, 9 oz. 7.00	Sherbet, Low Foot, Flared or Cupped, 3½ oz.
Goblet, Low Foot, 10 oz. (No. 69½) 7.00	(No. 69½) 5.00
Iced Tea, 11 oz. (straight, pressed) (No. 69½) 6.00	Sherbet, Regular, 4 oz. 5.00
Iced Tea, 12 oz. (blown) (No. 69½) 8.00	Side Water, 5 oz. (Old Fashioned shape) (No. 69½). . . 5.00
Jug & Cover, 60 oz. (blown) 35.00	Syrup & Cover, 12 oz. (blown) 25.00
Marmalade & Cover, 12 oz. (blown) 20.00	Tumbler, 12 oz. 6.00
Oil & Stopper, 6 oz. (No. 69½) 25.00	Tumbler, 5 oz. 5.00
Old Fashioned Cocktail, 6 oz. (No. 69½) 5.00	Tumbler, 9 oz. 6.00
Parfait, 5 oz. (No. 69½) 8.00	Tumbler, Table, 9 oz. (straight sided) (No. 69½) 6.00
Peach Melba, 9 oz. 7.00	Wine, 2½ oz. (small tumbler shape) 5.00
Plate, 6" 4.00	

Chapter 10
HUMAN FIGURES

CAMEO

Date: 1930 to 1934

Manufacturer: Hocking Glass Co., Lancaster, OH

Colors: Green, Yellow, Pink, Crystal with platinum edges

Reproductions: Reproductions of the salt shakers have a very faint design and are heavy—a lot of glass in the bottom cavity of the shaker. Colors made are green, pink and dark blue. Children's pieces have been made recently, but these were never made in old glass.

	Green	Yellow	Pink
Bowl, 3 Footed, 11"	$80.00	$95.00	$50.00
Bowl, 4½" (crystal only)	6.00		
Bowl, 5½"	35.00	32.00	160.00
Bowl, 7¼"	57.00		
Bowl, 8¼"	38.00		165.00
Bowl, Cream Soup, 4¾"	170.00		
Bowl, Oval, Vegetable, 10"	35.00	47.00	
Bowl, Soup, 9"	58.00		145.00
Butter & Cover	220.00	1,500.00+	
Cake Plate, 10½"	130.00		195.00
Cake Plate, 3 Footed, 10"	30.00		
Candlesticks, 4"	90.00		
Candy & Cover, Low, 4"	90.00	80.00	500.00+
Candy Jar & Cover, Tall, 6½"	165.00		
Cocktail Shaker (crystal only)	500.00+		
Cookie Jar & Cover	55.00		
Cream, 3¼"	24.00	22.00	
Cream, 4¼"	30.00		120.00
Cup & Saucer (two styles)	20.00	12.00	90.00
Decanter & Stopper, 10"	150.00		
Goblet	50.00		185.00
Ice Bowl	165.00		700.00+
Iced Tea, 11 oz.	35.00	58.00	100.00
Iced Tea, 15 oz.	70.00		130.00
Iced Tea, Footed, 11 oz.	62.00		130.00
Iced Tea, Footed, 15 oz.	470.00+		
Jam & Cover	170.00		
Juice, 5 oz.	32.00		100.00
Juice, Footed, 3 oz.	60.00		130.00
Mayonnaise, 5"	35.00		200.00
Pitcher, 20 oz.	220.00	2,100.00+	

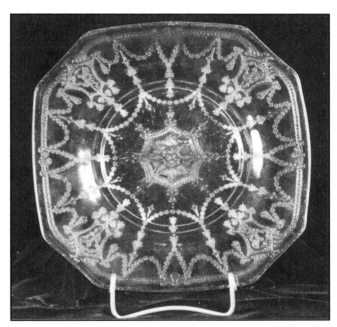

Cameo Plate

Cameo Salt Shaker

	Green	Yellow	Pink
Pitcher, 36 oz.	68.00		
Pitcher, 56 oz.	60.00		1,600.00+
Plate, 6"	6.00	5.00	95.00
Plate, 7" (crystal only)	5.00		

CAMEO *(continued)*

	Green	Yellow	Pink
Plate, 8"	12.00	14.00	42.00
Plate, 8" Square *(Illus.)*	42.00	270.00	
Plate, 9½"	20.00	10.00	80.00
Plate, 10"	20.00		45.00
Plate, Grill, 10½"	10.00	10.00	110.00
Plate, Grill, Handled, 10½"	70.00	10.00	
Plate, Handled, 10½"	14.00	15.00	
Platter, Handled, 12"	27.00	45.00	
Relish, 3 Compartment, Footed, 7½"	32.00	100.00	
Salt & Pepper, pr *(Illus. of salt)*	70.00		800.00+
Sandwich, Center Handled	5,000.00+		
Saucer, with Ring.	190.00		
Sherbet, (blown), 3"	18.00		80.00

	Green	Yellow	Pink
Sherbet, (molded), 3"	15.00	42.00	80.00
Sherbet, 4⅛"	36.00	45.00	120.00
Sugar, 3¼"	22.00	20.00	
Sugar, 4¼"	27.00		120.00
Tray, Domino Sugar, 7", with indent	175.00		
Tray, Domino Sugar, 7", without indent			270.00
Tumbler, 9 oz.	32.00		85.00
Tumbler, 10 oz.	32.00		100.00
Tumbler, Footed, 9 oz.	32.00	18.00	120.00
Vase, 5¾"	195.00		
Vase, 8"	40.00		
Water Bottle (dark green, Whitehouse Vinegar)	27.00		
Wine, 3½"	800.00+		900.00+
Wine, 4"	68.00		220.00

MARTELÉ—DANCING NYMPH

Dancing Nymph Plate

Date: 1926

Manufacturer: Consolidated Lamp & Glass Co., Coraopolis, PA

Colors: Crystal, Pink, Green, Deep Blue, Light Blue, Jade, Amethyst, Honey

This pattern is also sometimes called Dance of the Nudes, but Dancing Nymph is the original company name. Crystal pieces with all over satin were called Satin Crystal while French Crystal was the name for pieces with satin backgrounds and clear figures. It is thought that pieces which are not partially or all satin are unfinished. While Consolidated was closed for a period of time, much of this pattern was made by the nearby Phoenix Glass Co. At least three pieces may have only been made as samples or at least for a very short period of time: Candlestick (No. 2840), Palace Size Bowl (No. 2795B) and a Palace Size platter. For items in color add 25% to 75%.

	French Crystal
Bowl, 8" (No. 3098½)	$275.00
Bowl, Berry, 4½" (No. 3098)	85.00
Cocktail (No. 3091½)	100.00
Cup & Saucer (No. 3099, 3099½)	125.00
Goblet (No. 3080)	100.00
Plate, 6" (No. 3095)	70.00
Plate, 8" (No. 3096)	80.00
Plate, 10" (No. 3097) *(Illus.)*	150.00
Sherbet (No. 3094)	60.00
Vase, Crimped Top, 5" (3080C)	110.00
Vase, Fan, 5½" (No. 3080F)	120.00

ZODIAC, NO. 1590

Date: 1949

Manufacturer: A. H. Heisey & Co., Newark, OH

Colors: Crystal. Reissued by Imperial Glass Corporation, from 1969 to 1971; made by them in Crystal, Amberglo and Verde. The footed Candy Jar and Cover was made in nine or more colors.

Reproductions: Imperial Glass Corp. reproduced the stemware and several pressed pieces in Crystal, Amberglo, and Verde. Some pieces were also made in Rubigold and Peacock carnival.

This pattern was originally made only in Crystal by Heisey and the prices are for Crystal Heisey pieces. The design was done by Horace King, Heisey's designer in the 1940s and 1950s. The pattern is composed of the twelve signs of the zodiac. Many of the Heisey pieces are marked with the Diamond H, but the mark is often hidden in the design and hard to find.

Ashtray, Square, 3½"	$12.00
Bowl, Flower, 11"	55.00
Candlestick, 2 Light, pr.	160.00
Candy Jar & Cover, Footed *(Illus.)*	70.00
Claret, 4 oz.	15.00
Coaster, 3 ½"	12.00
Cocktail, 3½ oz.	15.00
Comport, 6"	35.00
Cream, Footed	22.00
Goblet, 10 oz.	22.00
Iced Tea, Footed, 12 oz.	20.00
Nappy, 4½"	8.00
Oyster Cocktail, 4 oz.	12.00
Plate, 8"	18.00
Relish, 4 compartment, 8"	35.00
Relish, Oval, 2 compartment, 10"	35.00
Salt & Pepper, pr.	50.00
Salver, (plate) 13"	70.00
Saucer Champagne, 5 oz.	15.00
Sherbet, 5 oz.	12.00
Soda, Tapered, 5 oz.	12.00
Soda, Tapered, 8 oz.	15.00
Soda, Tapered, 12 oz.	18.00
Sugar, Footed	22.00

Zodiac Tall Covered Candy

Chapter 11
MISCELLANEOUS

CATALONIAN

Two Catalonian Vases

Date: 1927

Manufacturer: Consolidated Lamp & Glass Co., Coraopolis, PA

Colors: Crystal, Spanish Rose, Jade, Honey, Emerald, Amethyst, Red, Reuben Blue, Ruby Stain and Rainbow

Designed and Patented by Reuben Haley. Light fixtures were also made similar in design to Catalonian. Contemporary company literature described the pattern as "The Glass of Old Spain." Prices given are for most colors. For Reuben Blue add 75%, for Red add 100% or more, and for Ruby Stain and Rainbow add 50% to 60%.

Ashtray $45.00	Sugar, No Handles 20.00
Bowl, Flower 90.00	Sundae, Low Foot, 7 oz. 18.00
Bowl, Lily, Cupped, 12" 95.00	Toilet Bottle 120.00
Bowl, Salad, Straight, 9" 80.00	Tray 110.00
Candlesticks, Low Foot, pr. 70.00	Tumbler, 7 oz. 25.00
Candlesticks, pr. 80.00	Tumbler, Iced Tea, 12 oz. 25.00
Cigarette Box & Cover 90.00	Tumbler, Iced Tea, Handled, 12 oz. 30.00
Cream 30.00	Tumbler, Tapered, 7 oz. 25.00
Cream, Triangle, 7 oz. 30.00	Tumbler, Tapered, 9 oz. 25.00
Cup & Saucer 45.00	Vase, Bottle 40.00
Dish, Oatmeal 30.00	Vase, Fan Shaped 45.00
Finger Bowl or Mayonnaise 20.00	Vase, Fan Shaped, 7" 45.00
Fish Bowl (in Emerald Green & Spanish Rose) 700.00	Vase, Flared Shape, 6" 40.00
Goblet, Iced Tea, Low Foot, 12 oz. 30.00	Vase, Flared, Footed 55.00
Goblet, Low Foot, 10 oz. 20.00	Vase, Nasturtium *(Illus. left)* 190.00
Ice Tub 95.00	Vase, Oblong, 6" 30.00
Jug, ½ gal. 145.00	Vase, Pinch Bottle 80.00
Jug, 72 oz. 185.00	Vase, Sweet Pea 80.00
Jug, Triangle, 20 oz. 140.00	Vase, Triangle, 4" 35.00
Jug, Triangle, 72 oz. 185.00	Vase, Triangle, 6" 55.00
Mayonnaise Boat 40.00	Vase, Triangle, 10" *(Illus. right)* 100.00
Plate, 13" 50.00	Vase, Tumbler-Shaped, 7" 60.00
Plate, Bread & Butter, 7" 15.00	Vase, Tumbler-Shaped, 8" 60.00
Plate, Salad, 8" 18.00	Vase, Violet 90.00
Plate, Service, 10" 25.00	Whiskey, 2½ oz. 25.00
Puff Box & Cover 150.00	Whiskey, Low Foot, 2½ oz. 40.00
Rose Jar, 8" 75.00	Whiskey Jug. 220.00
Sugar, 2 Handled 25.00	

COIN, NO. 1372

Date: 1958 to 1982

Manufacturer: Fostoria Glass Co., Moundsville, WV

Colors: Crystal, Amber, Olive, Blue, Ruby, Green

Reproductions: Some pieces are currently being made by Indiana Glass.

Lamps were also made electrified. Some pieces were made on special order with Canadian coins. Items were also made for Avon cosmetics. Pieces with unfrosted coins are considered to be unfinished. Some items are still being made in colors similar to Fostoria's, so beware when buying to make certain you have old pieces. Not all pieces were made in all colors.

Coin Jelly, Handled Nappy, 4½" Candleholder

	Crystal, Amber, Olive	Blue, Green, Ruby
Ashtray, 10" (No. 124)	$30.00	$50.00
Ashtray, Oblong, 3" x 4" (No. 115)	14.00	20.00
Ashtray, One Coin, 5" (No. 123) . .	14.00	20.00
Ashtray, Round, 7½" (No. 114) . . .	20.00	45.00
Ashtray, with Center Coin, 7½" (No. 119)	25.00	32.00
Bowl, 8" (No. 179)	40.00	60.00
Bowl, Oval, 9" (No. 189)	40.00	55.00
Bowl & Cover, Wedding, 8¼" (No. 162)	55.00	95.00
Candleholders, 4½", 1 Light, pr. (No. 316) *(Illus. of one)*	55.00	65.00
Candlesticks, 1 Light, 8", pr. (No. 326)	35.00	70.00
Candy Box & Cover, 6½" (No. 354)	35.00	65.00
Candy Jar & Cover, 6⁵⁄₁₆" (No. 347)	45.00	85.00
Cigarette Box & Cover, 5¾" (No. 374)	45.00	85.00
Cigarette Holder & Ashtray Cover.	45.00	85.00
Cigarette Urn, Footed, 3⅜" (No. 381)	20.00	48.00
Comport, Footed, 8½" (No. 199)	55.00	95.00
Cream, 3½" (No. 680)	18.00	24.00
Cruet & Stopper, 7 oz. (No. 531)	60.00	110.00
Decanter & Stopper (No. 400) . . .	110.00	170.00
Goblet, 10½ oz. (No. 2)	35.00	90.00
Iced Tea, 14 oz. (No. 58)	35.00	70.00

	Crystal, Amber, Olive	Blue, Green, Ruby
Jelly, Footed, 3¾" (No. 448) *(Illus.)*	18.00	50.00
Lamp, Coach, 13½" (No. 324) . . .	130.00	200.00
Lamp, Oil, 9¾" (No. 310)	110.00	160.00
Lamp, Patio, 16⅝" (No. 459)	150.00	250.00
Nappy, 4½" (No. 495)	20.00	
Nappy, Handled, 5¾" (No. 499) *(Illus.)*	20.00	35.00
Old Fashioned, Double (No. 23) . .	18.00	
Pitcher, Quart, 6⁹⁄₁₆" (No. 453) . . .	70.00	95.00
Plate, 8" (No. 550)	20.00	45.00
Punch Bowl, 14" (No. 600) (Crystal only)	280.00	
Punch Bowl Foot (No. 602).	120.00	
Punch Cup, 3½" (No. 615) (Crystal only)	35.00	
Salt & Pepper, pr. (No. 652)	45.00	70.00
Salver, Cake, 10" (No. 630)	120.00	200.00
Sherbet, 9 oz. (No. 7)	15.00	55.00
Sugar & Cover, 5⅜" (No. 673) . . .	35.00	50.00
Tray, Condiment, 9⅝" (No. 738)	40.00	70.00
Tumbler, Iced Tea, 12 oz. (No. 64) (Crystal only)	38.00	
Tumbler, Juice (No. 81) (Crystal only)	25.00	
Tumbler, Water, 9 oz. (No. 73) (Crystal only)	28.00	
Urn & Cover, Footed, 12¾" (No. 829)	85.00	175.00
Vase, Bud, 8" (No. 799)	16.00	30.00
Wine, 5 oz. (No. 26)	32.00	60.00

EL MEXICANO/CRINKLE

Crinkle, Footed Tumbler, Pitcher

Date: El Mexicano—1933; Crinkle—1962

Manufacturer: Morgantown Glass Works, Morgantown, WV

Colors: El Mexicano (All semi-opaque)—Ice (white), Seaweed (green), Pink Quartz, Hyacinth (lavender); Crinkle (All transparent)—Crystal , Topaz, Green, Pink, Blue, Amethyst, Violet, Amberina, Ruby, Steel Blue, Peacock Blue, Moss Green, Nutmeg, Bristol Blue. Also in Black and White.

This unusual pattern was designed as a copy of old, crudely made Mexican glass. Pieces are irregular in finish and final form. According to the company, the translucent colors were also made to emulate the appearance of the ancient glass which was worn by years of use and weathering. Crinkle used the same molds as El Mexicano but was made in later years by Morgantown Glass Guild and only in transparent colors. Several items were added to the Crinkle line which are not known in El Mexicano. For detailed information on El Mexicano, Crinkle, and other Morgantown products, we recommend the book Old Morgantown Glass *by Jerry Gallagher.*

	El Mexicano	Crinkle
Bowl, 4"	$35.00	$22.00
Bowl, 5"	35.00	22.00
Bowl, Flower, 13"	210.00	
Candlesticks, pr.	250.00	
Cocktail 5½ oz.		24.00
Cream	150.00	95.00
Iced Tea, 20 oz.	35.00	20.00
Ice Tub	200.00	
Icer & Insert	60.00	50.00
Jug, Liquor, & Stopper	210.00	210.00
Jug, Tankard, 34 oz.		110.00
Jug, Tankard, 54 oz.		125.00
Juice, Footed		24.00
Martini Pitcher		170.00
Old Fashioned, 12 oz.	32.00	20.00
Old Fashioned, 7 oz.	30.00	18.00
Old Fashioned, Roly Poly, 11 oz.		25.00
Pilsner, Hollow Stem, 16 oz.		26.00
Pitcher, Water (bulbous base)	250.00	175.00

	El Mexicano	Crinkle
Pitcher, Water (shouldered base) (Illus.)	180.00	165.00
Plate, 6½"	25.00	18.00
Plate, 7½"	30.00	18.00
Plate, 9¼"	35.00	20.00
Relish Dish, 3 part	100.00	100.00
Sherbet, Footed	20.00	18.00
Sugar	150.00	100.00
Tumbler, Beer, 8 oz.	35.00	20.00
Tumbler, Beverage, 14 oz.	40.00	25.00
Tumbler, Footed, 13 oz. (Illus.)	40.00	25.00
Tumbler, Liquor, 3 oz.	50.00	50.00
Tumbler, Orange Juice, 6½ oz.	24.00	16.00
Tumbler, Water, 10 oz.	35.00	20.00
Vase, 5"	95.00	70.00
Vase, 6"	135.00	
Vase, 6½"	135.00	
Vase, 7"	75.00	50.00
Wine, Footed, 4 oz.		50.00

NAUTICAL

Date: 1936

Manufacturer: Duncan & Miller Glass Co., Washington, PA

Colors: Crystal, Blue. Covered Jars in Blue Opalescent, Pink Opalescent, Yellow Opalescent.

A unique small line designed by Robert A. May for Duncan & Miller. All items are designed with nautical or ship motifs. While extremely attractive, it probably was not a good seller originally since pieces of the pattern are difficult to find today. Crystal and Blue items are often found with frosted highlights. The various sodas and tumblers were continued in the line simply as a barware line; the covered jars and ashtrays were continued in the Sanibel line.

	Crystal	Blue	Opalescent
Ashtray, 3" (Life Preserver)	$10.00	$30.00	$40.00
Ashtray, 6" (Life Preserver) (Illus.)	25.00	55.00	95.00
Cake Plate, 12"	30.00	95.00	
Candy Jar & Cover (Illus.)	95.00	250.00	350.00
Cigarette Holder	30.00	55.00	
Cigarette Jar & Cover	95.00	150.00	195.00
Cocktail	30.00	45.00	
Comport, Anchor Stem	125.00	240.00	275.00
Cream	30.00	60.00	
Decanter & Stopper	175.00	325.00	395.00
Hi-ball	30.00	45.00	
Ice Bucket (Illus.)	95.00	150.00	
Orange Juice	25.00	40.00	
Plate, 8"	18.00	30.00	
Plate, 6"	12.00	25.00	
Plate, Handled Cake or Candy (center handle), 6"	65.00	125.00	
Relish Tray, 7 Compartment, 12"	95.00	150.00	
Relish, 2 Compartment	55.00	95.00	
Salt & Pepper, (large), pr	175.00	350.00	
Salt & Pepper, (small), pr	150.00	300.00+	
Sugar	25.00	55.00	
Tray for Salt & Pepper	100.00	175.00	
Tumbler, Water, 9 oz.	35.00	50.00	
Whiskey & Soda, 8 oz.	30.00	45.00	

Nautical Candy Jar, Ice Bucket, 6" Ashtray

Nautical Original 1936 Drawing

Nautical Original 1936 Drawing

RAINDROPS

Raindrops Cream

Date: 1929 to 1933

Manufacturer: Federal Glass Co., Columbus, OH

Colors: Green, Crystal

A plain pattern with a small circular optic. Salt and pepper shakers are very hard to find.

	Crystal	Green
Bar Glass, 1 oz. (whiskey)	$4.00	$8.00
Bar Glass, 2 oz. (whiskey)	4.00	7.00
Bowl, 4½"	3.00	6.50
Bowl, 6"	5.00	9.00
Bowl, 7½"	18.00	35.00
Cream *(Illus.)*	4.00	8.00
Cup & Saucer (2 styles)	5.00	8.50
Iced Tea, 14 oz.	8.00	14.00
Juice, 4 oz.	3.00	5.00
Juice, 5 oz.	3.00	6.00
Plate, 6"	1.50	3.00
Plate, 8"	3.00	6.00
Salt & Pepper, pr.	100.00+	275.00+
Sherbet	3.00	7.00
Sugar & Cover	27.00	50.00
Tumbler, 9½ oz.	6.00	10.00
Tumbler, 10 oz.	6.00	10.00

ROULETTE

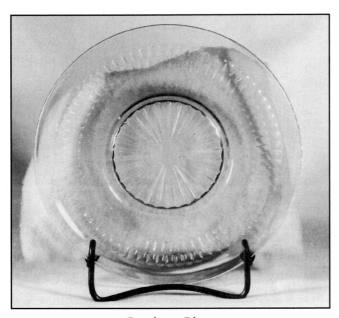

Roulette Plate

Date: 1935 to 1939

Manufacturer: Hocking Glass Co., Lancaster, OH

Colors: Green. Limited production in Pink and Crystal.

	Crystal	Pink, Green
Bar Glass, 1½ oz. (whiskey)	$7.00	$15.00
Bowl, 9"	8.00	15.00
Cup & Saucer	35.00	40.00
Iced Tea, 12 oz.	15.00	25.00
Juice, 5 oz.	7.00	20.00
Old Fashioned, 7½ oz.	20.00	37.00
Pitcher, 64 oz.	30.00	40.00
Plate, 6"	3.00	5.00
Plate, 8½" *(Illus.)*	5.00	7.00
Plate, Sandwich, 12"	10.00	12.00
Sherbet	3.00	6.00
Tumbler, 9 oz.	11.00	20.00
Tumbler, Footed, 10 oz.	12.00	24.00

RUBA ROMBIC

Date: 1928

Manufacturer: Consolidated Lamp & Glass Co., Coraopolis, PA

Colors: Smoky Topaz (transparent), Jungle Green (transparent), Silver Gray, Lilac (cased), Jade (cased), Sunshine (cased). Difficult to find in Opalescent Crystal, Black and Crystal.

Designed and Patented by Reuben Haley. Described in company literature as "An Epic in Modern Art." This is the strongest Art Deco influenced pattern in Depression/Elegant glass, making it very desirable for aficionados of this type of design. This creates a large demand with resulting high prices, making Ruba Rombic the most valuable of the patterns included in this book. Light fixtures were also made similar in design to Ruba Rombic and are valued from $1,100 to $2,400, depending on size and color. Add from 25% to 50% for cased colors. Values are given for transparent colors.

Ruba Rombic Toilet Bottle, Bowl

Almond	$750.00
Ashtray	750.00
Bonbon, 3 Compartment	250.00
Bouillon	160.00
Bowl, 9"	1,400.00
Bowl, Cupped, 8" *(Illus.)*	1,400.00
Bowl, Oblong, 12"	1,750.00
Candlesticks, 1 Light, pr.	550.00
Celery, 3 Compartment	950.00
Cigarette Box & Cover	800.00
Comport, 7"	1,000.00
Finger Bowl	90.00
Iced Tea, 12 oz.	160.00
Jug	2,300.00
Juice	110.00
Liquor Bottle	1,700.00

Plate, 15"	1,800.00
Plate, Bread & Butter, 7"	75.00
Plate, Salad, 8"	75.00
Plate, Service, 10"	230.00
Relish, 2 Compartment	325.00
Sundae	90.00
Toilet Bottle with Stopper *(Illus.)*	1,600.00
Tray	1,800.00
Tumbler, 9 oz.	110.00
Tumbler, Footed, 10 oz.	110.00
Tumbler, Footed, 15 oz.	300.00
Vase (several styles)	800.00 to 1,500.00
Vase, 16½"	9,000.00
Whiskey	90.00

CABOCHON, NO. 1951

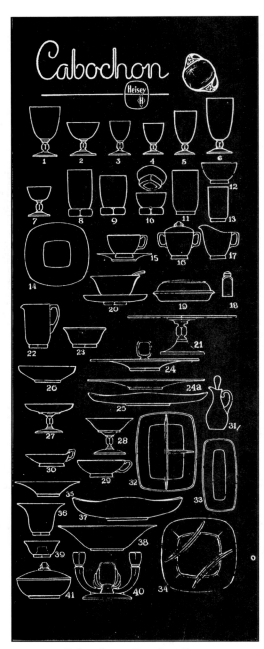

Cabochon Catalog Page

Date: 1951 to 1957

Manufacturer: A. H. Heisey & Co., Newark, OH

Colors: Crystal. Some production in Dawn (Charcoal gray). Limited items in Amber.

Reproductions: Pieces in the pattern, including the blown stemware, continued to be made by Imperial Glass Corporation after they bought the Heisey molds.

One of Heisey's last patterns. Cabochon (original name) was designed by Horace King who interpreted it as a combination of the classic forms of the circle and the square. The No. 6092 tumblers and sodas are desirable because of the thick amber bases. Note: Numbers with listings indicate pieces shown in this ad.

Bonbon, Handled, 6¼" (30). $15.00
Bowl, Cereal, 7" (26) 8.00
Bowl, Floral, Fruit or Salad, 13" 22.00
Bowl, Gardenia, 13" (37) 22.00
Butter & Cover, ¼ lb. (19). 35.00
Candelettes, 1 Light, pr (39). 45.00
Candlesticks, 2 Light, pr. (40). 150.00
Candy & Cover, 6¼" (41) 45.00
Cheese & Cracker, 2 pcs., 14" 32.00
Cream (17) 18.00
Cream, Cereal, 12 oz. (22) 55.00
Cup & Saucer (15). 18.00
Jelly, Handled, 6" (29) 15.00
Juice, 5 oz. (13) 22.50
Mayonnaise, 6" (20). 15.00
Mint, Footed, 5¾" 15.00
Nappy, 4½" or 5" (23). 7.00
Oil Bottle & Stopper, 3 oz. (31) 60.00
Pickle Tray, 8½" (33) 15.00
Plate, Mayonnaise, 8". 8.00
Plate, Salad, 8" (14) 8.00
Plate, Sandwich, 14" (24a) 20.00
Plate, Sandwich, Center Handled, 13" (24) 45.00
Plate, Torte, 14" (25) 20.00
Relish, Oblong, 3 Compartment, 9" (32) 20.00

(continued) CABOCHON, NO. 1951

Relish, Square, 3 Compartment, 9" (34) 22.00
Salt & Pepper, pr. (18) 90.00
Salver, Footed, 13" (21) 65.00
Sherbet, 6 oz. (12) 5.00
Sugar & Cover (16) 35.00
Tidbit, 7½" (35) 8.00
Tray for Sugar & Cream, 9" 10.00
Tumbler, 12 oz. (11). 40.00
Vase, Flared, 3½" (36) 15.00

BLOWN STEMWARE: (ALL NO. 6091)

Cocktail, 4 oz. (7) $6.00
Goblet, 10 oz. (1). 10.00
Iced Tea, Footed, 12 oz. (6) 10.00
Juice, Footed, 5 oz. (5) 8.00

Oyster Cocktail, 3 oz. (4) 6.00
Sherbet, 5½ oz. (2) 6.00
Wine, 3 oz. (3). 10.00

BLOWN TUMBLERS: SOLID CABOCHON BASES. (ALL NO. 6092)

These were made with crystal bowls and amber bases. Prices are for crystal bowls and amber bases.

Beverage, 10 oz. (8) $75.00
Iced Tea, 12 oz. 85.00
Juice, 5 oz.. . . . . 50.00
Sherbet, 6 oz. (10) 50.00
Soda, 14 oz.. . . . . 95.00
Tumbler, 10 oz. (9) 75.00

CANTERBURY, NO. 115, 5155

Date: Ca. 1938

Manufacturer: Duncan & Miller Glass Co., Washington, PA

Colors: Crystal, Sapphire Blue, Ruby, Chartreuse, Opalescent Blue, Opalescent Pink. Tiffin produced the pattern in Biscayne Green, Smoky Avocado, Teakwood Brown, Copen blue, Dawn (Twilight) and possibly others.

Reproductions: Many Canterbury pieces were continued by U. S. Glass/Tiffin who bought out the Duncan & Miller plant. Tiffin Twilight (actually Dawn) is quite desirable and expensive.

Basket measurements are diameters, not heights. This was an extensive pattern made by Duncan & Miller until it closed in 1955. Prices given are for pieces in Crystal. Names of pieces are taken from original company price lists and catalogs. Canterbury is the original name used by Duncan & Miller and continued by Tiffin.

Canterbury Pattern Folder

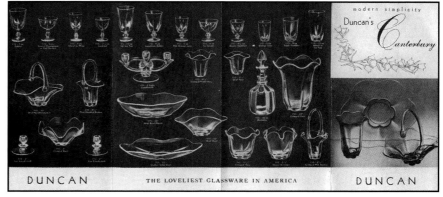

Canterbury Pattern Folder

CANTERBURY, NO. 115, 5155 *(continued)*

Ashtray, 3"	$8.00
Ashtray, 3½"x 2¼"	8.00
Ashtray, 4½"x 3½"	8.00
Ashtray, 5"	10.00
Ashtray, 6½"x 4¾"	8.00
Ashtray, Club, 3"	8.00
Ashtray, Club, 4½"	12.00
Ashtray, Club, 5½"	15.00
Basket, Crimped, Handled, 3"	30.00
Basket, Crimped, Handled, 3½"	30.00
Basket, Crimped, Handled, 4½"	35.00
Basket, Crimped, Handled, 10"	75.00
Basket, Oval, Handled, 3"	30.00
Basket, Oval, Handled, 3½"	30.00
Basket, Oval, Handled, 4½"	35.00
Basket, Oval, Handled, 10"	85.00
Basket, Oval, Handled, 11"	95.00
Bonbon, 6"	18.00
Bonbon, 8"	20.00
Bonbon & Cover, 6½"	25.00
Bowl, Crimped, 7½"	15.00
Bowl, Crimped, 8"	18.00
Bowl, Crimped, 9"	20.00
Bowl, Crimped, 10½"	25.00
Bowl, Flared, 8"	18.00
Bowl, Flared, 9" (No. 115½)	20.00
Bowl, Flared, 10"	25.00
Bowl, Flared, 11½"	25.00
Bowl, Flared, 12"	30.00
Bowl, Gardenia, 6½"	15.00
Bowl, Gardenia, 9"	18.00
Bowl, Miniature Flower, 6½"	15.00
Bowl, Miniature Flower, 8"	18.00
Bowl, Oval, 9"	30.00
Bowl, Oval, 10"	25.00
Bowl, Oval, 11½"	35.00
Bowl, Oval, 12"	35.00
Bowl, Oval, Flared, 13"	45.00
Bowl, Salad Dressing, 2 Compartment, 5"	18.00
Bowl, Salad, 10"	30.00
Bowl, Salad, Shallow, 12"	30.00
Candelabra, 1 Light, 7", pr.	30.00
Candelabra, 2 Light, 6¾", pr.	65.00
Candelabra, 3 Light, 7", pr.	75.00
Candlesticks, 1 Light, 3", pr.	25.00
Candlesticks, 1 Light, 6", pr.	20.00
Candlesticks, 2 Light, 6½", pr.	20.00
Candlesticks, 3 Light, 6", pr.	40.00
Candy Box & Cover, 7"	30.00
Candy Box & Cover, 3 Compartment, 7"	30.00
Candy Box & Cover, 3 Compartment, 3 Handled, 8"	35.00

Candy Jar & Cover, 9"	35.00
Candy Jar & Cover, Footed, 5½"	45.00
Celery & Relish, 2 Compartment, 2 Handled, 10½"	25.00
Celery & Relish, 3 Compartment, 11"	25.00
Celery & Relish, 3 Compartment, 2 Handled, 10½"	25.00
Celery & Relish, 5 Compartment, 12"	25.00
Celery Tray, 9"	35.00
Celery Tray, 11"	15.00
Cheese & Cracker, 2 pcs., 11"	20.00
Cigarette Box & Cover, 4½"x 3½"x 2½"	35.00
Cigarette Jar & Cover, 4" tall, 3" wide	15.00
Claret or Wine, 4 oz.	15.00
Cocktail, 3½ oz.	25.00
Comport, High Footed, 6"	20.00
Comport, Low Footed, Crimped, 7½"	20.00
Comport, Low Footed, Deep, 8"	20.00
Comport, Low Footed, Flared, 9"	10.00
Cream, 7 oz.	10.00
Cream, Individual, 3 oz.	10.00
Cup & Saucer, Tea, 6 oz.	20.00
Decanter & Stopper, 32 oz., 12" tall	65.00
Dessert Dish or Finger Bowl, 4¼"	10.00
Epergne Candelabrum, 2 Light with Vase	60.00
Epergne Candlestick, 2 Light with Vase	60.00
Finger Bowl	10.00
Flower Arranger, 5½"	20.00
Flower Arranger, 7"	25.00
Flower Arranger, 8½"	25.00
Flower Arranger, 10½"	30.00
Fruit, Handled, 5½"	15.00
Goblet, 9 oz.	12.00
Goblet, Luncheon, 9 oz.	10.00
Ice Bucket—See Vase	
Ice Cream, 6 oz.	9.00
Iced Tea, Footed, 13 oz.	15.00
Iced Tea or Hi-ball, Straight, 13 oz.	15.00
Jug, Juice, Handled, 32 oz.	35.00
Juice, Orange, Footed, 5 oz.	11.00
Juice, Straight, 5 oz.	10.00
Ladle, Mayonnaise	5.00
Marmalade Jar & Cover, 5½"	15.00
Martini Mixer, 32 oz., 9¾" tall	45.00
Martini Mixer, Handled, 32 oz., 9¼" tall	45.00
Mayonnaise, Crimped, 5½"	10.00
Mayonnaise, Flared, 5"	10.00
Mustard or Horseradish & Cover	15.00
Nappy, 2 Handled, 9"	15.00
Nappy, Fruit, 5"	8.00
Nappy, Heart Shape, 1 Handle, 5½"	15.00
Nappy, Round, 1 Handle, 5½"	15.00

*(continued)*CANTERBURY, NO. 115, 5115

Nappy, Round, 2 Handled, 6" 15.00	Tumbler, Table, Straight, 9 oz. 10.00
Nappy, Square, 1 Handle, 5½" 15.00	Vase or Ice Bucket, 6" 20.00
Nappy, Star Shape, 1 Handle, 5½" 18.00	Vase or Ice Bucket, 7" 25.00
Oil & Stopper, 3 oz. 25.00	Vase, 8" 25.00
Old Fashioned, 7 oz. 10.00	Vase, 9" 30.00
Olive, Oval, 6" 15.00	Vase, 12" 35.00
Pickle Tray, 8" 15.00	Vase, Clover Leaf, 3½" 15.00
Pitcher, ½ gal., 7¾" tall 55.00	Vase, Clover Leaf, 4" 15.00
Pitcher, 16 oz., 4¾" tall 22.00	Vase, Clover Leaf, 4½" 15.00
Plate, 2 Handled, 7½" 12.00	Vase, Clover Leaf, 6½" 18.00
Plate, 7½" 8.00	Vase, Crimped, 3½" 15.00
Plate, 8" 5.00	Vase, Crimped, 4" 15.00
Plate, 8½" 10.00	Vase, Crimped, 5" 18.00
Plate, Finger Bowl, 6" 8.00	Vase, Crimped, 5½" 15.00
Plate, Fruit, Handled, 6½" 10.00	Vase, Crimped, 7" 25.00
Plate, Sandwich, 2 Handled, 11½" 22.00	Vase, Crimped Violet, 3" 15.00
Plate, Service, Dinner or Torte, 11" 30.00	Vase, Crimped Violet, 3½" 15.00
Plate, T.C.S. Marmalade, 6" 20.00	Vase, Crimped Violet, 4½" 15.00
Plate, Torte, 14" 30.00	Vase, Flared, 9" 30.00
Relish, 3 Compartment, 7" 18.00	Vase, Oval, 3½" 15.00
Relish, 3 Compartment, 3 Handled, 8" 15.00	Vase, Oval, 4" 15.00
Relish, 3 Compartment, 3 Handled, 9" 15.00	Vase, Oval, 4½" 15.00
Relish, 2 Compartment, 2 Handled, 7" 18.00	Whiskey, 1½ oz. 12.00
Relish, Round, 2 Compartment, 2 Handled, 6" 15.00	
Relish, Star Shape, 2 Compartment, 2 Handled, 6" . . 18.00	**BLOWN ITEMS NO. 5115:**
Rose Bowl, 4" 20.00	Claret, 5 oz. $15.00
Rose Bowl, 5" 22.00	Cocktail, Footed, 5½ oz. 15.00
Rose Bowl, Tall Shape, 6" 25.00	Cocktail, Liquor, 3 oz. 12.00
Salt & Pepper, 3¾", pr. 25.00	Cordial, 1 oz. 25.00
Sea Food Cocktail, 4½ oz. 10.00	Finger Bowl 15.00
Sherbet (Champagne), 6 oz. 9.00	Goblet, 10 oz. 15.00
Sherbet, Crimped, 4½" 8.00	Goblet, Low, 12 oz. 15.00
Sherbet, Crimped, 5½" 10.00	Ice Cream Footed, 5 oz. 10.00
Sugar, 7 oz., 3" 9.00	Iced Tea, Footed, 12 oz. 15.00
Sugar, Individual, 3 oz. 10.00	Iced Tea, Footed, 15 oz. 15.00
Sweetmeat, Star Shape, 2 Handled, 6" 15.00	Juice, Footed, 7½ oz. 10.00
Top Hat or Cigarette Holder, 3" 25.00	Juice, Orange, Footed, 5 oz. 10.00
Tray, 2 Compartment, 2 Handled, 8" 15.00	Oyster Cocktail, 4 oz. 8.00
Tray, 4 Compartment, 9" 10.00	Saucer Champagne, 5 oz. 10.00
Tray, Celery, 2 Handled, 9" 15.00	Sherbet, Low, 8 oz. 8.00
Tray, Mint, Footed, 4" 15.00	Tumbler, Footed, 10 oz. 10.00
Tray, Pickle & Olive, 2 Compartment, 8" or 9" 15.00	Wine, 3½ oz. 15.00

CHARADE

Charade Luncheon Set

Date: Ca. 1930s

Manufacturer: Unknown

Colors: Crystal, Deep Blue, Amethyst, Pink, Black

The black set comes with crystal cups. Prices are for colored pieces. Prices for crystal are 75% of color.

Cream $12.00
Cup & Saucer 12.00
Plate, 8" 6.00
Sandwich, Center Handled, 10" 24.00
Sugar 12.00

Charade Handled Sandwich Tray

CHARM

Charm Cup & Saucer

Date: 1950 to 1954

Manufacturer: Anchor Hocking Glass Corporation, Lancaster, OH

Colors: Azur-ite, Jadite, Forest Green, Royal Ruby

Charm is a small tableware line made in several colors. Pieces are square shaped.

	Azur-ite	Jadite	Forest Green	Royal Ruby
Bowl, Salad, 7⅜"	$14.00	$25.00	$15.00	$17.00
Bowl, Soup, 6"	17.00	25.00	22.00	25.00
Cream	9.00	18.00	9.00	10.00
Cup & Saucer *(Illus.)*	8.00	18.00	9.00	10.00
Dessert, 4¾"	6.00	12.00	7.00	9.00
Plate, Dinner, 9¼"	17.00	32.00	37.00	40.00
Plate, Luncheon, 8¼"	9.00	13.00	10.00	12.00
Plate, Salad, 6½"	7.00	10.00	7.00	9.00
Platter, 11"	18.00	35.00	27.00	30.00
Sugar	10.00	18.00	9.00	11.00

CONTOUR

Date: 1955 to 1977

Manufacturer: Fostoria Glass Co., Moundsville, WV

Colors: Crystal, Pink opalescent

Contour is the original name of the pattern and piece names are taken from original company price lists and catalogs.

No. 2638:

Ashtray, 3"	$7.00
Ashtray, 6"	12.00
Ashtray, 7"	10.00
Bowl, 3 Cornered, 7½"	18.00
Bowl, 5 ½"	10.00
Bowl, Deep, 7"	18.00
Bowl, High, Flared, 10¾"	25.00
Bowl, Oblong, 10½"	22.00
Bowl, Oval, 8½"	20.00
Bowl, Square, 5½"	10.00
Bowl, Square, 8½"	18.00
Candlesticks, 4½", pr.	30.00
Tray, 7"	12.00

No. 2666:

Bonbon, 6⅞"	$15.00
Bowl, Oval, 8¼"	18.00
Bowl, Salad, 9"	22.00
Bowl, Salad, 11"	25.00
Butter & Cover, Oblong, 7"	35.00
Celery, 9"	16.00
Cream, 8½ oz.	12.00
Cream, Individual, 5½"	14.00
Cup & Saucer	18.00
Flora-Candles, 6", pr.	32.00
Mayonnaise, 3 piece set	38.00
Pitcher & Plate, Sauce, 8½"	38.00
Pitcher, pt., 5¼"	30.00
Pitcher, qt., 6⅞"	45.00
Pitcher, 3 pts., 8¾"	50.00
Plate, 7"	10.00
Plate, Canape, 7⅜"	12.00
Plate, Crescent Salad, 7¼"	18.00
Plate, Sandwich, 11½"	30.00
Plate, Snack, 10"	18.00
Plate, Torte, 14"	32.00
Plate, Torte, 16"	37.00
Preserve, Handled, 6½"	20.00
Relish, 2 Part, 7⅜"	15.00
Relish, 3 Part, 10¾"	20.00
Salt & Pepper, 2⅝", pr.	20.00
Salt & Pepper, 3¼", pr.	20.00
Salver, 11¼"	30.00
Sugar, 2⅝"	12.00
Sugar, Individual, 2½"	12.00
Tray, Lunch, Handled, 11¼"	30.00
Tray for Sugar & Cream	12.00

No. 6060 Stemware:

Cordial, 1 oz.	$30.00
Goblet, 10½ oz.	22.00
Goblet, Luncheon/Iced Tea, Footed, 14 oz.	22.00
Juice, Footed, 6 oz.	20.00
Plate, 7"	15.00
Plate, Coupe, 7"	15.00
Sherbet, 6½ oz.	12.00
Wine/Cocktail, 5 oz.	20.00

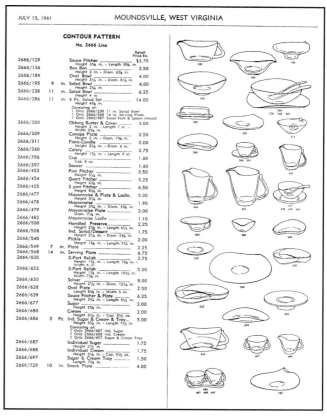

Contour Catalog Page

FOVAL (PEARL ART GLASS)

Foval Plate, Cup & Saucer

Date: Ca. 1922

Manufacturer: H. C. Fry Glass Co., Rochester, PA

Colors: Pearl glass, often with either Jade or Delft trim.

This "Heat Resisting Glass" was patented in May of 1922 and assigned to the H. C. Fry Glass Co. Most of the Pearl Art Glass pieces are found with Jade (green) or Delft (blue) accents, usually in the form of feet, handles and finials. Plates are solid color in Pearl, Jade or Delft. Some Pearl plates have Jade or Delft edges. Tea sets were decorated with blue or gold bands, silver overlay bands or gold overlay. Ice tea sets were also made with a "stippled" surface. In trade journal reports, the company stressed that the Pearl tableware was made of the same glass as their ovenware. Teapots and coffeepots were sturdy enough to hold boiling water without cracking. In the following list, we have listed which portions of each piece were made with the Jade or Delft trim. Do not be confused, the pieces were made entirely in Pearl and also with the trims as listed. Names and numbers of pieces are from original company price lists.

	Pearl	Jade or Delft Trim
Berry Saucer, Footed (sherbet shape) (No. 2503), colored foot	$125.00	$135.00
Bowl, Berry, 8" (No. 2503), colored foot	325.00	350.00
Bowl, Cereal, 7½", (No. 2100), colored edge	125.00	135.00
Bowl, Fruit, 10" (No. 2200), colored foot	375.00	400.00
Bowl, Fruit, 10" (low) (No. 2502), colored foot	400.00	425.00
Bowl, Fruit, 10" (No. 2505), colored foot	425.00	475.00
Bowl, Salad, 9½" (No. 2504), colored foot	450.00	500.00
Bouillon Cup & Saucer, 6 oz. (No. 2400 cup, 2000 saucer)	125.00	135.00
Cake Plate, Handled, 3 Ball Feet, 10" (No. 600) colored handles & feet	400.00	425.00
Candlesticks, 10" pr. (No. 1103) pearl post, colored buttons & stripe on post		600.00
Candlesticks, 10", pr. (No. 1105) pearl post, base & bobeches, jade buttons		600.00
Coffee Percolator (glass basket & stand) (No. 3000)	575.00	600.00
Coffeepot, Individual (No. 2000), colored handle, spout & knob	750.00	775.00

	Pearl	Jade or Delft Trim
Cologne & Stopper, colored knob	400.00	450.00
Compote, 6", (No. 2502), colored stem	300.00	325.00
Comport, Covered, 5½", (No. 100), colored stem and knob	375.00	400.00
Cream, (No. 2000)	150.00	160.00
Cream, (No. 2001), colored handle & foot	175.00	190.00
Cup & Saucer, Coffee, 6 oz. (No. 2400 cup, 2000 saucer), colored handles	120.00	125.00
Cup & Saucer, After Dinner Coffee (tall), (No. 2003), colored handles	90.00	95.00
Cup & Saucer, After Dinner (short), (No. 2002), colored handles	90.00	95.00
Cup & Saucer, Tea (No. 2000), colored handle *(Illus.)*	75.00	85.00
Cup & Saucer, Tea (tall) (No. 9003 cup, 2000 saucer), colored handle	90.00	100.00
Egg Cup, (No. 2300), colored foot	150.00	160.00
Fruit Saucer, 6½", (No. 2100), colored edge	125.00	135.00
Goblet, colored stem	125.00	135.00
Iced Tea, Handled, 12 oz. (No. 9416), colored handle	120.00	130.00
Iced Tea, Handled & Footed	125.00	135.00

FOVAL (PEARL ART GLASS) *(continued)*

	Pearl	Jade or Delft Trim
Jug & Cover, Hot Water, 12 oz. (No. 2000), colored handle & knob	250.00	275.00
Jug & Cover, (No. 11), colored handle & knob	400.00	475.00
Jug, Footed, (No. 4), colored handle & foot	500.00	550.00
Perfume & Atomizer, colored foot	500.00	550.00
Plate, Grill, 10½" (No. 1957)	25.00	
Plate, 7½", (No. 3101)	85.00	90.00
Plate, Breakfast, 8" (No. 2100)	100.00	125.00
Plate, Bread & Butter, 7", (No. 2100)	100.00	125.00
Plate, Salad, 8½", (No. 2504) *(Illus.)*	100.00	125.00
Plate, Soup, 8", (shallow soup bowl) (No. 2100), colored edge	135.00	150.00
Powder Box & Cover, colored foot & knob	350.00	375.00
Sherbet, colored stem	125.00	135.00
Sugar, (No. 2001), colored handles & foot	175.00	190.00
Sugar, (No. 2000)	150.00	160.00
Teapot, (No. 2001), colored handle, spout, & knob (3 cup)	450.00	475.00
Teapot, (No. 2000), colored handle, spout & knob (6 cup)	300.00	350.00
Teapot, English Shape, (No. 2005), colored handle, spout & knob (6 cup)	400.00	425.00
Teapot, Individual, (No. 2002), colored handle, spout & knob (2 cup)	400.00	425.00

	Pearl	Jade or Delft Trim
Toast Plate & Cover, (No. 2100), colored handles	350.00	375.00
Tray, Lemon, Handled, 6" (No. 600)	400.00	450.00
Tumbler, 9 oz. (No. 9416)	85.00	
Vase, 5" (No. 828), colored foot & edge	325.00	350.00
Vase, 6" (No. 826), colored foot & edge	300.00	350.00
Vase, 6½" (No. 831), colored button	275.00	300.00
Vase, 7" (No. 351), colored foot	350.00	375.00
Vase, 8" (No. 830), colored button	300.00	325.00
Vase, 9" (No. 1658), colored foot, button & edge	400.00	425.00
Vase, 10" (No. 353), colored foot, stem & edge	375.00	400.00
Vase, 10" jack-in-the-pulpit, (No. 821), colored edge	350.00	375.00
Vase, Bud, 10" (No. 804), colored foot	200.00	225.00
Vase, Bud, 10" (No. 814), colored button	175.00	200.00
Vase, Sweet Pea, 6" (No. 2502), colored foot	350.00	375.00
Vase, Trumpet, 8", 10", 12" (No. 1657), colored foot	375.00	400.00
Vase, Violet, 4" (No. 823), colored foot	300.00	325.00
Wine, colored stem	125.00	135.00

LAGUNA, NO. 154

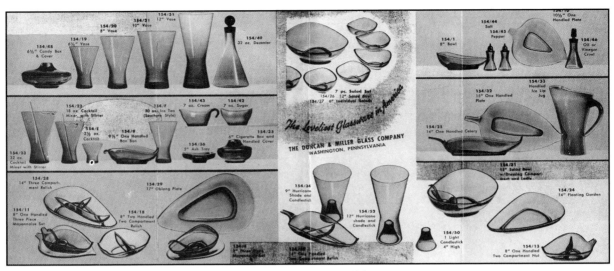

Laguna Pattern Folder

Date: Ca. 1950s

Manufacturer: Duncan & Miller Glass Co., Washington, PA

Colors: Crystal, Smoky Avocado, Teakwood Brown, Biscayne Green

A very modernistic, informal pattern typical of designs of the 1950s. Designed by James Rosati. In 1953 Laguna was selected by the Museum of Modern Art for its Good Design. Piece names are from original company price lists and catalogs. Laguna is the original name.

	Crystal	Colors
Ashtray, 5"	$7.00	$18.00
Ashtray, 7½"	9.00	22.00
Ashtray, 8"	9.00	22.00
Beverage, 14 oz.	14.00	32.00
Bonbon, 1 Handled, 9½"	12.00	25.00
Bonbon, 2 Handled, 9"	12.00	25.00
Bowl, 8"	12.00	25.00
Bowl, 1 Handled, 8"	12.00	25.00
Bowl, Individual Salad, 6"	7.00	18.00
Bowl, Salad, 12"	18.00	38.00
Bowl, Salad with Dressing Compartment, 12"	20.00	42.00
Candlesticks, 1 Light, 4", pr.	25.00	55.00
Candlesticks, 1 Light with Hurricane Shade, 9", pr.	50.00	110.00
Candlesticks, 1 Light with Hurricane Shade, 12", pr.	60.00	125.00
Candy Box & Cover, 6½"	25.00	55.00
Celery, 2 Handled, 10"	20.00	38.00
Celery, 1 Handled, 14"	22.00	42.00
Cigarette Box & Handled Cover, 6"	25.00	55.00

	Crystal	Colors
Cocktail, 3½ oz.	10.00	22.00
Cocktail Mixer, 18 oz.	35.00	75.00
Cocktail Mixer, 32 oz.	40.00	85.00
Cream, 7 oz.	12.00	28.00
Decanter & Stopper, 32 oz.	40.00	80.00
Dressing, Twin, 8"	15.00	25.00
Floating Garden, 14"	30.00	60.00
Iced Tea (Southern Style), 20 oz.	17.00	35.00
Jug, Handled, Ice Lip	50.00	110.00
Juice, 5 oz.	8.00	17.00
Mayonnaise, 1 handled, 8"	15.00	25.00
Nut, 1 Handled, 2 Compartment, 8"	15.00	25.00
Oil or Vinegar Cruet	25.00	75.00
Plate, 9"	10.00	25.00
Plate, Oblong, 17"	22.00	55.00
Plate, 1 Handled, 10½"	18.00	35.00
Plate, 1 Handled, 15"	20.00	50.00
Plate, 2 Handled, 10"	18.00	35.00
Relish, 1 Handled, 2 Compartment, 14"	20.00	50.00
Relish, 2 Handled, 2 Compartment, 8"	15.00	25.00
Relish, 3 Compartment, 14"	20.00	50.00
Salt & Pepper, pr.	22.00	60.00
Sugar, 7 oz.	12.00	28.00
Sherbet or Old Fashioned, 7 oz.	6.00	15.00
Water, 10 oz.	12.00	20.00
Vase, 6½"	12.00	22.00
Vase, 8"	15.00	30.00
Vase, 10"	18.00	35.00
Vase, 12"	20.00	40.00

MAYFAIR, NO. 2419

Date: 1930 to 1944

Manufacturer: Fostoria Glass Co., Moundsville, WV

Colors: Crystal, Azure, Green, Topaz/Gold Tint, Amber, Rose. Some pieces in Ebony, Wisteria and Ruby.

The ashtray was made in Regal Blue, Burgundy, Empire Green, Ruby, Ebony but not Azure. Tea cream and sugar were made in all colors but Ruby and Azure. For pieces in Wisteria, add 100% to Crystal prices.

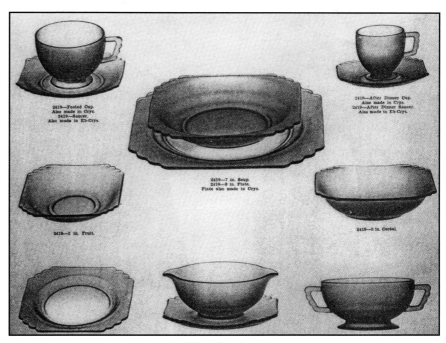

Mayfair Catalog Page

	Crystal	Topaz, Rose, Ebony	Ruby Azure, Empire Green		Crystal	Topaz, Rose, Ebony	Ruby Azure, Empire Green
Ashtray	$8.00	$12.00	$14.00	Pickle, 8½"	15.00	22.00	
Baker, Oval Vegetable, 10"	16.00	24.00		Plate, 6" or 7"	8.00	12.00	14.00
Bonbon, 2 Handled	15.00	22.00		Plate, 8"	10.00	15.00	
Cake Plate, 2 Handled, 10"	25.00	37.00		Plate, 9"	20.00	30.00	
Celery, 11"	14.00	21.00		Platter, 12"	25.00	37.00	
Cereal, 6"	9.00	12.00		Platter, 15"	40.00	60.00	
Comport, 6"	15.00	22.00		Relish, 2 part, 8½"	15.00	22.00	
Cream	12.00	18.00		Relish, 4 part, 2 Handled	15.00	22.00	
Cream, Footed (2419½)	12.00	18.00		Sauce Bowl (2 lips) & Stand			
Cream, Tea (small)	15.00	22.00	25.00	(1 pc.)	30.00	45.00	
Cream Soup, 2 Handled	16.00	24.00		Soup, 7"	14.00	21.00	
Cup & Saucer	15.00	22.00		Sugar	12.00	18.00	
Cup & Saucer, After Dinner	20.00	30.00		Sugar, Footed (2419½)	12.00	18.00	
Fruit, 5"	7.00	10.00		Sugar, Tea (small)	15.00	22.00	25.00
Jelly, 2 Handled	15.00	22.00	25.00	Syrup & Cover	30.00	45.00	
Lemon, 2 Handled	18.00	27.00		Tray, Condiment, 8¾"	25.00	37.00	
Lunch Tray, Center Handled	28.00	40.00		Underplate for Syrup	12.00	18.00	
Mayonnaise, 2 Handled	30.00	45.00					

MT. PLEASANT

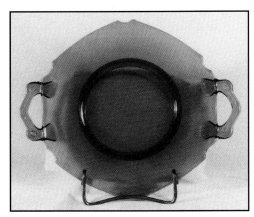

Mt. Pleasant 7" Handled Plate

Date: 1920s to 1934

Manufacturer: L. E. Smith, Mt. Pleasant, PA

Colors: Black, Amethyst, Deep Blue, Crystal, Pink, Green

	Pastels	Amethyst, Deep Blue, Black			Pastels	Amethyst, Deep Blue, Black
Bonbon, Handled, 7"	$15.00	$22.00		Cup & Saucer	14.00	20.00
Bowl, 10"		42.00		Mayonnaise, Footed	20.00	30.00
Bowl, 2 Handled, 8"	20.00	30.00		Mint Dish, Center Handled, 6" . . .	15.00	20.00
Bowl, 2 Handled, 10"		28.00		Plate, 8"	10.00	16.00
Bowl, Flared, 3 Footed, 7"	15.00	22.00		Plate, Grill, 9"		14.00
Bowl, Footed, 9"		25.00		Plate, Handled, 7" *(Illus.)*	10.00	15.00
Bowl, Square, 4"	12.00	18.00		Plate, Handled, 8"	10.00	17.00
Bowl, Square, Footed, 9¼"	20.00	28.00		Plate, Handled, 12"	22.00	35.00
Bowl, Square, Handled, 6"	12.00	17.00		Rose Bowl, 4"	20.00	27.00
Bowl, Square, 2 Handled, 8"	20.00	28.00		Salt and Pepper, pr.		40.00
Cake Plate, Handled, 10½"		35.00		Sandwich, Center Handled		40.00
Candlesticks, 1 Light, pr.	24.00	30.00		Sherbet	9.00	15.00
Candlesticks, 2 Light, pr.	27.00	48.00		Sugar		20.00
Cream	16.00	20.00		Vase, 7¼"		32.00

NEW ERA, NO. 4044

New Era Dinner Plate, Individual Nut, Cream,
Cup & Saucer, Goblet, Tumbler
(some pieces with satin highlights)

Date: 1934 to 1941. Stemware and candelabra were made from 1944 to 1957.

Manufacturer: A. H. Heisey & Co., Newark, OH

Colors: Crystal. Stiegel Blue in 1934 only, so it is very difficult to find.

A very Deco styled pattern based on an imported French china service. Used for cuttings and satin decorations by Heisey. New Era is the original name of the pattern and piece names are from original catalogs. The line was patented in 1934. Imperial Glass Corporation reproduced the candelabrum in crystal for about 14 years. Prices are for crystal pieces. For pieces in Stiegel Blue (Cobalt) add as much as 500%.

(continued) NEW ERA, NO. 4044

Ashtray or Individual Nut *(Illus.)* $35.00
Bowl, Floral, 11" 65.00
Candlesticks with Bobeches & Prisms, 2 Light, pr. . . 150.00
Celery Tray, 13" 35.00
Claret, 4 oz. 24.00
Cocktail, 3½ oz. 20.00
Cordial, 1 oz. 65.00
Cream *(Illus.)* 35.00
Cup & Saucer *(Illus.)* 50.00
Cup & Saucer, After Dinner 68.00
Finger Bowl 12.00
Goblet, 10 oz. *(Illus.)* 28.00

Oyster Cocktail, 3½ oz. 20.00
Pilsner, 12 oz. 55.00
Plate, 9" x 7" 35.00
Plate, Bread & Butter, 5½" x 4½" 22.00
Relish, 3 Compartment, 13" 35.00
Rye Bottle & Stopper 140.00
Saucer Champagne, 6 oz. 22.00
Sherbet, 6 oz. 17.00
Soda, Footed, 12 oz. 27.00
Sugar 35.00
Tumbler, Footed, 10 oz. *(Illus.)* 22.00
Wine, 3 oz. 35.00

No. 84000

Date: 1957

Manufacturer: Anchor Hocking Glass Corporation, Lancaster, OH

Colors: Turquoise Blue

No original name was found for this tableware pattern. It is likely a grouping of many of Anchor Hocking's standard pieces. It was marketed under the name of Turquoise Blue which is the original color name. Kitchenware was also made in this color. (See Kitchen section for some of these items.) A few pieces were made with gold trim on the edges as special items. Descriptions of pieces and numbers are from original company material.

Bowl, Vegetable, 8¼" (84078) $17.00
Cream (84054) *(Illus.)* 7.50
Cup & Saucer (84079, 84029) *(Illus.)* 7.00
Dessert, 4⅝" (84074) *(Illus.)* 7.00
Plate, Bread & Butter, 6¼" (84037) 14.00
Plate, Dinner, 9" (84041) *(Illus.)* 9.00
Plate, Salad, 7¼" (84038) *(Illus.)* 12.00
Plate, Serving, 10" (84046) 30.00
Soup Plate, 6⅝" (bowl) (84067) 17.00
Sugar (84053) *(Illus.)* 7.50

OTHER PIECES IN TURQUOISE BLUE:

Ashtray, Square, 3½" $7.00
Ashtray, Square, 4⅝" 10.00
Ashtray, Square, 5¾" 15.00
Bowl, 5" 15.00
Egg Plate, 9¾" 18.00
Mug, Coffee, 8 oz. 12.00
Plate, Cup Indent for Snack Set, 9" 8.00
Relish, 3 Compartment, 11" 15.00

No. 84000 Plate, Sugar & Cream, Dessert,
Salad Plate, Cup & Saucer

OVIDE

Ovide Cream & Sugar

Date: 1930 to 1950

Manufacturer: Hazel-Atlas Glass Co.

Colors: Platonite, solid enamel colors, including Burgundy, Chartreuse, Green, Gray (original color names). Also Pine Green, Red, Orange Yellow. Also borders of Pink with a charcoal rim, Blue with a charcoal rim, and Sierra Sunrise, a graduated orange rim.

This "pattern" is confusing to today's collectors and researchers. Hazel-Atlas, along with Anchor Hocking, often seems to have marketed various of their standard shapes with matching colors or decorations, often calling the new sets by the names of the decorations or colors, not the name of the blank, since they were not specific patterns, but only like pieces. Ovide is one of these "patterns," and actually Ovide appears to be the name of the shape of the cup. Many adjectives have been applied to the line as names. Hazel-Atlas referred to some of the colors as "Moderntone"— confusing because of another Hazel-Atlas pattern using this name. Prices below are for solid enamel colors on Platonite.

Bowl, 4¾"	$7.00
Bowl, deep, 5½"	14.00
Bowl, 8"	20.00
Cream *(Illus.)*	6.00
Cup & Saucer	6.00
Plate, 6"	3.00

Plate, 8"	5.00
Platter	20.00
Sherbet	3.00
Sugar *(Illus.)*	6.00
Tumbler	14.00

RESTAURANT WARE

Restaurant Ware Grill Plate, Coffee Mug

Date: 1950 to 1956

Manufacturer: Anchor Hocking Glass Corporation, Lancaster, OH

Colors: Jade-ite. Much was also made in Anchorwhite, and with many decorations.

This is a grouping of various items in Anchor Hocking's standard line and not a true pattern. Many collectors use these plain pieces to augment some of the other Jade-ite lines which have few accessory pieces. Also many people like the sturdiness and weight of the heavier restaurant ware. Prices are for pieces in Jade-ite. Piece names and numbers are from original company material. Anchorwhite prices are 50% of Jade-ite.

(continued) RESTAURANT WARE

Bowl, 10 oz. (G309). $15.00
Bowl, 15 oz. (G300). 20.00
Cup (narrow rim), 7 oz. & Saucer, 6" (G319,
   G295). 18.00
Cup, 6 oz. (G215) 9.00
Cup, Extra Heavy, 7 oz. (G299) 10.00
Fruit, 4¾" (G294) 9.00
Grapefruit or Cereal, 8 oz. (G305) (with flange) 20.00
Mug, Coffee (extra heavy), 7 oz. (G212) *(Illus.)*. 9.00

Plate, 3 Compartment, 9⅝" (G292) *(Illus.)*. 20.00
Plate, 5 Compartment, 9⅝" (G311) 25.00
Plate, Bread & Butter, 5½" (G315). 4.50
Plate, Dinner, 9" (G306) 18.00
Plate, Luncheon, 8" (G316) 10.00
Plate, Oval Partitioned, 8⅞" (G211). 22.00
Plate, Pie or Salad, 6¾" (G297) 8.00
Platter, Oval, 9½" (G307) 25.00
Platter, Oval, 11½" (G308) 20.00

YEOMAN, NO. 1184, 1185, 1187, 1189

Date: 1913 to 1957

Manufacturer: A. H. Heisey & Co., Newark, OH

Colors: Crystal, Moongleam, Flamingo, Sahara, Marigold, Hawthorne

Reproductions: Imperial Glass Corp. made most stemware and a few other pieces in crystal with diamond optic.

Extensive tableware line. Made in plain or diamond optic. Selected pieces were made in other colors and not all pieces were made in all colors listed. Yeoman borrowed some pieces from other patterns which were added to its line. Original Heisey numbers are listed after these entries, but Yeoman is a name given by researchers. Pieces are often found with Heisey etchings. Cuttings on Yeoman blanks were usually done by various decorating companies. Most, but not all, pieces are marked with the Diamond H. For a discussion of Marigold color, see Heisey's Twist pattern, in the "Swirl" chapter.

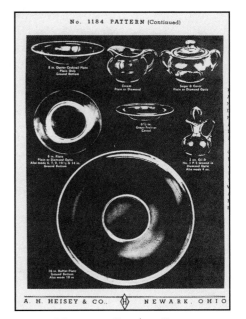

Yeoman Catalog Page

	Crystal	Moongleam, Flamingo, Sahara	Marigold	Hawthorne
Ashtray (No. 1187) 2 piece	$45.00	$85.00	$	$
Ashtray, Handled, 4"	24.00	48.00		
Ashtray, Individual (No. 1186)	10.00	35.00		75.00
Ashtray and Cigarette Holder	24.00	45.00		
Baker, Oval, 9".	18.00	30.00	45.00	
Banana Split, Footed.	17.00	35.00	55.00	
Bar, 2½ oz. (No. 236).	10.00	22.00		
Bonbon, Handled, 6½"	22.00	45.00		
Bonbon, 2 Handled, 5½"	18.00	24.00		
Bouillon, Footed.	22.00	48.00	80.00	
Bowl, Floral, 12"	22.00	35.00		
Candy Box & Cover, 6"	38.00	80.00	150.00	

YEOMAN, No. 1184, 1185, 1186, 1187, 1189 *(continued)*

	Crystal	Moongleam, Flamingo, Sahara	Marigold	Hawthorne
Candy Box & Cover, Deep, 6"	42.00	90.00	170.00	
Candy Dish, Handled, 8½" (bow tie shape)	24.00	55.00	100.00	
Celery, 9"	10.00	24.00	38.00	
Celery, 12" (No. 1185)	24.00	45.00		
Celery, 13"	12.00	25.00	45.00	
Celery Tray, 9" or 13" (No. 1189) . . .	22.00	50.00		
Cigarette Box with Ashtray Cover . . .	45.00	70.00		
Claret	18.00	28.00		
Coaster	9.00			
Cocktail, 3 oz.	15.00	27.00		
Comport, High Footed, 5"	24.00	35.00		
Comport, High Footed, 6" and 7" (No. 1186)	30.00	55.00		
Comport, Low Footed, Deep, 6"	22.00	35.00		
Cream (No. 1023)	24.00	45.00	65.00	65.00
Cream, Individual (No. 1189)	55.00	130.00		
Cream, Individual (restaurant)	35.00	48.00		
Cream Soup	17.00	30.00	60.00	65.00
Cup & Saucer (2 styles)	18.00	35.00	55.00	60.00
Cup & Saucer, After Dinner	35.00	55.00	90.00	
Dish, Berry, 2 Handled, 8½"	24.00	40.00		
Dish, Lemon, Oval, 5"	17.00			
Dish, Lemon & Cover, Round, 5" . . .	24.00	45.00		
Dish, Vegetable, 6"	8.00	15.00		
Dish, Vegetable & Cover, 9"	50.00	100.00	185.00	
Egg Cup	30.00	45.00	85.00	
Finger Bowl	12.00	25.00		
French Dressing Boat & Underplate . . .	35.00	75.00		
Fruit, Oval, 9"	24.00			
Fruit Cocktail, 4 oz.	10.00	17.00		
Goblet, 8 oz.	12.00	25.00		
Goblet, 10 oz.	15.00	27.00		
Grapefruit, Footed	18.00	30.00		
Hors' d'oeuvre Base, Center & Cover, 13"	145.00			
Jelly, Low Foot, 5"	15.00			
Jug, qt.	75.00	120.00		
Marmalade & Cover	30.00			
Mint, 3 Compartment, Center Handled, 8"	28.00	45.00	65.00	
Mixing Glass & Metal Cover, 28 oz. (cocktail shaker)	120.00			
Mustard & Cover	65.00	135.00		
Nappy, 4½"	8.00	15.00		
Nappy, Deep, 8"	18.00	24.00		
Oil & Stopper, 2 oz.	40.00	100.00	185.00	
Oil & Stopper, 4 oz.	35.00	85.00	175.00	
Oyster Cocktail, 2¾ oz.	10.00	22.00		

(*continued*) Yeoman, No. 1184, 1185, 1186, 1187, 1189

	Crystal	Moongleam, Flamingo, Sahara	Marigold	Hawthorne
Parfait, 5 oz.	17.00	35.00		
Pickle & Olive, 8"	27.00	40.00		
Pickle & Olive, 2 Compartment, 13" (No. 1189)	24.00	45.00		
Plate, 6"	8.00	15.00	25.00	
Plate, 7"	8.00	15.00	25.00	
Plate, 8"	10.00	15.00	35.00	
Plate, 9"	10.00	17.00	35.00	
Plate, 10½"	55.00	75.00	100.00	
Plate, 14"	35.00	50.00	75.00	
Plate, 4 Compartment, 11"	25.00	45.00		
Plate, Cheese, 2 Handled	10.00			
Plate, Coaster, 4½"	10.00			
Plate, Crescent Salad, 8"	30.00	55.00		200.00
Plate, Grapefruit, 6½"	8.00	15.00	25.00	
Plate, Grill, 9"	25.00	45.00		
Plate, Oval, 7"	15.00	22.00		
Plate, Oyster Cocktail, 8"	10.00	15.00		
Plate, Soup, 8" (bowl)	20.00			
Platter, 12"	22.00	40.00	55.00	
Platter, 15"	32.00	50.00	60.00	
Preserve, 6"	17.00			
Puff Box & Cover with Insert (No. 1186)	75.00	180.00		250.00
Relish, 3 Compartment, 13"	17.00	30.00	45.00	
Salver, Low Foot, 10"	38.00			
Sandwich, Handled, 10½"	22.00	40.00		
Saucer Champagne, 6 oz.	12.00	20.00		
Sherbet, 3½ oz. or 4½ oz.	8.00	12.00		
Smoking Set, Bridge—Handled Tray with 8 Ashtrays	70.00	120.00	150.00	170.00
Soda, 4½ oz.	6.00	12.00		
Soda, Footed, 5 oz.	10.00	14.00		
Soda, Footed, 12 oz.	12.00	16.00		
Soda, Straight, 8 oz.	8.00	12.00		
Soda, Straight or Cupped, 10 oz.	8.00	12.00		
Soda, Straight or Cupped, 12 oz.	8.00	12.00		
Sugar & Cover (No. 1023)	28.00	50.00	80.00	80.00
Sugar & Cover, Individual (No. 1189)	65.00	145.00		
Syrup, Saucer Foot (attached), 7 oz.	60.00			
Tray, 2 Compartment, Oval, 10½"	28.00	45.00		
Tray, 3 Compartment, Handled, 11"	35.00			
Tray, Oblong, 12"	23.00			
Tray, Relish, 7" x 10" with Inserts	95.00	140.00		
Tray, Spice, 3 Compartment, 12"— 4 pc. set (No. 1187)	45.00			
Tumbler Cover	35.00			
Tumbler, 8 oz.	8.00	12.00		

Chapter 13

RIBS

ANNIVERSARY

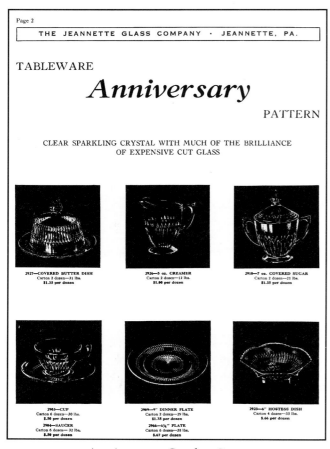

Anniversary Catalog Page

Date: 1947

Manufacturer: Jeannette Glass Co., Jeannette, PA

Colors: Pink. In the late 1950s in Crystal and Crystal iridescent.

	Crystal	Pink
Dish, Fruit, 4¾"	$6.00	$8.00
Bowl, Soup or Cereal, 7¼"	7.50	17.00
Bowl, Fruit, 9"	12.00	22.00
Butter & Cover.	40.00	60.00
Candy Jar & Cover	32.00	55.00
Comport, 3 Footed	7.00	12.00
Cake Plate, 12½"	8.00	15.00
Cake Plate, Square, 12¼"	8.00	15.00
Candlesticks, 5", pr.	20.00	
Cream	6.00	12.50
Cup & Saucer.	6.00	12.50
Dish, Hostess, 6"	7.00	15.00
Pickle, 9"	7.00	15.00
Plate, 6¼"	3.50	3.50
Plate, Dinner, 9"	7.00	14.00
Plate, Sandwich, 12½"	8.00	15.00
Relish, 8"	7.00	15.00
Sherbet.	5.00	9.00
Sugar & Cover	12.00	24.00
Vase, 6½"	15.00	40.00
Wall Pocket Vase	24.00	40.00
Wine, 2½ oz.	10.00	15.00

CARIBBEAN, NO. 112

Date: 1936

Manufacturer: Duncan & Miller Glass Co., Washington, PA

Colors: Crystal, Sapphire Blue. Occasionally found in Amber, Ruby, and Blue Opalescent. The punch cups and ladle in Crystal may have Amber, Blue or Ruby handles.

Duncan & Miller originally called this pattern "Wave." Prices are for Sapphire Blue items. For Crystal, deduct 75%.

Almond, Individual, 2½"	$25.00
Ashtray, 3" (cover for cigarette box)	25.00
Ashtray, 6"	35.00
Bar Glass, 2 oz.	50.00
Bowl, 5" x 3¾"	35.00
Bowl, 8½"	75.00
Bowl, Epergne, Flared, 9½"	100.00
Bowl, Flower, Oval, Handled, 10¾"	90.00
Bowl, Flower, Round, 12"	90.00
Bowl, Fruit Nappy, Handled, 5"	30.00
Bowl, Grapefruit, Footed and Handled, 7¼"	45.00
Bowl, Handled, 7"	45.00
Bowl, Oval, 7"	85.00
Bowl, Salad, 9"	75.00
Bowl, Soup, 6½"	42.00
Bowl, Vegetable, Flared, 9¼"	75.00
Bowl, Vegetable, Handled, 9¼"	75.00
Candelabra, with Prisms & Bobeche, 8", pr.	175.00
Candlesticks, 2 Light, 4¾", pr.	90.00
Candlesticks, 8", pr.	100.00
Candy Box & Cover, 7"	85.00
Cheese & Cracker Set, 2 pcs., 11"	70.00
Cigarette Box & Ashtray Cover	85.00
Cocktail, 3½ oz.	35.00
Cocktail Shaker, 32 oz.	200.00
Cordial, 1 oz.	150.00
Cream	25.00
Cruet & Stopper	100.00
Cup & Saucer *(Illus.)*	75.00
Finger Bowl, 4½"	35.00
Flower Ensemble, Vase, 2 Bowls and Plate, 4 pcs., 14"	450.00
Goblet, 8 oz.	25.00
Ice Bucket, Handled, 6½"	150.00
Ice Cream, 4½"	25.00
Iced Tea, 11½ oz	50.00
Iced Tea, Footed, 11 oz.	55.00
Jug, 1 pt.	250.00
Jug, with Ice Lip, 72 oz.	525.00
Juice, 5 oz.	30.00
Mayonnaise, 5¾"	50.00
Mayonnaise, 2 Compartment, 5¾"	75.00
Mustard & Cover, 4" *(Illus.)*	70.00

Caribbean Plate, Covered Mustard, Cup & Saucer

Oyster Cocktail, 2½ oz.	20.00
Plate, 6¼"	15.00
Plate, 8½" *(Illus.)*	35.00
Plate, 10½"	115.00
Plate, Handled, 6"	30.00
Plate, Handled, 11"	45.00
Plate, Mayonnaise, Handled, 8"	15.00
Plate, Rolled Edge, 7¼"	25.00
Plate, Salad, 7½"	20.00
Plate, Torte, 16"	115.00
Plate, Torte, Rolled Edge, 12" or 13"	100.00
Punch Bowl, 6¼ qt.	475.00
Punch Bowl, Flared, 6¼ qt.	475.00
Punch Bowl Plate, 18"	125.00
Punch Cup	20.00
Punch Ladle	100.00
Relish Tray	95.00
Relish, 2 Compartment, Round, 6"	75.00
Relish, 4 Compartment, Oblong, 9½"	80.00
Relish, 5 Compartment, 12¾" x 11"	95.00
Relish, 5 Compartment, Round, 12¾"	95.00
Relish, 7 Compartment, Round, 12¾"	95.00
Salt and Pepper, 3", pr.	75.00
Salt and Pepper, 5", pr.	85.00
Saucer Champagne, 6 oz.	25.00
Sugar	25.00
Syrup, 9 oz.	150.00
Tray, Mint, 2 Compartment, Handled, 6¼"	30.00
Tray, Round, 12¾"	55.00
Tumbler, Footed, 8½ oz.	40.00
Vase, 10"	110.00
Vase, Crimped Top, Footed, 5¾"	90.00
Vase, Crimped Top, Footed, 9"	110.00
Vase, Flared Top, 7¾"	105.00
Vase, Flared Top, Bulbous Base, 7½"	75.00
Vase, Flared Top, Footed, 7¼"	110.00
Vase, Straight, Footed, 7¾"	110.00
Vase, Straight, Footed, 8"	125.00
Wine, 3 oz.	100.00

CASCADE, NO. 15,365

Cascade Sugar & Cream

Date: Late 1937

Manufacturer: U. S. Glass Co., Tiffin, OH.

Colors: Crystal

This pattern was made at Factory R of U. S. Glass—Tiffin, Ohio. It is a very Art Deco inspired pattern with ribbed edges and ribbed sections. Several articles were made in a triangular shape, adding to the deco flavor.

Ashtray, Individual (triangular) $17.00	Jelly Dish & Cover. 48.00
Ashtray, Oblong. 17.00	Marmalade & Cover (triangular). 65.00
Bitters Bottle, 5¼" (blown) 95.00	Mayonnaise Bowl. 28.00
Bowl, 8¾" 35.00	Oil & Stopper (triangular) 75.00
Bowl, 13¼" 45.00	Plate, 15" (for punch bowl) 65.00
Bowl, Console, Oval. 48.00	Plate, Mayonnaise 12.00
Bowl, Low, 9" 35.00	Plate, Salad 12.00
Candlesticks, 2 Light with Bobeches, pr. 175.00	Plate, Service 45.00
Candy Jar & Cover 85.00	Punch Bowl 170.00
Cheese & Cracker with Cover. 85.00	Punch Cup 20.00
Cigarette Box & Cover (triangular) 65.00	Relish, Divided 30.00
Coaster, 3". 12.00	Salt & Pepper Shakers, Individual, 1¼" h., pr.. . . . . 65.00
Coaster, 3½" 12.00	Sugar, Oval *(Illus.)* 25.00
Comport 65.00	Tumbler, 10 oz. 28.00
Cream, Oval *(Illus.)* 25.00	Tumbler, 8 oz. 25.00
Cup & Saucer 30.00	Vase, 10" 125.00
Decanter & Stopper. 150.00	Vase, Small, 5⅜" h.. . . . . 55.00
Ice Tub & Cover 95.00	

COARSE RIB, NO. 406, 407

Coarse Rib Catalog Page

Date: 1923 to 1937

Manufacturer: A. H. Heisey & Co., Newark, OH

Colors: Crystal, Moongleam and Flamingo and limited number of items in Hawthorne.

Reproductions: A large one piece chip and dip was made by Imperial in Crystal and Cobalt, marked with the Diamond H. This piece was never made by Heisey.

Heisey used both No. 406 and 407 for items in Coarse Rib. All items are No. 407 unless otherwise noted. Be aware that a decorating company applied a marigold stain to some pieces of Coarse Rib. These are not the true Marigold color made by Heisey.

(continued) COARSE RIB, NO. 406, 407

	Crystal	Moongleam, Flamingo	Hawthorne		Crystal	Moongleam, Flamingo	Hawthorne
Celery Tray, 9"	$12.00	$35.00	$	Nappy, 9"	20.00		
Cream, Hotel	24.00			Nappy, 9" (No. 406) . . .	20.00		
Cream, Hotel				Oil & Stopper, 6 oz.	50.00		
(No. 406)	18.00	45.00	70.00	Pickle Jar & Cover	55.00		
Cream, Individual	25.00			Pickle Tray, 6"	12.00	32.00	
Custard	10.00			Plate, 8"	8.00	15.00	30.00
Dish, Lemon &				Preserve, 6"	12.00		
Cover, 5"	30.00			Saucer Champagne,			
Finger Bowl	9.00			5½ oz.		12.00	24.00
Goblet, 8 oz.	15.00	50.00		Sherbet, 6½ oz.	8.00		
Iced Tea, 12 oz.				Soda, 8 oz. (No. 406) . . .	12.00		
(No. 406)	15.00			Sugar & Cover, Hotel. . .	35.00		
Ice Tub	75.00	100.00		Sugar & Cover, Hotel			
Jelly, 2 Handled, 5"	18.00			(No. 406)	30.00	50.00	100.00
Jelly, High Footed, 5" . . .	22.00	55.00		Sugar, Individual	25.00		
Jelly, Low Footed, 5" . . .	16.00	40.00	65.00	Tankard, 3 pt.	85.00		
Jug, ½ gal.	85.00			Tumbler, 8 oz.			
Mustard & Cover	55.00			(No. 406)	17.00	50.00	
Nappy, 4½"	6.00			Tumbler, Straight,			
Nappy, 4½" (No. 406) . .	6.00	20.00		8 oz.	17.00		

CORONATION

Date: 1936 to 1949

Manufacturer: Hocking Glass Co., Lancaster, OH

Colors: Pink, Crystal, Red. Limited production in Green.

	Crystal	Pink	Red
Bowl, 4¼"	$4.00	$6.00	$10.00
Bowl, 6½"	5.00	8.00	27.00
Bowl, 8"	8.00	15.00	25.00
Bowl, Handled, 8"	7.00	10.00	18.00
Cup & Saucer	6.00	9.00	12.00 *(cup only)*
Pitcher, with or without			
Ice Lip, 68 oz.		400.00+	
Plate, 6" *(Illus.)*	2.00	3.50	
Plate, 8½"	5.00	8.00	12.00
Sherbet	4.00	9.00	
Tumbler, Footed, 10 oz.	12.00	32.00	

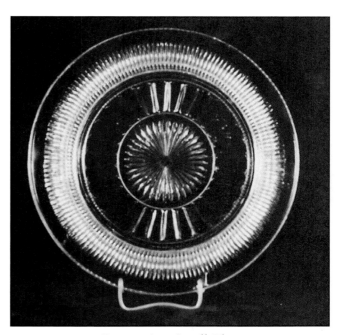

Coronation Small Plate

CRYSTOLITE, No. 1503

Crystolite Shell Torte Plate

Date: 1938 to 1957

Manufacturer: A. H. Heisey & Co., Newark, OH

Colors: Crystal

Reproductions: Imperial Glass Corp. made about 15 pieces in crystal, some with the Diamond H.

Inspired by a European cigarette box and ashtray set, Heisey first made this smoking set and called it No. 1503 Mahabar, available in Crystal, Sahara and Zircon. Within weeks, the set became a full pattern with the name changed to Crystolite. The popularity of this pattern helped the Heisey company survive the difficult years of World War II. Crystolite was made in a wide variety of pieces and many were made for only a short time, making them difficult to find today. Candy boxes are often found with metal lids with various glass finials, sometimes in fruit shapes, and sometimes using the Crystolite candleblock. This candleblock is also sometimes fitted with a cigarette lighter. These lids were made by other companies using Heisey parts.

Ashtray or Coaster, Round, 3½"	$7.00
Ashtray or Coaster, Round, 4"	7.00
Ashtray, 4" x 6"	75.00
Ashtray, Book Match, 5"	40.00
Ashtray, Square, 3½" or 4½"	7.00
Ball Vase (No. 1503½)	500.00
Basket, 6"	300.00
Bitter Bottle & Tube, 4 oz.	110.00
Bonbon, 2 Handled, 7"	15.00
Bonbon or Relish, Shell, 7"	30.00
Bowl, 1000 Island Dressing, 5", Crimped or Plain	24.00
Bowl, Combination Salad & Mayonnaise, Shell, 11"	200.00
Bowl, Floral, Round, 10"	55.00
Bowl, Floral, Round, 11½"	45.00
Bowl, Floral, Oval, Deep, 13"	60.00
Bowl, Floral, Touraine, 9"	40.00
Bowl, Fruit, 12"	45.00
Bowl, Gardenia, Square, 10"	125.00
Bowl, Gardenia or Floral, Shallow, 12"	45.00
Bowl, Oval, Hollandaise Sauce	24.00
Bowl, Oval, Shallow, 12"	50.00
Bowl, Salad, Round, 10" or 12"	45.00
Bowl, Salad, Shell, 11"	225.00
Bowl, Spring Salad, 10"	45.00
Breakfast Preserve (leaf shape), 5"	35.00
Candleblocks, 1 Light, pr. (rosette)	35.00
Candleblocks, 1 Light, (tall cylinder), pr. (No. 1503¾)	55.00

Candleblocks, Melon, 1 Light, pr. (No. 1503½)	120.00
Candleblocks, Square, 1 Light, pr. (No. 1503¼)	65.00
Candleblocks, Swirl, 1 Light, pr. (No. 1502)	50.00
Candlesticks with 5" Vase, 3 Light, pr.	180.00
Candlesticks, 2 Light, with Bobeches & Prisms, pr.	200.00
Candlesticks, 3 Light, pr.	120.00
Candlesticks, Footed, 1 Light, 4", pr.	55.00
Candy Box & Cover, 7"	50.00
Candy Box & Cover, 3 Footed, 6"	55.00
Candy Box & Cover, Shell, 5½"	60.00
Candy Box & Cover, 3 Compartment, 7"	60.00
Candy or Jelly, Swan, 6½"	45.00
Celery & Olive, 12"	35.00
Celery Tray, 12"	35.00
Centerpiece, 11" (garden tray)	225.00
Cheese & Cracker, 2 pcs., 14"	35.00
Cherry Jar & Cover	55.00
Chocolate, High Footed, 5½"	30.00
Cigarette Box & Cover, 4"	25.00
Cigarette Box & Cover, King Size, 4½"	35.00
Cigarette Holder, Footed	25.00
Cigarette Holder, Oval	20.00
Cigarette Holder, Round	20.00
Cigarette Lighter	75.00
Coaster, 4"	7.00
Coaster or Ashtray, Shell, 5"	20.00
Cocktail Shaker, 1 qt.	300.00
Cologne Bottle, 4 oz.	160.00

(continued) CRYSTOLITE, NO. 1503

Comport, Deep, Footed, 5" 40.00
Conserve, 2 Compartment, Center Handled, 8" 60.00
Cream (No. 1503½) 55.00
Cream, Oval 25.00
Cream, Oval, Individual 22.00
Cup, Plain Edge (No. 1503½) 12.00
Cup & Saucer 20.00
Ice Tub 70.00
Jam Jar & Cover 50.00
Jelly, 1 Handle, 5" 25.00
Jelly, 1 Handle, 3 Compartment 50.00
Jelly, 2 Compartment, 2 Handled, 6" 18.00
Jelly, 2 Handled, 6" 15.00
Jelly, High Footed, 5" 30.00
Jelly, Oval, 4 Footed, 5½" 65.00
Jug, Ice Lip, Blown, ½ gal., (No. 5003) 130.00
Jug, Swan (No. 1503½) 800.00
Lamp, Electric, 1 Light 150.00
Lamp, Hurricane, Square, 2 pcs., 1 Light, 10" 220.00
Lamp, Hurricane, Round, 2 pcs., 1 Light 220.00
Mayonnaise, Oval, Handled, 6" 30.00
Mayonnaise, Shell, 3 Footed, 5½" 40.00
Mayonnaise, 2 Compartment 50.00
Mustard & Cover 35.00
Nappy, 4½" or 5½" 8.00
Nappy, 8" 25.00
Nappy, 3 Footed, 7" 35.00
Nut Dish, Handled (leaf shape), 3" 25.00
Nut Dish, Individual Swan, 2" 25.00
Oil Bottle & Stopper, 3 oz. 45.00
Pickle, Leaf, 9" 45.00
Pickle, Oval, 6" 15.00
Plate, Cheese, Oval, 2 Handled, 8" 18.00
Plate, Coupe, 7½" 25.00
Plate, Demi-Torte, Shell, 10½" 180.00
Plate, Dinner, 10½" 125.00
Plate, Oval, 8" 15.00
Plate, Salad, 7" or 8½" 15.00
Plate, Sandwich, 12" 20.00
Plate, Sandwich, 14" 25.00
Plate, Shell, 7" 50.00
Plate, Snack, 2 Handled, 7" 20.00
Plate, Thousand Island Dressing, 7" 15.00
Plate, Torte, 11" 20.00
Plate, Torte, 13" 25.00
Plate, Torte, 14" 25.00
Plate, Torte, Shell, 13" (Illus.) 200.00
Praline, Shell, 7" 55.00
Preserve & Cover, 2 Handled, 6" 40.00
Preserve Dish, Oval, 7" 40.00

Puff Box & Cover, 4¾" 85.00
Punch Bowl, 7½ qt. 90.00
Punch Bowl Plate, 20" 65.00
Punch or Custard Cup 8.00
Relish, 3 Compartment, Oblong, 8" 35.00
Relish, 3 Compartment, Oval, 12" or 13"
     (No. 1503½) 35.00
Relish, 4 Compartment, Clover Leaf, 9" 45.00
Relish, 4 Compartment, Utility 45.00
Relish, 5 Compartment, Round, 10" 45.00
Relish, 5 Compartment, Shell, 13" 200.00
Rye Bottle & Stopper, 1 qt. 300.00
Salt & Pepper, pr. 40.00
Salt & Pepper, pr. (No. 1503½—straight sides) 90.00
Salver, Cake, Footed, 11" 225.00
Sugar (No. 1503½) 50.00
Sugar, Oval 25.00
Sugar, Oval, Individual 22.00
Syrup Bottle with Drip Cut Top 110.00
Thousand Island Dressing Bowl, Round, 5" 25.00
Tray for Individual Sugar & Cream, 5½" 28.00
Tray, Oval, 13" 40.00
Tumbler, 10 oz. 22.00
Urn, Flower, 7" 60.00
Vase, Footed, 6", Regular or Flared 32.00
Vase, Footed, 9", Regular or Flared 165.00
Vase, Short Stem Flower, 3" 40.00
Vase, Swing, 10" to 12" 225.00
Vase, Swing, Footed, 12" to 15" 260.00
Vase, Swing, Footed, 15" to 18" 325.00
Vase, Swing, Footed, 18" to 21" 400.00

BLOWN WARE: (ALL NO. 5003)

Bowl, 11" $550.00
Claret, 3½ oz. 20.00
Cocktail, 3½ oz. 20.00
Comport, 5" 450.00
Cordial, 1 oz. 120.00
Finger Bowl 225.00
Goblet, 10 oz. 28.00
Iced Tea, Footed, 12 oz. 28.00
Juice, Footed, 5 oz. 20.00
Oyster Cocktail, 3½ oz. 20.00
Sherbet or Saucer Champagne, 6 oz. 25.00
Soda, Regular, 5 oz. 18.00
Soda, Regular, 12 oz. 25.00
Tumbler, Footed, 10 oz. 25.00
Tumbler, Regular, 10 oz. 25.00

FORTUNE

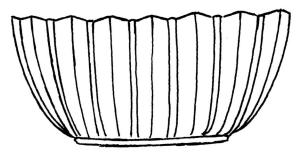

Fortune Bowl

Date: 1937 to 1938

Manufacturer: Hocking Glass Co., Lancaster, OH

Colors: Crystal, Pink

Prices are for pieces in Pink. Crystal is valued slightly less.

Bowl, 4"	$6.00
Bowl, 4½" *(Illus.)*	8.00
Bowl, 7¾"	16.00
Bowl, Flared Edge, 5¼"	12.00
Bowl, Handled, 4½"	7.00
Candy Dish & Cover	30.00
Cup & Saucer	10.00
Juice, 5 oz.	11.00
Plate, 6"	5.00
Plate, 8"	11.00
Tumbler, 9 oz.	7.50

HOMESPUN

Homespun Covered Butter

Date: 1939 to 1940

Manufacturer: Jeannette Glass Co., Jeannette, PA

Colors: Pink, Crystal

	Crystal	Pink
Bowl, 5"	$10.00	$24.00
Bowl, 8¼"	12.00	27.00
Bowl, Handled, 4½"	7.00	12.00
Butter & Cover *(Illus.)*	35.00	80.00
Coaster or Ashtray	5.00	10.00
Cream	7.00	14.00
Cup & Saucer	9.00	17.00
Iced Tea, 13 oz.	20.00	38.00
Iced Tea, Footed, (large), 15 oz.	20.00	38.00
Juice, Footed, 5 oz.	7.00	14.00
Plate, 6"	3.00	5.00
Plate, 9¼"	14.00	25.00
Platter, Handled, 13"	15.00	27.00
Sherbet	10.00	20.00
Sugar	8.00	17.00
Tumbler, 8 oz.	10.00	22.00
Tumbler, Footed, 9 oz.	15.00	28.00

CHILDREN'S DISHES

	Crystal	Pink
Cup & Saucer	$28.00	$45.00
Plate	7.00	14.00
Teapot & Cover		48.00

JANE RAY

Date: 1945 to 1963

Manufacturer: Anchor Hocking Glass Corporation, Lancaster, OH

Colors: Jade-ite, Ivory, Anchorwhite

Prices given are for Jade-ite, the most collectible color. Ivory and white sell for about 80% of Jade-ite prices.

Bowl, 5⅞"	$10.00
Bowl, Vegetable, 8¼"	18.00
Cream	8.00
Cup & Saucer *(Illus.)*	7.00
Cup & Saucer, After Dinner	55.00
Dessert, 4⅜" *(Illus.)*	7.00
Plate, Dinner, 9⅛" *(Illus.)*	10.00
Plate, Salad, 7¾"	9.00
Platter, 12"	17.00
Soup Plate, 7⅝" (bowl)	18.00
Sugar & Cover	15.00

Jane Ray Dessert, Plate, Cup & Saucer

LENOX

Date: 1920s

Manufacturer: McKee Glass Co., Jeannette, PA

Colors: Crystal

Very similar in both design and shapes of pieces to Heisey's Tudor and Double Rib and Panel.

Bonbon, 8"	$15.00
Bonbon, Partition, 8"	10.00
Bowl, Center, Flared, Footed, 12½"	25.00
Bowl, Center, Footed, 11½"	25.00
Candlesticks, 1 Light, 3", pr.	40.00
Celery Tray, 11½"	15.00
Celery Tray, Partition, 11½"	15.00
Cheese & Cracker, 10½"	24.00
Cocktail, 3 oz.	10.00
Cream, 10½ oz.	20.00
Cup & Saucer	20.00
Finger Bowl, 4½"	10.00
Goblet, High Footed, 8 oz.	14.00
Goblet, Low Footed, 8 oz.	14.00
Goblet, Low Footed, 10 oz.	14.00
Goblet, Low Footed, 12 oz.	14.00
Jug, 3 pt. (stuck handle)	35.00
Jug, Breakfast, 19 oz.	25.00

Lenox Catalog Page

LENOX *(continued)*

Mayonnaise Bowl	15.00
Nappy, 4½" or 5½"	9.00
Nappy, 8"	15.00
Oil & Stopper, 6 oz.	28.00
Parfait, Footed, 4½ oz.	12.00
Pickle, 9"	10.00
Plate, Bread & Butter, 6"	6.00
Plate, Lunch, Handled, 10½" (center handle)	24.00
Plate, Mayonnaise	8.00
Plate, Salad, 7" or 8"	8.00
Rose Bowl, Footed	25.00

Salt & Pepper, pr.	30.00
Sherbet or Oyster Cocktail, 3½ oz.	10.00
Soda or Hi-ball Tumbler, 8 oz.	12.00
Sugar & Cover	25.00
Sundae, High footed, 5 oz.	12.00
Sundae, Low Footed, 5 oz.	12.00
Tumbler, 3 oz.	15.00
Tumbler, Iced Tea, Tapered, 12 oz.	12.00
Tumbler, Lemonade, Straight, 10 oz.	12.00
Tumbler, Table, 9 oz.	10.00
Tumbler, Water, 6 oz.	10.00

MANHATTAN

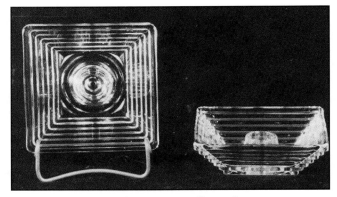

Manhattan Candlesticks

Manhattan 9½" Fruit Bowl, Footed, Handled

Date: 1938 to 1941

Manufacturer: Anchor Hocking Glass Co., Lancaster, OH

Colors: Crystal, Pink. Few pieces in Ruby and Green.

Popular with collectors of Art Deco patterns.

	Crystal	Pink
Ashtray, 4"	$18.00	$
Bowl, 4½"	12.00	85.00
Bowl, 7½"	21.00	32.00
Bowl, 9"	45.00	55.00
Bowl, 9½"	60.00	75.00
Bowl, Fruit, 9½" Footed, Handled (Illus.)	55.00	75.00
Bowl, Handled, 5¼"	30.00	37.00
Bowl, Handled, 8"	34.00	45.00
Candlesticks, Square, 1 Light, pr. (Illus.)	22.00	

	Crystal	Pink
Candy Dish, 3 Footed		14.00
Coaster, 3½"	20.00	
Comport, 5¾"	38.00	50.00
Cream	15.00	21.00
Cup & Saucer	40.00	190.00 (cup only)
Pitcher, 24 oz.	30.00	
Pitcher, 80 oz.	75.00	110.00
Plate, 6" (saucer)	8.00	
Plate, 8½"	21.00	58.00
Plate, 10¼"	28.00	
Plate, Sandwich, 14"	34.00	
Relish Tray, 4 Compartment, 14"	22.00	
Relish Tray, 5 Inserts, 14"	55.00	55.00
Salt & Pepper, Square, pr.	40.00	65.00
Sherbet	15.00	20.00
Sugar	15.00	20.00
Tumbler, Footed, 10 oz.	22.00	28.00
Vase, 8"	30.00	

OLD CAFE

Date: 1936 to 1940

Manufacturer: Hocking Glass Co., Lancaster, OH

Colors: Pink, Crystal, Royal Ruby

Several pieces are Crystal combined with Royal Ruby including Crystal cups with Royal Ruby saucers and the candy dish with a Royal Ruby lid.

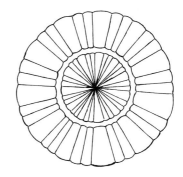

Old Cafe Plate

	Crystal	Pink	Royal Ruby
Bowl, 1 Handle, 5"	$4.00	$9.00	$
Bowl, 2 Handled, 5"	6.00		
Bowl, 3¾"	3.00	7.50	6.00
Bowl, 5½"	6.00	11.00	17.00
Bowl, Handled, 9"	12.00	24.00	28.00
Candy Dish & Cover, 8"	10.00	20.00	17.00
Cup & Saucer	12.00	17.00	25.00
Juice, 3"	25.00	15.00	
Lamp	20.00	32.00	45.00
Olive, Oblong, 6"	5.00	10.00	
Pitcher, 36 oz.	30.00	75.00	

	Crystal	Pink	Royal Ruby
Pitcher, 80 oz.	40.00	96.00	
Plate, 6"	3.00	5.00	
Plate, 10" *(Illus.)*	20.00	37.00	
Sherbet	5.00	10.00	15.00
Tumbler	12.00	18.00	
Vase, 7¼"	12.00	17.00	22.00

PARTY LINE, NO. 191, 191½, 192

Date: 1927 to 1951

Manufacturer: Paden City Glass Manufacturing Co., Paden City, WV

Colors: Crystal, Cheriglo (pink), Blue, Green, Amber, Mulberry, Black

This Paden City pattern was made for quite a long time and so there are many variations in pieces, resulting in different numbers for similar items of differing shapes. Much of the line was made for use in soda fountains and restaurants so some interesting pieces are found in this pattern. Since it was made for so long a time, pieces were added to the line and dropped from the line over this period which should result in some pieces being much more difficult to find than others. This probably is also true of the color production, with colors not made for the entire length of time. Also all pieces were most likely not made in all colors. Many of the pieces were available either plain or with a wide vertical optic, adding interest to this heavy horizontal ribbed pattern. Prices are for Crystal pieces. For colors, add 100% to 200% depending on color and piece.

Party Line 1928 Ad

Party Line, No. 191, 191½, 192 *(continued)*

Banana Split, 8¼" $8.00
Berry, 4½" 4.00
Berry, 8" or 9" 8.00
Bowl, Flared, 9" 15.00
Bowl, High Footed, Regular or Flared, 10½"
    (compote) 12.00
Bowl, Mixing, 7" 6.00
Bowl, Mixing, 8" 7.00
Bowl, Mixing, 9" 8.00
Butter Box & Cover 30.00
Candy Jar & Cover, ½ lb. (footed) 18.00
Champagne, High Footed, 6 oz. 6.00
Cheese & Cracker & Cover, 10½" 24.00
Cheese & Cracker & Cover, 12" 28.00
Cigarette Holder & Cover
    (footed, plain straight sides) 16.00
Cocktail Liner, 2½ oz. or 3½ oz. (No. 191½) 5.00
Cocktail Shaker, Footed, 18 oz. 22.00
Cocktail, Footed, 1½ oz. 7.00
Cocktail, Footed, 2½ oz. (No. 192) 5.00
Cocktail, Footed, 2½ oz. 5.00
Cocktail, Footed, 3½ oz. 5.00
Cologne, No. 5, 1½ oz. 18.00
Comport, Flared or Rolled Edge, Low Footed, 9" . . . 18.00
Comport, Low Footed, Flared or Rolled Edge, 11" . . 18.00
Comport, Low Footed, Flared or Rolled Edge, 14" . . 20.00
Cream, 7 oz. 7.00
Crushed Fruit Bowl & Cover, Hi 45.00
Cup & Saucer 12.00
Custard, 6 oz. 4.00
Goblet, 9 oz. 8.00
Grape Juice, Footed, 6 oz. 6.00
Iced Tea, 12 oz. or 14 oz. (No. 191½) 7.00
Iced Tea, Blown, 12 oz. (No. 192) 7.00
Ice Tub, Deep, 6½" 20.00
Ice Tub, No. 1, 6" or 7 ½" 18.00
Ice Tub & Pail, No. 2 . . . . 20.00
Jug, 74 oz. 35.00
Jug, Grape Juice & Cover, 34 oz. (No. 193) 30.00
Jug, Iced Tea & Cover, 52 oz. (No. 192) 35.00
Jug & Cover, 74 oz. 35.00
Jug & Cover, Hospital, 36 oz. (No. 191½) 35.00

Marmalade & Cover, 12 oz. 15.00
Mayonnaise, Footed, Flared or Rolled Edge, 6" 12.00
Measuring Cup & No. 10 Reamer 12.00
Measuring Jug, 36 oz. & 5½" Juice Extractor 18.00
Molasses Can, 8 oz. (metal top) 20.00
Nappy, 4½" 4.00
Orange Juice, 4½ oz. 5.00
Orange Juice, 4½ oz. (No. 191½) 5.00
Parfait, 5 oz. 7.00
Plate, 6" 4.00
Salt & Pepper, pr. 20.00
Sandwich Tray, Center Handled, 10" or 12" 17.00
Sherbet, Footed, 4½ oz. 4.00
Sherbet, High Footed, 6 oz. 5.00
Sherbet, Low Footed, 3½ oz. or 4½ oz. 4.00
Soda, 5 oz. or 6 oz. (No. 191½) 4.00
Soda, 7 oz. or 8 oz. (No. 191½) 5.00
Soda, 10 oz. or 12 oz. (No. 191½) 6.00
Soda, Footed, Flared or Cupped, 6 oz. 4.00
Soda, Footed, Flared or Cupped, 8 oz. or 10 oz. 5.00
Soda, Footed, Flared or Cupped, 12 oz. or 14 oz. . . . 7.00
Sugar & Cover, Hotel, 10 oz. (No. 191½) 15.00
Sugar Shaker 20.00
Sugar, 7 oz. 7.00
Sundae, 4 oz. 4.00
Sundae, Tulip, 6 oz. 7.00
Syrup, 8 oz. 20.00
Syrup & Cover, 12 oz. (glass cover) 20.00
Tumbler, 2½ oz. (No. 192) 6.00
Tumbler, 7 oz. or 9 oz. (No. 191½) 5.00
Tumbler, 7 oz. or 9 oz. (pressed, tapered sides) 7.00
Tumbler, 8 oz. (No. 192) 5.00
Tumbler, 10 oz. or 12 oz. (No. 192) 6.00
Tumbler, Barrel, 9 oz. 5.00
Tumbler, Blown, 8 oz. 5.00
Tumbler, Wine, 3 oz. 5.00
Vase, Crimped Top, 7" 10.00
Vase, Fan, 6" or 7" 15.00
Water Bottle, 48 oz. 20.00
Wine Bottle & Stopper (decanter), 22 oz. 20.00
Wine, Footed, 1½ oz. or 2½ oz. 7.00

PILLAR FLUTE, NO. 682

Date: 1930s

Manufacturer: Imperial Glass Corporation, Bellaire, OH

Colors: Crystal, Stiegel Green, Ritz Blue, Amber, Rose Pink, Imperial Green, Black

Prices are for items in color. All items may not have been made in all colors. Crystal items are valued at 50% less.

Bonbon, Crimped, 7" $15.00
Bouquet, 6" (vase) 20.00
Bowl, Console 40.00
Bowl, Flared, 7" 18.00
Bowl, Flower, 5" 18.00
Bowl, Salad, 8½" 30.00
Bowl, Salad, 10" 35.00
Candlesticks, 2 Light, pr. 50.00
Celery Tray, Oval, 8½" 22.00
Compote, 4½" 18.00
Compote, Shallow, 7" 15.00
Cream, Footed 15.00
Cup & Saucer 25.00
Dish, Square, 5½" 12.00
Jelly, 2 Handled, 4¾" 15.00
Mayonnaise Set, 2 pcs. 35.00
Nappy, 1 Handled, 4½" 15.00
Nappy, Belled, 6½" 15.00
Pickle, 2 Handled, 6¼" 18.00
Plate, 6" 12.00
Plate, 10½" 35.00
Plate, Cake, 12" 20.00

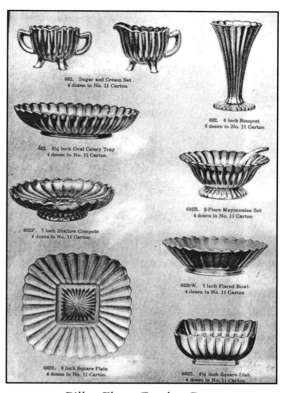

Pillar Flute Catalog Page

Plate, Salad, 8" 12.00
Plate, Square, 8" 12.00
Relish, Partitioned, 2 Handled, 6½" 18.00
Sugar, Footed 15.00

PLEAT & PANEL, NO. 1170

Date: 1925 to 1937

Manufacturer: A. H. Heisey & Co., Newark, OH

Colors: Crystal, Moongleam, Flamingo. Occasional pieces in Hawthorne and Sahara. Rare in Amber.

	Crystal	Moongleam, Flamingo
Bouillon Cup & Plate	$15.00	$38.00
Cheese & Cracker, 10½"	30.00	60.00
Chow Chow, 4"	14.00	20.00
Comport & Cover, Low Footed, 6"	45.00	70.00
Compotier & Cover, High Footed, 5"	65.00	150.00
Cream, Hotel	20.00	38.00
Cup & Saucer	30.00	45.00

Pleat and Panel Covered Lemon Dish, Luncheon Goblet

PLEAT & PANEL, NO. 1170 *(continued)*

Pleat & Panel Vase

	Crystal	Moongleam, Flamingo
Dish, Lemon & Cover, 5" *(Illus.)*	30.00	55.00
Dish, Vegetable, 9"	28.00	50.00
Goblet, 8 oz.	20.00	40.00
Goblet, Luncheon, 7½ oz. *(Illus.)*	18.00	38.00
Grapefruit or Cereal, 6½"	12.00	22.00
Iced Tea, 12 oz.	17.00	35.00
Jelly, 2 Handled, 5"	16.00	22.00
Jug, 3 pt.	70.00	135.00
Jug, Ice, 3 pt.	70.00	150.00
Marmalade, 4¼"	14.00	28.00
Nappy, 8"	22.00	35.00
Oil & Stopper, 3 oz.	40.00	95.00
Plate, 8"	12.00	15.00
Platter, Oval, 12"	30.00	45.00
Saucer Champagne, 5 oz.	15.00	28.00
Sherbet, 5 oz.	12.00	18.00
Sugar & Cover, Hotel	24.00	45.00
Tray, Spice, 5 Compartment, 10"	35.00	60.00
Tumbler, 8 oz.	18.00	35.00
Vase, 8" *(Illus.)*	28.00	65.00

QUEEN MARY

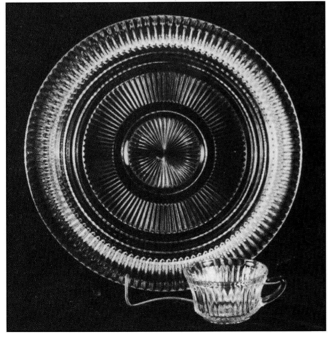

Queen Mary Sandwich Plate, Cup

Date: 1936 to 1949

Manufacturer: Hocking Glass Co., Lancaster, OH

Colors: Crystal, Pink. Limited production in Royal Ruby.

	Crystal	Pink
Ashtray, Oval	$5.00	$7.50
Ashtray, Round	6.00	
Bowl, 2 Handled, 5½"	8.00	10.00
Bowl, 4"	6.00	8.00
Bowl, 5"	7.00	9.00
Bowl, 6"	20.00	28.00
Bowl, 7"	10.00	20.00
Bowl, 8¾"	26.00	30.00
Butter & Cover	48.00	110.00
Candlesticks, 2 Light, 4½"	38.00	
Candy & Cover	28.00	45.00
Celery Tray, 10"	10.00	22.00
Cigarette Holder, Oval	7.00	9.00
Coaster, 3½"	5.00	6.00
Coaster, Square, 4"	5.00	6.00
Comport, 5¾"	9.00	18.00
Cream	12.00	17.00

(continued) QUEEN MARY

	Crystal	Pink		Crystal	Pink
Cup & Saucer *(Illus. of cup)*	10.00	15.00	Relish, 3 compartment, 12"	15.00	18.00
Jelly, Handled, 4"	6.00	8.00	Relish, 4 compartment, 14"	17.00	21.00
Juice, 5 oz.	18.00	27.00	Salt & Pepper, pr.	25.00	85.00
Plate, 6"	5.00	7.00	Sherbet	7.00	10.00
Plate, 6½"	6.00	8.00	Sugar	9.00	12.00
Plate, 8½"	7.00	9.00	Tray, 14"	22.00	32.00
Plate, 9¾"	22.00	55.00	Tumbler, 9 oz.	15.00	25.00
Plate, Sandwich, 12" *(Illus.)*	16.00	27.00	Tumbler, Footed, 10 oz.	37.00	67.00

RADIANCE, NO. 113, 113½, 5113

Date: Ca. 1938

Manufacturer: Duncan & Miller Glass Co., Washington, PA

Colors: Crystal, Amber, Sapphire Blue, Royal Blue (Cobalt), Green, Ruby. Ladles and punch cups sometimes have colored handles.

This pattern is often confused with Heisey's Crystolite pattern. Most of Duncan's pieces are of different shapes than Heisey's. Prices are for pieces in crystal. For colored pieces add these amounts to crystal prices: Cobalt 75%, Red 50%, Green 40%, Amber 20% and Sapphire Blue 40%. Sometimes found in Duncan opalescent colors.

Ashtray, 6"	$15.00
Bowl, Flower, 9"	20.00
Bowl, Flower, 12"	25.00
Candlesticks, 1 Light, 4", pr.	35.00
Cream, 6 oz.	15.00
Cup & Saucer, Tea	25.00
Plate, 8"	15.00
Plate, Torte, 14" *(Illus.)*	35.00
Punch Bowl, 2½ gal.	60.00
Punch Cup (No. 113½), Pressed Handle	10.00
Punch Ladle	35.00
Punch Tray, Rolled Edge, 18"	40.00
Sugar, 7 oz.	15.00
Vase, 8"	40.00
Vase, Footed, 9"	45.00

Radiance Torte Plate, Pitcher

NO. 5113 BLOWN ITEMS:

Iced Tea, 12 oz.	$10.00
Iced Tea, 14 oz.	12.00
Juice, Orange, 5 oz.	8.00
Old Fashioned, 7 oz.	10.00
Pitcher, Ice Lip, ½ gal. *(Illus.)*	50.00
Rose Bowl, 6"	30.00
Rose Bowl, 9"	35.00
Tumbler, 10 oz.	10.00

RIDGELEIGH, NO. 1469, 1469¼, 1469½

No. 1469 RIDGELEIGH PATTERN (Continued)

12 in. Celery & Olive
2 in. Candlestick
12 in. Celery Tray
3 oz. Oil Bottle & No. 103 P.S.
12 in. Fruit Bowl Also make 10 in.
11½ in. Floral Bowl Also make 10 in.
11 in. Punch Bowl
2 lt. Candlestick Bobeche & "A" Prisms

A. H. HEISEY & CO., NEWARK, OHIO

Ridgeleigh Catalog Page

Date: 1935 to 1944

Manufacturer: A. H. Heisey & Co., Newark, OH

Colors: Crystal. Limited items in Zircon and Sahara.

Reproductions: Imperial Glass Corp. made the cigarette holder and ashtrays in heather and charcoal and the coaster in crystal. Imperial also modified the coaster into a ring tree—never made by Heisey.

Items marked with an asterisk (*) were made in Zircon and Sahara. Compare Ridgeleigh with Fenton's Sheffield. The two patterns are often confused, although Ridgeleigh is a much more extensive line and many of the pieces are marked with the Diamond H.

Ashtray, 4" (No. 1469½)	$25.00
Ashtray, Bridge	18.00
Ashtray, Club	20.00
Ashtray, Diamond	20.00
Ashtray, Heart	25.00
Ashtray, Round	20.00
Ashtray, Spade	20.00
Ashtray, Square *	7.00
Ashtray, Square, 6"	30.00
Bar, 2½ oz.	40.00
Bonbon, 6" (No. 1469½)	20.00
Bottle, Bitters, 5 oz.	65.00
Bottle, French Dressing & Stopper	85.00
Bottle, Rock & Rye with Stopper	160.00
Bowl, Berry Cupped, 8½"	40.00
Bowl, Cone Beverage. 11"	100.00
Bowl, Cone Floral, 13"	65.00
Bowl, Floral, 11½"	60.00
Bowl, Floral, Oblong (swan handled), 14"	290.00

Bowl, Fruit, 12"	60.00
Bowl, Orange	70.00
Bowl, Oval Floral, 12" *	50.00
Bowl, Punch, 11"	160.00
Bowl, Salad, 9"	40.00
Bowl, Salad, 11"	45.00
Bowl, Oblong Floral, 14"	80.00
Candelabra with Bobeche, 7", pr. (bell shaped foot)	225.00
Candelabra with Prisms, 1 Light, pr. (No. 1469½)	185.00
Candelabra with Prisms, 2 Light, pr.	400.00+
Candle Vase, 6", pr. *	70.00
Candlesticks with Center Bobeche, 2 Light, pr.	220.00
Candlesticks, Cylinder. 5" (No. 1469½), pr.	65.00
Candlesticks, Square, 2", pr.	55.00
Celery & Olive Tray, 12"	35.00
Celery Tray, 12"	30.00
Centerpiece, 8" (No. 1469½)	60.00
Cheese, 6" (No. 1469½)	20.00

(continued) RIDGELEIGH, No. 1469, 1469¼, 1469½

Cigarette Box & Cover, 4" 45.00
Cigarette Box & Cover, Oval 75.00
Cigarette Holder & Cover 75.00
Cigarette Holder, Round 17.00
Cigarette Holder, Square. 17.00
Cigarette Holder/Ashtray, Oval, 2 Compartment
    (1469¼) 85.00
Claret 27.00
Coaster or Cocktail Rest. 24.00
Coaster, 3½" (No. 1469½) * 10.00
Cocktail. 20.00
Cocktail Shaker, 1 qt. 165.00
Cologne & Stopper, 4 oz. 130.00
Comport & Cover, Low Footed, 6". 70.00
Comport, Low Footed, Flared, 6" 35.00
Cream, Oval 28.00
Cream, Oval, Individual. 25.00
Cup & Saucer 40.00
Cup, Beverage 20.00
Custard or Punch Cup 12.00
Decanter & Stopper, 1 pt. (icicle shape) 165.00
Dessert, 2 Handled, 10". 40.00
Dish, Lemon & Cover, 5" 55.00
Floral Box, 8" 60.00
Goblet. 50.00
Hors d'oeuvre, Oval 45.00
Ice Tub, 2 Handled 75.00
Jelly, 2 Compartment, 6" (No. 1469½). 24.00
Jelly, 3 Handled 25.00
Jelly, 6" (No. 1469½) 24.00
Jelly, Individual Oval 20.00
Jug, ½ gal. 170.00
Jug, Ice, ½ gal. 170.00
Marmalade & Cover. 75.00
Mayonnaise 30.00
Mustard & Cover. 75.00
Nappy, 4½" 12.00
Nappy, 5" 17.00
Nappy, Scalloped, 5½" 12.00
Nappy, Square, 5" 17.00
Nut, Individual (No. 1469½) 18.00
Nut, Individual, 2 Compartment (No. 1469½) 20.00
Oil & Stopper, 3 oz. 55.00
Old Fashioned, 8 oz. 25.00
Oyster Cocktail 16.00
Perfume & Stopper, 5 oz. 170.00
Plate, 6". 15.00
Plate, Ice Tub, 2 Handled 45.00
Plate, Round, 8" 20.00
Plate, Round, 8" (plain edge) 25.00

Plate, Round, 14". 45.00
Plate, Sandwich, 13½" 45.00
Plate, Square, 8". 50.00
Plate, Torte, 13" 45.00
Plate, Torte, 14" 50.00
Plate, Torte, Footed, 13½" (No. 1469½). 55.00
Puff Box & Cover, 5". 65.00
Relish, 2 Compartment, 7" (No. 1469½) 35.00
Relish, 3 Compartment, 11". 50.00
Relish, 5 Compartment (star), 10" 60.00
Roly Poly with Rest 80.00
Salt & Pepper, pr. 45.00
Salt & Pepper, pr. (No. 1469½) 40.00
Salt, Individual. 15.00
Salver, Footed, 14" 55.00
Saucer Champagne. 25.00
Sherbet 17.00
Soda, 5 oz. (No. 1469½) 25.00
Soda, Cupped or Flared, 12 oz (No.1469½). 25.00
Soda, Footed, 12 oz. 35.00
Sugar, Oval 28.00
Sugar, Oval, Individual. 25.00
Tray, 3 Compartment, Oblong, 10½" 45.00
Tray for Individual Cream and Sugar. 45.00
Tray, Oblong, 10½" 45.00
Tumbler, 10 oz. (No. 1469½) 28.00
Vase, 3½" 30.00
Vase, 6" 30.00
Vase, 8" (No. 1469½) 70.00
Vase, 8" (Triangular) (No. 1469¼) 60.00
Vase, 9". 75.00
Vase, 10" 70.00
Vase, Ball 90.00
Vase, Ball, Flared Top, 7" 100.00
Vase, Flared, 9" 75.00
Vase, Individual, (5 shapes). 32.00
Wine 35.00

BLOWN STEMWARE, No. 4069:

Claret, 4 oz. $40.00
Cocktail, 3½ oz. 30.00
Cordial, 1 oz. 130.00
Goblet, 8 oz. 60.00
Goblet, Luncheon, 8 oz. 50.00
Oyster Cocktail, 4 oz. 22.00
Saucer Champagne, 5 oz. 35.00
Sherbet, 5 oz. 22.00
Sherry, 2 oz. 80.00
Soda, 5 oz. 22.00
Wine, 2½ oz. 60.00

SHEFFIELD, NO. 1800

Sheffield Crimped Bowl

Date: 1936 to 1938

Manufacturer: Fenton Art Glass Co., Williamstown, WV

Colors: Crystal, Aquamarine, Mermaid Blue, Gold, Ruby and Amber. Limited pieces in Wisteria and Royal Blue.

This pattern is very similar to Heisey's Ridgeleigh and Imperial's No. 779. Most pieces are not confusing because the shapes are different, but the plates and some bowls are remarkably similar to the Heisey and Imperial patterns. Remember that Heisey's Ridgeleigh came only in crystal except for a very few pieces, so when you find pieces in color, most likely they are Fenton or Imperial.

	Crystal, Gold	Ruby, Aquamarine
Ashtrays, different styles	$5.00	$6.50
Bonbon, 6½"	9.00	20.00
Bonbon, 3 Footed, Covered, 7" . . .	35.00	50.00
Bonbon, 3 Footed, Flared, 7"	10.00	22.00
Bonbon, 3 Footed, Shallow, 7½" . .	10.00	22.00
Bonbon, Triangle, 6½"	9.00	20.00
Bowl, 10"	20.00	42.00
Bowl, Crimped, 11" *(Illus.)*	24.00	45.00
Bowl, Flared, 12"	24.00	45.00
Bowl, Square, 12"	24.00	45.00
Candlesticks, pr.	25.00	40.00
Cigarette Box & Cover	18.00	27.00
Cream	10.00	17.00
Hi-ball, 12 oz. (flat)	8.00	18.00
Juice, 5 oz. (flat)		15.00
Mayonnaise, 5"	11.00	17.00
Plate, 6"	4.00	6.00
Plate, 8"	8.00	12.00
Plate, 9"	14.00	24.00
Plate, 10"	16.00	30.00
Plate, 14"	25.00	42.00
Plate, 3 Footed, 8¼"	14.00	
Rose Bowl.	10.00	25.00
Sugar	10.00	17.00
Tumbler, 9 oz. (flat)	8.00	15.00
Vase, 6½" (several shapes)	15.00	25.00
Vase, Square, 10"	24.00	45.00
Vase, Square, Flared, 8"	15.00	40.00
Whiskey	5.00	15.00

SUN-RAY, NO. 2510

Sun-Ray Tray, Four Part Relish, Handled Nappy

Date 1935 to 1944

Manufacturer: Fostoria Glass Co., Moundsville, WV

Colors: Crystal. The goblet, sherbet and footed tumbler were made in Azure, Amber, Green, Topaz/Gold Tint. Limited production in Ruby.

When ribs are frosted, or acid etched (Silver Mist decoration), the pattern is called Glacier. These items are valued 20% over Crystal. For pieces in color, add 50%. For Ruby, add at least 100%.

(continued) SUN-RAY, NO. 2510

Ashtray, Footed, Individual $10.00	
Ashtray, Individual 8.00	
Ashtray, Square 6.00	
Bonbon, 3 Toed 12.00	
Bonbon, Handled 12.00	
Bowl, Handled, 10" 45.00	
Bowl, Rolled Edge, 13" 40.00	
Bowl, Salad, 12" 35.00	
Butter & Cover or Cheese & Cover, 6" x 3⅜" 35.00	
Candelabrum, 2 Light, pr. 45.00	
Candlesticks, 3", pr. 20.00	
Candlesticks, 5½", pr. 35.00	
Candlesticks, Duo, pr. 65.00	
Candy Jar & Cover 27.00	
Celery, Handled, 10" 15.00	
Cigarette Box & Cover 24.00	
Claret, 4½ oz. 10.00	
Coaster, 4" 6.00	
Cocktail, Footed, 4 oz. 9.00	
Comport 15.00	
Cream, Footed 10.00	
Cream, Individual 12.00	
Cup & Saucer 12.00	
Decanter & Stopper, Oval, 18 oz. 65.00	
Decanter & Stopper, Rectangular, 26 oz. 55.00	
Dessert, Frozen, 2¼" tall 8.00	
Fruit Cocktail, 3½ oz. 7.00	
Fruit, 5" 7.00	
Goblet, 9 oz. 12.00	
Ice Bucket 28.00	
Iced Tea, 13 oz. (No. 2510½) 12.00	
Iced Tea, Footed, 13 oz. 15.00	
Jelly 12.00	
Jelly & Cover 20.00	
Jug, 2 qt. 70.00	
Jug, Ice Lip, 2 qt. 70.00	
Juice, 5 oz. (No. 2510½) 9.00	
Juice, Footed, 5 oz. 10.00	
Mayonnaise 20.00	
Mustard & Cover 25.00	
Nappy, 3 Cornered, Handled 16.00	

Nappy, Flared, Handled, 9½" 18.00	
Nappy, Handled 16.00	
Nappy, Handled, Footed 16.00	
Nappy, Square, Handled *(Illus.)* 16.00	
Oil & Stopper, 3 oz. 30.00	
Old Fashioned, 6 oz. (No. 2510½) 10.00	
Pickle, Handled, 6" 10.00	
Pitcher, pt. 35.00	
Plate, 6", 7" or 8" 8.00	
Plate, 9" 15.00	
Plate, Cream Soup 8.00	
Plate, Mayonnaise 8.00	
Plate, Sandwich, 12" 20.00	
Plate, Torte, 11" 25.00	
Plate, Torte, 15" or 16" 35.00	
Relish, 2 part 12.00	
Relish, 3 part 14.00	
Relish, 4 part *(Illus.)* 16.00	
Rose Bowl, 3½" 20.00	
Rose Bowl, 5" 25.00	
Salt & Pepper, 4", pr. 22.00	
Salt & Pepper, Individual, 2¼", pr. (No. 2510½) . . . 25.00	
Salt Dip 8.00	
Sherbet, Low, 5½ oz. 7.00	
Soup & Cover, Onion, or Candy, 4" 35.00	
Soup, Cream 20.00	
Sugar, Footed 10.00	
Sugar, Individual 12.00	
Sweetmeat, Divided, Handled 12.00	
Tray for Cheese or Butter, 8½" 20.00	
Tray for Sugar & Cream 20.00	
Tray, Oblong, 10½" 45.00	
Tray, Oval, Handled, 7" *(Illus.)* 20.00	
Tray, Square, 10" 55.00	
Tumbler, 9 oz. (No. 2510½) 12.00	
Tumbler, Footed, 9 oz. 12.00	
Vase, 7" 25.00	
Vase, Crimped, 6" 30.00	
Vase, Square, Footed, 9" 30.00	
Vase, Sweet Pea 25.00	

TERRACE, NO. 111, 5111½

Terrace Original Advertisement for Pressed and Blown Items

Date: 1935

Manufacturer: Duncan and Miller Glass Co., Washington, PA

Colors: Crystal, Ruby, Royal Blue (Cobalt), Amber

A patented design (No. 97082) available in a moderate variety of pieces. Very popular because of its Art Deco flavor and the strong colors of Royal Blue and Red. Plates are square and bases of many pieces are of graduated rings of fine ribs. Prices are for Crystal pieces. For Amber pieces add approximately 20%. For Royal Blue and Red pieces, add at least 200% to 300%. Not all pieces were made in all colors.

Bowl, Deep Salad, 9"	$40.00
Bowl, Flared, 11"	40.00
Bowl, Flared Flower, 11"	40.00
Bowl, Shallow Salad, 11"	40.00
Bowl, Footed, Flared, 12"	50.00
Candlesticks, Low, 4", pr.	55.00
Celery & Relish, 2 Handled, 5 Compartment, 10½"	25.00
Celery Tray, 2 Handled, 8"	20.00
Cheese & Cracker Set, 2 Handled, 11"	30.00
Cream	24.00
Cup & Saucer	25.00
Cup & Saucer, Demitasse	30.00
Mayonnaise, Footed, Handled, 5½"	17.00
Nappy, Square, 5½"	8.00
Nappy, 2 Handled, Basket Shape, 6"	14.00
Nappy, 2 Handled, Regular Shape, 6"	14.00
Nappy, Square, 7"	16.00
Nappy, 2 Handled, 10"	18.00
Plate, Mayonnaise	6.00
Plate, 2 Handled, Lemon, 6"	12.00
Plate, Round, 7"	6.00
Plate, Round Salad, 8½"	8.00
Plate, Square Salad, 6"	6.00
Plate, Square Salad, 7½"	8.00
Plate, Sandwich, 2 Handled, 11"	22.00
Plate, Torte, Flat Edge, 13"	25.00
Plate, Torte, Rolled Edge, 13"	25.00
Relish, 2 Handled, 2 Compartment, Diamond Shape, 6"	15.00
Relish, 2 Handled, 2 Compartment, Round Shape, 6"	15.00
Relish, 2 Handled, 2 Compartment, Square Shape, 6"	15.00
Relish, 2 Handled, 4 Compartment, 9"	18.00
Salad Dressing Bowl, Flared, 2 Compartment, 6"	17.00
Sugar	24.00
Urn & Cover	85.00
Vase, Footed, 10"	55.00

TUDOR, NO. 411, 412, 413

Date: 1923 to 1939

Manufacturer: A. H. Heisey & Co., Newark, OH

Colors: Crystal, Moongleam, Flamingo. Limited items made in Hawthorne.

Compare this pattern with McKee's Lenox which is very similar. All items are No. 411 unless otherwise noted. Pieces marked with an asterisk (*) have only handles in color.

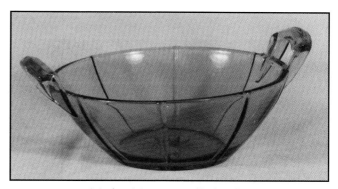

Tudor Two Handled Jelly

	Crystal	Moongleam, Flamingo	Hawthorne
Almond, Individual	$40.00	$	$
Banana Split, Footed, 8" (No. 412)	28.00		
Bar Tumbler, 2½ oz.	22.00		
Bonbon, 2 Handled	17.00	28.00	50.00
Bowl, Floral, Footed, 12½" . .	40.00	85.00	
Bowl, Nut, 4½"	30.00		
Celery Tray, 12"	25.00		
Cheese, 2 Handled, 6".	17.00	28.00	50.00
Cigarette Box & Cover (No. 412)	60.00	120.00	210.00
Cigarette Jar & Ashtray	75.00	140.00	210.00
Cream, Hotel	28.00	40.00*	75.00
Custard or Punch Cup, 4½ oz.	15.00		
Dish, Fruit, 10"	40.00		
Dish, Lemon & Cover, 5" . . .	35.00	60.00	
Finger Bowl	10.00		
Finger Bowl (No. 412)	10.00		
Goblet, 7½ oz. (No. 412) . . .	22.00		
Goblet, 8 oz.	20.00	48.00	
Goblet, 8 oz. (No. 412)	22.00		
Goblet, 8 oz. (No. 413)	22.00		
Goblet, Heavy, 10 oz. (No. 413)	28.00		
Goblet, Luncheon, 7 oz.	20.00	60.00	
Grapefruit, 6½"	17.00		
Grapefruit, Footed, 5"	24.00		
Iced Tea, Handled & Footed, 12 oz. (No. 412)	30.00	55.00	
Jelly, 2 Handled, 5" *(Illus.)* . .	17.00	28.00	50.00
Jelly, High Footed, 5"	32.00	48.00	100.00
Jug Cover	25.00		
Jug, ½ gal.	85.00	125.00*	
Marmalade, 7"	24.00		
Mayonnaise & Plate	45.00	75.00	120.00
Mint, 2 Handled, 6"	17.00	28.00	50.00
Mug (No. 412)	70.00		
Mustard & Cover	48.00		
Nappy, 8"	30.00		
Oil & Stopper, 6 oz.	55.00		
Orange Juice Glass, 4½ oz. . .	20.00		
Oyster Cocktail, 4 oz.	10.00		
Parfait, 4 oz.	24.00		
Parfait, 4½ oz. (No. 412) . . .	24.00		
Pickle Tray, 7"	18.00		
Plate, 5½"	10.00	14.00	24.00
Plate, 7"	12.00		
Plate, 8"	12.00	22.00	
Preserve & Cover, Footed, 5"	45.00	65.00	140.00
Preserve, 6½"	24.00		
Punch Bowl with Foot, 20" . .	270.00		
Salt & Pepper, pr.	40.00		
Saucer Champagne, 5½ oz. . .	17.00		
Saucer Champagne, 6 oz. (No. 412)	17.00		
Saucer Champagne, 6 oz. (No. 413)	18.00		
Sherbet, 5 oz.	10.00		
Sherbet, 5½ oz. (No. 412) . . .	12.00		
Sherbet, Low Footed, 5½ oz. (No. 413)	12.00		
Soda, 12 oz.	15.00	35.00	
Soda, Footed, 10½ oz. (No. 413)	17.00		
Sugar & Cover, Hotel	40.00	60.00*	100.00
Sugar & Cover, Hotel (No. 412)	45.00		
Sugar Dispenser	45.00		
Tankard, Footed (No. 412) . .	100.00	200.00	
Tumbler, 8 oz.	15.00		
Tumbler, 8 oz. (No. 412)	15.00		
Vase, 8"	45.00	115.00	
Water Bottle	60.00		
Wine, 3 oz.	22.00		

TWENTIETH CENTURY, NO. 1415

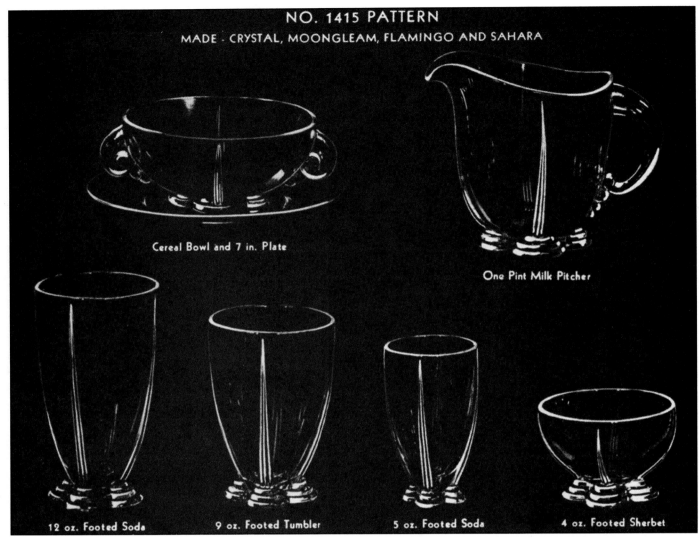

NO. 1415 PATTERN
MADE - CRYSTAL, MOONGLEAM, FLAMINGO AND SAHARA

Cereal Bowl and 7 in. Plate

One Pint Milk Pitcher

12 oz. Footed Soda   9 oz. Footed Tumbler   5 oz. Footed Soda   4 oz. Footed Sherbet

Twentieth Century Catalog Page

Date: 1931 to 1937; 1955 in Dawn.

Manufacturer: A. H. Heisey & Co., Newark, OH

Colors: Crystal, Flamingo, Moongleam, Sahara, Stiegel Blue (cobalt) and Dawn (charcoal gray)

Reproductions: Heisey Collectors of America has produced several styles of baskets in several colors from the sodas.

Most pieces in this short pattern are marked with the Diamond H. Cobalt sodas are valued at $120.00.

	Crystal	Moongleam, Flamingo, Sahara	Dawn
Bowl, Cereal	$35.00	$75.00	$
Pitcher, Milk, 1 pt.	55.00	100.00	135.00
Plate, 7"	10.00	15.00	
Sherbet, Footed, 4 oz.	15.00	45.00	50.00
Soda, Footed, 5 oz.	22.00	60.00	65.00
Soda, Footed, 12 oz.	22.00	60.00	65.00
Tumbler, Footed, 9 oz.	22.00	60.00	65.00

Chapter 14
SQUARES

BLOCK OPTIC

Date: 1929 to 1933

Manufacturer: Hocking Glass Company, Lancaster, OH

Colors: Crystal, Green, Pink. Limited production in Yellow.

Sometimes found with a frosted finish. Other companies also produced similar items which go nicely with Block Optic.

Block Optic Catalog Page

	Green	Pink
Bar Glass, 1 oz. or 2 oz.		
(whiskey)	$35.00	$35.00
Bowl, 4½"	12.00	12.00
Bowl, 5¼"	18.00	27.00
Bowl, 7"	50.00	50.00
Bowl, 8½"	40.00	40.00
Butter & Cover	60.00	
Candlesticks, Tall, 1¾" pr.	110.00	100.00
Candy & Cover, Tall, 2¼"	72.00	60.00
Candy Jar & Cover, Tall, 6¼"	72.00	110.00
Cocktail, 4"	32.00	32.00
Cream (3 styles)	16.00	20.00
Cup & Saucer (4 styles)	15.00	12.00
Goblet, 9 oz.	28.00	35.00
Ice Bucket	38.00	45.00
Iced Tea, 13 oz.	40.00	
Ice Tub	45.00	95.00
Juice, 5 oz.	20.00	
Mug	36.00	
Night Set: Bottle & Tumbler	85.00	95.00

	Green	Pink
Pitcher, 54 oz.	45.00	48.00
Pitcher, 80 oz.	72.00	85.00
Pitcher, Round Bottom, 68 oz.	70.00	60.00
Plate, 6"	3.50	3.50
Plate, 8"	6.50	5.00
Plate, 9"	22.00	45.00
Plate, Grill, 9"	14.00	18.00
Plate, Sandwich, 10¼"	75.00	60.00
Salt & Pepper, pr.	90.00	
Salt & Pepper, Footed, pr.	45.00	70.00
Sandwich, Center Handled	52.00	42.00
Sherbet (3 styles)	5.00 to 15.00	12.00
Soda, 12 oz.	30.00	
Sugar (3 styles)	12.00	15.00
Tumbler, 9 oz.	22.00	20.00
Tumbler, 10 oz.	25.00	22.00
Tumbler, Footed, 9 oz.	25.00	21.00
Vase, 5¾"	220.00	
Wine, 4½"	295.00+	

CAMBRIDGE SQUARE, NO. 3797, 3798

Cambridge Square 3797 Goblet,
Cream, Sugar, Salt, Pepper

Date: 1949

Manufacturer: Cambridge Glass Co., Cambridge, OH

Colors: Crystal. Limited availability in Carmen (Red) and Ebon (Black).

Reproductions: Some items were made by Imperial Glass Corporation after they bought out the Cambridge Glass Co. in 1955.

This modernistic line was patented by Cambridge and all pieces feature a square in the design. No. 3797 items are made with a bowl set directly on a square foot; No. 3798 items have a square stem between bowl and foot. Coffee cups are shallower and broader than tea cups—all have open handles for stacking.

Ashtray, 3½"	$9.00
Ashtray, 6½"	12.00
Bonbon, 7"	15.00
Bonbon, 8"	25.00
Bowl, Individual Salad, 6½"	15.00
Bowl, Salad, 9"	25.00
Bowl, Salad, 11"	40.00
Bowl, Shallow, 10"	30.00
Bowl, Shallow, 12"	38.00
Candleblocks, 1¾", pr.	30.00
Candleblocks, 2¾", pr.	32.00
Candleblocks, 3¾", pr.	35.00
Candleholders, Cupped, pr.	32.00
Candy Box & Cover	34.00
Celery, 11"	25.00
Celery & Relish, 3 part, 10"	28.00
Cigarette Urn	18.00
Cocktail (No. 3797)	20.00
Cocktail (No. 3798)	12.00
Cocktail Icer, 2 pcs.	38.00
Comport, 6"	27.00
Cordial (No. 3797)	30.00
Cordial (No. 3798)	30.00
Cream *(Illus.)*	12.00
Cream, Individual	12.00
Cup & Saucer, Coffee	18.00
Cup & Saucer, Tea	18.00
Decanter & Ball Stopper, 32 oz.	90.00
Dessert, 4½"	12.00
Dish, Oval, 10"	25.00
Dish, Oval, 12"	32.00
Goblet (No. 3797) *(Illus.)*	15.00
Goblet (No. 3798)	15.00
Iced Tea, 12 oz (No. 3798)	14.00
Iced Tea, 14 oz. (No. 3797)	20.00
Ice Tub, 7½"	38.00
Juice, 5 oz. (No. 3797)	14.00
Juice, 5 oz. (No. 3798)	12.00
Lamp, Hurricane, 2 pcs.	45.00
Mayonnaise Bowl	18.00
Oil & Stopper, 4½ oz.	24.00
Plate, 11½"	27.00
Plate, 13½"	32.00
Plate, Bread & Butter, 6"	9.00
Plate, Dinner, 9½"	30.00
Plate, Salad, 7"	12.00
Plate, Tidbit, 9½"	22.00
Relish, 2 part, 6½"	20.00
Relish, 3 part, 8"	25.00
Rose Bowl, 7½"	35.00
Rose Bowl, 9½"	45.00
Salt & Pepper, pr. *(Illus.)*	25.00
Sherbet (No. 3797)	12.00
Sherbet (No. 3798)	12.00
Sugar *(Illus.)*	12.00
Sugar, Individual	12.00
Tray, Oval, 8"	20.00
Vase, 6"	25.00
Vase, Belled, 5"	24.00
Vase, Belled, 5½"	27.00
Vase, Bud, Footed, 8"	25.00
Vase, Footed, 7½"	40.00
Vase, Footed, 8"	25.00
Vase, Footed, 9½"	22.00
Vase, Footed, 11"	30.00
Wine (No. 3797)	20.00
Wine (No. 3798)	18.00

LINCOLN INN, No. 1700

Date: 1928 to 1940

Manufacturer: Fenton Art Glass Co., Williamstown, WV

Colors: Amber, Ebony, Royal Blue, Crystal, Light Green, Jade Green, Aquamarine, Rose, Ruby, Emerald Green, and Green Opalescent

A small assortment was made with intaglio fruit centers in Crystal. Not all pieces were made in all colors.

	Crystal*	Ebony**
Ashtray	$15.00	$
Bonbon, Handled Oval	9.00	20.00
Bonbon, Handled Square	9.00	20.00
Bowl, 7⅝"	10.00	
Bowl, 9"	18.00	
Bowl, Cereal, 6"	7.00	18.00
Bowl, Footed, 10"	20.00	55.00
Bowl, Fruit, 5"	5.00	10.00
Bowl, Ruffled Edge, 6"	8.00	18.00
Cigarette Holder	16.00	30.00
Comport, Oval, Flat, Shallow Cupped, Mint, Nut (5)	11.00	24.00
Cream	12.00	25.00
Cup & Saucer	11.00	25.00
Finger Bowl	8.00	22.00
Goblet *(Illus.)*	15.00	25.00
Iced Tea, Footed, 12 oz.	15.00	25.00
Juice, 5 oz. (flat)	9.00	28.00
Juice, Footed, 4 oz.	12.00	30.00
Olive, Handled	8.00	20.00
Pitcher, 46 oz.		500.00+
Plate, 6"	4.00	7.00
Plate, 8"	7.00	12.00
Plate, 10"	20.00	45.00
Plate, 12"	14.00	32.00
Plate, 14"	22.00	35.00
Plate, Finger Bowl	4.00	8.00.
Salt & Pepper, pr.	60.00	200.00+
Sherbet	7.00	20.00
Sugar	12.00	25.00
Tumbler, Footed, 7 oz.	12.00	30.00
Vase, 12"		150.00
Wine	15.00	35.00

Lincoln Inn Goblet, Decorated Foot

*Also includes Amber, Rose, Green and Emerald Green.

**Also includes Aquararine, Ruby, Jade Green, Royal Blue and Green Opales.

MONTICELLO, NO. 698

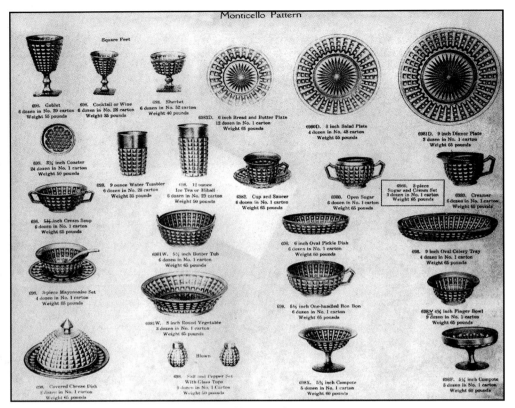

Monticello Catalog Page

Date: 1930s

Manufacturer: Imperial Glass Corporation, Bellaire, OH

Colors: Crystal. Basket in Rose Marie, Milk Glass, possibly others.

The cheese dish and cover looks like an old-fashioned round butter and cover. The molds for this pattern were sold to Mexico in the early 1950s.

Basket, 10"	$55.00
Bonbon, 1 Handle, 5½"	15.00
Bowl, Flower with Wire Holder, 7"	20.00
Bowl, Lily, 5", 6"	15.00
Bowl, Lily, 7", 8"	20.00
Bowl, Salad, Square, 7½"	18.00
Buffet Set, 3 pcs. (16" plate)	50.00
Butter Tub	20.00
Celery Tray, Oval, 9"	15.00
Cheese Dish & Cover	25.00
Coaster, Round, 3¾"	4.00
Cocktail or Wine	12.00
Compote, 5¼", 5¾"	15.00
Cream Soup, 5½"	20.00
Cream	15.00
Cup & Saucer	18.00
Finger Bowl	8.00
Goblet	15.00
Iced Tea or Hi-ball, 12 oz.	15.00
Mayonnaise Set, 3 pcs.	25.00
Pickle, Oval, 6"	12.00
Pitcher, Ice Lip, 52 oz.	45.00
Plate, Bread & Butter, 6"	6.00
Plate, Dinner, 9"	20.00
Plate, Round, 10"	18.00
Plate, Round, 12"	22.00
Plate, Salad, 7½", 8"	8.00
Plate, Square, 10½"	18.00
Relish, 3 part, 8¼"	18.00
Salt & Pepper, Blown, pr.	25.00
Sherbet	8.00
Sugar	15.00
Tid Bit, 2 Tier	25.00
Tumbler, Water, 9 oz.	15.00
Vase, 6"	15.00
Vase, 10½"	22.00
Vegetable, Round, 8"	18.00

VICTORIAN, NO. 1425

Date: 1933 to 1953

Manufacturer: A. H. Heisey & Co., Newark, OH

Colors: Crystal, Sahara, Stiegel Blue (Cobalt). Goblets and sherbets in Moongleam and Flamingo.

Reproductions: Imperial Glass Corp. made the stemware, a nappy, plate and a small compote (which was never made by Heisey) in crystal, amber, azalea and verde. All pieces are marked with the Diamond H.

This tableware pattern in a moderate number of pieces is a copy of early pressed glass but in modern shapes. Heisey marked most pieces with the Diamond H. A very similar pattern was made by Geo. Duncan & Sons in the 1880s. Study the handles of cruets and other details to avoid buying look-alike pieces.

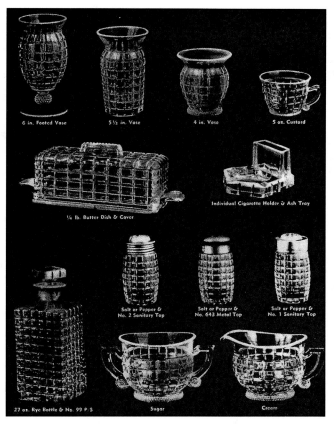

Victorian Catalog Page

	Crystal	Sahara	Cobalt
Bar, 2 oz.	$25.00	$95.00	$165.00
Bottle, French Dressing & Stopper	55.00		
Bottle, Rye & Stopper, 27 oz.	110.00	275.00	500.00+
Bowl, Floral, 10½"	48.00	100.00	350.00
Bowl, Triplex	60.00		
Butter Dish & Cover, ¼ lb.	55.00		
Candlesticks, 2 Light, pr.	190.00	330.00	750.00+
Celery Tray, 12"	25.00	65.00	165.00
Cheese & Cracker, 2 pcs.	85.00	160.00	400.00
Cigarette Box & Cover, 4"	50.00		
Cigarette Box & Cover, 6"	55.00		
Cigarette Holder/Ashtray, Individual	35.00	90.00	175.00
Claret, 4 oz.	22.00	50.00	120.00
Cocktail, 3 oz.	18.00	50.00	120.00
Comport, 5"	35.00		
Condiment Set: Tray, Salt, Pepper, Mustard & Cover	145.00		
Cream	24.00	65.00	300.00
Custard or Punch Cup, 5 oz.	14.00		
Finger Bowl	15.00	45.00	100.00
Goblet, 9 oz.	24.00	75.00	180.00
Goblet, High Footed, 9 oz.	24.00	85.00	180.00
Nappy, 8"	30.00	78.00	300.00
Oil & Stopper, 3 oz.	65.00		
Old Fashioned Cocktail, 8 oz.	18.00	50.00	120.00
Oyster Cocktail, 5 oz.	16.00		
Plate, 6" or 7"	18.00	40.00	110.00
Plate, Buffet, 21"	100.00		
Plate, Sandwich, 13"	35.00	95.00	275.00
Punch Bowl	250.00		
Relish, 3 Compartment, 11"	48.00		
Rose Bowl	250.00		
Salt & Pepper, pr.	50.00	110.00	300.00
Saucer Champagne, 5 oz.	18.00	60.00	140.00
Sherbet, 5 oz.	15.00	50.00	130.00
Soda, 12 oz.	18.00		
Soda, Footed, 12 oz.	18.00	90.00	170.00
Sugar	24.00	65.00	300.00
Tumbler, Footed, 10 oz.	20.00	70.00	190.00
Vase, 4"	25.00	60.00	120.00
Vase, 5½"	25.00		
Vase, Footed, 6"	40.00		
Vase, Footed, 9"	65.00		
Wine, 2½ oz.	25.00	80.00	175.00

ADAM

Adam Butter Dish with Cover

Adam Plate

Date: 1932 to 1934

Manufacturer: Jeannette Glass Co., Jeannette, PA

Colors: Crystal, Pink, Green, Yellow. Limited production in Delphite.

Reproductions: *Butter and cover reproductions exist. The large veins of the leaves on the new cover do not touch in the center as they do in the original. On the bottom, the long, slender leaves do not point to the corners as they do on the old.*

	Pink	Green
Ashtray, 4¼".	$32.00	$28.00
Bowl & Cover, 9"	0.00	110.00
Bowl, 7¾"	28.00	35.00
Bowl, 9"	54.00	35.00
Bowl, Berry, 4¾"	20.00	22.00
Bowl, Cereal, 5¾".	48.00	52.00
Bowl, Oval, 10"	40.00	47.00
Butter & Cover *(Illus.)*	125.00	400.00+
Cake Plate, Footed, 10".	35.00	45.00
Candlesticks, 4", pr.	100.00	120.00
Candy Dish & Cover	110.00	125.00
Coaster, 3¼".	28.00	27.00
Cream	25.00	30.00
Cup & Saucer, Square	40.00	37.00
Iced Tea	82.00	75.00
Lamp	500.00+	500.00+
Pitcher, Round Base, 32 oz.	75.00	
Pitcher, Square Base, 32 oz.	47.00	52.00
Plate, 6"	12.00	15.00
Plate, Grill, 9".	26.00	25.00
Plate, Round, 7¾"	65.00	
Plate, Square, 7¾"	18.00	22.00
Plate, Square, 9" *(Illus.)*	37.00	32.00
Platter, 11¾"	35.00	45.00
Relish, Divided, 8"	30.00	35.00
Salt & Pepper, pr.	87.00	150.00
Sherbet.	28.00	38.00
Sugar & Cover	47.00	67.00
Tumbler	35.00	35.00
Vase, 7½.	290.00	100.00

AMERICAN SWEETHEART

Date: 1930 to 1936

Manufacturer: Macbeth-Evans Glass Co., Charleroi, PA

Colors: Monax, Pink, Red, Blue. Limited production in Cremax and Monax with enameled rims.

As with many other patterns, sugar lids are quite rare, being valued at $350.00+.

American Sweetheart Cereal Bowl, Plate, Cup & Saucer

	Pink	Monax
Bowl, Berry, 3¾"	$47.00	$
Bowl, Berry, 9"	50.00	75.00
Bowl, Cereal, 6" *(Illus.)*	18.00	20.00
Bowl, Console, 18"		450.00+
Bowl, Cream Soup, 4½"	95.00	125.00
Bowl, Flat Soup		85.00
Bowl, Oval, Vegetable, 11"	85.00	100.00
Cream, Footed	17.00	14.00
Cup & Saucer *(Illus.)*.	20.00	17.00
Juice, 5 oz.	95.00	
Lamp Shade		750.00+
Pitcher, 60 oz.	800.00+	
Pitcher, 80 oz.	650.00+	
Plate, 6"	8.00	6.00
Plate, 8"	14.00	12.00
Plate, 9" *(Illus.)*.		15.00
Plate, 9¾"	40.00	35.00
Plate, 10¼"	40.00	35.00
Plate, 15½"		250.00
Plate, Chop, 11"		16.00

	Pink	Monax
Platter, Oval, 13"	60.00	72.00
Salt & Pepper, pr.	425.00+	375.00+
Salver, 12"	28.00	24.00
Sherbet, Footed, 3¾"	22.00	
Sherbet, Footed, 4¼"	20.00	24.00
Sugar, Footed	17.00	12.00
Tidbit Server, 3 Tier		300.00
Tidbit, 2 Tier		100.00
Tumbler, 9 oz.	85.00	
Tumbler, 10 oz.	95.00	

BOWKNOT

Date: 1920s or 1930s

Manufacturer: Unknown

Colors: Green

The footed tumbler also has an all-over pattern on the underside of the base not shown in the drawing.

Bowl, Deep, 4½"	$18.00
Bowl, 5½"	22.00
Cup	10.00
Plate, 7"	14.00
Sherbet, Footed	18.00
Tumbler, 10 oz.	23.00
Tumbler, Footed, 10 oz. *(Illus.)*	23.00

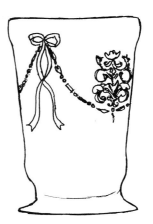

Bowknot Footed Tumbler

HARP

Harp Coaster

Date: 1954 to 1957

Manufacturer: Jeannette Glass Co., Jeannette, PA

Colors: Crystal. Limited production in pink and pale blue. Crystal sometimes decorated with gold edges.

Ashtray or Coaster $6.00
Coaster *(Illus.)* 5.00
Cup & Saucer 25.00
Plate, 7" 12.00
Salver, Footed, 9" (cake stand) 24.00
Tray, Rectangular 35.00
Vase, 7½" 25.00

HERITAGE

Heritage 12" Sandwich Plate, 10½" Bowl

Date: Late 1930s to 1960s

Manufacturer: Federal Glass Co., Columbus, OH

Colors: Crystal. Limited production in Pink, Blue, and Green.

Prices are for Crystal items.

Bowl, Berry, 5" $10.00
Bowl, Berry, 8½" 38.00
Bowl, 10½" *(Illus.)* 23.00
Cup & Saucer 11.00
Cream 28.00

Plate, 8" 7.00
Plate, 9¼" 11.00
Plate, Sandwich, 12" *(Illus.)* 17.00
Sugar 28.00

HORSESHOE, NO. 612

Date: 1930 to 1933

Manufacturer: Indiana Glass Co., Dunkirk, IN

Colors: Crystal, Green, Yellow, Pink

	Green	Yellow
Bowl, Berry, 4½"	$38.00	$27.00
Bowl, Berry, 9½"	42.00	48.00
Bowl, Cereal, 6½".	38.00	32.00
Bowl, Oval, Vegetable, 10½"	27.00	34.00
Bowl, Salad, 7½"	32.00	28.00
Bowl, Vegetable, 8½"	38.00	42.00
Butter & Cover.	900.00+	
Candy Dish & Cover		
in Metal Holder	270.00	
Cream	25.00	
Cup & Saucer.	17.00	22.00
Iced Tea, Footed, 12 oz..	220.00	200.00
Pitcher, 64 oz. *(Illus.)*	360.00	420.00
Plate, 6"	15.00	15.00
Plate, 8¼"	8.00	9.00
Plate, 9¼"	12.00	12.00
Plate, 10¼"	22.00	20.00
Plate, Grill, 10¼	95.00	42.00
Plate, Sandwich, 11¾"	27.00	27.00
Platter, 10¾"	30.00	28.00
Relish, 3 part, Footed	22.00	35.00

Horseshoe Pitcher

	Green	Yellow
Sherbet.	18.00	15.00
Sugar	15.00	14.00
Tumbler, 9 oz..	150.00	
Tumbler, Footed, 9 oz.	30.00	32.00

LORAIN, NO. 615

Date: 1929 to 1932

Manufacturer: Indiana Glass Co., Dunkirk, IN

Colors: Green, Yellow. Limited production in Crystal.

	Green	Yellow
Bowl, Cereal, 6"	$65.00	$75.00
Bowl, Salad, 7¼"	47.00	75.00
Bowl, Berry, 8"	100.00	185.00
Bowl, Oval, Vegetable, 9¾"	55.00	68.00
Cream *(Illus.)*	22.00	27.00
Cup & Saucer.	20.00	25.00
Plate, 5½"	11.00	15.00
Plate, 7¾"	12.00	18.00
Plate, 8¼"	24.00	37.00
Plate, 10¼"	55.00	78.00
Platter, 11½"	40.00	60.00
Relish, 4 part, 8".	22.00	3.00
Sherbet, Footed.	22.00	27.00

Lorain Cream

	Green	Yellow
Snack Tray	28.00	
Sugar	22.00	27.00
Tumbler, Footed, 9 oz.	30.00	38.00

193

MADRID

Madrid Cup & Saucer

Date: 1932 to 1939

Manufacturer: Federal Glass Co., Columbus, OH

Colors: Crystal, Green, Pink, Amber, Light Blue

Reproductions of many pieces have been made beginning in 1976. These older repros have the number 76 worked into the design, but current ones do not. The amber and blue of the reproductions are darker than the original colors, the pink is somewhat lighter, and teal was never originally made. New pieces include a grill plate divided in half, low footed goblet, vase or hurricane lamp, short salt and pepper shakers, and an 11 oz. tumbler. None of these were originally made. The candlestick was also used as a foot for a plate, making a cake stand, and with the butter to make a preserve dish.

	Amber	Blue	Green	Pink
Ashtray, 6"	$200.00	$	$150.00	$
Bowl, 5"	10.00	22.00	12.00	11.00
Bowl, 8"	18.00	68.00	22.00	
Bowl, 9¼"	24.00			34.00
Bowl, Console, 11"	22.00			20.00
Bowl, Cream Soup, 4¾"	20.00			
Bowl, Deep, 9½"	36.00			
Bowl, Oval, Vegetable, 10"	22.00	50.00	28.00	27.00
Bowl, Soup, 7"	20.00	40.00	24.00	
Butter & Cover	90.00		100.00	
Candlesticks, 2", pr.	32.00			38.00
Cookie Jar & Cover	55.00			55.00
Cream	12.00	28.00	15.00	
Cup & Saucer *(Illus.)*	12.00	22.00	15.00	12.00
Gravy Boat & Underplate	1,500.00+			
Hot Plate, (2 styles)	55.00		55.00	
Iced Tea, (2 styles)	32.00	55.00	42.00	
Jam Dish, 7"	25.00	45.00	25.00	
Jello Mold, 2"	16.00			
Juice, 5 oz.	20.00	48.00	45.00	
Juice, Footed, 5 oz.	37.00		52.00	
Pitcher, Juice, 36 oz.	54.00			
Pitcher, Square, 60 oz.	54.00	180.00	150.00	50.00
Pitcher, 80 oz. with or without Ice Lip	78.00		250.00	
Plate, 6"	5.00	12.00	5.00	5.00
Plate, 7½"	13.00	27.00	12.00	12.00
Plate, 8¾"	13.00	27.00	12.00	12.00
Plate, 10½"	65.00	95.00	55.00	47.00
Plate, Cake, 11¼"	20.00			20.00
Plate, Grill, 10½"	14.00		20.00	14.00
Plate, Relish, 10¼"	18.00		20.00	20.00
Platter, 11½"	22.00	38.00	30.00	27.00
Salt & Pepper, pr.	52.00		74.00	
Salt & Pepper, Footed, pr.	85.00	175.00	95.00	
Sherbet (2 styles)	12.00	20.00	15.00	15.00
Sugar & Cover	60.00	210.00	60.00	
Tumbler, 9 oz.	22.00	35.00	32.00	27.00
Tumbler, Footed, 10 oz.	28.00		42.00	

PATRICIAN

Date: 1933 to 1937

Manufacturer: Federal Glass Co., Columbus, OH

Colors: Pink, Amber, Green, Crystal

Again, sugar lids are scarce and are valued at $55.00+ in all colors.

Patrician Sugar, Plate, Cream

	<u>Crystal</u>	<u>Amber</u>	<u>Pink</u>	<u>Green</u>
Bowl, Cream Soup, 4¾".........	$15.00	$20.00	$22.00	$22.00
Bowl, 5".....................	10.00	14.00	16.00	15.00
Bowl, 6".....................	17.00	28.00	28.00	32.00
Bowl, 8½"...................	35.00	50.00	40.00	45.00
Bowl, Oval, Vegetable, 10".......	32.00	45.00	32.00	40.00
Butter & Cover	100.00	125.00	275.00	160.00
Cookie Jar & Cover	110.00	120.00		525.00+
Cream *(Illus.)*.................	10.00	14.00	15.00	16.00
Cup & Saucer	12.00	18.00	20.00	22.00
Iced Tea, 14 oz.	32.00	52.00	42.00	52.00
Jelly, 6½"...................		36.00		45.00
Juice, 5 oz....................	28.00	35.00	32.00	40.00
Pitcher, 75 oz.	110.00	125.00	140.00	155.00
Pitcher, Applied Handle, 75 oz.....	135.00	155.00	180.00	200.00
Plate, 6"....................	9.00	12.00	14.00	15.00
Plate, 7½"...................	13.00	20.00	22.00	24.00
Plate, 9" *(Illus.)*..............	12.00	15.00	16.00	18.00
Plate, 10½".................	12.00	16.00	50.00	51.00
Plate, Grill, 10½"..............	11.00	16.00	16.00	16.00
Platter, 11½"	24.00	34.00	38.00	38.00
Salt & Pepper, pr...............	52.00	62.00	100.00	78.00
Sherbet......................	10.00	15.00	15.00	16.00
Sugar *(Illus.)*.................	9.00	12.00	14.00	14.00
Tumbler, 9 oz.	25.00	35.00	35.00	35.00
Tumbler, Footed, 8 oz.	40.00	60.00		65.00

PHILBE

Philbe Plate

Date: 1937 to 1938

Manufacturer: Hocking Glass Company, Lancaster, OH

Colors: Crystal, Light Blue, Pink, Green

Part of the Fire-King line.

	Crystal	Pink Green	Blue
Bowl, 5½"	$20.00	$45.00	$65.00
Bowl, 7¼"	28.00	55.00	90.00
Bowl, Oval, Vegetable, 10" . .	55.00	85.00	160.00
Candy Jar & Cover, 4"	225.00	750.00+	800.00+
Cookie Jar & Cover	650.00+	1,000.00+	1,500.00+
Cream	40.00	120.00	140.00
Cup & Saucer.	90.00	175.00	225.00
Goblet, 9 oz..	80.00	185.00	235.00
Iced Tea, Footed, 15 oz..	45.00	80.00	80.00
Juice, Footed.	45.00	160.00	185.00
Pitcher, 36 oz..	300.00+	650.00+	900.00+

	Crystal	Pink Green	Blue
Pitcher, 56 oz..	400.00+	1,000.00+	1,200.00+
Plate, 6"	35.00	60.00	80.00
Plate, 8"	22.00	40.00	50.00
Plate, 10" *(Illus.)*.	25.00	70.00	110.00
Plate, 10½"	25.00	60.00	85.00
Plate, 11½"	25.00	65.00	100.00
Plate, Grill, 10½"	25.00	50.00	80.00
Platter, Handled, 12".	35.00	130.00	180.00
Sugar	45.00	115.00	135.00
Tumbler, 9 oz..	45.00	110.00	135.00
Tumbler, Footed, 10 oz..	35.00	75.00	95.00

PRINCESS

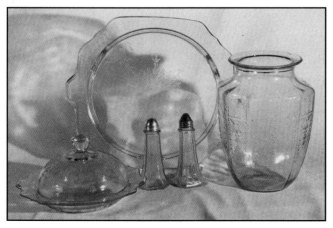

Princess Covered Butter, Cake Plate,
Salt & Pepper, Vase

Date: 1931 to 1935

Manufacturer: Hocking Glass Co., Lancaster, OH

Colors: Green, Pink, Topaz. A few pieces available in Blue.

Reproductions: The plain footed candy and cover exist in low quality glass. Both pink and green colors do not match those of the old. Salt and pepper shakers are made in new garish colors in poor quality glass.

There are two shades of Topaz yellow, so care must be taken when trying to match pieces. A popular pattern because of the many different pieces made.

(continued) PRINCESS

	Green	Pink	Topaz
Ashtray, 4½"	$80.00	$95.00	$100.00
Bowl, 4½"	28.00	28.00	50.00
Bowl, 5"	35.00	30.00	35.00
Bowl, Flared Rim, Deep, 9½"	50.00	45.00	130.00
Bowl, Octagonal, 9"	42.00	40.00	130.00
Bowl, Oval, Vegetable, 10" . . .	30.00	28.00	70.00
Butter & Cover *(Illus.)*	100.00	100.00	700.00+
Cake Plate, 10" *(Illus.)*	30.00	35.00	
Candy & Cover	70.00	75.00	
Coaster	40.00	70.00	100.00
Cookie Jar & Cover *(Illus.)* . . .	60.00	70.00	
Cream, Oval	15.00	15.00	15.00
Cup & Saucer	25.00	25.00	14.00
Iced Tea, 13 oz.	40.00	30.00	30.00
Iced Tea, Footed, 10½ oz.	90.00	90.00	160.00
Juice, 5 oz.	30.00	30.00	30.00
Pitcher, 36 oz.	55.00	70.00	600.00+
Pitcher, 60 oz.	60.00	60.00	100.00
Pitcher, Footed, 24 oz.	550.00+	500.00+	
Plate, 5½" (saucer)	12.00	12.00	5.00
Plate, 8"	17.00	17.00	12.00
Plate, Dinner, 9½"	27.00	25.00	17.00
Plate, Grill, 9½"	15.00	15.00	7.00
Plate, Grill, Handled, 10¼" . .	12.00	14.00	7.00
Plate, Sandwich, Handled, 10¼"	15.00	27.00	165.00
Platter, Handled, 12"	25.00	25.00	65.00

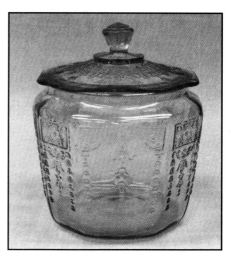

Princess Covered Cookie Jar

	Green	Pink	Topaz
Relish, 7½" (no divider)	120.00	180.00	160.00
Relish, Divided, 7½"	28.00	30.00	110.00
Salt & Pepper, pr., 4½" *(Illus.)*	60.00	60.00	80.00
Sherbet	24.00	24.00	40.00
Sugar	12.00	14.00	10.00
Tumbler, 9 oz.	28.00	28.00	25.00
Tumbler, Footed, 10 oz.	35.00	30.00	25.00
Tumbler, Square, Footed, 9 oz.	70.00	70.00	
Vase, 8" *(Illus.)*	40.00	45.00	

PRINCESS FEATHER, NO. 201

Date: Ca. 1924, until at least the late 1940s (in crystal).

Manufacturer: Westmoreland Glass Co., Grapeville, PA

Colors: Crystal, Pink, Green, Blue (Pale Aqua)

This pattern was Westmoreland's pattern similar to Hocking's and Indiana's Sandwich, but lacking the flower motif of both of those (See Flowers, Fruits & Leaves chapter for these and Early American Sandwich by Duncan & Miller). There are probably pieces other than those listed. This pattern is under-appreciated today, but should gain in popularity with the increasing interest in Westmoreland patterns.

Princess Feather Table Setting, Original Ad

PRINCESS FEATHER, NO. 201 *(continued)*

	Crystal	Colors
Bowl, Console.	$20.00	$35.00
Candlesticks, 1 Light, pr.	22.00	35.00
Candlesticks, 2 Light, pr.	30.00	50.00
Champagne, High Footed	10.00	16.00
Cocktail, 3 oz.	10.00	16.00
Cream, Footed	10.00	17.00
Cup & Saucer.	18.00	28.00
Decanter & Stopper	40.00	65.00
Finger Bowl	6.00	12.00
Ginger Ale, 5 oz. (flat—juice)	8.00	15.00
Goblet, 8 oz.	10.00	16.00
Grapefruit, 6½"	10.00	15.00
Iced Tea, 10 oz. (flat).	8.00	15.00

	Crystal	Colors
Nappy, Round, 5" or 6"	6.00	12.00
Plate, 7" or 8".	8.00	12.00
Plate, 13"	17.00	22.00
Plate, Finger Bowl, 6½"	5.00	10.00
Plate, Service, 10½"	15.00	25.00
Relish, 3 Compartment.	15.00	24.00
Salt & Pepper, pr.	30.00	45.00
Sherbet.	8.00	15.00
Sherbet, High Footed	10.00	16.00
Sugar, Footed	10.00	17.00
Tray for Cream & Sugar	12.00	20.00
Tumbler, Footed, 8 oz.	10.00	16.00
Wine	12.00	18.00

S PATTERN

S Pattern Small Bowl, Salad Plate, Cup & Saucer

Date: 1930 to 1933

Manufacturer: MacBeth-Evans Glass Co., Charleroi, PA

Colors: Crystal, Green, Amber, Monax, Yellow. Crystal with various fired-on colors.

	Crystal	Yellow
Bowl, 5½" *(Illus.)*	$7.00	$10.00
Bowl, 8½"	20.00	26.00
Cream (2 styles)	9.00	11.00
Cup & Saucer (2 styles) *(Illus.)* . . .	5.00	7.00
Iced Tea, 12 oz.	16.00	22.00
Juice, 5 oz.	78.00	
Pitcher, 80 oz. (2 styles).	37.00	
Plate, 6"	4.00	5.00
Plate, 8" *(Illus.)*.	5.00	6.00
Plate, 9¼"	9.00	10.00
Plate, 11"	75.00	85.00
Plate, 13"	3.00	4.00
Plate, Grill	8.00	.00
Sherbet.	6.00	8.00
Sugar (2 styles)	8.00	9.00
Tumbler, 9 oz.	9.00	10.00
Tumbler, 10 oz.	9.00	11.00

Chapter 16

SWAGS

CAPRICE, NO. 3550

Date: 1936

Manufacturer: Cambridge Glass Co., Cambridge, OH

Colors: Crystal, Moonlight (light blue), La Rosa (Pink). Limited number of items in Pistachio (pale green), Milk, Amethyst, Royal Blue, Mandarin Gold, Emerald (pale green) and Mocha (pale amber). Later production in late Imperial colors.

Reproductions: These began when Imperial Glass Corp. bought the Cambridge Glass Co. and made some of the Caprice items as their Curlicue line. After the failure of Imperial, the Caprice molds were sold to several customers who have since produced some pieces. Several pieces have been made in crystal, light blue and other colors. Some repros have a small dot in the center of the bottom. Be careful when buying Caprice—most pieces were never reproduced, but some have been. After the close of Imperial Glass, Fenton Art Glass Co. purchased some of the Caprice molds and made pieces of the pattern.

Caprice is the most extensive line made by the Cambridge Glass Co. The pattern was referred to as Alpine when it was decorated with satin finish portions. Caprice was covered by several patents granted to the company in 1936. For detailed information on Caprice, we recommend Cambridge Caprice *by The National Cambridge Collectors, Inc.*

Caprice Assortment—Imperial Glass Photo—
Sold as Curlicue Crystal by Imperial

CAPRICE, NO. 3550 *(continued)*

	Crystal	Moonlight
Almond, 4 Footed, 2" (No. 95) . . .	$27.00	$70.00
Ashtray w/Card Holder, 2¾" (No. 213)	12.00	20.00
Ashtray, Round, 3", 4" & 5"	10.00	25.00
Ashtray, Triangular, 3" & 4½" (Nos. 206, 210)	15.00	25.00
Ball Vase, 4½" (No. 237)	50.00	120.00
Ball Vase, 6½" (No. 238)	70.00	175.00
Ball Vase, 8½" (No. 239)	100.00	220.00
Ball Vase, 9¼" (No. 240)	150.00	310.00
Basket, Low Footed, 7" (No. 134)	30.00	60.00
Basket, Square, 2 Handled, 4" & 5" (Nos. 146, 153)	18.00	42.00
Bitters Bottle (No. 186)	190.00	420.00
Bonbon, Oval, 2 Handled, 4½" & 6" (Nos. 148, 155)	45.00	120.00
Bonbon, Oval, Low Footed, 6" (No. 132)	22.00	55.00
Bonbon, Square, 2 Handled, 4" & 6" (Nos. 147, 154)	22.00	45.00
Bonbon, Square, Low Footed, 6" (No. 133)	22.00	55.00
Bowl, Banana (No. 66A)	45.00	100.00
Bowl, Belled, 3 Footed, 10½" (No. 54)	38.00	
Bowl, Belled, 4 Footed, 10½" (No. 54)	40.00	110.00
Bowl, Belled, 4 Footed, 12½" (No. 62)	38.00	80.00
Bowl, Belled, 4 Footed, 12½" (No. 62)	38.00	95.00
Bowl, Crimped, 3 Footed, 10½" (No. 53)	42.00	
Bowl, Crimped, 3 Footed, 12½" (No. 61)	40.00	
Bowl, Crimped, 4 Footed, 10½" (No. 53)	42.00	120.00
Bowl, Crimped, 4 Ftd., 11", 12½", 13", (Nos. 60, 61, 66)	38.00	150.00
Bowl, Crimped, 9½" (No. 52)	42.00	120.00
Bowl, Deep, Tapered, 4 Footed, 11" (No. 59)	55.00	140.00
Bowl, Deep, 4 Footed, 9½" (No. 51)	52.00	130.00
Bowl, Oval, Handled, 4 Footed, 9" (No. 64)	75.00	140.00
Bowl, Oval, Handled, 4 Footed, 11" (No. 65)	42.00	120.00
Bowl, Salad, 15" (No. 84)	58.00	160.00
Bowl, Salad, 4 Footed, 8" (No. 49)	42.00	120.00

	Crystal	Moonlight
Bowl, Salad, 4 Footed, 10" (No. 57)	45.00	135.00
Bowl, Salad, Cupped, 13" (No. 80)	80.00	185.00
Bowl, Shallow, 3 or 4 Footed, 11½" (No. 81)	40.00	110.00
Bowl, Shallow, 3 or 4 Footed, 13½" (No. 82)	45.00	125.00
Bowl, Square, 4 Footed, 8½" (No. 50)	52.00	130.00
Bowl, Square, 4 Footed, 10" (No. 58)	38.00	170.00
Bowl, Twin Salad Dressing, 6" (No. 110)	80.00	200.00
Bowl, Twin Salad Dressing (No. 112)	165.00	450.00
Butter Dish, ¼ lb. (No. 52)	245.00	
Candelabra, 2 Light (shell bobeches), 7½", pr. (No. 69)	220.00	900.00+
Candelabra, 2 Light, 6", pr. (No. 78)	185.00	310.00
Candelabra, 2 Light, 7½", pr. (No. 71)	350.00	700.00+
Candlesticks with Prism, 1 Light, 7", pr. (No. 70)	60.00	160.00
Candlesticks, 1 Light, 2½", pr. (No. 67)	40.00	75.00
Candlesticks, 2 Light, 6", pr. (No. 72)	90.00	220.00
Candlesticks, 2 Light, 7½", pr. (No. 69)	325.00	1,100.00-
Candlesticks, 3 Light, pr. (No. 74)	85.00	275.00
Candlesticks, Reflector, pr. (No. 73)	275.00	
Candy & Cover, 2 part, 6" (No. 168)	40.00	110.00
Candy & Cover, 3 Footed, 6" (No. 165)	50.00	140.00
Candy & Cover, Low Footed, 6" (No. 167)	60.00	140.00
Celery & Relish, 3 part, 8½" (No. 124)	22.00	50.00
Celery & Relish, 3 part, 12" (oblong) (No. 125)	52.00	160.00
Celery, 12" (No. 103)	90.00	215.00
Cigarette Box & Cover, 3½" or 4½" (Nos. 207, 208)	28.00	65.00
Cigarette Holder, Triangular, 3" x 3" & 2" x 2¼" (204, 205)	22.00	65.00
Claret, 4½ oz. (No. 5)	70.00	200.00+
Cloverleaf (No. 173)	35.00	100.00

(continued) CAPRICE, No. 3550

	Crystal	Moonlight
Club, 6½" (No. 170)	35.00	100.00
Coaster, 3½" (No. 13).	17.00	48.00
Cocktail (No. 200)	15.00	40.00
Cocktail, 3½ oz. (No. 3)	25.00	65.00
Comport, Low Footed, 7"		
(No. 130).	25.00	55.00
Comport, Tall, 7" (No. 136)	45.00	125.00
Cracker Jar & Cover (No. 202) . . .	275.00	1,200.00+
Cream, Individual (No. 40)	15.00	30.00
Cream, Large Size (No. 41)	15.00	35.00
Cream, Medium Size (No. 38). . . .	12.00	25.00
Cup & Saucer (No. 17).	18.00	52.00
Decanter, 35 oz. (tilted)		
(No. 187).	160.00	450.00
Diamond, 6" (No. 171).	35.00	100.00
Finger Bowl (No. 16)	35.00	110.00
Fruit, 5", (straight edge or crimped)		
(Nos. 18, 19)	32.00	80.00
Goblet (No. 200)	16.00	45.00
Goblet, 10 oz. (No. 1).	30.00	65.00
Goblet, 19 oz. (No. 400).	85.00	
Heart, 6" (No. 169)	35.00	100.00
Ice Bucket, 4 Footed (No. 201) . . .	65.00	185.00
Iced Tea, Footed (No. 200)	16.00	45.00
Jelly, 2 Handled, 4" & 5"		
(Nos. 144, 151)	18.00	40.00
Jelly, Crimped, Low Footed, 7"		
(No. 135).	28.00	75.00
Jug, 32 oz. (No. 179)	120.00	400.00
Jug, 80 oz. (No. 183)	110.00	380.00
Jug, Doulton, 80 oz. (No. 178) . . .	800.00+	4100.00+
Marmalade & Cover (No. 89)	70.00	220.00
Mayonnaise Bowl, 6" (No. 105). . .	40.00	95.00
Mayonnaise Plate,		
6½" (No. 128).	7.00	25.00
Mayonnaise, 5" (No. 127)	35.00	90.00
Mustard & Cover (No. 87)	60.00	225.00
Nut Dish, Individual, 2 part,		
2½" (No. 94)	28.00	80.00
Nut Dish, Individual,		
2½" (No. 93)	25.00	75.00
Oil & Stopper, 3 oz. (open handle)		
(No. 117).	50.00	110.00
Oil & Stopper, 3 oz. (solid handle)		
(No. 101) cone.	35.00	100.00
Oil & Stopper, 3 oz. (tilted)		
(No. 98).	25.00	70.00
Oil & Stopper, 5 oz. (solid handle)		
(No. 100)	75.00	220.00
Pickle, 9" (No. 102)	27.00	65.00
Plate, 16" (No. 40)	45.00	115.00

	Crystal	Moonlight
Plate, 3 or 4 Footed,		
11½" (No. 26)	35.00	75.00
Plate, 3 or 4 Footed,		
14" (No. 28)	40.00	90.00
Plate, Bread & Butter,		
5½" & 6½" (Nos. 20, 21)	10.00	27.00
Plate, Cabaret, 16" (No. 35)	45.00	140.00
Plate, Cabaret, 3 or 4 Footed,		
11" (No. 32)	35.00	75.00
Plate, Cabaret, 3 or 4 Footed,		
14" (No. 33)	40.00	90.00
Plate, Cake, 13" (No. 36)	160.00	375.00
Plate, Dinner, 9½" (No. 24)	48.00	150.00
Plate, Finger Bowl (No. 16).	18.00	25.00
Plate, Lemon, 2 Handled,		
5" & 6" (Nos. 145, 152).	14.00	38.00
Plate, Low Footed, 8" (No. 131) . .	28.00	48.00
Plate, Salad, 7½" & 8½"		
(Nos. 23, 22)	15.00	32.00
Punch Bowl (No. 498)	2,300.00+	
Relish, 2 Compartment,		
5½" (No. 119).	30.00	55.00
Relish, 2 part, 6" (No. 115).	45.00	90.00
Relish, 2 part, 6 ¾" (No. 120). . . .	30.00	55.00
Relish, 3 part, 8" (No. 122).	25.00	60.00
Relish, 4 part, 12" (No. 126).	85.00	240.00
Rose Bowl, 4 Footed,		
6" (No. 235)	80.00	160.00
Rose Bowl, 4 Footed,		
8" (No. 236)	110.00	220.00
Rose or Ivy Ball, 5" (No. 232)	65.00	280.00
Salt & Pepper, Individual, pr.		
(ball shape) (No. 90).	50.00	220.00
Salt & Pepper, Individual,		
pr. (No. 92)	45.00	140.00
Salt & Pepper, pr. (No. 96)	30.00	110.00
Salt & Pepper, pr. (ball shape)		
(No. 91).	45.00	125.00
Salver, Cake, 2 pcs. (No. 31)	170.00	500.00+
Seafood Cocktail,		
4½ oz. (No. 7).	36.00	95.00
Sherbet, Low, 5 oz. (No. 4)	32.00	90.00
Sherbet, Tall (No. 200)	16.00	40.00
Sherbet, Tall, 7 oz. (No. 2)	20.00	45.00
Sherbet, Tall, 7 oz. (No. 400).	85.00	
Spade, 6" (No. 172)	35.00	100.00
Sugar, Individual (No. 40).	15.00	30.00
Sugar, Large Size (No. 41)	15.00	35.00
Sugar, Medium Size (No. 38).	12.00	25.00
Tray, Oval, 6" (No. 37)	20.00	45.00
Tray, Oval, 9" (No. 42)	25.00	55.00
Tumbler, 12 oz. (No. 184).	28.00	55.00

CAPRICE, NO. 3550 *(continued)*

	Crystal	Moonlight
Tumbler, 2 oz. (No. 188)	25.00	70.00
Tumbler, 5 oz. (No. 180)	25.00	62.00
Tumbler, Flat, Iced Tea, 12 oz. (No. 15)	42.00	100.00
Tumbler, Flat, 9 oz. (No. 14)	45.00	120.00
Tumbler, Footed, 10 oz. (No. 10)	22.00	45.00
Tumbler, Footed, Iced Tea, 12 oz. (No. 9)	25.00	50.00
Tumbler, Footed, 3 oz. (No. 12)	30.00	110.00
Tumbler, Footed, Juice, 5 oz. (No. 11)	22.00	55.00
Tumbler, Footed, 5 oz. (No. 200)	15.00	40.00
Vase (squat), 4½" (No. 244)	70.00	160.00
Vase (squat), 5½" (No. 245)	75.00	175.00
Vase (squat), 7½" (No. 246)	110.00	190.00
Vase, 4¼" (No. 241)	50.00	95.00
Vase, 6" (No. 242)	100.00	150.00
Vase, 8½" (No. 243)	120.00	235.00
Wine (No. 200)	22.00	50.00
Wine, 3 oz.(No. 6)	40.00	135.00

BLOWN PIECES

	Crystal	Moonlight
Ball Vase, 4½" (No. 337)	$55.00	$130.00
Ball Vase, 6" (No. 338)	70.00	170.00
Ball Vase, 8½" (No. 339)	100.00	240.00
Ball Vase, 9¼" (No. 340)	150.00	500.00+
Bubble Ball, 4" (No. 256)	95.00	220.00
Claret (No. 301)	40.00	
Claret, 4½ oz. (No. 300)	75.00	240.00
Cocktail (No. 301)	22.00	
Cocktail, 3 oz. (No. 300)	25.00	65.00
Cocktail, Low (No. 301)	20.00	
Cordial (No. 301)	45.00	
Cordial, 1 oz. (No. 300)	45.00	190.00
Finger Bowl (No. 300)	40.00	120.00
Goblet (No. 301)	20.00	
Goblet, 9 oz. (No. 300)	20.00	50.00
Iced Tea (No. 301)	22.00	

	Crystal	Moonlight
Iced Tea, 12 oz. Flat (No. 310)	40.00	95.00
Juice (No. 301)	18.00	
Marmalade & Cover	100.00	220.00
Old Fashioned Cocktail, Flat, 7 oz. (No. 310)	40.00	130.00
Oyster Cocktail, 4½ oz. (No. 300)	22.00	70.00
Parfait, 5 oz. (No. 300)	85.00	240.00
Sherbet (No. 301)	15.00	
Sherbet, Low, 6 oz. (No. 300)	14.00	30.00
Sherbet, Tall, 6 oz. (No. 300)	15.00	35.00
Tumbler, Flat, 5 oz. (No. 310)	30.00	140.00
Tumbler, Footed, 10 oz. (No. 300)	22.00	50.00
Tumbler, Footed, 12 oz. (No. 300)	22.00	50.00
Tumbler, Footed, 2½ oz. (No. 300)	45.00	240.00
Tumbler, Footed, 5 oz. (No. 300)	20.00	45.00
Tumbler, Footed, Stemmed, 12 oz. (No. 300/2)	25.00	55.00
Tumbler, Table, Flat, 10 oz. (No. 310)	35.00	110.00
Tumbler, Tall, Flat, 10 oz. (No. 310)	30.00	80.00
Vase, (squat) 4½" (No. 344)	75.00	125.00
Vase, (squat) 5½" (No. 345)	80.00	200.00
Vase, (squat) 7½" (No. 346)	115.00	290.00
Vase, 3½" (2 styles) (Nos. 249, 250)	85.00	270.00
Vase, 4" (No. 251)	85.00	250.00
Vase, 4¼" (No. 341)	55.00	95.00
Vase, 4½" (No. 252)	80.00	230.00
Vase, 4½" (No. 253)	95.00	270.00
Vase, 6" (No. 254)	180.00	600.00
Vase, 6" (No. 342)	125.00	220.00
Vase, 8½" (No. 343)	125.00	250.00
Wine (No. 301)	30.00	
Wine, 2½ oz. (No. 300)	30.00	80.00

CASCADE

Date: Ca. 1940s

Manufacturer: Cambridge Glass Co., Cambridge, OH

Colors: Crystal. Limited production in Crown Tuscan, Mandarin Gold, Milk and Emerald.

Assigned Patent Nos. 140826-141034. A moderate size tableware line with most production in Crystal. For pieces in color, add 50% to 75%. Prices given are for Crystal.

Ashtray, 4½" $5.00
Ashtray, 6" 6.00
Ashtray, 8" 9.00
Bonbon, 6" 7.00
Bonbon, 2 Handled, Footed, 7" 10.00
Bonbon Plate, 2 Handled, Footed, 8" 9.00
Bowl, Flared, 4 Footed, 10" 15.00
Bowl, Flared, 4 Footed, 12½" 18.00
Bowl, Oval, 4 Footed, 12" 18.00
Bowl, Shallow, 4 Footed, 10½" 15.00
Bowl, Shallow, 4 Footed, 13" 17.00
Candlesticks, 1 Light, 5", pr. 20.00
Candlesticks, 2 Light, 6", pr. 32.00
Candy Box & Cover 22.00
Celery & Relish, 3 part, 10" 12.00
Cigarette Box & Cover 18.00
Cocktail 8.00
Comport, 5½" 14.00
Cream 7.00
Cup & Saucer 11.00
Fruit Saucer, 4½ oz. 6.00
Goblet 10.00
Ice Tub 18.00
Mayonnaise Bowl 10.00
Plate, 4 Footed, 11½" 15.00
Plate, Bread & Butter, 6½" 6.00
Plate, Salad, 8½" 8.00
Plate, Torte, Rolled Edge, 14" 20.00
Punch Bowl & Foot, 15" (10 qt.) 45.00
Punch Bowl Plate, 21" 25.00
Punch Cup 6.00
Relish or Pickle, 6½" 8.00
Relish, 2 part, 6½" 9.00
Salt & Pepper, pr. 27.00
Sherbet 8.00
Sugar 7.00
Tumbler, 5 oz. 8.00
Tumbler, 12 oz. 10.00
Tumbler, Footed, 5 oz. (juice) 8.00
Tumbler, Footed, 12 oz. (iced tea) 10.00
Vase, 9½" 22.00
Vase, Oval 9½" 20.00

Cascade
by Cambridge

sturdy, modern, magnificent

Glory in the splendor of this dazzling, rich table crystal, bountiful with brilliance and created for every-day use! For Cascade is definitely modern and robust in design — fashioned in shapes you'll find as practical as they are beautiful. Make your personal acquaintance with this fine new Cambridge crystal soon. Choose from open stock items, including stemware, flatware and serving pieces. Moderately priced at good stores.

The Cambridge Glass Company, Cambridge, Ohio

Cascade 1949 Ad

NEWPORT

Newport Sandwich Plate & Salad Plate

Date: 1936 to 1940

Manufacturer: Hazel-Atlas Glass Co.

Colors: Deep Blue, Amethyst, Pink; Platonite white.

Platonite is often decorated with fired-on enamel colors. Formerly called Hairpin.

	Deep Blue	Amethyst	Platonite with Colors
Bowl, Berry, 4¼"	$20.00	$17.00	$6.00
Bowl, Cream Soup, 4¾"	25.00	22.00	9.00
Bowl, Cereal, 5¼"	42.00	62.00	
Bowl, Berry, 8¼"	48.00	42.00	15.00
Cup & Saucer	17.00	16.00	8.00
Cream	20.00	16.00	8.00
Plate, Salad 6" *(Illus.)*	9.00	8.00	2.00
Plate, 8½"	14.00	11.00	6.00
Plate, Sandwich, 11½" *(Illus.)*	48.00	42.00	15.00
Platter, 11½"	52.00	42.00	20.00
Salt and Pepper, pr.	57.00	52.00	25.00
Sherbet	16.00	14.00	7.00
Sugar	18.00	18.00	8.00
Tumbler, 9 oz.	42.00	38.00	17.00

ROYAL LACE

Royal Lace Dinner Plate

Date: 1934 to 1941

Manufacturer: Hazel-Atlas Glass Co.

Colors: Deep Blue, Green, Pink, Crystal. A few items in Amethyst.

A sherbet in a metal holder was also made. This popular pattern is eagerly sought by many collectors for the wonderful blue color made.

	Crystal	Blue	Green	Pink
Bowl, Berry, 5"	$16.00	$55.00	$32.00	$38.00
Bowl, Berry, 10"	24.00	85.00	47.00	48.00
Bowl, Cream Soup, 4¾.	14.00	48.00	38.00	40.00
Bowl, Oval, 11"	27.00	75.00	48.00	55.00
Bowl, 3 Footed, Crimped Rim, 10" . . .	42.00	525.00	85.00	70.00
Bowl, 3 Footed, Rolled Rim, 10"	140.00	350.00	90.00	85.00
Bowl, 3 Footed, Straight Rim, 10"	30.00	110.00	65.00	75.00
Butter & Cover.	100.00	625.00+	300.00	200.00
Candlesticks, Straight Edge, pr.	45.00	150.00	85.00	95.00
Candlesticks, Crimped Edge, pr.	60.00	265.00	95.00	120.00
Cookie Jar & Cover	45.00	450.00+	110.00	100.00
Cream, Footed	20.00	70.00	35.00	40.00
Cup & Saucer.	20.00	70.00	40.00	30.00
Iced Tea, 12 oz.	28.00	125.00	70.00	70.00

(continued) ROYAL LACE

	Crystal	Blue	Green	Pink
Juice, 5 oz.	24.00	60.00	48.00	48.00
Pitcher, Straight Sided, 48 oz.	65.00	220.00	170.00	170.00
Pitcher, 68 oz.	65.00	235.00	140.00	140.00
Pitcher, 86 oz.	75.00	230.00	170.00	135.00
Pitcher, 96 oz.	80.00	340.00	220.00	160.00
Plate, 6"	7.00	17.00	15.00	15.00
Plate, 8½"	12.00	54.00	24.00	24.00
Plate, 10" *(Illus.)*.	15.00	50.00	38.00	38.00
Plate, Grill, 9¾".	12.00	40.00	35.00	35.00
Platter, 13".	28.00	77.00	32.00	60.00
Salt & Pepper, pr.	48.00	315.00	160.00	120.00
Sherbet, Footed.	11.00	50.00	35.00	35.00
Sugar & Cover	45.00	225.00	90.00	95.00
Tumbler, 9 oz.	20.00	55.00	45.00	45.00
Tumbler, 10 oz.	38.00	180.00	95.00	95.00

STANHOPE, No. 1483

Date: 1936 to 1941

Manufacturer: A. H. Heisey & Co., Newark, OH

Colors: Crystal

Reproductions: Imperial Glass made the vase in their Stiegel Green (a deep green) for the Smithsonian Institution in 1980.

Designed by Walter Von Nessen for Heisey. Pieces may come with flat inserts or "T" knobs as handles made of plastic for which Heisey won an award from the Modern Plastics Competition. Blown stemware was made to match this pattern and pieces may be found with various Heisey etchings and cuttings. The ball vase may be found as a lamp base.

Stanhope Sugar, Covered Cigarette Box, 7" Plate, Cup & Saucer, Cocktail

Ashtray, Individual	$ 25.00
Bowl, Floral, 2 Handled, 11"	70.00
Bowl, Salad, 11"	50.00
Candelabra, 2 light with prisms, pr.	350.00
Candy Box & Cover, 6"	75.00
Celery, 12"	40.00
Cigarette Box & Cover *(Illus.)*	75.00
Cocktail, 3½ oz. *(Illus.)*.	20.00
Cream & Sugar, pr. *(Illus.)*.	50.00
Cup & Saucer *(Illus.)*.	30.00
Goblet, 9 oz.	30.00
Ice Tub, 2 Handled	55.00
Jelly, 3 Compartment, Handled, 6".	30.00
Jelly, Handled, 6".	25.00
Mayonnaise, 2 Handled	35.00
Mint, 2 Compartment, 2 Handled, 6".	35.00

Nappy or Porringer, 4½".	20.00
Nut, Individual	35.00
Oil & Stopper, 3 oz.	195.00
Plate, 7" *(Illus.)*.	22.00
Plate, 15".	65.00
Plate, Torte, 15".	70.00
Plate, Torte, 2 Handled, 12".	55.00
Relish, 4 Compartment, 2 Handled, 12".	45.00
Relish, 5 Compartment, 2 Handled, 12".	55.00
Relish, Triplex, 2 Handled, 11".	45.00
Salt & Pepper, pr.	100.00
Saucer Champagne, 5½ oz.	20.00
Sugar	25.00
Vase, 2 Handled, 9".	60.00
Vase, Ball, 7".	75.00

COLONIAL SPIRAL, NO. 40, 40½

Colonial Spiral Flower Box, Tall Candlestick

Date: 1924

Manufacturer: Duncan & Miller Glass Co., Washington, PA

Colors: Crystal, Green, Rose (in 1926), Amber. Crystal decorated with Amber stain.

Collectors know this pattern as Spiral Flutes, but Colonial Spiral is its original name. Prices are given for pieces in Crystal. Pieces in color are valued at 150% of Crystal. Amber-stained Crystal is valued at 150% to 175% of Crystal prices.

Almond, Individual, Footed, 2¼" $9.00
Baked Apple 20.00
Bowl, Flower with Foot 35.00
Bowl, Low Flower (40½) 35.00
Bowl, Nappy, 5½" 8.00
Bowl, Oval, Vegetable, 10¼" 15.00
Bowl, Round, Flared, 10" 15.00
Bowl, Round, Flared, 12" 25.00
Bowl, Vegetable, Covered 35.00
Candlesticks, 1 Light, 3½" (No. 40½), pr. 15.00
Candlesticks, 7½", pr. 60.00
Candlesticks, 9½", pr. 90.00
Candlesticks, 11½", pr. *(Illus. of one)* 135.00
Celery Tray 17.00
Chocolate Jar & Cover. 35.00
Cigarette Holder 30.00
Cocktail or Footed Ice Cream, 3½ oz (No. 40½). 9.00
Cocktail, Footed, 2½ oz. 10.00
Comport, High Footed, 6" 15.00
Comport, Low Footed, 6" 12.00
Comport, Low Footed, Flared, 9" 18.00
Cream Soup, 2 Handle, 3⅞" Tall 13.00
Cream, Oval 7.00
Cup, Bouillon, 2 Handled 12.00

Cup & Saucer, Tea. 15.00
Cup & Saucer, After Dinner (demitasse) 30.00
Dish, Bake, 10" 15.00
Finger Bowl. 6.00
Flower Box, Footed, 10" x 5½" *(Illus.)* 315.00
Goblet, 6¼" 15.00
Grapefruit 8.00
Grapefruit, Footed 10.00
Ice Cream, Footed, 5 oz. 9.00
Ice Cream, Footed, 6 oz. 12.00
Iced Tea, Flat, 11 oz. 50.00
Iced Tea, Footed, Handled 15.00
Ice Tub, Handled. 20.00
Juice, Footed, 5½ oz. (No. 40½). 10.00
Lamp, Countess, Kerosene, 10½" 55.00
Mayonnaise 10.00
Nappy & Cover, 2 Handled 18.00
Nappy, 2 Handled, 6" 10.00
Nappy, 7" 8.00
Nappy, 8" 18.00
Nappy, 9" 20.00
Oil & Stopper, 6 oz.. . . . . 145.00
Oyster Centre 18.00
Parfait, 5⅜" 16.00

(continued) COLONIAL SPIRAL, NO. 40, 40½

Pickle, Oval, 8⅝"	12.00	Saucer, Bouillon	5.00
Pitcher, ½ gal.	125.00	Saucer, Cream Soup	5.00
Plate, Dinner, 10½"	35.00	Sherbet, Tall, 5"	12.00
Plate, Finger Bowl	7.00	Sugar, Oval	7.00
Plate, Luncheon, 8⅜"	6.00	Sweetmeat & Cover	60.00
Plate, Mayonnaise, 6"	4.00	Tumbler, 7½ oz. (flat)	10.00
Plate, Oyster, 8½" (bowl, wide rim)	27.00	Tumbler, Footed, 5⅛" h. (No. 40½)	8.00
Plate, Salad, 7⅜"	6.00	Tumbler, Footed, 9 oz., 4¼" h.	10.00
Plate, Sandwich, 14"	30.00	Tumbler, Table, Flat, 4⅞"	30.00
Platter, Oval, 11"	25.00	Vase, 6½"	14.00
Platter, Oval, 12¾"	35.00	Vase, 8½"	25.00
Relish, Oval, 3 pcs.	25.00	Vase, 10½"	35.00

COLONY, NO. 2412

Date: 1938 to 1979

Manufacturer: Fostoria Glass Co., Moundsville, WV

Colors: Crystal

Fostoria's first swirled pattern was produced in the late 1890s and called Cascade. By the 1920s, they made a swirl pattern called Queen Anne which was the forerunner of Colony. Some pieces in Queen Anne were produced in color. Eventually in the early 1980s, some pieces of Colony were again introduced in colors as Maypole.

Almond, Footed, 2¾"	$18.00
Ashtray, 3½"	14.00
Ashtray, 4½"	17.00
Ashtray, Individual	12.00
Ashtray, Round, 3"	12.00
Ashtray, Round, 4½"	15.00
Ashtray, Round, 6"	20.00
Bonbon, 3 Toed	16.00
Bonbon, 5"	15.00
Bowl, Lily Pond, 10" or 13"	55.00
Bowl, Centerpiece, 13"	55.00
Bowl, Cupped, 8"	48.00
Bowl, Flared, 8¼"	52.00
Bowl, Fruit, 10½"	50.00
Bowl, Fruit, Footed, 10½"	60.00
Bowl, Fruit, High Footed	75.00
Bowl, Fruit, Low, 14"	65.00
Bowl, High Foot, 10½"	85.00
Bowl, Ice Cream, Square, 5½"	35.00
Bowl, Low Foot, 10½"	72.00
Bowl, Nut	18.00
Bowl, Oval, Vegetable, 10½"	45.00

Colony 1940 Ad

COLONY, NO. 2412 *(continued)*

Bowl, Oval, Footed, 11" 80.00
Bowl, Rolled Edge, 9" 45.00
Bowl, Salad, 9¼" 30.00
Bowl, Serving, Handled, 8½" 40.00
Bowl, Whipped Cream, Handled, 4¾" 28.00
Butter & Cover, 7½" 52.00
Cake Plate, Handled, 10" 45.00
Candlesticks, 1 Light, 3", pr. 38.00
Candlesticks, 7", pr. 55.00
Candlesticks, Duo, 6¼", pr. 65.00
Candy & Cover, 6½" 52.00
Celery, 9½" 22.00
Celery, 10½" 44.00
Cheese & Cracker, 12½", 2 pcs. 45.00
Cigarette Box & Cover 85.00
Cocktail, 3½ oz. 18.00
Comport, Low, 4" 25.00
Comport & Cover, Low, 6⅜" 40.00
Cornucopia Vase, 9¼" 130.00
Cream 10.00
Cream, Individual 12.00
Cream Soup 48.00
Cup & Saucer 15.00
Finger Bowl, 4¾" 12.00
Goblet, 9 oz. 20.00
Ice Bowl, 6¼" 120.00
Iced Tea, Footed, 12 oz. 22.00
Jelly & Cover, 6" 42.00
Juice, Footed, 5 oz. 18.00
Lemon Dish, 6½" 20.00
Lusters (Candlesticks), 1 Light, 7½", pr. 125.00
Lusters (Candlesticks), 1 Light, 14½", pr. 250.00
Mayonnaise, 4½" 40.00
Nappy, Round, 4½", 5" 11.00
Oil & Stopper, 4½ oz. 60.00
Olive, 6¼" 17.00
Oyster Cocktail, 4 oz. 20.00
Pickle, 8" 16.00
Pickle, 9½" 22.00

Pitcher, Cereal, 1 pt. 75.00
Pitcher, Ice Lip, 2 qt. 135.00
Pitcher, Ice Lip, 3 pt. 150.00
Plate, 6", 7" or 8" 9.00
Plate, 9" 25.00
Plate, Mayonnaise, 6¾" 8.00
Plate, Torte, 13" 35.00
Plate, Torte, 15" 45.00
Plate, Torte, 18" 120.00
Platter, 12½" 50.00
Punch Bowl, 2 gal. 420.00
Punch Cup 17.00
Relish, 2 part, 7¼" 17.00
Relish, 3 part, 10" 34.00
Rose Bowl, 6" 50.00
Salt & Pepper, 2¾", pr. 18.00
Salt & Pepper, Individual, 1⅞", pr. 20.00
Salver, 12" 65.00
Sherbet, 5 oz. 10.00
Sugar 12.00
Sugar, Individual 15.00
Sweetmeat, Divided 30.00
Sweetmeat, Handled, 5" 15.00
Tid Bit, 3 Toed 22.00
Tid Bit, Footed, 7" 32.00
Tray for Individual Salt & Pepper 4½" 11.00
Tray for Individual Cream & Sugar 6¾" 18.00
Tray, Luncheon, Center Handled, 11½" 30.00
Tray, Muffin, Handled, 8⅜" 30.00
Tray, Snack, 10½" 22.00
Tumbler, Flat, 5 oz. (No. 2412½) 22.00
Tumbler, Flat, 9 oz. (No. 2412½) 24.00
Tumbler, Flat, 12 oz. (No. 2412½) 26.00
Urn & Cover 50.00
Urn & Cover, Footed 60.00
Vase, Bud, Flared, Footed 20.00
Vase, Cupped, Footed, 7" 60.00
Vase, Flared, Footed, 7½" 70.00
Wine, 3½ oz. 25.00

DIANA

Date: 1937 to 1941

Manufacturer: Federal Glass Co., Columbus, OH

Colors: Pink, Amber, Crystal

	Pink	Amber	Crystal
Ashtray, 3½"	$4.00	$	$2.50
Bowl, Cereal, 5"	10.00	14.00	5.00
Bowl, Fruit, 11"	42.00	20.00	6.00
Bowl, Cream Soup, 5½"	24.00	18.00	6.00
Bowl, Crimped Rim, 12"	30.00	20.00	8.00
Bowl, Salad, 9"	21.00	21.00	7.00
Candy Box & Cover	42.00	37.00	17.00
Coaster, 3½"	8.00	12.00	3.00
Cream	14.00	10.00	4.00
Cup & Saucer	18.00	12.00	6.00
Cup & Saucer, Demitasse	48.00		15.00
Plate, Bread & Butter, 6"	5.00	3.00	2.00
Plate, Dinner, 9½"	17.00	10.00	6.00
Plate, Sandwich, 11½" *(Illus.)*	27.00	12.00	6.00
Platter, 12"	30.00	15.00	6.00
Salt & Pepper, pr.	75.00	110.00	30.00
Sherbet	12.00	10.00	4.00
Sugar	14.00	9.00	4.00
Tumbler, 9 oz.	45.00	28.00	25.00

Diana Sandwich Plate

FLAIR, NO. 150

Date: Ca. 1940

Manufacturer: Duncan & Miller Glass Co., Washington, PA

Colors: Crystal

This modernistic design was designed by Robert May who designed many of Duncan & Miller's patterns. The pattern shows a Swedish influence popular during the 1940s and 1950s with its flowing lines and unusual shapes.

Basket, Crimped, Handled, (tall)	$50.00
Basket, Crimped, Handled, 10"	50.00
Basket, Oval, Candy, Handled, 6½"	32.00
BonBon, Oblong, Flared, 6½"	17.00
Bowl, 2 Compartment, Salad Dressing, 7½"	18.00
Bowl, Crimped Flower, 11½"	27.00
Bowl, Gardenia, 12"	28.00
Bowl, Gardenia, 13"	30.00
Bowl, Oval, 11"	25.00
Bowl, Oval, Flared, 7½"	18.00
Bowl, Pretzel, 8"	22.00

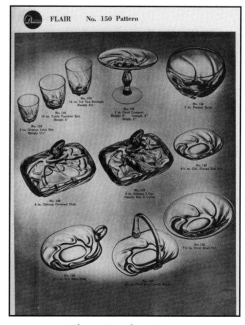

Flair Catalog Page

FLAIR, NO. 150 *(continued)*

Bowl, Rolled Edge, 10½" 25.00
Bowl, Salad, Twin Dressing, 12" 20.00
Candelite Garden, Oblong (candlestick) 6" 35.00
Candelite Garden, Oblong with
   Hurricane Shade 6" 50.00
Candy Box & Cover, Oblong, 2 Compartment, 8" . . 35.00
Celery & Relish, 3 Compartment, 14" 22.00
Celery, Oblong, 11" 20.00
Comport, Oval, 6" Tall 18.00
Cream, Oval, 7 oz. 15.00
Dish, Oblong, Covered, 8" 22.00
Floating Garden, Oblong, 14" x 8" 32.00
Floating Garden, Oblong, 8" x 6" 22.00
Goblet, 10 oz. 18.00
Iced Tea, Footed, 14 oz. 15.00
Iced Tea, Straight, 14 oz. 14.00
Juice, Orange, Footed, 5 oz. 12.00
Juice, Orange, Straight, 5 oz. 10.00
Mayonnaise, Oval, 7½" 17.00
Oyster Cocktail, 5 oz. 8.00
Plate, 8" 8.00
Plate, Bread & Butter, 6" 6.00

Plate, Hors d'oeuvre, 15" x 9" 35.00
Plate, Mayonnaise, Oval, 8" 9.00
Plate, Oval, 8" 9.00
Plate, Torte, Flat Edge, 14" 30.00
Plate, Torte, Rolled Edge, 14" 30.00
Relish, Oblong, 2 Compartment, 8" 18.00
Relish, Oblong, 2 Compartment, 11" 20.00
Relish, Oval, 2 Compartment, Flared, 7½" 17.00
Rose Bowl, 6½" 24.00
Saucer Champagne, 6 oz. 14.00
Sugar, Oval, 7 oz. 15.00
Tray, 4 Compartment, Buffet or Relish, 13" 24.00
Tray, 5 Compartment, Celery & Relish, 13" 24.00
Tray, Handled, Mint, 6½" 12.00
Tray, Oblong, Lemon, 7" 12.00
Tumbler, Table, Straight, 10 oz. 15.00
Vase, Crimped, 3" 18.00
Vase, Crimped, 4" 18.00
Vase, Crimped, 5" 20.00
Vase, Crimped, 6" 20.00
Vase, Crimped, 10" 35.00
Vase, Flared, 10" 35.00
Vase, Regular, 10" 30.00

JAMESTOWN, NO. 2719

Jamestown Goblet, Iced Tea, Sherbet

Date: 1958 to 1985

Manufacturer: Fostoria Glass Co., Moundsville, WV

Colors: Crystal, Ruby, Green, Pink, Blue, Brown, Amber, Amethyst

Items marked with an asterisk (*) were not made in Ruby.

	Crystal, Brown, Amber	Green, Amethyst	Ruby, Blue, Pink
Bowl, Dessert, 4½"	$10.00	$15.00	$18.00
Bowl, Handled, 10"	35.00	50.00	*60.00
Bowl, Salad, 10"	30.00	45.00	*60.00
Butter & Cover, ¼ lb.	45.00	68.00	*80.00
Cake Plate, Handled, 9½"	30.00	45.00	*55.00
Celery, 9¼".	18.00	27.00	*32.00
Cream.	15.00	22.00	*26.00
Goblet, 9½ oz. *(Illus.)*	15.00	22.00	26.00
Iced Tea, 12 oz.	16.00	24.00	28.00
Iced Tea, Footed, 11 oz. *(Illus.)*.	16.00	24.00	28.00
Jelly & Cover	40.00	60.00	*70.00
Juice, Footed, 5 oz.	12.00	18.00	21.00

(continued) JAMESTOWN, No. 2719

	Crystal, Brown, Amber	Green, Amethyst	Ruby, Blue, Pink
Pickle, 7½"	15.00	22.00	*26.00
Pitcher, Ice Lip, 48 oz.	95.00	140.00	*165.00
Plate, 8"	7.00	10.00	12.00
Plate, Torte, 14"	32.00	48.00	*56.00
Relish, 2 Compartment, 9" . . .	18.00	27.00	*30.00
Salt & Pepper, pr.	24.00	36.00	*42.00
Salver, 10"	65.00	85.00	*110.00

	Crystal, Brown, Amber	Green, Amethyst	Ruby, Blue, Pink
Sauce Dish & Cover, 4½"	35.00	48.00	*60.00
Sherbet, 6½ oz. *(Illus.)*.	10.00	15.00	18.00
Sugar	15.00	22.00	*26.00
Tray, Muffin, 2 Handled, 9⅜"	35.00	50.00	*60.00
Tumbler, 9 oz.	15.00	22.00	16.00
Wine, 4 oz.	15.00	22.00	26.00

SPIRAL

Date: 1928 to 1930

Manufacturer: Hocking Glass Co., Lancaster, OH

Colors: Crystal, Green, Pink

	Crystal	Green, Pink
Bowl, Berry, 4¾"	$3.00	$9.00
Bowl, Berry, 8"	8.00	20.00
Bowl, Mixing, 7"	12.00	28.00
Cream, Footed or Flat	5.00	12.00
Cup & Saucer.	6.00	12.00
Ice Tub	18.00	32.00
Juice, 5 oz.	3.50	7.00
Pitcher, 58 oz. *(Illus.)*	22.00	40.00
Plate, Luncheon, 8"	3.00	7.00
Plate, Sherbet, 6"	2.00	4.00
Platter.	15.00	35.00
Preserve & Cover	22.00	45.00
Salt & Pepper, pr.	25.00	50.00
Sandwich Plate, Center Handled . .	17.00	35.00
Sherbet.	4.00	9.00
Sugar, Footed or Flat	5.00	12.00
Tumbler, 9 oz.	5.00	10.00
Tumbler, Footed	11.00	22.00

Spiral Pitcher

SWIRL

Swirl (Jeannette) Sugar & Cream, Salt Shaker

Date: 1937 to 1938

Manufacturer: Jeannette Glass Co., Jeannette, PA

Colors: Ultramarine Blue, Pink. Limited production in Amber, Delphite and pale blue.

	Pink	Ultramarine
Ashtray, 5¼"	$10.00	$18.00
Bowl, Cereal, 5"	16.00	33.00
Bowl, Console, Footed, 10½"	35.00	45.00
Bowl, Footed & Handled, 10"	38.00	45.00
Bowl, Salad, 9"	28.00	33.00
Butter & Cover.	180.00	325.00
Candleholders, 2 Light, pr.	75.00	55.00
Candy Dish, 3 Footed	16.00	22.00
Candy Dish & Cover	110.00	165.00
Coaster, 3¼"	10.00	18.00
Cream, & Sugar, Footed, pr. *(Illus.)*.	30.00	44.00
Cup & Saucer.	14.00	22.00
Iced Tea, 12 oz..	55.00	150.00+

	Pink	Ultramarine
Pitcher, Footed, with Ice Lip, 48 oz		1,500.00+
Plate, Sherbet 6½"	7.00	10.00
Plate, 7¼"	8.00	12.00
Plate, Salad, 8"	10.00	18.00
Plate, 9¼"	18.00	27.00
Plate, 10½"		32.00
Plate, Sandwich, 12½"	27.00	42.00
Salt & Pepper, pr. *(Illus. of one)* . . .		58.00
Sherbet	12.00	21.00
Soup, Handled	28.00	55.00
Tumbler, 9 oz. (2 types).	26.00	45.00
Tumbler, Footed, 9 oz.	34.00	50.00
Vase, Footed, 6½"	27.00	
Vase, Footed, 8½" (2 styles).		44.00

SWIRL, NO. 4100, LATER NO. 2300

Swirl (Anchor Hocking) Plate, Cup & Saucer

Date: 1950s to 1970s

Manufacturer: Anchor Hocking Glass Corporation, Lancaster, OH

Colors: No. 4100: Azur-ite, Ivory, Pink, Ivory White (later called Anchorwhite) No. 2300: Anchorwhite, Jadite

In No. 4100 Ivory White (Anchorwhite) was decorated with 22 Karat gold and called Golden Anniversary. Ivory was decorated with red rims and called Sunrise. Add 25% to Ivory White prices for Golden Anniversary pieces. Sunrise decorated Ivory is valued about the same as Azur-ite and Pink.

	Ivory Anchorwhite	Azur-ite Pink
Bowl, Vegetable, 7¼" (No. 4177)	$	$15.00
Bowl, Vegetable, 8¼" (No. 4178)	6.00	16.00
Cream (No. 4154) & Sugar (4153), pr.	8.00	14.00

(continued) SWIRL, NO. 4100, LATER NO. 2300

	Ivory Anchorwhite	Azur-ite Pink
Cup, 8 oz. & Saucer, 5¾" (Nos. 4179, 4129) *(Illus.)*	4.00	8.00
Dessert, 4⅞" (No. 4174)	3.00	5.00
Plate, Dinner, 9⅛" (No. 4141) *(Illus.)*	4.00	8.00
Plate, Salad, 7¾" (No. 4138)	3.00	5.00
Platter, 12" x 9" (No. 4147)	8.00	18.00
Soup Plate, 7⅝" (bowl) (No. 4167) . .	3.00	9.00
Sugar (No. 4153)	4.00	7.00

In the early 1960s this pattern was redesigned with more strongly scalloped edge on many pieces. Shapes of sugars, creams and cups were also restyled and have slightly different shapes. The line number was changed to No. 2300. Anchorwhite decorated with gold was now called No. 31 Golden Shell and a peach lustre was applied and called simply Lustre Shell.

	Golden Shell	Jade-ite Shell	Lustre Shell
Bowl, Vegetable, 8½" (No. 2378)	$6.00	$8.00	$8.00
Cream (No. 2354)	4.00	6.00	6.00
Cup & Saucer, 5¾" (Nos. 2379, 2329)	5.00	6.00	6.00
Cup & Saucer, Demitasse			15.00
Dessert, 4¾" (No. 2374)	2.00	3.50	3.50
Plate, Dinner, 10" (No. 2346)	5.00	7.00	8.00
Plate, Salad, 7¼" (No. 2338) . .	3.00	3.00	4.00
Platter, 13" x 9½" (No. 2347)	9.00	14.00	
Soup Plate (Bowl), 6⅝" (No. 2367)	6.00	7.50	6.00
Sugar & Cover (No. 2353) . . .	7.50	12.00	12.00

SWIRL AND BALL, NO. 1842

Date: Ca. 1940

Manufacturer: Westmoreland Glass Co., Grapeville, PA

Colors: Crystal

Swirl and Ball is the original name for this pattern. The list below is taken from factory price lists. Pieces have been found with a cranberry stain on the swirls. Because of the timing of the introduction of this pattern (during World War II), it is somewhat scarce today.

Swirl and Ball Small Comport, Cranberry Stain

Basket, Round, Handled, 7"	$25.00
Basket, Tri Handled, 7"	20.00
Bowl, Bell, 10"	22.00
Bowl, Cupped, 7½"	12.00
Bowl, R. E., 9½"	18.00
Bowl, T. E., 11"	20.00
Candelabra, 2 light, pr.	48.00
Candlesticks, Low, 4", pr.	27.00
Candy Jar & Cover, ½ lb. (low footed)	25.00
Cocktail, 3 oz.	12.00
Comport & Cover, 6½" (tall, footed) *(Illus. without cover)*	35.00
Comport, T. E., 7½"	15.00
Cream	12.00
Goblet, 8 oz.	15.00
Iced Tea, Footed, 12 oz.	15.00
Iced Tea, Straight, 10 oz.	10.00
Jug, Ice Lip, 3 pt.	45.00
Mayonnaise, Footed	15.00

Nappy, Bell, 6"	10.00
Nappy, Bell, Handled, 6"	15.00
Nappy, Heart, Handled, 5"	18.00
Nappy, Round, 4"	7.00
Nappy, Round, 7"	10.00
Plate, 7" or 8"	8.00
Plate, 9"	10.00
Plate, 10"	30.00
Plate, 13"	24.00
Plate, 18"	40.00
Plate, Bread & Butter, 6"	5.00
Salver, Cake, 9"	35.00
Sherbet, Low Foot	8.00
Sugar	12.00
Tumbler, Bell, 8 oz.	15.00
Vase, Bell, Footed, 9½"	35.00
Vase, Fan, 6"	18.00
Vase, Flared, Footed, 8½"	25.00

TWIST, NO. 1252

Twist Candlestick, Celery, Iced Tea

Date: 1928 to 1937

Manufacturer: A. H. Heisey & Co., Newark, OH

Colors: Crystal, Moongleam, Flamingo, Marigold. Limited production in Sahara.

Reproductions: Imperial Glass Corp. made the small nappy in crystal.

Twist is not the original name as Heisey referred to the pattern only as No. 1252. Pieces in this extensive tableware line usually carry the Heisey mark. Twist is very Art Deco in its design; notice the lightning handles and the square stems and feet of stemmed pieces. Twist was patented in 1928 and 1929. Be aware that the Marigold color may deteriorate into a "spun sugar" effect. This begins as fine scratches and grades to a coarse sandpaper finish. It cannot be repaired, but not all pieces are affected.

	Crystal	Sahara, Flamingo, Moongleam	Marigold
Almond, Footed (individual sugar)	$25.00	$50.00	$75.00
Baker, Oval, 9"	20.00	35.00	
Bonbon, 2 Handled, 6"	15.00	22.00	28.00
Bonbon, Individual	20.00	40.00	65.00
Bottle, French Dressing & Stopper	45.00	95.00	130.00
Bowl, Floral, Oval, 12"	37.00	60.00	100.00
Bowl, Floral, Rolled Edge, 9"	30.00	50.00	80.00
Bowl, Floral, Round, 12"	35.00	70.00	135.00
Bowl, Low Footed, 8"	25.00	60.00	85.00
Bowl, Nasturtium, 8"	40.00	85.00	135.00
Candlesticks, 2", pr.	45.00	90.00	160.00
Celery, 10"	22.00	35.00	45.00
Cheese, 2 Handled, 6"	12.00	22.00	27.00
Cocktail, 3 oz.	18.00	27.00	40.00
Cocktail Shaker, 1 qt. (threaded top)		900.00	
Comport, High Footed, 7"	35.00	85.00	140.00
Cream Soup or Bouillon	20.00	35.00	65.00
Cream & Sugar, Cover, pr.	67.00	80.00	
Cream & Sugar, Footed, pr.	70.00	100.00	
Cream & Sugar, Individual, pr.	50.00	100.00	150.00
Cream & Sugar, Oval Hotel, pr.	70.00	80.00	135.00
Cup & Saucer	25.00	45.00	65.00
Goblet, 9 oz.	30.00	55.00	80.00
Goblet, Luncheon, 9 oz.	30.00	50.00	70.00
Grapefruit, Footed	17.00	30.00	50.00
Iced Tea (2 types) 12 oz.	25.00	45.00	70.00
Ice Tub	58.00	100.00	185.00
Jelly, 2 Handled, 6"	15.00	22.00	28.00

	Crystal	Sahara, Flamingo, Moongleam	Marigold
Jug, 3 pt.	80.00	125.00	200.00
Mayonnaise, Footed (No. 1252½)	25.00	38.00	70.00
Mint & Cover, 3 Cornered (No. 1253)	35.00	58.00	75.00
Mint, 2 Handled, 6"	15.00	22.00	28.00
Mustard & Cover	45.00	95.00	150.00
Nappy, 8"	24.00	50.00	80.00
Nut, Individual	155.00	30.00	50.00
Oil Bottle & Stopper, 4 oz.	50.00	110.00	170.00
Oyster Cocktail, 3 oz.	15.00	27.00	40.00
Pickle Tray, 7"	15.00	25.00	45.00
Plate, 4½"	10.00	17.00	25.00
Plate, 6" or 7", each	10.00	15.00	25.00
Plate, 8"	10.00	17.00	30.00
Plate, 9"	16.00	32.00	50.00
Plate, 10½"	50.00	130.00	200.00
Plate, 12"	45.00	60.00	90.00
Plate, Kraft Cheese, 8"	25.00	40.00	60.00
Plate, Muffin, 2 Handled, 12"	24.00	48.00	55.00
Plate, Sandwich, 2 Handled, 12"	24.00	32.00	40.00
Plate, Utility, 3 Feet, 10"	25.00	40.00	65.00
Platter, 12"	25.00	40.00	48.00
Relish, 3 Compartment, 13"	18.00	30.00	50.00
Salt & Pepper (No. 54), pr.	45.00	60.00	110.00
Salt & Pepper, Footed, pr.	70.00	120.00	250.00
Saucer Champagne, 5 oz.	20.00	32.00	50.00
Sherbet, 5 oz.	15.00	27.00	35.00
Tumbler, 8 oz.	20.00	40.00	70.00
Wine, 2½ oz.	25.00	55.00	80.00

TWISTED OPTIC

Date: 1927 to 1930

Manufacturer: Imperial Glass Corporation, Bellaire, OH

Colors: Pink, Green, Amber. Limited production in Blue and Canary.

Compare this with Spiral. The swirls in Twisted Optic twist to the right while in Spiral they swirl to the left.

	Amber, Green Pink	Canary, Blue
Basket, 10"	$25.00	$45.00
Bowl, Cereal, 5"	8.00	14.00
Bowl, Console, 10½"	45.00	80.00
Bowl, Cream Soup, 4¾"	14.00	20.00
Bowl, Salad, 7"	13.00	18.00
Bowl, Small, Crimped Edge (Illus.)	12.00	16.00
Candlesticks, 1 Light, 3", pr. (2 styles)	28.00	55.00
Candy Jar & Cover (3 styles)	45.00	75.00
Candy Jar & Cover, Footed	50.00	80.00
Cologne & Stopper	28.00	42.00
Cream	10.00	15.00
Cup & Saucer	10.00	18.00
Iced Tea, 12 oz.	12.00	
Mayonnaise	45.00	80.00
Pitcher, 64 oz.	45.00	
Plate, Luncheon, 8"	5.00	9.00

Twisted Optic Small Bowl, Crimped Edge

	Amber, Green Pink	Canary, Blue
Plate, Oval 7½" x 9"	8.00	12.00
Plate, Salad, 7"	5.00	9.00
Plate, Sherbet, 6"	4.00	8.00
Powder Jar & Cover	24.00	35.00
Preserve & Cover (notched cover)	35.00	
Sandwich Server, 2 Handled	16.00	24.00
Sandwich Server, Center Handled	25.00	40.00
Sherbet	10.00	15.00
Sugar	8.00	
Tumbler, 9 oz.	85.00	50.00

U.S. SWIRL

Date: 1920

Manufacturer: U. S. Glass Co.

Colors: Crystal, Pink, Green

	Crystal	Colors
Bowl, Berry, 4¼"	$4.00	$9.00
Bowl, Berry, 8"	10.00	20.00
Bowl, Oval, 8½" (2 styles)	28.00	65.00
Butter & Cover (Illus.)	70.00	130.00
Candy & Cover, Handled	18.00	38.00
Cream	10.00	20.00
Iced Tea, 12 oz.	9.00	18.00
Jelly, 1 Handle	7.50	12.00
Pitcher, 48 oz.	40.00	65.00
Plate, 6"	3.00	4.00
Plate, 8"	5.00	8.00
Salt & Pepper, pr.	30.00	55.00

U.S. Swirl Covered Butter

Sherbet	3.50	7.50
Sugar & Cover	22.00	40.00
Tumbler, 8 oz.	8.00	14.00
Vase, 6½"	12.00	24.00

Chapter 18
TRIANGLES

MOUNT VERNON

Mount Vernon Covered Butter

Date: Mid Teens through 1930s

Manufacturer: Imperial Glass Corporation, Bellaire, OH

Colors: Crystal, Imperial Green. Possibly other colors.

Prices are for Crystal pieces, for colors add 50%. The triangles making up the pattern are depressed rather than raised.

Bowl, Console, 12"	$28.00
Bowl, Fruit, 3 Toed, 10"	18.00
Bowl, Lily or Nut, 6", 7", 8"	18.00
Bowl, Orange, 10"	25.00
Butter & Cover, Round, Low, 5"	20.00
Butter & Cover, Table Set *(Illus.)*	25.00
Butter or Ice Tub, 8"	22.00
Candlesticks, 1 Light, 9", pr.	50.00
Celery Tray, 10½"	15.00
Cocktail, 3 oz.	12.00
Cream, Individual	12.00
Cup & Saucer	18.00
Custard	8.00
Decanter & Stopper, Blown, 36 oz.	65.00
Finger Bowl	10.00
Goblet	18.00
Iced Tea, 12 oz.	12.00
Jug, Ice Lip and Cover, 69 oz.	70.00
Oil & Stopper, 6 oz.	45.00
Old Fashioned, 7 oz.	8.00

Nappy & Cover, Round, Handled, 5¾"	18.00
Pickle Jar & Cover	40.00
Pitcher, 54 oz.	40.00
Pitcher, 69 oz.	55.00
Plate, Bread & Butter or Finger Bowl, 6"	6.00
Plate, Cake, 11"	15.00
Plate, Sandwich, 12½"	16.00
Plate, Square or Round, 8"	8.00
Plate, Torte (plain edge), 13½"	18.00
Salt & Pepper, pr.	35.00
Sherbet	8.00
Spoon Holder, Table Set	18.00
Sugar, Individual & Cver	12.00
Sugar & Cover Table Set	20.00
Sugar, Tall	16.00
Syrup with Lock Cover	50.00
Tidbit Set, 2 Tier	25.00
Tumbler, Table, 9 oz.	12.00
Wine, 2 oz.	12.00

KITCHEN GLASS

Chapter 19

Kitchen glassware made from the 1920s through the 1960s comprises a myriad of items. The variety of pieces made runs from the more familiar baking dishes, mixing bowls, measuring cups, and reamers to canister sets, range sets, refrigerator dishes, rolling pins, napkin holders and a variety of small or large glass parts used with mechanical or electrical appliances such as percolator tops, bowls for electric mixers, beater jars and others. Kitchen collectibles have now also encompassed items which were originally made as soda fountain glassware such as sugar dispensers, straw jars, and beverage dispensers, among others. Colors include pale green, deep green, jadite, Delphite, pale custard, milk glass, blue, amber and others. Most items were also made in crystal, but fewer people collect these and they have considerably less value.

Entire collections can be assembled of many individual categories. Certainly many collectors decorate their kitchens with various glass kitchen items and often use these for their original purposes—at least the less expensive examples!

It would be impossible for us to list all of the kitchen items made by many, many companies. However, we are including several of the more extensive types and also a small sampling of the more unusual items so that you, the reader, can see the variety of items you might find. You can expect to find many unlisted kitchen items because of the long period of time they were made, the number of companies making the items and the wide variety of items made. Some of these present puzzles today when found, as often their exact use is not apparent. Many glass parts were made for specific mechanical kitchen tools, and if these are now missing from the glass often the glass piece is not easily identified.

MANUFACTURERS' MARKS

A within an H = Hazel-Atlas
Anchor with an H superimposed = Anchor Hocking
F in a Shield = Federal
Fire King = Anchor Hocking
GlasBake = McKee Glass Co.
McK in a Circle = McKee Glass Co.
O-I = Owens-Illinois Glass Co.
Pyrex = Corning Glass Works
Vitrock = Hocking's opal or milk glass

Collectors need to realize that most kitchen items received hard, often day-to-day, use in a family setting. These pieces were the tools of the housewife, and did not receive the same care that tableware did. Expect to find pieces in less than perfect condition with wear marks and even small chips.

If your item is marked, the accompanying table may help you identify its manufacturer quickly.

Note the interesting "copying" of a name by Anchor Hocking. Corning had introduced their Pyrex oven glass in the early 1920s. When Anchor Hocking started making their ovenware, they chose the literal translation—Fire King!

CANISTERS AND STORAGE JARS

The Jeannette Glass Co. appears to have made the first glass canister sets of the Depression Glass era as evidenced by the following trade announcement from December 25, 1922:

"The Jeannette Glass Co., of Jeannette, Pa., have just put out a new and distinct line, never before attempted by any glass manufacturer. It is a 15-piece cereal set, fashioned after the imported earthenware sets, as far as shape goes, being oblong, but when it comes to a question of price and attractiveness in the kitchen, it is far more interesting. The pieces of the set are six large jars, six small ones, oil and vinegar bottles, with glass stopper, and salt box, with wooden top. Not only are these sets lower in price than anything before put on the market, but they are sanitary inasmuch as they can be kept clean very easily. Another advantage is the fact of always being

217

CANISTERS AND STORAGE JARS *(continued)*

Fig. 19.1

Fig. 19.2

Fig. 19.3

Fig. 19.4

Fig. 19.5

Fig. 19.6

Fig. 19.7

able to see stock on hand at a glance. The jars are labeled by means of raised frosted letters…. The sets sell at wholesale for about $2 per set, each set packed in a separate carton."

Soon many DG era companies were making glass canister sets, including Hazel-Atlas, Hocking Glass, Jeannette Glass, McKee Glass, Owens-Illinois Glass and others. A great variety of canister sets were made in light green, dark green, crystal (many for "Hoosier" cupboards) and opaque colors including jadite, blue (similar to delphite), a light custard, milk glass and a paler version sometimes called clambroth. Crystal items were also sometimes given coats of fired-on paint, especially in red and black. Labels on canister jars vary—some had none originally, others had foil labels, while most had painted-on permanent labels. Prices given are for complete jars—lids and labels intact. There are fewer collectors for the crystal glass jars, except for the Hoosier cabinet jars, so crystal items are much less valuable.

Interest in kitchen glassware continues to increase with values increasing steadily. The difficulty in finding complete sets in good condition adds to the increase in cost.

HAZEL-ATLAS

Fig. 19.1—*Round, paneled with glass lids and silk screen labels in a vertical format. These are hard to find and desirable for collectors of blue glass. Each canister in Hazel-Atlas blue, complete, is valued at $500.00+.*

HOCKING

Fig. 19.2—*Square canisters with vertical ribbed sides, metal or glass lids and diagonal foil labels.*
Cookie, 1 gallon, transparent light green $80.00
48 oz., glass lid, transparent light green 60.00
Salt & pepper, transparent light green, pr. 38.00

Fig. 19.3—*Square canisters. Flat plain sides, square. Metal lids. Painted øn labels, either in straight line or angled down.*
40 oz., fired red, green or blue 30.00
40 oz. opaque custard yellow (pale) 120.00
Salt & pepper, opaque custard yellow (pale), pr. 45.00

INDIANA

Fig. 19.4—Large, crystal. $35.00
Medium, crystal. 25.00

JEANNETTE

Fig. 19.5—*Canisters with round, straight sides with equal sized ribbed horizontal grooves on bottom 2/3 of canister. Salts and peppers are slightly tapered outward to the top. May have either black painted lettering or foil labels. This variety has metal screw tops.*

(continued) CANISTERS AND STORAGE JARS

Delphite (Opaque Blue)

40 oz.	$450.00
Salt & pepper, pr.	250.00
Drippings bowl & cover	190.00

Jadeite

40 oz.	95.00
Salt & pepper, pr.	35.00

Fig. 19.6—Canisters with square, tapering sides slightly larger towards the top. Glass lids with recessed handles. Painted black lettering.

Delphite (Opaque Blue)

29 oz.	300.00
Salt & pepper, metal tops	200.00

Jadeite

48 oz.	85.00
29 oz.	75.00
Spice jar.	90.00
Salt & pepper, pr.	55.00

JENKINS

Fig. 19.7—No. 1, 8 oz.	$15.00
No. 2, 13 oz.	20.00
No. 3, 37 oz.	25.00
No. 4, 3 lb.	30.00

McKEE

McKee canister sets are found in a variety of colors and decorations of fired color, often in red. Labels are usually fired color to match any decoration but vary widely from initials (S & P) to block letters to a semi-script style. Decal labels (non-permanent) were also used. Skokie green is the original name for McKee's jadeite color; Seville yellow is a medium opaque custard color. Dots decoration has dots in graduated sizes with the smallest at the bottom and the largest at the top placed at an angle (left to right) from the bottom to the top. Sailboat shows a sailboat with a ship's wheel, anchor and flying birds. McKee made several shapes of sets—a representation is listed below.

Fig. 19.8—Square canisters with plain sides, metal screw tops.

48 oz., Seville Yellow (opaque)	$100.00
48 oz., Seville Yellow (opaque) with painted dots	110.00
Salt & pepper, Skokie green, pr.	35.00

Fig. 19.9—Square canister, 2 plain sides, 2 sides with 3 graduated, raised arches (Roman). Metal tops. Labels either fired paint or decals.

Milk glass	40.00
Salt & pepper, Skokie green, pr.	50.00
Salt & pepper, black, pr.	100.00

Fig. 19.8

Fig. 19.9

 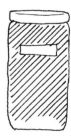

Fig. 19.10   Fig. 19.11

OWENS-ILLINOIS

Fig. 19.10—Owens-Illinois green is very similar to Forest Green, being much deeper than most green Depression glass. Canisters in oval shape, straight sided, with fine, vertical ribs. Metal screw lids. Jars have a plain vertical panel where labels were placed. It is difficult to find these jars with the original labels intact.

Large, deep green	$80.00
Medium, fired red color	70.00
Salt & pepper, deep green, pr.	50.00

Fig. 19.11—Square canisters with diagonal ribs from base to top. Metal screw tops.

40 oz., deep green	45.00
20 oz., deep green	35.00
Salt & pepper, deep green, pr.	25.00

219

KNIVES

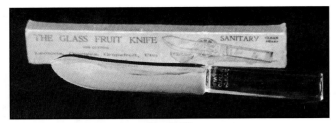

Fig. 19.12

Fig. 19.13

Fig. 19.14

Glass knives became popular in the 1920s and were promoted as perfect for slicing acidic foods such as fruits and tomatoes because they were sanitary and stainless. Cutting cake was another suggested use for the knives. Most are not yet identified as to manufacturer. Colors include crystal (the most common), pink, green, blue and amber. Other colors are considered rare. Several styles are available for collectors, probably indicating several manufacturers. Handles may be plain or have several types of flowers or other decorative motifs. Blades also are of various shapes. As a general guideline, the following values are representative for most styles.

Crystal . . . . $ 8.00 to 15.00
Pink. . . . . 18.00 to 30.00
Green. . . . . 15.00 to 25.00
Blue . . . . 20.00 to 35.00
Amber . . . . 125.00+
Fig. 19.12—Plain glass knife with original box 15.00
Fig. 19.13—Westmoreland, No. 1800, 9″ 12.00
Fig. 19.14—Westmoreland, No. 1801, 9″ 12.00

LADLES

Fig. 19.15

Crystal . . . . $10.00+
Pink . . . . .15.00 to 20.00
Green . . . . .15.00 to 20.00
Blue . . . . 20.00+
Amber . . . . .15.00 to 20.00
Cobalt . . . . 25.00+
Black . . . . 25.00+

Specific ladles are valued at:
Heisey:

No. 6, Crystal, marked with Diamond H $38.00
No. 6, Flamingo, marked with Diamond H 55.00
No. 6, Moongleam, marked with Diamond H. 55.00
No. 6, Sahara, marked with Diamond H. 65.00
No. 6, Hawthorne, marked with Diamond H 100.00
No. 6, Alexandrite, marked with Diamond H 180.00
No. 1567 Plantation, Crystal 50.00

Cambridge:

Dianthus (Pink) $25.00
Green 25.00
Moonlight Blue 50.00
Amber 22.00
Crystal. 15.00
Opaque Colors . . . . .50.00+

MAYONNAISE LADLES

Most ladles are mayonnaise ladles to complete a three piece mayonnaise set, comprising an underplate, bowl and ladle. Twin mayonnaise or dressing bowls had a ladle for each compartment. Often these ladles have become separated from the mayonnaise sets and have actually become a collectible category in themselves. Many companies, including Heisey, Duncan, Fostoria and Cambridge, made ladles to match specific patterns and in many of their colors. Many companies made ladles similar to Westmoreland's No. 1837 (center). We are illustrating several Westmoreland ladles to show the usual variety of shapes of mayonnaise ladles.

Westmoreland Mayonnaise

Fig. 19.15—*Typical shapes. In general, the following prices are for mayonnaise ladles in color.*

PUNCH LADLES

Many companies made glass punch ladles. Early examples had glass cups with wooden handles. This type was made as early as the turn of the century by U. S. Glass and some others. All-glass ladles were made during the Depression era. Some, like Heisey, made plain ladles to be used with any of their punch sets. Others, such as Duncan & Miller, made ladles to match both the pattern and the color of the punch set.

Caribbean (Duncan & Miller), colored handles $65.00
Caribbean (Duncan & Miller), blue 100.00
Hobnail (Duncan & Miller), colored handles 60.00
Hobnail (Duncan & Miller), opalescent colors. 100.00
Radiance (New Martinsville), blue 100.00
Heisey, crystal 60.00
Cambridge, crystal 50.00

SALAD FORKS AND SPOONS

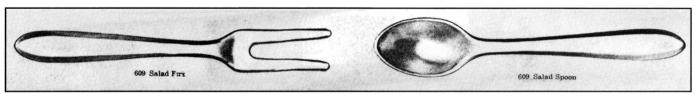

Fig. 19.17

Many types of salad forks and spoons were made during the Depression period. The most popular are those with various colored handles or completely colored. Particularly attractive are those with chandelier prism-type handles. Many of these sets are probably of foreign manufacture, but Heisey and Cambridge also made salad sets.

These sets usually sell for approximately the following prices.
Various colors . . . .$50.00 to 75.00
Crystal. 25.00
Fig. 19.16—Heisey, No. 2 (2 styles), Crystal 85.00
Fig. 19.17—Cambridge, No. 609, Crystal 55.00
Cambridge, various colors . . . . .135.00+
Fig. 19.18—Westmoreland, No. 1801, Crystal 50.00

Fig. 19.16

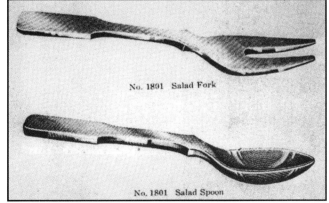

Fig. 19.18

MEASURING CUPS, PITCHERS AND GLASSES

Fig. 19.19

Fig. 19.20

Fig. 19.21a

Fig. 19.21b

Fig. 19.22

Fig. 19.23

Fig. 19.24

Fig. 19.25

Measuring cups, jars and other graduated devices form a varied group of kitchen collectibles. Many different styles were made from graduated measures in the familiar ¼ cup size to 1 cup size to 2 cup size and even larger. Most have the measuring gradations raised on the exterior of the piece. The most common style is the handled cup with pouring spout. However, variations include cups with multiple spouts, pitchers in quart and ½ gallon sizes, and tapered measuring glasses with or without pouring spouts. Measuring cups or glasses without spouts are for dry ingredients. Note should be made of reproduction measures marked Kellogg's *in both pink and green.*

The following are general guidelines for the values of most cups. Of course, as in most collectibles, there are exotic colors and rare examples which fetch much higher prices.

1 cup, crystal, common styles . . . .$5.00 to 8.00
1 cup, marked *Kellogg's*, pink or green (old) 30.00

ANCHOR HOCKING (FIRE KING)
1 cup, blue, 1 or 3 spouts 22.00

CAMBRIDGE
1 cup, transparent colors, pink or green . . . . .250.00+

FEDERAL
Fig. 19.19—1 cup measuring glass, 3 spouts,
　　no handle, green or pink . . . . .35.00+

FRY
Fig. 19.20—1 cup, pearl glass, 3 spout 85.00
1 cup, pearl glass, 1 spout 50.00

HAZEL-ATLAS
1 cup, opaque white, with or without
　　colored decor .60.00 to 70.00
Fig. 19.21a—1 cup, green or pink,
　　3 spouts . . . . .25.00 to 40.00
1 cup, yellow (rare) . . . . .290.00+
Fig. 19.22—Jumbo, No. 3041, 2 cup,
　　green or pink .30.00 to 60.00
Jumbo, No. 3041, 2 cup, blue or yellow . . . . .200.00+

HOCKING
1 cup, green 30.00
Fig. 19.21b—2 cup, green 25.00
2 cup, pink 45.00

IMPERIAL
Fig. 19.23—1 qt. Jug, graduated, crystal 40.00

(continued) MEASURING CUPS, PITCHERS AND GLASSES

JEANNETTE
4 piece sets, (¼ cup, ⅓ cup, ½ cup, 1 cup) in
   opaques and transparent colors of ultramarine,
   pink, delphite, and jadeite . . . . .75.00 to 200.00
*Delphite is the most sought after color followed by ultramarine
and jadite.*

JENKINS
Fig. 19.24—1 cup, No. 100 or No. 375, green 40.00

MCKEE
1 cup, GlasBake, crystal 25.00
1 cup, GlasBake, opaque white 50.00
Fig. 19.25—1 qt. Measuring jar, crystal 35.00

PADEN CITY
1 cup, green 130.00

U. S. GLASS
1 cup, pink 75.00
1 cup, green 45.00
Fig. 19.26—2 cup, pink or green, tall . . . . .190.00+
Large, Slick handle, pink or green 50.00

**The Handiest Measuring Cup
on the Market**

and on account of its convenience it is meeting with a
hearty welcome by housewives the country over. It
is plainly graduated in ounces, cups and pints, and is
large enough to be used for mixing purposes. The
substantial handle is a help when measuring large
quantities and the lip makes pouring easy.   A ready
seller, and a profitable item.

Include this in your next order

UNITED STATES GLASS COMPANY
General Offices and Salesrooms
South Ninth and Bingham Sts. Pittsburg Pa.

Fig. 19.26

MIXING BOWLS

*Sets of glass mixing bowls began to be popular in the early 1920s
in crystal or crystal with fired-on colors. As transparent colors
became popular, mixing bowls, too, began to appear in colors. By
the 1940s and 1950s, milk glass (opaque white) bowls were
popular. These were made with all-over fired-on colors and
various fired-on decorations. Often entire sets were made in these
designs from salt and pepper shakers to baking dishes to reamer
sets. So, if you find a favorite design in mixing bowls, be sure to
check out other items when you're shopping to find matching
pieces. Bowl sets were usually made in 4 sizes, often nesting one
into the other.*

MISCELLANEOUS
Fig. 19.27—Dutch & Ship decoration, various styles,milk
   glass . . . . $10.00 to 20.00
Pale blue opaque (Chalaine), any size . . . . .90.00+
Jadeite, plain . . . . 20.00 to 40.00

ANCHOR HOCKING, (FIRE KING)
1950S AND 1960S
Dots . . . . 7.00 to 15.00
Floral, Fruits, Modern Tulip, or KitchenAids
   decoration on milk glass. . . . . 10.00 to 20.00

Fig. 19.27

Fig. 19.28

223

MIXING BOWLS *(continued)*

Fig. 19.29

Fig. 19.30

Fig. 19.31

Fig. 19.32

Fig. 19.33

Fig. 19.34

Fig. 19.35

Fig. 19.36

Fig. 19.37

Jadeite, Swirl (See color plate for shape). . . . 10.00 to 20.00
Fig. 19.28—Jadeite, teardrop shape. . . . . . . 20.00 to 40.00
Tulips decoration . . . . 10.00 to 20.00
Turquoise blue . . . . 10.00 to 20.00

CORNING (PYREX)
Fig. 19.29—4 piece set: yellow, green, red, blue, each . .25.00+
Delphite . . . . 10.00 to 20.00
Fig. 19.30—Pennsylvania Dutch decoration,
    milk glass . . . . 10.00 to 20.00

FEDERAL
Fig. 19.31—Golden Glow, paneled lower half,
    square base . . . . 15.00 to 30.00
Green, paneled lower half, square base. . . . . 15.00 to 30.00
Pink, paneled lower half, square bases . . . . . 15.00 to 65.00
Green, plain. . . . . 10.00 to 22.00
Fig. 19.32—Fired-on color, ribbed,
    round base. . . . . 8.00 to 20.00

HAZEL-ATLAS
Criss Cross, blue . . . . .30.00 to 120.00
Criss Cross, green or pink . . . . .20.00 to 30.00
Dots, milk glass .10.00 to 25.00
Pink, fluted bases . . . . .12.00 to 35.00
REST-WELL, yellow . . . . .25.00 to 50.00

HOCKING
Apple or Dots designs . . . . .8.00 to 20.00
Fig. 19.33—Batter bowl, Jadeite 24.00

JEANNETTE
Delphite, horizontal ribbed base . . . . .70.00 to 100.00
Delphite, plain . . . . .50.00 to 80.00
Fired-on colors, (see color plate) . . . . .10.00 to 25.00
Jadeite, horizontal ribbed base . . . . .15.00 to 45.00
Jadeite, vertical paneled base . . . . .15.00 to 25.00
Jennyware, ultramarine or pink . . . . .25.00 to 130.00
Fig. 19.34—Plain, transparent colors . . . . . .10.00 to 22.00

McKEE
Fig. 19.35—Dots, French Ivory
    (pale custard) . . . . .15.00 to 25.00
Dots, white . . . . .10.00 to 20.00
Fig. 19.36—French Ivory,
    (pale custard), plain . . . . .15.00 to 30.00
Ship decoration, milk glass . . . . .15.00 to 25.00

U. S. GLASS
Amber, plain or horizontal ribbed base . . . .20.00 to 50.00
Green, plain . . . . .12.00 to 25.00
Fig. 19.37—Green, Slick handle . . . . .35.00 to 45.00

OVEN GLASS

Oven glass had its beginnings in the late Teens when Corning introduced its first Pyrex line. At this time it made only crystal, but eventually ovenware was made in many colors. Pyrex was patented and so for several years only Corning could make ovenware. After the idea was no longer under patent, many other companies started making ovenware, notably McKee (GlasBake), Anchor Hocking (Fire King) and others. The following is a short list of typical pieces.

ANCHOR HOCKING (FIRE KING)
Fig. 19.38—Anchorwhite, Wheat design, utility pan . $17.00
Fig. 19.39—Swirl casserole & lid, shell lustre 15.00

CORNING (PYREX) See color plates for examples
Casserole & Cover, large. 18.00
Casserole, Individual 5.00
Deep Baking Dish, 1½ qt., Flamingo 12.00
Oblong Dish, 1½ qt., Lime 12.00

FRY
Fig. 19.40—Covered casserole, Pearl glass, cut lid . . . 40.00
Fig. 19.41—Loaf dish, grape cover, Pearl glass 70.00

MCKEE
Fig. 19.42—Casserole & Cover, Optic, Crystal 12.00
Fig. 19.43—Tube cake pan, Optic, Crystal 45.00

Fig. 19.38

Fig. 19.39

Fig. 19.40

Fig. 19.41

Fig. 19.42

Fig. 19.43

REAMERS

Reamers made of glass date back to the late 1800s when simple styles first appeared. Reamers are used to extract juice from citrus fruits. Most glass companies made reamers, and the reamers are available in a wide range of both styles and colors, both opaque and transparent. Today interest is mainly concentrated in these reamers with crystal ones being less sought after unless they are of an unusual type. However, the crystal reamers make good everyday kitchen utensils and are valued at $5.00 to $8.00. Orange reamers are the larger sized reamers, while the smaller are termed lemon reamers. There are also reamers made in a small size specifically for use to prepare baby's orange juice. Because of the "cuteness" of these, they have suffered from reproductions, so be careful about buying them. Full size reamers come in two basic styles: solid base in which the juice and seeds accumulate in the base and are poured off and a perforated base in which the juice will run

through into a container below leaving the seeds in the reamer. Often these reamers were sold with a 2 cup measuring pitcher to catch the juice. Glass companies, however, sold the two pieces as a set and also separately.

In addition to the 2-piece styles described, some companies made other variations. Notably, U. S. Glass made reamers to fit the tops of pitchers and sold these with juice glasses as breakfast sets. Other companies combined the reamers with cocktail shakers.

As with any popular collectible, someone eventually makes reproductions, and there are many reproduction reamers now on the market. It takes study and experience to make sure you have old reamers. Fortunately, most of the colors made do not truly reproduce the old colors. Do not be afraid to collect reamers, but learn about your collectible first to avoid a mistake.

REAMERS *(continued)*

Fig. 19.44

Fig. 19.45

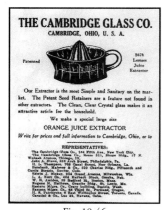

Fig. 19.46

Fig. 19.47

Fig. 19.48

Fig. 19.49

Fig. 19.50

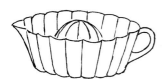

Fig. 19.51

Fig. 19.52

Fig. 19.53

BARTLETT-COLLINS

Fig. 19.44—Lemon, No. 1, 1 piece, tab handle, spout
90° from handle, green .18.00

Fig. 19.45—Orange, No. 2, 1 piece, loop handle with
thumb grip, green 18.00

CAMBRIDGE

Fig. 19.46—Lemon, No. 2674, 1 piece, fluted
body, loop handle, seed retainer, ...15.00

Orange, same as above but larger 15.00

FEDERAL

Fig. 19.47—Lemon, No. 2520, 1 piece, tab handle,
spout 90° from handle, seed retainer

Amber 22.00

Pink 35.00

Green 20.00

Fig. 19.48—Orange, No. 2521, 8½", 1 piece,
fluted body, loop handle with thumb grip

Green 24.00

Amber 22.00

Crystal . . . . 5.00 to 10.00

FENTON

Fig. 19.49—2 piece, plain bulbous bodied pitcher
with large loop handle (colors) . . . . .1,200.00+

FRY

Fig. 19.50—Fruit, 1 piece, paneled sides,
flat horizontal handle

Green . . . . 20.00 to 30.00

Pink . . . . .50.00+

Amber . . . . .340.00+

Pearl (opalescent crystal) 25.00

Fig. 19.51—Fruit, 1 piece, "Jell-O mold"
style, loop handle

Canary yellow 300.00

Dark green 500.00

Pearl (opalescent crystal) 40.00

HAZEL-ATLAS

Fig. 19.52—2 piece, 2 cup size. No. 3043 pitcher and No.
2954 reamer. Has been reproduced in cobalt blue, pink,
and an unusual shade of green—almost olive.

Yellow or cobalt blue . . . . .300.00+

Green 35.00

Pink . . . . .140.00+

Fig. 19.53—Criss Cross. One piece.
Swirled cone, loop handle.

Crystal 10.00

Green 24.00

Cobalt blue 160.00

HAZEL-ATLAS (CONTINUED)

Fig. 19.54—Lemon, No. 71, 1 piece, tab handle, spout 90° from handle, seed retainer
Crystal 8.00
Green 22.00

Fig. 19.55—Orange, No. 72, 1 piece, paneled body, tab handle with thumbrest, spout 90° from handle
Crystal 8.00
Green 22.00

HOCKING

Fig. 19.56—2 piece, 2 cup size, green 30.00
Fig. 19.57—Green, fluted .70.00
Crystal, fluted 30.00

INDIANA

One piece, 2 styles. Paneled bodies, loop handles. Spout either directly across from handle or 90° from handle.
Amber . . . . .300.00+
Green 40.00
Pink . . . . .70.00 to 120.00

JEANNETTE

Fig. 19.58—1 piece, No. 379, large, paneled sides with thumbrest, loop handle
Crystal 12.00
Green 25.00

Fig. 19.59—2 piece, 2 cup size,
No. 287 jug, No. 245 reamer
Jadeite, light 25.00
Jadeite, deep 70.00

Fig. 19.60—Lemon, No. 5019, green 15.00

1 piece, plain sides, loop handle with thumbrest
Delphite. . . . . 1,000.00+
Jadeite. 30.00

1 piece, small. Paneled sides, loop handle with thumbrest.
"Jennyware" Pink or crystal . . . . 75.00 to 100.00+
Ultramarine. 125.00

JENKINS

Fig. 19.61—Lemon, No. 160, green 12.00
Fig. 19.62—Lemon, No. 170, green 12.00
Fig. 19.63—Orange, No. 180, green. 12.00
Fig. 19.64—Baby, 4 oz., No. 181, crystal 45.00
Fig. 19.65—2 piece, No. 55, paneled pitcher, handled, crystal. 40.00

L. E. SMITH

Fig. 19.66—Lemon juicer & cup, 2 piece, plain body, tab handle, crystal 35.00

Fig. 19.54

Fig. 19.55

Fig. 19.56

Fig. 19.57

Fig. 19.58

Fig. 19.59

5019
LEMON REAMER

Fig. 19.60

No. 160—Lemon Reamer

Fig. 19.61

No. 170—Lemon Reamer with seed catcher

Fig. 19.62

No. 180—Orange Reamer

Fig. 19.63

Reamer Set

Fig. 19.64

Fig. 19.65

LEMON JUICER AND C

Fig. 19.66

REAMERS *(continued)*

Fig. 19.67

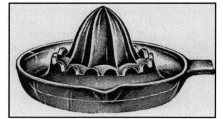

Fig. 19.68

Fig. 19.69

Fig. 19.70

Fig. 19.71

Fig. 19.72

Fig. 19.73

Fig. 19.74

Fig. 19.75

Fig. 19.76

Fig. 19.78

Fig. 19.77

Fig. 19.79

LANCASTER
19.67 1 piece, crystal 8.00

MCKEE
Fig. 19.68—Lemon, No. 2, 1 piece, plain body,
   tab handle, spout 90° from handle, green 25.00
Fig. 19.69—Orange, No. 34, 1 piece, plain, loop
   handle with thumbrest, green 25.00
Fig. 19.70—Lemon, No. 35, 1 piece, plain, loop
   handle with thumbrest, milk glass 40.00
Fig. 19.71—Grapefruit, No. 36, 1 piece, plain, loop
   handle with thumbrest, Seville yellow (opaque) . . 265.00
"SUNKIST," transparent green or vaseline yellow . . . 50.00
"SUNKIST," Skokie green 35.00
"SUNKIST," various shades of Seville
   yellow . . . . 35.00 to 75.00

U. S. GLASS
Fig. 19.72—No. 9431, 1 piece, paneled body, straight sides,
   loop handle with thumb rest, spout 90° from handle.
Lemon, green. 35.00
Orange, pink 85.00
Grapefruit, green 45.00
Fig. 19.73—Orange, No. 9437, 1 piece, paneled body,
   tab handle, spout 90° from handle, opal 35.00
Fig. 19.74—Orange, No. 9214, 14 oz., 1 piece, plain body,
   patented Slick handle, spout 90° from handle
Crystal. 20.00
Green 35.00
Pink 45.00
Jade Green. 95.00
Fig. 19.75—No. 15359, 2 piece. Pitcher with vertical
   ribbed panels, alternating with panels of measuring
   lines. Slick handle, crystal 65.00
Fig. 19.76—No. 346, 2 piece. Horizontal lines with
   measuring lines between. Slick handle, green. 45.00

WESTMORELAND
Fig. 19.77—Orange, No. 73, 1 piece, paneled body,
   elongated loop handle with flat thumbrest, pink . . . 95.00
Fig. 19.78—Orange, No. 74, 2 piece set. Pitcher has
   embossed oranges on 2 sides, loop handle.
   (has been reproduced) 200.00

MISCELLANEOUS
Fleur de lis, "VALENCIA," white . . . . .100.00+
Fleur de lis, "VALENCIA," crystal or green . . . . . . .200.00+
Fleur de lis, any type in slags of red, orange,
   or yellow . . . . .400.00+
"LINDSAY" or "LINDSEY" in pink or green . . . . .100.00+
Fig. 19.79—2 cup measure in metal frame 65.00

REFRIGERATOR GLASS

All refrigerator/left-over jars are priced with lids unless noted.
Several of the stacking sets were sold with one lid for the set.

BARTLETT-COLLINS
Fig. 19.80—Jar & Cover, oval, green . . . . . $30.00 to 40.00
(Hocking also made oval covered jars)

CORNING (PYREX)
Fired-on color, crystal lids (see color plate) . . . 8.00 to 20.00

FEDERAL
Fig. 19.81—Ribbed sides, smooth corners and ribbed lids.
Square, large, green 50.00
Square, small, green 25.00
Oblong, green 30.00

HAZEL-ATLAS
Fig. 19.82—No. 759, round, green, each 20.00
No. 759, round, green, with lid 50.00
Fig. 19.83—No. 2015, square, green, each 20.00
No. 2015 square, green, with lid 50.00

HOCKING
Fig. 19.84—Square, ribbed, small, green 25.00

JEANNETTE
Fired-on colors, crystal lids, (see color plate) . . . 8.00 to 20.00

McKEE
Fig. 19.85—No. 257, square, Skokie green (opaque) . . 65.00
Fig. 19.86—No. 257, oblong, Dots 35.00
Fig. 19.87—No. 263, round, Dots 35.00
Round canisters, tapering larger to top, glass lids.
48 oz., Seville Yellow (opaque) with dots 85.00
32 oz., Seville Yellow (opaque) with dots 85.00
48 oz., white with sailboat 80.00
48 oz., Delphite 175.00
16 oz., Skokie green 80.00

Fig. 19.80

Fig. 19.81

Fig. 19.82

Fig. 19.84

Fig. 19.83

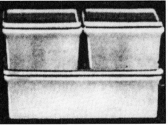

Fig. 19.85

Fig. 19.87

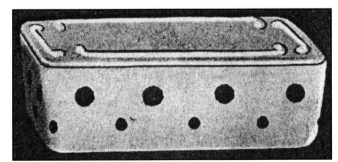

Fig. 19.86

REFRIGERATOR GLASS—(continued)

Fig. 19.88

Fig. 19.89

Fig. 19.90

Fig. 19.91

Fig. 19.92

Fig. 19.94

Fig. 19.95

Fig. 19.93

U. S. Glass

Fig. 19.88—No. 6493, square, patterned lid, green . . 65.00
Fig. 19.89—No. 8135, covered bowls, pink, each . . . 85.00

Miscellaneous

Many other accessories were made for refrigerator/ice box use. Most companies that made canister sets also made refrigerator bottles for water or juice. Most of these are flat oblong bottles able to be stored alongside the small freezer in early refrigerators.

Cambridge, No. 1570, Cheese preserver & cover,
    round, crystal (has been reproduced) $40.00
Fig. 19.90—Cambridge, No. 1571, Cheese
    preserver & cover, square, crystal (has been
    reproduced). 40.00
Fig. 19.91—Hocking, covered refrigerator jar,
    green frosted 40.00
Fig. 19.92—Indiana, Kontainerette, with tray,
    crystal. 225.00
Fig. 19.93—Indiana, Conserv-O-Jars, with tray,
    crystal. 225.00
Fig. 19.94—L. E Smith, water jar & cover,
    deep blue . . . . 500.00+
Fig. 19.95—McKee, No. 24 water jar & cover,
    Jade Green 150.00

ROLLING PINS

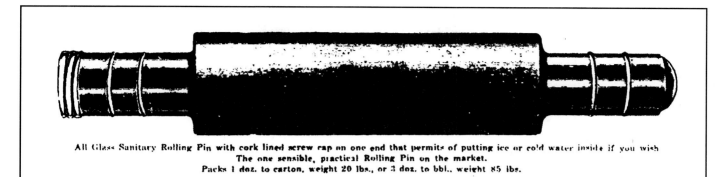

All Glass Sanitary Rolling Pin with cork lined screw cap on one end that permits of putting ice or cold water inside if you wish
The one sensible, practical Rolling Pin on the market.
Packs 1 doz. to carton, weight 20 lbs., or 3 doz. to bbl., weight 85 lbs.

Fig. 19.96

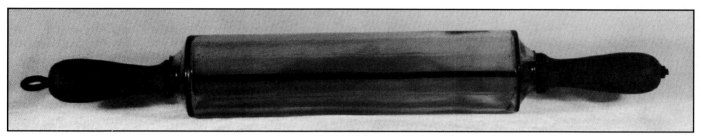

Fig. 19.97

Glass rolling pins have been made since at least Victorian times. Many early pins are in unusual glasses, including drawn opalescent loops, opaque and transparent colors.

Rolling pins of the DG and post-DG era can be found made entirely of glass, bodies of glass with wooden handles, or a screw cap on the end of one handle. The screw cap pins are of most recent manufacture and even more recently have been reproduced in several colors—none of which were originally made.

The following is a general guide to evaluate your rolling pin.

One-piece blown (glass handles) in opaque
    blue or black . . . . $500.00+
One-piece blown (glass handles) in transparent
    blue . . . . .200.00+
One-piece blown (glass handles) in transparent
    amethyst, dark green, amber,
    light blue. . . . . 150.00 to 200.00+
One piece, blown, with screw cap in
    McKee colors of Skokie green, pale custard,
    and yellow. . . . . 300.00 to 400.00+
Fig. 19.96—Indiana, crystal 35.00
Fig. 19.97—Blown body with wooden handles,
    various types, in transparent colors or
    opaques. 300.00 to 400.00+
Fig. 19.98—Blown body with wooden
    handles, white opalite. . . . . 50.00 to 75.00

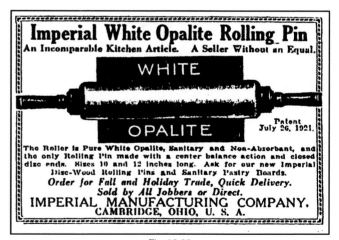

Fig. 19.98

MISCELLANEOUS

The following are examples of many other types of kitchen glass available to the collector.

Fig. 19.99—Beater Jar, green, stippled. $55.00

Fig. 19.100—Beater Jar, Crystal 25.00

Fig. 19.101—Beater Bowl, Hazel-Atlas, green 15.00

Fig. 19.102—Cracker Bowl, McKee No. 39,
   4½ x 2½, Jade green 18.00

Fig. 19.103—Dripping Jar & cover,
   red on milk glass 9.00

Fig. 19.104—Nut Chopper, crystal. 15.00

Fig. 19.105—Promotional Glasses, each . . . . . 5.00 to 8.00

Fig. 19.106a—Salt Shaker, tulip on milk glass 10.00

Fig. 19.106b—Salt Shaker, plain milk glass 6.00

Fig. 19.107—Soap Dish, "Patent Applied For,"
   dark blue. 35.00

Fig. 19.108—Spice Jars, blue Dutch design on
   milk glass, each . . . . 5.00 to 7.00

Fig. 19.109—Teapots, Corning (Pyrex) crystal,
   ca. 1922, each . . . . 125.00 to 160.00

Fig. 19.103

Fig. 19.102

Fig. 19.105

Fig. 19.104

Fig. 19.106a   Fig. 19.106b

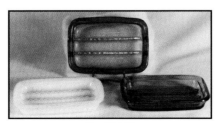

Fig. 19.107

Fig. 19.109

Fig. 19.99   Fig. 19.100

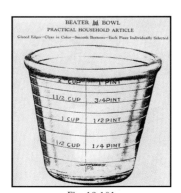

Fig. 19.101

Fig. 19.108

Chapter 20
BARWARE & BEVERAGE SETS

Barware is becoming increasingly collectible with more and more people focusing on this aspect of American Glass. Beverage or water sets have been collectible for some time, with examples back into Victorian pressed glass and even prior to that. With that in mind, we wanted to present an overview of this interesting branch of collecting.

Barware, in the sense of decanters and drinking vessels, was made prior to the DG era. However, with the repeal of Prohibition in 1933 making drinking again legal, most American glass companies began producing lines of barware. This included various cocktail shakers, ice tubs, stemware, tumblers, sodas, old fashioneds and other specialized glasses for serving liquor. In addition, Tom and Jerry sets were offered, especially by McKee Glass Co. Heisey patented their all-glass cocktail shaker, and it was so popular that it remained for sale until the company closed and was continued for several years by Imperial Glass. Much of this is blown ware, not pressed ware, so the Elegant companies predominate in the Barware category. This adds to the difficulty in identifying much of this ware.

Beverage or Water Sets are likewise an interesting collectible. Many of the DG and Elegant companies had extensive lines of pitchers with matching tumblers or sodas. Fenton's exotic stretch glass lemonade sets are eagerly sought. In addition, many lines of sodas and tumblers were made, either plain or decorated.

Each of these categories could more than fill a book, but as in Kitchen Glass, we are attempting to give a general profile of pieces which might be found. While your item may not be shown exactly, we hope that the general forms and values given will help you to decide on values for yourself.

COCKTAIL SHAKERS & MARTINI MIXERS

Cocktail shakers are containers, usually holding about 1 quart, for preparing mixed drinks. They may have either glass tops (as in the Heisey one) or more often, chrome tops with a pouring spout. Decanters, on the other hand, are bottles to hold liquors and have a stopper. They are used for wines and other liquors which are not being mixed for serving.

Fig. 20.1—*Photo of the queen of the Glass Festival in Weston, WV in the late 1930s. Note the products of either Louie Glass Co. or West Virginia Glass Specialty Co. both of Weston, WV. Both of these companies made much blown ware such as cocktail shakers, pitchers, tumblers and vases during the 1930s and later. Little has been written about either, so often their products are unrecognized or erroneously attributed. – Photo courtesy of Dave Bush.*

Fig. 20.1

COCKTAIL SHAKERS & MARTINI MIXERS (continued)

Fig. 20.2   Fig. 20.3   Fig. 20.4   Fig. 20.5   Fig. 20.6

Fig. 20.7   Fig. 20.8   Fig. 20.9   Fig. 20.10   Fig. 20.11

Fig. 20.12   Fig. 20.13 a,b   Fig. 20.14

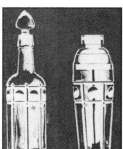

Fig. 20.15   Fig. 20.16   Fig. 20.17   Fig. 20.18

Fig. 20.19   Fig. 20.20   Fig. 20.21 a, b, c

CAMBRIDGE GLASS CO.
Fig. 20.2—No. 101, Pristine, 32 oz, Crystal...... $30.00
Fig. 20.3—No. 102, Pristine, 48 oz., Crystal...... 40.00
Fig. 20.4—No. 1393 mixer, Crystal 35.00
Fig. 20.5—No. 1394 mixer, Carmen............. 75.00
Fig. 20.6—No. 1395 mixer, Blue 75.00
Fig. 20.7—No. 3400/157, Crystal 35.00
Fig. 20.8—No. 3400/158, Carmen............. 75.00
Fig. 20.9—No. 3500/159, Blue 75.00
Fig. 20.10—Tally Ho, Footed, 50 oz.,
No. 1402/48, Crystal 55.00
Fig. 20.11—Tally Ho, Handled, No. 1402/51, Crystal.. 70.00

DUNBAR GLASS CO.
Fig. 20.12—No. 3085 .... 75.00
Made in Rose Pink or Bermuda Green satin, with Golfing, Fishing, Hunting, Yachting, Coaching, or Assorted Dogs handpainted decoration of black silhouettes.

DUNCAN & MILLER GLASS CO.
Fig. 20.13a—Chanticleer, 16 oz., Ruby.......... 150.00
Fig. 20.13b—Chanticleer, 32 oz., Cape Cod Blue .. 250.00
Fig. 20.14—No. 11, colors................... 75.00
All made in Crystal, Ruby, Green, Blue, Amber. Chanticleers also made in opalescent Cape Cod Blue, Shell Pink and Jasmine Yellow.

FENTON ART GLASS CO.
Fig. 20.15—Plymouth, Crystal................ 65.00
This pattern was made in a complete barware assortment and in several Fenton colors.

FOSTORIA GLASS CO.
Fig. 20.16—No. 2518, 38 oz. (also 28 oz.),
    Crystal .... 85.00 to 100.00
Fig. 20.17—No. 2525, 42 oz. (also 30 oz).
    Crystal .... 65.00 to 75.00

HAZEL-ATLAS
Fig. 20.18—Fish silk screen decor, Blue 45.00
Fig. 20.19—Hunting dogs tumblers, Blue........ 28.00
Sail Boat silk screen decor, Blue 45.00
These cocktail shakers are also found with various other decorations such as Windmills, Dancers and various sporting motifs.
Fig. 20.20—No. 386 beverage shaker, Crystal 24.00

A. H. HEISEY & CO.
Fig. 20.21c—Cobel 1 pt. Cocktail shaker, "Us" etch 190.00
Fig. 20.21b—Cobel 1 qt. Cocktail shaker 55.00
Fig. 20.21a—Cobel 2 qt. Cocktail shaker 70.00
Fig. 20.22—Coronation Cocktail shaker, 1 qt. 80.00
Fig. 20.23a—Crystolite, 1 qt., Crystal.......... 300.00

(continued) COCKTAIL SHAKERS & MARTINI MIXERS

A. H. HEISEY & CO. (CONTINUED)
20.23b—Crystolite, Rock & Rye bottle,
　　1 qt., Crystal 300.00
20.24—Ipswich, No. 1405, 1 qt. 275.00
20.25—No. 4036 . . . . 45.00
Twist, 1 qt. (not shown) 350.00
The Cobel (No. 4225) and No. 4036 cocktail shakers were also
sold with Rooster Head, Girl's Head, Ram's Head and two styles
of Horsehead stoppers. These stoppers greatly add to the value of
the shakers. Coronation was a full barware line.

HOCKING GLASS CO.
20.26—Pinch, No. G151 . . . . 50.00
Pinch was made in a full line of barware.

IMPERIAL GLASS CORPORATION
20.27—Reeded, 1 qt., Crystal 35.00
Reeded in colors . . . . .65.00+
20.28—No. 142 . . . . .45.00
20.29—No. 451 . . . . .45.00

PADEN CITY GLASS CO.
20.30—Aristocrat, colors 75.00
Made in Crystal, Amber, Ritz Blue, Cheriglo, and Ruby.

STEUBEN GLASS CO.
20.31—Martini pitcher with Gold Ruby threading
　　and stopper 550.00

WEST VIRGINIA SPECIALTY GLASS CO.
20.32—Cobalt with silver stripes, 1 qt. 60.00
20.33—Lady's Leg, Ruby 390.00
20.34—Barbell, vertical, Royal Blue 110.00
20.35—Martini mixer & glasses, set of 3 . . . . 28.00

WESTMORELAND GLASS CO.
20.36—No. 15, Crystal 35.00

MISCELLANEOUS
20.37—Polar Bears, Cocktail shaker only 65.00

Fig. 20.23a　　　　Fig. 20.23b

Fig. 20.24　　　　Fig. 20.25

• The Class of All Glass •
Stepping far ahead of the field to take the "Mixing World" by storm is this aristocratic drinking service. Its rich appearance belies its moderate cost. Shown are 6-oz. Old Fashioned, 23-oz. Bar Bottle with ground stopper, 12-oz. whisky and soda, and chromium topped cocktail shaker. These may be had in Crystal, Amber, Ritz Blue, Cheriglo and Ruby.
PADEN CITY GLASS MFG. CO.
PADEN CITY　　　　　　　　W. VA.

Fig. 20.30

Fig. 20.22

Fig. 20.26　　　　Fig. 20.27

Fig. 20.31　　　　Fig. 20.28　　　　Fig. 20.29

Fig. 20.32　　Fig. 20.33　　Fig. 20.34　　　　Fig. 20.35　　　　　　Fig. 20.37　　　　　Fig. 20.36

DECANTERS

Fig. 20.38

Fig. 20.39

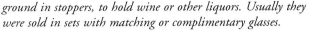

Fig. 20.41

Fig. 20.40

Fig. 20.43

Fig. 20.45

Fig. 20.46

Fig. 20.42

Fig. 20.47

Fig. 20.48

Fig. 20.44

Fig. 20.49

Decanters are bottles, usually with narrow necks and often ground in stoppers, to hold wine or other liquors. Usually they were sold in sets with matching or complimentary glasses.

CAMBRIDGE GLASS CO.
Fig. 20.38—No. 1388, 28 oz., Crystal $35.00
Fig. 20.39—No. 3145, 32 oz., Crystal 25.00
Fig. 20.40—Pinch, No. 1070, 36 oz., Carmen 60.00
Cambridge made many styles of decanters, most in crystal and colors.

COOPERATIVE FLINT GLASS CO.
Fig. 20.41—Conical, 24 oz., plain or optic 25.00

DUNBAR GLASS CO.
Fig. 20.42—Aristocrat, 39 oz., Frost/22k Gold 35.00

DUNCAN & MILLER GLASS CO.
Fig. 20.43—Canterbury, No. 115, Crystal. 65.00
Fig. 20.44—Hobnail, No. 118, Crystal. 75.00
Fig. 20.45—No. 55, 16 oz., Sienna. 40.00
Fig. 20.46—Pall Mall, No. 30, Crystal 50.00
Fig. 20.47—Teardrop, No. 301, bottle, Crystal 120.00

FENTON ART GLASS CO.
Fig. 20.48—Franklin, No. 1935, Crystal. 55.00
Fig. 20.49—No. 1934, flower stopper, Royal Blue . . 100.00
Plymouth, No. 1620, Crystal
    (see illustration 20.15) 60.00

A. H. HEISEY & CO.
Fig. 20.50b—Christos, No. 4027, 32 oz., Crystal . . 100.00
Fig. 20.51—Gascony, No. 3397, 1 pt., Crystal 120.00
Fig. 20.52—Prism Band, No. 367, Crystal 125.00
Fig. 20.50c—Robinson, No. 4028, 30 oz., Crystal . . 90.00
Fig. 20.50a—Spencer, No. 4026, 16 oz., Crystal 85.00

HOCKING GLASS CO.
Fig. 20.53—Circle, handled, Green 45.00
Fig. 20.54—Pinch, G102. . . . . 45.00

Fig. 20.50a

Fig. 20.50b

Fig. 20.50c

Fig. 20.51

Fig. 20.52

Fig. 20.53

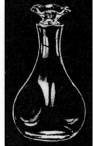

Fig. 20.54

IMPERIAL GLASS CORPORATION

Fig. 20.55—Cape Cod, No. 160, Crystal 100.00
Fig. 20.56—Georgian, No. 451, jigger stopper,
  Crystal 90.00
Made in crystal, Stiegel Green, Ritz Blue, Amber
Fig. 20.57—Horseshoe, No. 7, Flask Brown 65.00
Fig. 20.58—No. 110, 26 oz., Crystal 65.00
Fig. 20.59—Tomorrow, No. 76C, Crystal 65.00

LOUIE GLASS CO.

Fig. 20.60—Nos. 1, 2 or 3, Crystal . . . . . . 20.00 to 30.00
Fig. 20.61—Barbell, horizontal, Royal Blue 250.00

MCKEE GLASS CO.

Fig. 20.62—Jolly Golfer 350.00
Fig. 20.63—Jolly Golfer tumblers 75.00
Fig. 20.64—Life Saver 350.00
*These decanters were made in many McKee colors including
Crystal, Amber, Rose Pink, Blue, Canary and Green, also the
Golfer is known in satin glass.*

MORGANTOWN

Fig. 20.65—Canteen, No. 58, Meadow Green 425.00
Fig. 20.66a—Circlet, No. 24, Ruby, platinum
  bands 400.00
Fig. 20.66b—Tumbler 50.00
Fig. 20.66c—Shot glass 70.00
Fig. 20.67a—Lynward, No. 10 ½, pineapple optic,
  Anna Rose. 360.00
Fig. 20.67b—Shot glass 35.00
Fig. 20.68a—Victory, No. 2, Black 260.00
Fig. 20.68b—Shot glass 35.00

Fig. 20.55   Fig. 20.56   Fig. 20.57   Fig. 20.58

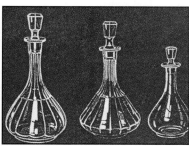

Fig. 20.59   Fig. 20.60   Fig. 20.61

Fig. 20.62

Fig. 20.64   Fig. 20.65   Fig. 20.66a, b, c

Fig. 20.67a, b   Fig. 20.68a, b

Fig. 20.63

DECANTERS *(continued)*

Fig. 20.69

Fig. 20.71

Fig. 20.74

Fig. 20.75

Fig. 20.76

Fig. 20.70

Fig. 20.73

Fig. 20.77

Fig. 20.78

Fig. 20.79

Fig. 20.80

NEW MARTINSVILLE GLASS CO.

Fig. 20.69—Cozy Cordial, Ruby 55.00
Fig. 20.70—Hostmaster, No. 38, Crystal 35.00
Fig. 20.71—Michael, Crystal 40.00
Fig. 20.72—No. 10, in colors 45.00
Fig. 20.73—Silly Toby, Crystal 75.00
Fig. 20.74—Volstead Pup, No. 1926, figural dog,
    Green 85.00
*Most of these decanters were made in colors of Crystal, Ruby,
Ritz Blue, Amethyst, Amber, Evergreen, Rose and Crystal.*

PADEN CITY

Fig. 20.75—Decanter, etched and gold filled 55.00
Fig. 20.76—Decanter, etched 55.00

TIFFIN GLASS CO.

Fig. 20.77—Just a few examples of many types
    available, value (*each*) 75.00

MISCELLANEOUS

*Many examples are available in many different decorations. The
following are a few examples of different types.*
Fig. 20.78—Donut shaped, enamel bands 50.00
Fig. 20.79—Light Blue, blown, blown stopper 50.00
Fig. 20.80—Plain, enamel bands 20.00
Fig. 20.81—Samovar, Blue satin 700.00
Fig. 20.82—Spirit of St. Louis, complete, Blue 900.00

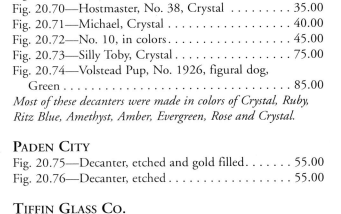

Fig. 20.72

Fig. 20.81

Fig. 20.82

BEVERAGE SETS

Water or Beverage Sets are combinations of pitchers and tumblers or sodas for serving drinks such as lemonade, iced tea and other non-alcoholic beverages. The pitchers usually hold about ½ gallon, although smaller juice sets are also available in which the capacity is about 1 quart. The tumblers are often sodas or iced teas (taller than standard tumblers), sometimes with handles. The juice sets, of course, have matching small juice glasses. Almost every glass company produced these sets. They are available in cheaper glass and in very expensive glass. Many of the more recent sets are decorated with fired enamel decorations and spray-painted designs. These types of decorations allowed a wide range of design and color while not making the set overly expensive. Water sets usually had 6 tumblers and a pitcher, but some companies sold either 4 or 8 tumblers with a set, and some had matching or accompanying trays. Most companies made water sets, but we will concentrate on just a few of the lesser known sets because of space limitations and to show many of the now unrecognized designs.

DUNCAN & MILLER

Old Charlie pitcher (not shown) $110.00
Fig. 20.83—Old Charlie mug. 65.00
For pieces in Shell Pink opalescent or Cobalt, add 400% to 500%.

DUNBAR GLASS CO.

Fig. 20.84—For any style in Crystal, set 70.00
Fig. 20.85—For any style in Crystal, set 70.00
For pastel colors add 50%, for deep colors of blue or red add 75% to 100%.
Fig. 20.86—1950s style pitchers, Crystal,
    each . . . . 28.00 to 35.00

FEDERAL GLASS CO.

"Water and Iced Tea Sets" from 1934 catalog. Often pitchers were sold with different styles of glasses.
Figs. 20.87, 20.88, 20.88a&b—Any set, Crystal 70.00
For pastel colors, add 50%. Hazel Marie Weatherman named some of these sets in her book, Colored Glassware of the Depression Era, Book 2 *as follows:*

Fig. 20.84

Fig. 20.83

Fig. 20.86

Fig. 20.85

Fig. 20.87

Fig. 20.88

BEVERAGE SETS *(continued)*

Fig. 20.88a

Fig. 20.88b

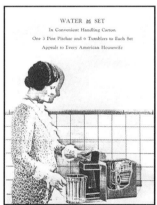

Fig. 20.89

Fig. 20.90

Fig. 20.91

Fig. 20.92

FEDERAL GLASS CO. (CONTINUED)

No. 20—Mutt n' Jeff
No. 50—Squat
No. 70—Tall Boy
No. 170, Tudor Ring is the original company name.

HAZEL-ATLAS GLASS CO.

Fig. 20.89—Water set, Crystal, from 1934 catalog. . . 60.00
Note the interesting original packaging.

JEANNETTE GLASS CO.

All these decorated water sets are valued in the range of $35.00 to $55.00. Original numbers and descriptions are as follows:

Fig. 20.90—Decoration No. 31—Dutch Scene
Decoration No. 62—Red Chrysanthemum
Decoration No. 152—Blue or Red Mayflower*
Decoration No. 199—Clematis, Blue, Red or White
Decoration No. 221—Red Peacock*

Fig. 20.91—Decoration No. 58—White Cosmos
Decoration No. 81—Red Tomatoes+
Decoration No. 82—Yellow Oranges+
Decoration No. 242—New Orleans (Red and White)
Decoration No. 247—Red Flower, White Butterfly
Decoration No. 249—Red Barn, White Fence
* = made as a water set or a juice set.
+ = made in a juice set only.

20.92—"Golden Iridescent" sets are valued at $45.00 to $55.00.
White Cosmos*
White Glass Flower*
Purple Glass Flower*
Plain 13 pc. or 7 pc. set.
* = made in both 7 piece water set or juice set.

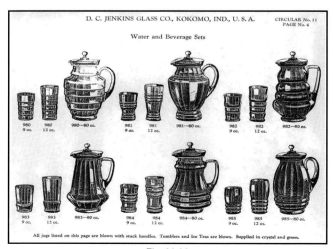

Fig. 20.93

(continued) BEVERAGE SETS

D. C. JENKINS GLASS CO.

Fig. 20.93—*These pitchers from D. C. Jenkins are valued at $45 in crystal with the correct lid. Deduct at least 25% if the lid is missing. Tumblers and iced teas are valued at $5.00 to $8.00 each in crystal. For pieces in Green add 50%.*

LOUIE GLASS CO.

These pitchers in standard Louie shapes are valued from $20.00 to $45.00 in crystal. With correct lids they are valued at the higher amount. If found in pastel colors add at least 50%; in rich colors such as blue or red, add 100%.
Figs. 20.94, 20.95, 20.96, 20.97, 20.98 Harpo, 20.99 Chico, 20.100

MORGANTOWN GLASS CO.

Morgantown made many styles of water sets. Here is one.
Fig. 20.101a—No. 37 Barry Jug,
Meadow Green cased 500.00
Fig. 20.101b—No. 7637 Belton tumblers, each. . . . 110.00

WEST VIRGINIA GLASS SPECIALTY CO., INC.

See color plates
Blendo, various colors, set. 55.00

MISCELLANEOUS TUMBLERS

See color plates
Figs. 20.102, 20.103, 20.104, 20.105
These colorful tumblers were made in water sets in a wide variety of colors and styles. Any of these are valued from $5.00 to $7.00 each.

Fig. 20.94

Fig. 20.95

Fig. 20.96

Fig. 20.97

Fig. 20.98

Fig. 20.99

Fig. 20.100

Fig. 20.101a, b

Fig. 20.102

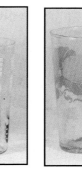

Fig. 20.103

Fig. 20.104

Fig. 20.105

ICE TUBS & ACCESSORY PIECES

Fig. 20.106

Fig. 20.107

Fig. 20.108

Fig. 20.109

Fig. 20.110

Fig. 20.111

Fig. 20.112

Fig. 20.113

Fig. 20.114

Fig. 20.115

Fig. 20.116

In addition to cocktail shakers, decanters and other liquor items, companies sometimes added accessories to the line. Ice tubs are probably the most common. But additional pieces were also sold, such as bowls for serving snacks and bitter bottles. Heisey even made a pretzel jar using a pretzel as the finial for the lid.

ICE TUBS AND BOWLS

Fig. 20.106—Amber, metal handle $25.00
Fig. 20.107—Green, 2 handled 30.00
Fig. 20.108—Red decorated 10.00
Fig. 20.109—Stars & Bunting, bowl only 25.00

CAMBRIDGE GLASS CO.

Fig. 20.110—Cascade, No. 4000, Crystal 20.00
Fig. 20.111—No. 845, Crystal 24.00
Fig. 20.112—Pristine, Crystal. 15.00

DUNBAR GLASS CO.

Fig. 20.113—various shapes/colors 25.00

DUNCAN & MILLER GLASS CO.

Fig. 20.114—Canterbury, No. 115, Crystal. 25.00
Fig. 20.115—Teardrop, No. 301, Crystal 120.00

FOSTORIA GLASS CO.

Fig. 20.116—No. 2375 . . . . 40.00
This style came plain, optic and with cuttings and etchings.

HAZEL-ATLAS GLASS CO.

Fig. 20.117—Sailors, Blue 75.00
Ice tubs are available in many Hazel-Atlas designs. This is one of the most rare.

A.H. HEISEY & CO.

Fig. 20.118—Empress, No. 1401, Crystal 70.00
Fig. 20.119—Octagon, No. 500, Crystal. 50.00

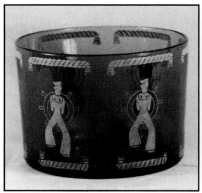

Fig. 20.117

Fig. 20.118

(continued) ICE TUBS & ACCESSORY PIECES

WESTMORELAND GLASS CO.
Fig. 20.120—Doreen, No. 1211, Crystal 25.00

MISCELLANEOUS
Bowling Ball, Imperial
Fig. 20.121a—Snack bowl, Black, No. 857 . . . . . . 145.00
Fig. 20.121b—Bowling Pin stems, No. 846, each . . . 65.00
Fig. 20.122—Ice crusher, Crystal decorated. 15.00
Odd Ball, No. 3010, Morgantown, Black
Fig. 20.123a—Pretzel bowl. 130.00
Fig. 20.123b—Old Fashioned. 45.00
Fig. 20.124—Game Set, Cambridge, each set 145.00

BEER MUGS
Fig. 20.125—Duncan & Miller, colored handles 35.00
Fig. 20.126—Heisey No 4163,
 with colored handles . . . . 200.00 to 350.00
Fig. 20.127—Heisey No. 3408,
 with colored handles 250.00

Fig. 20.121a, b

Fig. 20.122

Fig. 20.123a, b

Fig. 20.124

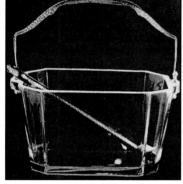

Fig. 20.119

Fig. 20.120

Fig. 20.125

Fig. 20.126   Fig. 20.127

COCKTAIL STIRRERS, GLASS STRAWS, & COCKTAIL PICKS

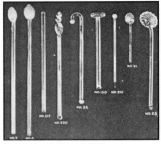

Fig. 20.128

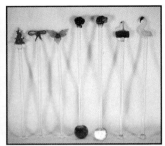

Fig. 20.130

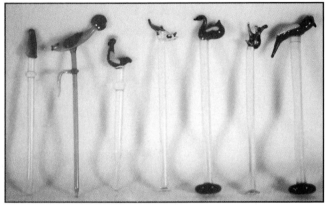

Fig. 20.129

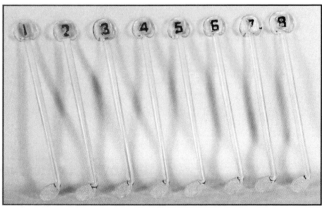

Fig. 20.131

Fig. 20.132

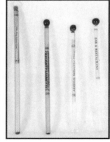

Fig. 20.133

Fig. 20.134

This category is attracting new collectors regularly as they become interested in the wide variety available. Stirrers have the added interest in being hand done (often lamp work to make elaborate figures) and take up little room for a large collection.

The simplest stirrers are solid glass rods. These are made in many colors, and some have advertising either etched or painted on them. Usually the advertising is for hotels or bars. A similar variety looks solid on first glance, but is actually hollow with a small paper advertisement inside. These are much more difficult to find. Elaborate stirrers are also available in many styles, often figurals. These are done in many colors and are actually miniature glass sculptures. These comprise the most popular of the stirrers.

Glass straws are made from glass tubing with an added piece of fancy hollow glass often in the form of berries or fruit. They are used to sip drinks.

Cocktail picks are made much like the figural cocktail stirrers, involving multicolored, sometimes fanciful, animals and other subjects. They are short, about 4 inches in length, with a sharp end used to spear various vegetables and fruit in drinks. They can also be used as picks for snacks.

Most of these pieces cannot be identified as to manufacturer. Many are imported, but also large numbers were American made. In fact, some are still being made with unusual, colorful subjects, including Christmas, Hawaiian and animal themes. The Cavalier Glass Co. made a wide variety of straws and stirrers in the 1940s.

The following are representative examples of each of the varieties. Values are based on how elaborate or colorful the decorations are. Prices given are for individual pieces.

Fig. 20.128—Cavalier Glass Co., all items. . $5.00 to 10.00
Fig. 20.129—Cocktail Picks or muddlers . . 15.00 to 25.00
Fig. 20.130—Cocktail Stirrers, figural. . . . . 12.00 to 20.00
Fig. 20.131—Cocktail Stirrers, golf set of eight 60.00
Fig. 20.132—Cocktail Stirrers, rods with
    advertising. . . . . 10.00 to 15.00
Fig. 20.133—Cocktail Stirrers, rods with paper
    advertising inserts 20.00
Fig. 20.134—Glass Straws . . . . 8.00 to 15.00

INDEX